THE MORNING OF THE MAGICIANS

The MORNING
of the MAGICIANS

by Louis Pauwels and Jacques Bergier

Translated from the French by Rollo Myers

DORSET PRESS
New York

First published in France under the title *Le Matin des Magiciens*.
Copyright © 1960 by Editions Gallimard

The Morning of the Magicians was published in England
as *The Dawn of Magic*.

Translation copyright © 1963 by Anthony Gibbs & Phillips Ltd.

This edition published by Dorset Press,
a division of Marboro Books Corporation,
by arrangement with
Stein & Day/Publishers.
1988 Dorset Press

ISBN 0-88029-191-5

Printed in the United States of America

M 9 8 7 6 5 4 3 2 1

To the fine soul, to the warm heart of Gustave Bouju,
a worker, a real father to me. In memoriam.

L.P.

CONTENTS

THE EXAMPLE OF ALCHEMY

THE VANISHED CIVILIZATIONS

Part Two

A FEW YEARS IN THE ABSOLUTE ELSEWHERE

Part Three

THAT INFINITY CALLED MAN . . .

CONTENTS

PREFACE

Physically I am a clumsy person and I deplore the fact. I think I would be a happier man if I had worker's hands – hands capable of making useful things, of plunging into the depths of nature to tap sources of goodness and peace. My adopted father (I always refer to him as my father because it was he who brought me up) was a journeyman tailor. He was great-hearted and possessed a truly questing mind. He used to say, with a smile, that betrayal by the intellectuals began with the first artist who depicted a winged angel – it is by our *hands* that we attain heaven!

In spite of my lack of manual dexterity I did once manage to bind a book. I was sixteen at the time, a student at a vocational class in a suburb of Juvisy. On Saturday afternoons we had the choice between wood and metal work, modelling, and book binding. Poetry was then my favourite reading, Rimbaud my favourite poet. And yet – after an inner struggle, I admit – I abandoned the idea of binding his *Une Saison en Enfer*. My father possessed some thirty books ranged in a narrow cupboard in his workroom along with bobbins, chalk, shoulder pads and patterns. There were also, in this cupboard, thousands of notes which he had jotted down in his scholar's hand at a corner of his bench during innumerable nights working at his trade. Among these books I had read Flammarion's *Le Monde avant la Création de l'Homme* (The World before the Creation of Man) and was just discovering Walter Rathenau's *Ou va la Monde?* (Where is the World Going?) I set out to bind Rathenau's book, not without difficulty. Rathenau was among the first victims of the Nazis, and the year was 1936. So, each Saturday, I struggled over my task in the little workshop of the vocational school, and on the first of May I presented my father with the finished book, and a spray of lilies of the valley out of regard for him and the working class.

My father had underlined in red pencil in this book a passage I still remember:

'Even the most troubled epoch is worthy of respect, because it is the work not just of a few people but of humanity; and thus it is the work of creative nature – which is often cruel but never absurd. If this epoch in which we are living is a cruel one it is more than ever our duty to love it, to penetrate it with our love till we have removed the heavy weight of matter screening the light that shines on the farther side.'

'Even the most troubled epoch . . .'

My father died in 1948 without ever having ceased to believe in creative nature, without ever having ceased to love and to penetrate with his love the sad world in which he lived, without ever having lost the hope of seeing the light behind the heavy weight of matter.

i

He belonged to the generation of romantic socialists who had as their idols Victor Hugo, Romain Rolland, Jean Jaurès, wore widebrimmed hats, and kept a little blue flower in the folds of the red flag. Just at the edge of pure mysticism on the one hand and the cult of social action on the other, my father (he worked fourteen hours a day at his bench: and yet we lived in near misery) succeeded in reconciling an ardent trade union activity with a search for an inner liberation. He had introduced into the humble actions demanded by his work a sort of method of concentration and purification of the mind on which he left hundreds of pages of notes. Stitching button holes or pressing cloth, his face yet bore a radiant expression. Every Thursday (a school holiday in France) and Sunday my friends would gather round his workbench to listen to him and to savour his strength, and nearly all of them felt their life changed in some way.

Full of confidence in progress and science, believing in the coming to power of the proletariat, he had constructed a powerful philosophy for himself. The reading of Flammarion's study of prehistory had been a sort of revelation for him. Guided only by feeling he went on to read books on palaeontology, astronomy and physics. Although with little formal education he yet managed to penetrate to the heart of these subjects. When he talked it was as if it might have been Teilhard de Chardin (whom we hadn't even heard of in those days):

'The experience of our century is going to be something considerably more than the birth of Buddhism! It is no longer a question of endowing such and such a god with human faculties. The religious power of the Earth will undergo in us a final crisis: that of its own discovery. We are beginning to understand, and for ever, that the only acceptable religion for man is the one that will teach him first of all to recognize, love and passionately serve this universe of which he is the most important element.'*

My father believed that the evolutionary process is not to be confused with selection, which is a purely superficial process, but that it is all-inclusive and ascendant, augmenting the 'psychic density' of our planet, preparing it to make contact with the intelligences of other worlds, to draw nearer to the very soul of the Cosmos. For him the human species is not something completed. By virtue of the spread of communal living and the slow creation of a universal psyche, it is progressing toward a state of superconsciousness. He used to say that man is not yet perfect and saved, but that the laws of condensation of creative energy permit us to nourish, at the cosmic level, a tremendous hope. And he never lost sight of this hope. It was from that viewpoint that he judged, serenely and with a religious dynamism, the affairs of this world, seeking far and high an immediate and truly effective optimism and courage. In 1948 the war was over, and new battles – atomic ones,

* 'Teilhard de Chardin tel que je l'ai connu' (Teilhard de Chardin as I knew him), by G. Magloire, in *Synthèse*, November 1957.

ii

this time – were threatening. Nevertheless he considered the disquieting and painful times to be no more than the negative of a magnificent image. It was as if he were in communication with the spiritual destiny of the Earth, and for the troubled epoch in which he ended his life of labour, and despite numerous personal setbacks, he felt nothing but confidence and love.

He died in my arms during the night of 31 December, and before dying he said to me:

'One must not count too much on God, but perhaps God counts on us. . . .'

How did things stand with me at that moment? I was twenty-eight years old. I was twenty in 1940 at the time of France's collapse. I belonged to a critical generation which had seen a world fall apart, which was sundered from the past and mistrustful of the future. I was certainly far from believing that our shattered world was worthy of respect and that it was my duty to penetrate it with love. Rather it seemed to me that a clear head led to refusal to participate in a game where everyone was cheating.

During the war I sought refuge in Hinduism – that was my way of resisting, and I lived in absolute Resistance.

Don't look for help in a study of history, nor among people – they'll let you down every time. Look for it in yourself. Live in this world without being of it. One of my favourite images was the Bhagavad Gita diving bird: 'down, skim the water, and up – without having even wet its wings'. Act in such a way that events too powerful to be modified by us will at least not affect us. I existed in a rarefied air, sitting – lotus fashion – on a cloud borne from the Orient. . . . When I had gone to sleep my father would quietly thumb through my bedside reading, trying to understand the source of my strange ideas which yawned like a gulf between us.

Some time later, just after the Liberation, I found a new master to model myself on and to live for. I became a follower of Gurdjieff. I worked hard to separate myself from all emotion, sentiment, impulse, hoping to find, beyond them, a state of – how shall I say it? – of immobility and of permanence, a silent presence, anonymous, transcendant, which would console me for all that I lacked and for the world's absurdity. I thought of my father with pity. *I* possessed the secrets of controlling the mind; all knowledge was mine. In fact, I possessed nothing except the illusion of possessing, and an overwhelming contempt for those who did not share my illusion.

My father despaired of me. I despaired of myself. I steeped myself to the very bone in a position of refusal. I was reading René Guénon, and believed it was our disgrace to be living in a completely perverted world bent on the Apocalypse. The words spoken by Cortes to the Spanish Chamber of Deputies in 1849 became mine: 'The cause of all your mistakes, gentlemen, is your unawareness of the direction being taken by civilization and the world. You believe that civilization and the world progress. No, they go

iii

backwards!' For me our modern age was the dark ages. I spent my time listing the crimes committed by the modern mind against Mind. Since the twelfth century the Western World, having abandoned the Principals, has been rushing to disaster. To have any hope, however small, was a betrayal. I had energy only for refusal, for the breaking of contact. In this stricken world where priests, thinkers, politicians, sociologists and manipulators of all kinds seemed to me like dung-eaters the only dignified behaviour lay in traditional studies and unconditional resistance to the spirit of the age.

Looked at from such a point of view, evidently, my father appeared the veriest simpleton. His sense of belonging, of affection, of vision irritated me as something unbelievably absurd. The hope he placed in a growing communal life inspired by infinitely more than purely political motives incited my deepest contempt. My standards were those of the ancient theocracies.

Einstein founded a 'committee of despair' of atomic scientists; the menace of total war bore down on a humanity divided into two blocs. Yet my father died with his faith in the future intact; I no longer understood him. I do not intend to raise the problems of the existence of social classes in this book – it isn't the place. But I know very well the reality of these problems: they crucified the man who loved me.

I never knew my real father. He belonged to the old bourgeoisie of Ghent. My mother, like my second father, came from the working class. It was the inheritance from my Flemish ancestors, sensualists, artists, layabouts, and proud, that separated me from a generous, dynamic way of thinking, forcing me into myself and into a misapprehension of the virtue of participation. The barrier between my second father and me had already existed a long time. He who had never wished other child than me (who came of another's blood), solicitous for me, sacrificed much so that I should become an intellectual. Having given everything, he fell into the trap of thinking that we were kindred spirits. He saw in me a beacon, someone capable of lighting a way for others, of giving them courage and hope – of showing them, as he used to say, the light within us. But I knew of no sort of light – except some sort of dark lamp, perhaps – in me or in humanity. I was simply one intellectual among a multitude of intellectuals.

I pushed the conviction of being an outsider and of the need for revolt – ideas reflected in the literary reviews around 1947 when they wrote of 'metaphysical disquiet' – to their extreme limits. Such ideas were the difficult heritage of my generation. How, then, to be a beacon in such circumstances? This typical Victor Hugo thought only caused me to smile sneeringly. My father reproached me with having sold the pass, gone over to the side of the mandarins and those proud of their very powerlessness.

The atom bomb, for me the sign of the end of everything, was for him herald of a new dawn: matter was spiritualizing itself and man was discovering in his surrounding and within himself completely unsuspected forces. The bourgeois sentiment, which sees

iv

this world as nothing but a comfortable habitation, was to be swept away in the gale of a new spirit – the spirit of the 'workers of the Earth' for whom the world is a going machine, an organism in process of becoming, a unity to be achieved, a Truth to be realized. For him humanity is only at the beginning of its evolution. It has received only its primary instruction on the role assigned to it by the Intelligence of the Universe. We are only now beginning to understand the meaning of the phrase 'love of the world'.

The human adventure had a direction, for my father. He judged events as they moved or not in this direction. History made sense: it was leading to some kind of ultra-human being and promised a super-consciousness. But this cosmic philosophy did not isolate him from his century. He was a 'leftist' in his day-to-day living. This irritated me; particularly as I did not then understand that he put more spirituality in his progressiveness than I of progressiveness in my spirituality.

I was suffocating within the closed system of my thinking; I sometimes felt myself to be no more than a little, arid intellectual and envied him his large free-ranging thoughts. Evenings, sitting by his bench, I used to contradict him, provoke him, yet hoping inwardly that he would manage to confound and change me. But, tired, he would lose his temper with me and with a destiny which had given him such splendid conceptions without giving him the means to pass them on to this child of another, mutinous, blood. We would quit each other in anger and sad, I to my meditations and my literature of despair, he back to his work under the raw electric light that yellowed his hair. From my little bedroom I could hear his breathing, his mutterings. Then suddenly, between his teeth he would begin to whistle quietly the opening bars of Beethoven's 'Hymn to Joy' – saying to me in my little bedroom that love will always find its way back. Each evening, round about the hour when we used to have those arguments, I think of him and I hear again those mutters which invariably terminated in song, in that sublime hymn.

He has been dead twelve years. If I had understood then as I understand now I would have managed my intelligence and my heart more skilfully. Then, I was an incessant seeker. Now I have rallied to him after many often sterile and dangerous journies. I would have been able, much sooner, to conciliate the attraction subjectivity has for me with an affection for the world in all its movement. I would have been able to throw up – and perhaps with greater success in the vigour of my youth – a bridge between mysticism and the modern mind. I would have been able to feel myself at once, religious and yet part of the great drive of history. Earlier, much earlier, I would have acquired faith, hope, and charity.

This book sums up five years of questing, through all the regions of consciousness, to the frontiers of science and tradition. I flung myself into this enterprise – and without adequate equipment – because I could no longer deny this world of ours and its future, to which I so clearly belong.

v

Yet, every extremity illuminates. I should have found a means of communication with my epoch more quickly, yet it may be that in approaching things in my own way I did not altogether waste my time. Men get not what they merit but what they resemble. I have always been seeking for, as Rimbaud expressed it, the 'Truth in a soul and a body' I have not found it. In the pursuit of this Truth I lost sight of numerous small truths which would have made of me, certainly not the superman I yearned to be, but at least a better and more integrated person than I am. However, I did learn some things about the fundamental behaviour of the mind, about the various possible states of consciousness, about memory and intuition – some precious things I would not have otherwise learnt and which one day may help me to comprehend those things that are grandiose, essentially revolutionary, in the modern mind at its peak: its questionings on the nature of consciousness and the urgent need for a sort of transmutation of the intelligence.

When I came out of my Yogi's retreat to take a look at the modern world – I knew of its existence, of course, but did not understand the first thing about it – I was immediately struck by its air of the marvellous. My backward-looking preoccupations, fed on pride and hate, had at least this useful result: I no longer saw this world from its bad side, from the point of view of a 'beat-up' nineteenth-century rationalism, of a demagogic radicalism. They had also stopped me from simply accepting the world just because it was there, the place where I happened to live, in that semi-conscious way most people accept it. My viewpoint refreshed by the long visit I had made outside the frontiers of my period, I saw this world to be as rich in a real fantasy as I had supposed the traditional world to be. Better still, my fresh way of looking at the modern world reacted back on and deepened my understanding of the ancient mind. Old and new, I saw both from a fresh angle.

I met Jacques Bergier just about the time I was finishing my book on Gurdjieff's little group. Our meeting (something more than chance I have always thought) was to prove of great consequence. I had just devoted two years to a study of an esoteric school and my experiences in it. But new experiences were beginning for me and this is what I explained to readers of that book on taking my leave of them. With the story of a certain method of trapping monkeys in mind (a handful of nuts in a narrow-mouthed gourd attached to a tree, the monkey slides in his paw, balls it into a fist around the nuts, and so cannot withdraw his paw, and is trapped) I wrote:

'Examine the bait by all means, test it with your hand, then discreetly disengage. Curiosity satisfied, return your attention to the world, resume your liberty, your lucidity, your place on the route leading into our world of Man. The important thing is to discover the extent to which the rhythms of the so-called traditional mode of thinking merge with the movements of contemporary thinking. At their present farthest limits physics, biology, mathematics touch on certain traditional concepts: certain aspects of esoterism, visions of the Cosmos, of the relation between energy and matter. Modern science, once freed from conformism, is seen to have ideas to exchange with the magicians, alchemists and wonder-workers of antiquity. A revolution is taking place before our eyes – the unexpected remarriage of reason, at the summit of its victories, and intuition. For the really attentive observer the problems facing contemporary intelligence are no longer problems of progress. The concept of progress has been dead for some years now. Today it is a question of a change of state, of a transmutation. From this point of view those concerned with the domain of the interior life and its realities are in step with the pioneering savants who are preparing the birth of a world that will have nothing in common with our present world of laborious transition in which we have to live for just a little while longer.

– And that is the precise argument we shall develop in this present book. Before launching into the undertaking I told myself that as a preliminary to understanding the present, one must be capable of projecting one's intelligence far into the past and far into the future. Formerly I had felt a dislike for those described as 'moderns', but I had disliked them for the wrong reasons. They are to be condemned because their minds are occupied with so small a portion of the time-scale. Scarcely have they arrived on the scene than they are anachronisms. Only a contemporary of the future can truly be of the present. Even the distant past may be conceived of as an undertow tending toward the future. Thus interrogating the present from this point of view I received some strange but promising replies.

The American writer, James Blish, wrote that Einstein's glory was to have swallowed Newton alive and kicking. An admirable formula! A preliminary to any raising of our sights toward a higher vision of life is that our thinking should have absorbed – alive and kicking – the truths of the previous level. This is the one certainty that has emerged from my studies. Does this sound banal? But when one has been living with methods of thinking that claim to be on the very peaks of human endeavour, such as René Guénon's wisdom and the Gurdjieff system with their contempt for the greater part of social and scientific reality, this new way of looking at things changes the intentions of the mind and its needs. 'Lower things', said Plato, 'will be found again in higher things – though in another form.' I am convinced that any advance in philosophy which does not *vitally* include in itself the realities of the level it claims to have superseded, is an imposture.

So I passed a long exploratory period in the domain of physics, of anthropology, mathematics, biology before making any attempt to fashion an idea of Man, his nature, his force, his destiny. Formerly I sought to comprehend the 'totality of the concept Man' and was contemptuous of science. I suspected the mind's ability to scale the highest summits. And yet, what did I know of its advances in the field of science? Had it not there manifested its power in certain ways that I might be inclined to accept? And so,

I reflected, the need is to surmount the apparent contradiction between the material and the spiritual. But was the scientific approach the way to achieve this? The least I could do was to investigate the possibility – a more reasonable attitude after all, for a twentieth-century man than undertaking a bare-foot pilgrimage across India! The territory to be explored lay immediately around me.

It was my simple duty to discover whether scientific thinking at its extreme limit resulted in a revision of the idea Man. I further decided that any conclusions I might henceforth come to about the possibilities of intelligence and the significance of the human adventure were to be retained only in so far as they did not run counter to the overall movement of modern consciousness.

I discovered an echo of my attitude in Oppenheimer's reflection that nowadays our poets, historians, and philosophers are actually proud of their ignorance of anything to do with the sciences; our philosophy – in so far as we still have one – is anachronistic, completely out of step with the times in which we live.

Now, for one whose intellectual muscles are in good condition it is no more difficult to attain to the attitude that has inspired nuclear physics than to appreciate Marxist economics or Thomism, no more difficult to grasp the theory of cybernetics than to analyse the causes of the Chinese revolution or the nature of Mallarmé's poetics. Our mandarins refuse to make the effort not because effort as such intimidates them but because they prefer their present modes of thinking, their present values.

As Oppenheimer suggested, a more subtle understanding of the nature of human knowledge and of Man's relations with the Universe is necessary and has been necessary for some time now.

So I commenced my ransacking of the treasures of science and modern technique, inexpertly, certainly; with an ingenuousness and a sense of wonder perhaps dangerous but yet productive of illuminating comparisons, correlations, and attunements. In this way I rediscovered some convictions concerning Man's infinite grandeur that I had held when I was immersed in esoterism and mysticism. But I found them wearing a new look. This time, these convictions had absorbed – alive and kicking – the style and drive of a contemporary intelligence, an intelligence bent on the study of realities. They were no longer backward-looking; they smoothed out antagonisms instead of exciting them. Erstwhile massive antagonisms – the material *versus* the spiritual, individual *versus* collective life – fused as under a tremendous heat. So conceived they were no longer expressions of a choice (that is to say, *of a rupture*) but of a becoming, an overtaking, of a renewing, so to speak, of existence.

The apparent incoherence of bees in flight, the dances executed by them, are, so it is thought, precise mathematical figures and constitute a language. I would like to write a novel wherein all the experiences of a life, the fleeting ones and the significant ones, chance

viii

ones and inevitable ones, would equally compose precise figures – would in fact disclose themselves for what they may well be: a subtle discourse addressed to the soul to help it accomplish itself: a discourse of which the soul comprehends, in its entire life, only a few disjointed phrases.

There are moments when it seems that I comprehend the inner meaning of the human ballet surrounding me, that someone is speaking to me by means of this ceaseless movement of people approaching, people pausing for a second, and then moving away. And then I lose the thread, as who does not, until the next equally fleeting moment of illumination.

At the time I left the Gurdjieff circle I had a very great friend in André Breton. Through him I met René Alleau, the historian of alchemy. One day I was looking for a scientific journalist to contribute to a current-events series. Alleau introduced me to Bergier. (It was bread-and-butter work, and in any event science, popularized or not, interested me little.) This chance meeting was to shape my life for many years. Under its influence I rearranged and orientated the various intellectual and spiritual experiences which I had exposed myself to – from Vivekananda to Guénon, to Gurdjieff, to Breton – and found myself at the point where I had started: my father!

Though dissimilar in many ways Bergier and I worked closely and happily together during five years of study and speculation, arriving at a point of view which I believe is novel and rich in its possibilities. This was how the surrealists worked thirty years ago. But unlike them we were exploring not the regions of sleep and the subconscious but their very opposites: the regions of ultra-consciousness and the 'awakened state'. We call our point of view *fantastic realism*. It has nothing to do with the bizarre, the exotic, the merely picturesque. There was no attempt on our part to escape the times in which we live. We were not interested in the 'outer suburbs' of reality: on the contrary we have tried to take up a position at its very hub. There alone we believe, is the fantastic to be discovered – and not a fantastic leading to escapism but rather to a deeper participation in life.

Artists who seek for the fantastic outside reality in the clouds, lack imagination. They return from their explorations with nothing more than counterfeits. As it is with rare minerals so with the fantastic; it has to be torn out from the very bowels of the Earth, from the heart of reality. True imagination is something other than a leap into the unreal. 'No other aspect of the mind *dives* as deeply as the imagination.'

The fantastic is usually thought of as a violation of natural law, as a rising up of the impossible. That is not how we conceive it. It is rather a manifestation of natural law, an effect produced by contact with reality – reality perceived directly and not through a filter of habit, prejudice, conformism.

Modern science has shown us that behind the visible there is an extremely complicated invisible. A table, a chair, a starry sky are in fact radically different from our ideas of them: they are systems in motion, suspended energy. . . . This is what Valéry meant when he said that 'the marvellous and the actual have contracted an astonishing alliance' in the modern mind. As we hope to show in this book the alliance between the marvellous and the actual is meaningful not only in the fields of physics and mathematics but equally, for example, in anthropology, contemporary history, or sociology. That which is effective in the physical sciences should be fruitful in the humanities – but there will be difficulties of application. The humanities have become the last refuge of prejudice (as well the prejudices long since abandoned by the physical sciences). Not only that, but in this field, still so fluid, there have been attempts to reduce everything to a *system*: Freud explains all, *Das Kapital* explains all, etc. When we say 'prejudice' we are really saying 'superstition'. Just as the ancients were superstitious so are we. For some people every phenomenon of civilization finds its origin in the existence of Atlantis. For others Marxism has a complete explanation of Hitler. Some see the motive force of genius as the breath of God; others think it is sex. Our task then is to fashion this alliance between the marvellous and the actual in the individual and in social man as it already exists in biology, physics, and mathematics (which openly and quite directly refer to such concepts as an 'absolute elsewhere', the 'forbidden light', the 'quantity strangeness number').

As Teilhard de Chardin has stated, only the fantastic is likely to be true at the cosmic level. We believe that human phenomena must also be measured against the cosmic scale. The thinkers of antiquity said this. Our modern world, with its planetary rockets and its efforts to contact other intelligent beings, is saying it. So then, Bergier and I are no more than witnesses to the realities of our epoch.

A close scrutiny will show that our point of view – the extension of fantastic realism as it exists in the physical sciences to the humanities – is by no means original. Nor do we claim originality. The idea of applying mathematical method to the sciences was not a particularly shattering one but its consequences were novel and important. The idea that the Universe may not be quite what it seems is not original: but see what Einstein did with that idea!

It follows from our attitude that a book such as the present one, prepared with scrupulous honesty and a minimum of naïveté, may well spring more questions than answers. A working method is not a system of thought. We do not believe that even the most ingenious of systems could completely illuminate life in its totality, which is our subject. You can work over your Marxism as much as you wish without managing to fit into it Hitler's conviction that the Unknown Master had visited him on occasion. Manipulate the medical theories previous to Pasteur as you will: they have absolutely nothing to say about illness being caused by animal life too minute to be seen. Yet it is possible that there is an overall, final response to the questions we are posing – and that we have not yet heard it.

For Bergier and I, nothing is excluded, neither the yes nor the no. We have not discovered still one more Eastern sage; we have not become the disciples of a new Messiah; we are not expounding a doctrine. We simply propose to open the greatest possible number of doors to our readers, and as most of these doors open outward we have stood back a pace so that the reader may enter.

Let me repeat: the fantastic is not to be equated with the imaginary. But a powerful imagination working on reality will discover that the frontier between the marvellous and the actual – between the visible and the invisible Universe, if you wish – is a very fine one. There may be other Universes parallel to our own. Indeed, perhaps this book would not have been written if Bergier and I had not on more than one occasion had an impression of being in contact – actually, physically – with another world. Bergier had one such experience when he was in Mauthausen. Something similar happened to me when I was a Gurdjieff disciple. In each case the circumstances were different but the essential facts the same.

The American anthropologist, Loren Eiseley, whose attitude is somewhat similar to ours, tells a story which perfectly illustrates what I have been trying to say.

He, too, believes that the impression of being in contact with another world is not always the result of a too-fertile imagination. People have had such experiences. Not only people, animals too! For the space of a moment the frontier dissolves; it is simply a question of being there at that moment. Eiseley was actually present when such an experience befell a crow. Although the crow was, so to speak, a neighbour of his it took good care to avoid all contact with humanity, keeping to the tree-tops and the upper air, keeping to *its* world. But one unusually foggy morning our anthropologist was feeling his way to the station when suddenly, at eye level, two great, black wings preceded by a cruel beak loomed up in front of him and then swept by with a great cry of anguish. The cry haunted Eiseley for the rest of the day; he even found himself before his mirror – wondering whether indeed he could be so repulsive a sight! And then the explanation for that terrible cry dawned on him. The frontier had slipped its position because of the fog. Suddenly, before the eyes of the crow (which reasonably believed itself to be flying around at its usual height) there surged up a fact contrary to nature – a man walking on air, in the very heart of the crow's domain. A veritable manifestation of the marvellous from the crow's point of view: a flying man! Ever after, when it saw Eiseley making his normal way along the ground it would give little cries of distress, of regret for a Universe that could never be the same again.

This book is not a romance, although its intention may well be romantic. It is not science-fiction, although it cites myths on which that literary form has fed. Nor is it a collection of bizarre facts, though the Angel of the Bizarre might well find himself at home in it. It is not a scientific contribution, a vehicle for an exotic teaching, a testament, a document, a fable. It is simply an account – at times figurative, at times factual – of a first excursion into some as yet scarcely explored realms of consciousness. In this book as in the diaries of Renaissance navigators, legend and fact, conjecture and accurate observation intermingle. Lacking the time and the means we were not able to push our exploration far inland, so all we do here is suggest hypotheses and rough out a scheme for communication between those various regions which are still for the most part forbidden territory. Later, fuller investigation may well make hay of some of our impressions, as happened to Marco Polo's narrative. We willingly face this eventuality. 'There certainly were some howlers in that book of Bergier's and Pauwels'!' So be it. But if it is this book that has inspired our critics to themselves take a first-hand look, we shall have done what we set out to do.

The words of Fulcanelli might well have been ours: 'I leave to the reader of these enigmatic notes the task of comparing, of co-ordinating versions, of extracting verity from its allegorical setting.'

However, our documentation owes nothing to esoteric masters, hidden books or secret archives. Vast it may be but it is accessible to everyone. But, so as not to weigh down the book too much, we have avoided a multiplicity of references, footnotes and bibliographies. And sometimes we have developed our argument by way of image or allegory – but always for the purpose of more efficiently making our point and never for the sake of that mystification beloved of the esoterists and which makes one think of the Marx brothers' story:

'Say, there's a million bucks buried in the house next door.'

'There isn't a house next door.'

'No? Then let's build one.'

As I have said, this book owes much in its general theory and its documentation to Jacques Bergier. Everyone who has met him and experienced his extraordinary memory, his insatiable curiosity, his (a rare quality, this) invariable presence of mind, will at once believe me when I say that five years with Bergier have saved me perhaps twenty years of private reading. His brain includes a formidable library: selection, classification, complex cross-references take place with an electronic rapidity. Watching him thinking out a problem never failed to produce in me an excitation of my own faculties without which I would have found the conceiving and preparing of this book impossible.

We brought together an imposing collection of books, reviews, reports, and newspapers in various languages, at an office in the rue de Berri at Paris and dictated thousands of pages of notes: quotations, translations, reflections. The week-end we met at my place at Mesnil-le-Roi to continue our discussions, breaking off from time to time only to refer to some book or other. The evening I would spend in noting down our conclusions, fresh ideas that had occurred to us, fresh lines of research. For five years I was at my desk every day at dawn (the greater part of the day being spent in bread-and-butter work). Things being what they are in this world we yet so stubbornly cleave to, the question of time becomes a question of energy. Had we had ten years before us, better working conditions, and a team of assistants, we would certainly have produced a vastly superior book. One day (should we ever have the money, got from whatever source!) we would like to set up and direct an . . . institute, perhaps, is the word, to continue the studies here initiated. I hope this book may prove of sufficient worth to help us in that aim. As G. K. Chesterton has it, if an idea does not strive to express itself in words then it is an inept idea, and if words do not result in action it is because they too are inept.

Both Jacques Bergier and I are caught up in a multitude of other activities – mine being very demanding. This despite the fact that when I was young I knew people who literally died from over-work; so, 'How do you manage it all?' I don't know; perhaps these Zen words are some sort of explanation: 'I go on foot and yet I am mounted on an ox.'

Difficulties, obligations to be met, obstructions of all kinds continually rose up on every side to the point where I almost despaired. I am not one of those geniuses who pretend a vast indifference to everything not to do with their work. My responses are large and wide; a concentration of passion, however splendid the result, strikes me as somehow being a mutilation. Agreed, if one participates in life to the full one risks being swamped. I fall back on a thought of Vincent de Paul: 'The greatest aims suffer continuing distraction. Flesh and blood insist on abandoning the mission. Listen to them not. God, once resolved, does not change his mind whatever the occasional seeming to the contrary.'

When I was a student at Juvisy (I referred to this period of my life earlier in this preface) I one day had to comment on a phrase of Vigny: 'A life that has achieved itself is a dream of adolescence realized in maturity.' At that time my dream was to serve and to deepen my father's philosophy of progress. After many retreats, side-trackings, and equivocation, this is now, finally, what I am trying to do. May my struggle bring peace to his ashes long since scattered in the thought that 'matter is no more than one of the masks worn by the Great Visage'.

THE MORNING OF THE MAGICIANS

Part One

THE FUTURE PERFECT

I

*Salute to the reader in a hurry – A resignation in 1875 –
Birds of ill-omen – How the nineteenth century closed the
doors – The end of science and the repression of fantasy –
Poincaré's despair – We are our own grandfathers – Youth,
Youth!*

How can an intelligent man today not feel in a hurry? 'Get up, sir;
you've got important things to do!' But one has to rise earlier every
day. Speed up your machines for seeing, hearing, thinking, remembering and imagining. Our best reader, the one we value the most,
will have finished with us in two or three hours.

There are men I know who can read with the greatest profit one
hundred pages of mathematics, philosophy, history, or archaeology
in twenty minutes. Actors learn how to 'place' their voice. Who will
teach us to 'place' our attention? At a certain height everything
changes speed. So far as this work is concerned, I'm not one of
those writers who want to keep their readers with them as long as
possible and lull them to sleep. I'm not interested in sleep, only in
waking. Get on with it quickly; take what you want and go. There's
plenty to do outside. Skip chapters if you want to; begin where you
like and read in any direction; this book is a multiple-use tool, like
the knives campers use. For example, if you're afraid of arriving too
slowly at the heart of the subject that interests you, skip these first
pages. You should understand, however, that they show how the
nineteenth century had closed its doors against fantasy as a positive
element in man and the world and the Universe, and how the twentieth
has opened them again, although our morality, our philosophy and
our sociology, which ought to be contemporary with the future, are
nothing of the kind and remain attached to the out-of-date nineteenth century. The bridge between the era of muskets and that of
rockets hasn't yet been built; but it's being thought about. And the
object of this book is to make people think about it harder. If we're
in a hurry, it's not because we're crying over the past but are
worried about the present, and getting impatient. There you have
it. You know enough now to be able, if necessary, to skim through
this introduction and push on further.

His name is not recorded in the history books – unfortunately. He
was a Director of the American Patent Office and it was he who
first sounded the alarm. In 1875 he sent in his resignation to the
Secretary of the Board of Trade. What's the good of going on, is the
gist of what he said; there's nothing left to invent.

9

Twelve years later, in 1887, the great chemist Marcellin Berthelot wrote: 'From now on there is no mystery about the Universe.' To get a coherent picture of the world science had cleared everything up: perfection by omission. Matter consisted of a certain number of elements, none of which could be turned into another. But while Berthelot in his learned work was rejecting the dreams of the alchemists, the elements, which knew nothing about this, continued to transmute themselves as a result of natural radio-activity. In 1852 the phenomenon had been described by Reichenbach, but was immediately repudiated. Scientists before 1870 had referred to a 'fourth state of matter', observed in gases. Any kind of mystery, however, had to be suppressed. Repression is the right word; some nineteenth century thinking ought to be psychoanalysed.

A German named Zeppelin, returning home after fighting with the Southerners, tried to get the industrialists interested in a dirigible balloon. . . . 'Unhappy man! Don't you know that there are three subjects which can no longer be the subject of a paper submitted to the French Academy of Science: the squaring of the circle, the tunnel under the Channel and dirigible balloons.'

Another German, Herman Gaswindt, had the idea of building flying machines heavier than air to be propelled by rockets. On his fifth blueprint the German War Minister, after consulting the technicians, wrote, with the habitual moderation of his race and office: 'How long will it be before this bird of ill-omen is finally bumped off?'

The Russians, on their side, had got rid of another bird of ill-omen. Kibaltchich who was also in favour of rocket-propelled flying machines: a firing-squad saw to that. It is true that Kibaltchich had used his technical skill to fabricate the bomb that had just cut up into little pieces the Emperor Alexander II. But it wasn't necessary to execute Professor Langley, of the Smithsonian Institute, who had imagined flying machines propelled by the recently invented internal combustion engine. It was enough for him to be dishonoured, ruined and expelled from the Smithsonian. Professor Simon Newcomb proved mathematically the impossibility of a heavier-than-air machine. A few months before the death of Langley, who died of grief, a little English boy came back from school one day in tears. He had shown his companions the photograph of a design that Langley had just sent to his father. He declared that men would one day be able to fly. His comrades had laughed at him. And the schoolmaster had asked him how his father could be such a fool. The name of this 'fool' was H. G. Wells.

And so all the doors were closing with a bang. There was, in fact, nothing left to do but to resign, and M. Brunetière in 1895 was able calmly to speak of the 'bankruptcy of science'. The celebrated Professor Lippmann told one of his pupils, about the same time, that physics was a subject that had been exhausted and was finished and done with, and that he would do better to turn his attention in other directions. This pupil's name was Helbronner who later was to become the greatest authority in Europe on physical chemistry and make remarkable discoveries relating to liquid air, ultra-violet rays and colloidal metals. Moissan, a chemist of genius, was forced to recant and declare in public that he had not manufactured diamonds, but had made a mistake during an experiment. It was useless to seek any further: the great discoveries of the century were the steam-engine and the gas lamp, and no greater human inventions were possible. Electricity? A mere technical curiosity. A mad Englishman, Maxwell, had pretended that invisible light rays could be produced by means of electricity: this couldn't be taken seriously.

A few years later Ambrose Bierce wrote in his *Devil's Dictionary*, 'No one knows what electricity is, but in any case it gives a better light than a horse-power and travels quicker than a gas jet.'

As for energy, this was something quite independent of matter and devoid of mystery. It was composed of fluids. These fluids filled everything up, could be described in equations of great formal beauty and were intellectually satisfying: they could be electric, luminous, calorific, etc. Here was a continuous and obvious progression: matter in its three states, solid, liquid and gaseous, and the various energy-fluids, more elusive even than gases. To preserve a 'scientific' image of the world it was only necessary to reject as philosophic dreams the theories about the atom that were beginning to take shape. Planck's and Einstein's 'grains of energy' were still a very long way off.

The German Clausius maintained that no source of energy other than fire was conceivable. And though energy may be preserved quantitatively, it deteriorates in quality. The Universe has been wound up once for all, like a watch, and will run down when the spring is worn out. No surprises are to be expected. Into this Universe, whose destiny is foreseeable, life entered by chance and developed according to the simple laws of natural selection. At the apex of this evolution came man – a mechanical and chemical compound endowed with an illusion – consciousness. Under the influence of this illusion man invented time and space: concepts of the mind. If you had told an official nineteenth century scientist that physics would one day absorb space and time and would study experimentally the curvature of space and the contraction of time, he would have summoned the police. Space and time have no real existence; they are the mathematician's variables and subjects for philosophers to discuss at their leisure. There can be no connection between man and such immensities. Despite the work of Charcot, Breuer, Hyslop, extra-sensory or extra-temporal perception is an idea to be rejected with scorn. Nothing unknown in the universe, nothing unknown in man.

It was quite useless to attempt any internal exploration; nevertheless there was one fact that defied simplication: hypnotism. People like the naïve Flammarion, the sceptical Edgar Poe and the suspect H. G. Wells were interested in this phenomenon. And yet, fantastic as this may seem, the nineteenth century proved officially that there was no such thing as hypnotism. Patients tend to tell lies and pretend in order to please the hypnotizer. That is true. However, since Freud and Morton Price, we know that there is such a thing as a split personality. Thanks to a generally critical attitude this century succeeded in creating a negative mythology, in eliminating any trace of the unknown in man and in repressing any suggestion of mystery.

Biology, too, was finished. M. Claude Bernard had exhausted its possibilities, and the conclusion had been reached that the brain secreted thoughts as the liver secretes bile. Doubtless it would soon be possible to analyse this secretion and write out its chemical formula to fit in with the pretty patterns of hexagons for which M. Berthelot was famous. As soon as we discover how the hexagons of carbon combine to create mind the last page will have been turned. Let's get on with the job! and have all the madmen shut up. One fine day in 1898 a certain seriously-minded gentleman forbade the governess to allow his children to read Jules Verne. These false ideas would only deform their young minds. The gentleman's name was Edouard Branly. He had just decided to abandon his experiments with sound-waves as being devoid of interest, and take up the career of a general practitioner.

Scientists have to give up their throne. But they also have to get rid of the 'adventurers' – that is to say, people who think and dream and are endowed with imagination. Berthelot attacked the philosophers – 'fencing with their own ghosts in the solitary field of abstract logic' (a good description that, of Einstein, for example). And Claude Bernard declared that 'a man who discovers the simplest fact does a greater service than the greatest philosopher in the world'. Science can only be experimental; without it we are lost. Shut the gates; nobody will ever be the equal of the giants who invented the steam-engine.

In this organized, comprehensible and yet doomed universe the place assigned to man was that of an epiphenomenon. There could be no Utopia and no hope. Coal deposits would be exhausted in a few hundred years, and humanity would perish by cold and starvation. Men would never fly and would never travel through space. Nor would they ever explore the bottom of the sea. Strange that this ban should have been imposed on any investigation of the ocean depths! From a technical point of view there was nothing, in the nineteenth century, to prevent Professor Picard from constructing his bathyscaphe. Nothing but an extreme timidity and concern that man should 'stay in his proper place'.

Turpin, who invented melinite, was promptly jailed. The inventors of the internal combusion engine were discouraged, and an attempt was made to show that electric machines were merely forms of perpetual motion. Those were the days when the great inventors were persecuted, isolated and in revolt. Hertz wrote to the Dresden Chamber of Commerce that research into the transmission of the Hertzian waves should be discouraged, as they could not be used for any practical purpose. Napoleon III's experts proved that Gramme's dynamo could never function.

As for the first automobiles, the submarine, the dirigible balloon and electric light ('one of that fellow Edison's swindles') the learned societies were not interested. There is an immortal entry in the Minutes of the Paris Academy of Sciences recording the reception of the first phonograph: 'No sooner had the machine emitted a few words than the Permanent Secretary threw himself upon the impostor (presenting it) seizing his throat in a grip of iron. "You see, gentlemen," he exclaimed, "what it is . . ." But, to the stupefaction of everyone present, the machine continued to utter sounds.'

Nevertheless, some great minds, profoundly discontented with the situation, were secretly preparing the most formidable revolution in human knowledge in the history of mankind. For the time being, however, every avenue was barred.

Barred in every direction – in front and in the rear. The fossils of pre-human creatures that were beginning to be discovered in large numbers were not taken seriously. Did not the great Heinrich Helmholtz prove that the Sun derived its energy from its own contractions – that is to say, from the only force, its own combustion, existing in the Universe? And did not his calculations show that the Sun had not been in existence for more than about a hundred thousand years? How, then, could there have been a long process of evolution? Moreover, it would never be possible to fix a date for the beginning of the world. In the short interval between two states of nothingness we human 'epiphenomena' must be serious. Facts, facts! – nothing but facts!

As their researches into matter and energy had met with little encouragement, the best among the inquiring minds turned to explore an *impasse* – the ether, a substance that permeates matter in all its forms and acts as a vehicle for luminous and electromagnetic waves. It is at once both infinitely solid and infinitely tenuous. Lord Rayleigh, who at the end of the nineteenth century represented official English science in all its splendour, formulated the theory of a gyroscopic ether – an ether consisting of a mass of spinning-tops turning in all directions and reacting on one another. Aldous Huxley has remarked since that 'if it is possible for a human invention to convey the idea of absolute ugliness, then Lord Rayleigh's theory has succeeded'.

Scientists everywhere were engaged in speculations on the ether on the eve of the twentieth century. Then in 1898 came a catastrophe: the Michelson-Morley experiment shattered the hypothesis of the ether. All the work of Henri Poincaré bears witness to this collapse. Poincaré, a mathematician of genius, felt crushed by the enormous weight of this nineteenth century prison, the destroyer of all fantasy. He would have discovered the theory of relativity, had he dared. But he did not dare. His books – *La Valeur de la Science*, *La Science et l'Hypothèse*, are expressions of despair and abdication. For him, a scientific hypothesis is never true and can at best be useful. Like the Spanish inn – you only find there what you bring yourself. According to Poincaré, if the Universe contracted a

13

million times and ourselves with it, nobody would notice anything. Such speculations are therefore useless because they have no connection with reality as we perceive it.

This argument, up to the beginning of this century, was cited as a model of profound reasoning. Until one day a practical engineer pointed out that the butcher, at any rate, would notice it, as all his joints would fall down. The weight of a leg of mutton is proportional to its volume, but the strength of a piece of string is proportional only to its length. Therefore, were the universe to contract by only a millionth of a degree, there would be no more joints hanging from the ceiling! Poor, great and dear Poincaré! It was this great thinker who wrote: 'Common sense alone is enough to tell us that the destruction of a town by a pound of metal is an evident impossibility.'

The limited nature of the physical structure of the Universe; the non-existence of atoms; restricted sources of fundamental energy; the inability of a mathematical formula to yield more than it already contains; the futility of intuition; the narrowness and absolutely mechanical nature of Man's internal world: these were the things the scientists believed in, and this attitude of mind applied to everything and created the climate which permeated every branch of knowledge in this century. A minor century? No; a great century, but narrow – a dwarf stretched out.

But suddenly the doors so carefully closed by the nineteenth century in the face of the infinite possibilities of man, of matter, of energy, of time and of space are about to burst asunder. Science and technical skills will make enormous progress, and a new assessment will be made of the very nature of knowledge.

Not merely progress, this, but a transformation. In this new state of the world, consciousness itself acquires a new status. Today, in every domain, all forms of imagination are rampant – except in those spheres where our 'historical' life goes on, stifled, unhappy and precarious, like everything that is out of date. An immense gulf separates the man of adventure from humanity, and our societies from our civilization. We are living with ideas of morality, sociology, philosophy and psychology that belong to the nineteenth century. We are our own great-great-grandfathers. As we watch rockets rising to the sky and feel the ground vibrating with a thousand new radiations, we are still smoking the pipe of Thomas Graindorge. Our literature, our philosophical discussions, our ideological conflicts, our attitude towards reality – all this is still slumbering behind the doors that have been burst open. Youth! Youth! – go forth and tell the world that everything is opened up and already the Outside has come in!

Bourgeois delights – A crisis for the intelligence, or the hurricane of Unrealism – Glimpses of another reality – Beyond logic and literary philosophies – The idea of an Eternal Present – Science without conscience or conscience without science ? – Hope

'THE Countess had her tea at five o'clock': Valéry said something to the effect that that kind of thing could not be written by anyone who had gained an entrance to the world of ideas, a thousand times stronger, more romantic and more *real* than the world of the heart and senses. 'Anthony loved Mary who loved Paul; they were very unhappy and had lots of little nothings.' A whole literature! – to describe the palpitations of a mass of amoeba and infusoria, whereas human Thought gives rise to tragedies and gigantic dramas, transmutes human beings, alters the course of whole civilizations and enrols in its service vast sections of the human race. As to soporific pleasure and bourgeois delights – we workers of the earth, devotees of intellectual enlightenment, are well aware of all that they contain in the way of insignificance, decadence and rottenness. . . .

At the end of the nineteenth century the 'bourgeois' theatre and novel were in their hey-day, and for a time the literary generation of 1885 paid homage to Anatole France and Paul Bourget.

Nevertheless, about the same time, a much more important and exciting drama than any in which the characters of *Divorce* or *Le Lys Rouge* were involved was being played out in the sphere of pure knowledge. The dialogue between materialism and spiritualism, science and religion, suddenly entered on a new and exciting phase.

The scientists, who had inherited the positivism of Taine and Renan, were confronted with staggering discoveries which were to demolish the strongholds of incredulity. Where hitherto only a reality that was well vouched for could be believed in, suddenly the unreal became a possibility, and things were viewed from the standpoint of a romantic intrigue, with the transformation of characters, the intrusion of traitors, conflicting passions and illusory discussions.

The principle of the conservation of energy was established as a certainty, solid as a rock. And yet here was radium, producing energy without acquiring it from any source. No one doubted that light and electricity were identical: they could only proceed in a straight line and were incapable of traversing any obstacle. And yet here were X-rays which could go through solid objects. In the discharge tubes matter seemed to disappear or be transformed into particles of energy. The transmutation of the elements was taking place in nature: radium turns into helium or lead. And so the Temple of Consecrated Beliefs is ready to collapse; Reason no longer reigns supreme! It seemed that anything was possible. The scientists who were supposed to have the monopoly of knowledge suddenly ceased to make a distinction between physics and metaphysics – between fact and fantasy. The pillars of the Temple dissolve into clouds, and the High Priests of Descartes are dumbfounded. If the theory of the conservation of energy is false, what is there to prevent a medium from manufacturing an ectoplasm out of nothing? If magnetic waves can traverse the earth, why should thought-transmission not be possible? If all known bodies emit invisible forces, why should there not be astral bodies? If there is a fourth dimension, could this be the spirits' world?

Mme Curie, Crookes and Lodge go in for table-turning; Edison tries to construct a machine for communicating with the dead. Marconi, in 1901, thought he had intercepted messages from Mars. Simon Newcomb was not surprised when a medium materialized sea-shells fresh from the Pacific. The seekers after reality are bowled over by strong blasts of the fantastic and the un-real.

But the stalwarts, the Old Guard, endeavour to stem the flood. The Positivists, in the name of Truth and of Reality, reject everything *en bloc*: X-rays, ectoplasms, atoms, spirits of the dead, the fourth phase of matter and the idea of there being inhabitants on Mars.

And so begins a conflict between fantasy and reality – a conflict often seemingly absurd, blind and confused, but one which will soon have repercussions on all forms of thought in every sphere: literature, sociology, philosophy, morals and aesthetics. But in the physical sciences order will be re-established, not through retreat or the whittling down of claims, but thanks to fresh advances. A new conception of physics takes shape, due to the efforts of titans such as Langevin, Perrin, Einstein. A new science is born, less dogmatic than the old one. Doors are opened on to a different *kind* of reality. As in all great novels, in the end there are neither good nor bad characters, and all the heroes are right so long as the novelist's ideas are directed towards a complementary dimension where all their destinies converge and become one, and are raised, together, to a higher level.

How do we stand today? Doors have been thrown open in almost all the strongholds of science, but that of physics has lost almost all its walls to become a cathedral entirely built of glass wherein can be seen the reflections of another world, infinitely near.

Matter has been shown to be as rich, if not richer in possibilities than the spirit. The energy it contains is incalculable; its resources can only be guessed at; it can undergo an infinite number of transformations. The term 'materialist' in its nineteenth century connotation, has become meaningless; and so has the expression 'rationalist'. The logic of 'common sense' is no longer valid. In the new physics a proposition can be both true and false. A.B. no longer equals B.A. An entity can be at once continuous and discontinuous. Physics can no longer be relied on to determine what is or is not possible. One of the most astonishing signs of the breach that has been made in the domain of physics is the introduction of what has been called the 'strangeness quantum number'. What has happened is roughly as follows. At the beginning of the nineteenth century it was believed, somewhat naïvely that two, or at most three, numbers were enough to define a particle, referring respectively to its mass, its electric charge and its magnetic moment. This turned out to be very far from the truth. In order to define completely a particle, another dimension, which cannot be expressed in words, had to be allowed for, known as *spin*. It was believed at first that this 'dimension' corresponded to a period in the particle's rotation on itself, rather like the period of twenty-four hours which, in the case of the planet Earth, regulates the alternation of night and day. However, it soon became clear that the explanation could not possibly be as simple as that. The spin was simply the spin – a quantity of energy connected with the particle, envisaged mathematically as a rotation, although nothing whatever within the particle actually turns.

In spite of erudite research carried out, notably by Professor Louis de Broglie, the mystery of the spin has only been partially explained. Then suddenly the discovery was made that among the three known particles – protons, electrons and neutrons (and their mirror-reflections, the negative anti-proton, positron and anti-neutron) there were at least thirty other particles. The cosmic rays, the great accelerators, produced them in enormous quantities. But to describe these particles the three numbers used hitherto, mass, 'charge', 'magnetic moment' no longer sufficed. It was necessary to create a fourth, perhaps a fifth number, or even more. And so, quite naturally, the physicists called these new dimensions 'strangeness quantum numbers'. There is something supremely poetic about this salute to the angel of the bizarre. Like many other expressions used in modern physics – 'forbidden radiation', 'absolute elsewhere', 'strangeness quantum number', has overtones which seem to go beyond physics to rejoin the profounder regions of the human mind.

Take a sheet of paper. Pierce two holes in it, near together. Obviously, common sense tells us, an object small enough to go through these holes will go through either one or the other. By the same criterion, an electron is an object. It has a definite weight and produces a ray of light when it strikes a television screen and a shock when it hits a microphone. Here we have, then, an object small enough to go through one of our two holes. Now, the electronic microscope will tell us that the electron has gone through both holes at the same time. What? If it has gone through one, it can't have gone through the other at the same time. But indeed it *has* gone through both. It sounds crazy, but the experiment has been made. Attempts to explain it have led to the formulation of various theories, notably that of wave mechanics. But this theory is still not a complete explanation of a fact that defies reason, which can only function in terms of Yes or No, A or B. In order to understand it, the very structure of our reason will have to be changed.

Our philosophy is based on thesis and antithesis. But it looks as if, in the philosophy of the electron, thesis and antithesis are both true at the same time. Are we talking about absurdities? The electron seems to obey laws, and television, for example, is a reality. Does the electron exist, or not? What nature calls existence is not existence in our eyes. Is an electron something or nothing? The question is meaningless. And so, at the extreme limits of knowledge, our normal methods of thought and the 'literary' philosophies, born of an outdated outlook on the world, simply disappear.

The Earth is part of the Universe; Man is not only in contact with the planet he inhabits. Cosmic rays, radio-astronomy and theoretical physics reveal the contacts he has with the Cosmos as a whole. We no longer live in a closed world, as no intelligent person in tune with our times can have failed to notice. How, then, in these circumstances, is it possible for a thinking man to be still pre-occupied with problems that are not even planetary, but narrowly regional and provincial? And how can our psychology, as revealed in works of fiction, remain so enclosed and confined to the analysis of the subconscious impulses of human sensuality and senti-mentality? While millions of civilized people read books and go to the cinema or the theatre to see how Françoise can be in love with René and yet, through her hatred of her father's mistress, revenge herself by becoming a Lesbian, there are scientists, making a celestial music out of mathematics, who are speculating as to whether space does not contract around a vehicle. The whole universe would then be accessible; one could visit the farthest star in the space of a lifetime. If equations like these could be verified, human thinking would be revolutionized. If mankind is no longer confined to this Earth, new questions will have to be asked with regard to the deeper aspects of Initiation and the possibility of making contact with intelligent beings from Beyond.

What, then, is our position today? As regards research into the structure of space and time, our notions of past and future are no longer valid. Where particles are concerned, time travels in the two directions simultaneously – past and future. At very high speeds, at the velocity of light, for example, where does time come in? We are in London in October 1944. A V2 rocket, travelling at 5,000 km. per hour is over the city. It is about to fall. But to what does this 'about to' apply? As regards the occupants of the house which in a moment will be destroyed and who have only their eyes and ears, the V2 is, indeed, 'about to' fall. But from the point of view of the radar operator, using waves travelling at 300,000 km. per second (a speed which makes the rocket appear to be crawl-ing) the trajectory of the bomb is already traced. He can only watch; there is nothing he can do. Humanly speaking, nothing can now intercept the engine of death; no warning can be given. In the eyes of the operator the rocket has already crashed. At the speed of radar time is practically non-existent. The occupants of the house are 'about to die'; in the radar's eye they are already dead.

Another example: when the cosmic rays reach the Earth's surface, they are found to contain particles, the μ mesons which live on Earth only for a millionth of a second, destroying themselves by radio-activity. Now, these particles are born thirty kilometres up in the air when the atmosphere of our planet is beginning to be dense. So, by the time they have covered this distance, they have already exceeded their life span by our reckoning. But their time is not ours. Their journey was made in eternity, and they only entered time when they lost their energy on arriving at sea level. Apparatus, it is thought could be built to reproduce these conditions. In this way drawers of time, as it were, could be created in which objects enjoying only a brief span of life would be placed and preserved in the fourth dimension. This receptacle would be a hollow glass ring placed in a field of intense energy in which the particles would rotate so rapidly that for them time would practically have ceased to exist. A life-span of a millionth of a second might thus be maintained and observed for minutes, or even hours. . . .

'It must not be supposed that past time vanishes into the void; time is one and eternal, of which past, present and future are only different aspects – different "pressings", if you like – of a continuous, invariable recording of perpetual existence.'

The modern disciples of Einstein recognize nothing but an eternal present, which was also what the ancient mystics believed. If the future exists already, then precognition is a fact. The whole trend of advanced knowledge is to place the laws of physics, and biology and psychology as well, in a four-dimensional continuum – that is to say, in the eternal present. Past, present and future *are*. Perhaps it is only our consciousness that moves. For the first time, consciousness is admitted in its own right into the equations of theoretical physics. In this eternal present, matter appears as a slender thread stretched between past and future. Along this thread glides human consciousness. By what means it it able to modify the tensions of this thread so as to have an influence on events ? One day we shall know, and psychology will then become a branch of physics.

And no doubt there is a place for freedom within this eternal present. 'The traveller in a boat on the Seine knows in advance what bridges he will encounter. He none the less has freedom of action and is capable of foreseeing anything that could happen *en route.*'*

Freedom to *become* in the midst of an eternity which *is*! A double vision, an admirable vision of human destiny bound up with that of the whole Universe!

If I had my life to live again I should certainly not choose to be a writer and spend my days in a backward society where adventure is kept under the bed like a dog. I should want a lion-like adventure: I would go in for theoretical physics in order to live at the very heart of true romance.

The new world of physics explicitly contradicts the philosophies

* R. P. Dubarle, in a broadcast discussion, 12 April, 1957.

19

of despair and non-sense. Science without conscience spells ruin for the soul. But conscience without science means ruin too.

These philosophies which were all the rage in Europe in the twentieth century were nothing but phantoms of nineteenth-century creeds dressed up in the new fashions. Real, objective knowledge in the field of technology and science, which sooner or later englobes the domain of sociology, teaches us that the history of mankind follows a definite path, accompanied by an increase in man's powers, a rise in the general level of intelligence and a compulsive force which acts on the masses transforming them into active thinkers and giving them access to a civilization where life will be as much superior to ours as ours is now to that of the animals. The literary philosophers had been telling us that man is incapable of understanding the world. André Maurois, in *Les Nouveaux Discours du Docteur O'Grady*, for example, wrote as follows: 'Yet you will admit, Doctor, that nineteenth-century man believed that science would one day be able to explain the universe. Renan, Berthelot, Taine, early in their lives, hoped that this would come about. Twentieth-century man has no such hopes. He knows that discoveries only make the mystery deeper. As to progress, we have seen how man, with all his powerful resources, has only succeeded in producing famine, terror, disorder, torture and confusion in the mind. What hope is there left? Why do you go on living, Doctor?' In point of fact, however, the problem could no longer be stated in these terms. Though the protagonists in this discussion were unaware of it, the circle was already closing round the mystery, and the 'progress' so bitterly decried, was opening the gates of heaven. We do not turn to Berthelot or Taine for enlightenment on the future of mankind, but rather to men like Teilhard de Chardin. At a recent discussion between representatives of the various scientific disciplines the following idea was put forward: one day, perhaps, the ultimate secrets of the elementary particles will be revealed to us by what takes place deep down in the brain, for it is here that the most complex reactions in our region of the universe are finally registered, and the brain, no doubt, contains in itself the laws which govern the profoundest mysteries of this region. The world is not absurd, and the mind is surely not incapable of understanding it. On the contrary; it may well be that the human mind *has already understood the world*, but doesn't know that - yet.

III

Brief reflections on the backwardness of sociology – Talking cross-purposes – Planetary versus provincial – Crusader in the modern world – The poetry of science

THE outlook in modern physics, mathematics and biology is limitless. Sociology, on the other hand, is barred from new horizons by the monuments of the last century. I remember how astonished and disappointed we were, Jacques Bergier and myself, in 1957

20

when we were following the correspondence between the celebrated Soviet economist Eugene Varga and the American magazine *Fortune*. This luxurious publication expounds the views of an enlightened capitalism. Varga is an intelligent writer, and is respected by the powers that be. A public discussion between two such authorities might have done much, one would have thought, to bring about a better understanding of the times we live in. In the event, however, it proved a ghastly failure.

Mr. Varga stuck faithfully to his gospel. Karl Marx had predicted the inevitable collapse of capitalism, and Mr. Varga thought this collapse was imminent. The fact that the economic situation of the United States was steadily improving and that the great problem from now on would be how the workers' leisure time could best be employed had escaped the notice of this theoretician who, in these days of radar, was still looking at the world through Karl's spectacles.

The idea that the predicted collapse might not happen according to the prearranged schedule, and that it was possible that a new society was coming into being across the Atlantic did not for a moment enter his head. Neither did the editor of *Fortune*, for his part, foresee any change in the structure of society in the U.S.S.R., and made it clear that the America of 1957 was the expression of a perfect and unchangeable ideal. All that the Russians could hope for was to attain, if they behaved themselves, a similar state of perfection in a century, or a century and a half. Nothing worried or disturbed the theoretical adversaries of Mr. Varga – not even the multiplicity of new cults springing up everywhere in American intellectual circles (Oppenheimer, Aldous Huxley, Gerald Heard, Henry Miller and many others seduced by ancient Oriental philosophies) nor yet the existence in the great cities of millions of young 'rebels without a cause' going about in gangs, nor yet again the twenty million individuals unable to support modern life without absorbing drugs as dangerous as morphine and opium. The problem of finding a *purpose* in life did not seem to exist for them. When all American families possess two cars, they will then have to buy a third. When the market for television sets is saturated, motor-cars will have to be equipped with them.

And yet, compared to French sociologists, economists and thinkers, Mr. Eugene Varga and the editors of *Fortune* are more advanced. They are not paralysed by the complex of decadence. They do not indulge in morbid pleasures, or believe that the world is absurd and life not worth living. They firmly believe in the virtues of progress, and are confident that man's domination over nature will increase indefinitely. They have energy and a certain grandeur, and their outlook is broad, if not very elevated. To say that Mr. Varga is in favour of free enterprise and the editors of *Fortune* are all progressists might seem outrageous; and yet, from a strictly doctrinal, European point of view, it is true. Mr. Varga is not a communist; *Fortune* is not capitalist, according to our narrow, provincial ideas. What the Russian and the American in this case have in common is ambition, the will to power and an unshakeable

21

optimism. These are the forces at work in science and technology which will demolish the old sociological order established in the nineteenth century. Even if Western Europe became involved in and were destroyed by some Byzantine struggle (which God forbid!) the forward march of humanity would still go on, bursting open the old structure of society and setting up a new form of civilization between the two new poles of militant thought represented by Chicago and Tashkent, while the vast hordes in the East and in Africa would launch out into industry.

While one of our best French sociologists sheds tears over *Le Travail en Miettes* (the title of one of his books) American syndicates are studying the twenty-hour week. And while Parisian so-called *avant-garde* intellectuals are wondering whether Marx is not perhaps a back number, or whether existentialism is or is not a revolutionary form of humanism, the Sternfeld Institute in Moscow is examining the possibility of settling human beings on the moon. While Mr. Varga awaits the collapse of the United States announced by the Prophet, American biologists are preparing to create life artificially. While the problem of co-existence is still being debated, communism and capitalism are being transformed by the most sweeping technological revolution this planet has ever known. Our eyes are in the back of our heads; it is time to put them in their right place.

The last sociologist with any imagination or drive was no doubt Lenin. He had accurately defined the communism of 1917 as 'socialism plus electricity'. After nearly half a century, the definition still holds good for China, Africa and India, but is obsolete as regards the modern world. Russia awaits the thinker who will describe the new order: communism *plus* atomic energy, *plus* automation, *plus* the synthetic creation of fuel and food from water and air, *plus* the physics of solid bodies, *plus* the conquest of the stars, etc., etc. John Buchan, after attending the funeral of Lenin announced the coming of another Seer who would promulgate a 'four-dimensional communism'.

If the U.S.S.R. lacks a sociologist of sufficient eminence, America is no better off. The reaction against the 'red historians' at the end of the nineteenth century has led economic observers to indulge in uninhibited praise of the great capitalist dynasties and powerful institutions. This is a healthy reaction up to a point, but a short-sighted one. Critics of the 'American way of life' are rare, and their attitude is 'literary' and purely negative. None of them seems to have enough imagination to see, beyond this 'solitary crowd', a civilization that belies its external forms, or to sense the collapse of old values and the advent of new myths. And yet the astonishing and abundant production of what is known as 'science-fiction' points to the emergence of a new spirit, leaving adolescence behind, unfolding on a planetary level, preoccupied with cosmic speculations and adopting an entirely new approach to the question of the destiny of mankind within the vast universe. But this kind of literature, having so much in common with the oral tradition of the story-tellers of ancient times and so clearly indicating a profound change in people's mental habits, is not taken seriously by the sociologists.

As regards European sociology, it is still quite provincial in outlook, and preoccupied with inessentials. It is therefore not surprising that the more sensitive sections of society take refuge in a philosophy of despair. Everything is absurd, and the H-bomb has put an end to history. It is easier to live with this philosophy which appears to be at once sinister and profound, than to attempt the arduous task of analysing the world of reality. It is a temporary sickness of mind among civilized people who have not adapted the ideas they have inherited about such things as the freedom of the individual, human personality, happiness, etc., to the new set of values envisaged by the civilization of the future. It is a sign of nervous fatigue affecting the human spirit at a time when, fully occupied in coping with its own conquests, it is important that it should not give up the struggle, but change its own structure. After all, it is not the first time in the history of humanity that human consciousness has had to switch to another level. All operations are painful; but if there is to be any future, it is worth investigating. And, at the rate things are moving today, our criterion should not be the immediate past. Our immediate future is as different from anything we have known as the nineteenth century was from the Maya civilization. We must therefore proceed by projecting ourselves farther and farther into space and time instead of making trivial comparisons within an infinitely small period where the past we have just been living in bears no resemblance to the future, and where the present has no sooner come into being than it is swallowed up by this unusuable past.

The first really fruitful idea is that there has been a change in what our civilization is aiming at. A Crusader from the past revisiting the world would immediately ask why we are not using the atomic bomb against the Infidels. Stalwart-hearted and intelligent, he would in the last resort be less disconcerted by our modern techniques than by the fact that the Infidels still hold half the Holy Sepulchre, the other half being in the hands of the Jews. He would find it harder still to understand why the wealth and power of a powerful and wealthy civilization are not being devoted to the service and glory of Jesus. What would our sociologists have to say to this? That the exclusive aim of all these immense efforts, conflicts and discoveries has been to raise the 'standard of living' of the human race? He would find that absurd since, for him, such a life would seem to him an aimless one. They would talk to him about Justice, Liberty and the Rights of Man, and recite to him the humanistic-materialist gospel of the nineteenth century. And our Crusader no doubt would reply: 'But liberty to do what? And justice in what cause? And what are the rights of man?' If we want our knight to look upon our civilization as a worthy setting for a human soul, it is useless to talk to him in the retrospective language of our sociologists. We must use a forward-looking vocabulary, and

23

present to him, as evidence of the beginning of a triumphant new crusade, the achievements, material and intellectual, of our progressive world.

Once again, it's a question of saving the Holy Sepulchre – spirit weighed down by matter – and repulsing the Infidel – everything that is unfaithful to the infinite might of the spirit. It is still a religious question: making manifest everything that binds man to his own greatness, and that greatness to the laws of the Universe. We should have to show our Crusader a world in which cyclotrons are like cathedrals, and mathematics like Gregorian plain-chant; where transmutations take place not only in matter, but in the brain; where human beings of all races and colours are on the march; where man in his quest for knowledge extends his antennae into cosmic space, and where the soul of our planet is awakening. Perhaps, then, our Crusader would ask to go back to the past. Perhaps he would feel at home here, but placed as it were, on a different level. Perhaps, on the other hand, he would march eagerly towards the future, just as long ago he marched towards the East, inspired once again by faith, but this time of a different kind.

You see now the adventure on which we are engaged. Make sure your eyes are in their right place! It is time to turn darkness into light!

AN OPEN CONSPIRACY

I

The generation of the 'workers of the Earth' – Are you a behind-the-times modern, or a contemporary of the future? – A poster on the walls of Paris in 1622 – The esoteric language is the technical language – A new conception of a secret society – A new aspect of the 'religious spirit'

GRIFFIN, H. G. Wells's Invisible Man, said: 'People, even cultivated people, have no idea of the forces concealed in scientific books. These volumes contain marvels and miracles.'

They have now, however; and the man in the street knows it better than the clever people, always one revolution behind. There are marvels and miracles, and terrifying things too. The powers of science since Wells have extended beyond our planet, and threaten even its existence. A new generation of scientists is born. These are men who believe themselves to be, not disinterested seekers after truth and spectators, but, as Teilhard de Chardin has so finely described them, 'ouvriers de la terre', who have linked their destiny to that of humanity and made themselves largely responsible for that destiny.

Joliot-Curie hurls bottles of petrol against the German tanks during the fighting for the liberation of Paris. Norbert Wiener the cybernetician, reprimands the politicians: 'We have given you unlimited power, and you have created Bergen–Belsen and Hiroshima!'

These are the 'new-look' scientists who have linked their destiny with that of the world itself.*

They are the direct heirs of the great seekers of the first quarter of our century: the Curies, Langevin, Perrin, Planck, Einstein, etc. It has not been sufficiently proclaimed that the flame of genius during those years rose to greater heights than at any period since the miracle of Greece. These great men had had to wage war against the inertia of the human spirit, and had been violent in their campaigns. 'Truth never prevails,' said Planck, 'but her adversaries always perish in the end.' And Einstein: 'I do not believe in education. Your only model ought to be yourself, however frightful that model may be.' But the struggles these men were engaged in had nothing to do with the Earth and its history, or with day-to-day happenings.

They felt themselves responsible only to truth. And yet political events overtook them. Planck's son was assassinated by the Gestapo, Einstein driven into exile. The present generation, everywhere and in all circumstances, is made aware that the scientist is closely connected with world affairs. Almost all useful knowledge is

* 'The scientist has had to admit that, like any other human being, he is as much a spectator as an actor in the great drama of existence.' (Bohr)

concentrated in his hands, and very soon all power will be too. He is the key figure in the adventure on which humanity has embarked. Enmeshed by politics, harassed by the police and information services, supervised by the military, he has about an equal chance of ending his career with the Nobel Prize or facing a firing squad. At the same time his work leads him to scorn the trivialities of the individual and the particular, and enables him to think on a planetary, even cosmic level. Between his own power and the powers that be there is a misunderstanding. Only an arrant coward could hesitate between the risk he runs himself and the risks to which he exposes the world. Kurchatov broke the seal of silence and revealed what he knew to the British physicists at Harwell. Pontecorvo fled to Russia to carry on his work there. Oppenheimer got into trouble with his Government. The American atomic scientists took sides against the Army and published their extraordinary Bulletin: the cover drawing represented a clock whose hands move towards midnight every time some formidable experiment or discovery falls into the hands of the military.

'This is my prediction for the future,' wrote the British biologist J. B. S. Haldane: 'whatever hasn't happened will happen! And no one will be safe from it!'

Matter liberates its energy, and the way to the planets is open. Events such as these seem to be unprecedented in history. 'We are living at a time when history is holding its breath, and the present is detaching itself from the past like an iceberg that has broken away from its icy moorings to sail across the boundless ocean.'*

If the present is detaching itself from the past, this means a rupture, not with all past periods, and not with those that reached maturity, but only with the most recent past, i.e., what we have called 'modern civilization'. This civilization which emerged from the welter of ideas circulating in Western Europe in the eighteenth century, reached its highest development in the nineteenth and spread its benefits throughout the world in the first half of the twentieth, is becoming more and more remote from us. We are conscious of this all the time, and have reached the point of rupture. Our conscience and our intelligence tell us that between being an out-of-date modern and a contemporary of the future there is a big difference.

The ideas on which this modern civilization of ours is founded are outworn. During this period of rupture, or rather of transmutation, we must not be surprised if great changes take place in regard to the role of science and the scientist's mission in life.

What are these changes? A vision from the distant past may enable us to throw some light upon the future. Or, to put it more precisely, it may help us to see more clearly where to look for a new point of departure.

One day, in the year 1622, the inhabitants of Paris woke to find the walls of their city covered with posters bearing the following
* Arthur Clarke: *The Children of Icarus.*
26

message: 'We, deputies of the principal College of the Brethren of the Rosy Cross (Rosicrucians) are amongst you in this town, visibly and invisibly, through the grace of the Most High to whom the hearts of all just men are turned, in order to save our fellow-men from the error of death.' This was considered by most people to be a joke, but, as M. Serge Hutin reminds us today: 'The Rosicrucian Brethren were credited with possession of the following secrets: the transmutation of metals, the prolongation of life, knowledge of what is happening in distant places and the application of the occult sciences to the discovery of even the most deeply hidden objects.'*

Eliminate the term 'occult', and you find yourself confronted with the powers that modern science possesses or is on the way to possess. . . . According to the legend, already firmly established at that time, the Rosicrucians claimed that man's powers over nature and over himself would become limitless, that immortality and control of all natural forces were within his grasp, and that he would be able to know everything that happened in the universe.

There is nothing absurd in this, and the progress of science has to some extent justified these claims. Therefore the poster of 1622, couched in modern terms, might well appear on the walls of Paris today, or in a newspaper, if there was to be a congress of scientists to warn men of the dangers to which they are exposed, and the necessity of adopting a new approach to all their social and moral activities. Certain statements by Einstein, charged with emotion; a speech by Oppenheimer, a leading article in the bulletin of the American atomic scientists have exactly the same undertones as this Rosicrucian manifesto. Here, for example, is a recent Russian pronouncement. Referring to the conference on radio-isotopes held in Paris in 1957 the Soviet writer Vladimir Orlov, wrote as follows: 'The "alchemists" of today would do well to remember the statutes of their predecessors in the Middle Ages, now preserved in a Parisian Museum, in which it is laid down that no man shall devote himself to alchemy who is not "pure in heart and inspired by the loftiest intentions".'

The notion of a secret international society composed of men of the highest intelligence, spiritually transformed by the profundity of their knowledge, desirous of protecting their scientific discoveries against officialdom and the curiosity and greed of other men, and reserving for themselves the right to use their discoveries at the right moment, or else to conceal them for a number of years or to allow only an insignificant fraction of them to be published – such a notion is both an extremely ancient and an ultra-modern one. It would have been inconceivable in the nineteenth century, or even twenty-five years ago. Today it is quite conceivable. I would even dare to state that, on a certain level, such a society exists today. Some of us who have been received at Princeton (I am thinking especially of my friend Rajah Rao) may have formed the same opinion. Though there is nothing to prove that the secret Rosicrucian society

* Serge Hutin: *Histoire de la Rose-Croix*, Paris.

27

existed in the seventeenth century, we have every reason to believe that a society of this nature is being formed today by the pressure of events, and that there is bound to be one in the future. We should explain, however, what is meant by secret society, the idea of which, seemingly so remote, has its own significance today.

To return to the Rosicrucians. The historian Serge Hutin tells us that: 'They then represented a group of human beings who had reached a higher state than the mass of humanity, and thus possessed similar internal characteristics which enabled them to recognize one another at all times.'

This definition, in our opinion at least, has the merit of being free from high-falutin' occult terminology. That is because we have a clear, almost scientific, practical and optimistic idea of what is meant by a 'higher state'.*

Scientific research has reached the stage where we can envisage the possibility of artificial mutations that will improve living beings, including man himself. 'Radio-activity', according to a British biologist, 'may create monsters, but it will also give us geniuses.' The aim of the alchemist's researches was the transmutation of the operator himself; perhaps it is also that of the modern scientist. We shall see presently that, up to a point, this has already happened in the case of certain contemporary scientists.

Advanced studies in psychology seem to have proved the existence of a state of hyper-consciousness different from sleep and wakefulness, in which a man's intellectual faculties may be increased ten-fold. To the psychology of the subconscious, which we owe to psychoanalysis, must now be added a psychology of the heights which opens up a vista of super-intellectuality. Genius may be merely one of the stages through which man must pass in order to achieve the fullest use of his faculties.

In normal life, we only use a tenth of our potential resources of attention, prospection, memory, intuition and co-ordination. We may well be on the point of discovering, or rediscovering the keys that will enable us to open within ourselves doors behind which a mass of new knowledge is awaiting us. In this context, the idea of an imminent mutation in humanity is nearer reality than it is to some occult dream.

We shall be dealing at length with this point later. No doubt there are already among us the products of this mutation, or at all events men who have already taken some steps along the road on which we shall all be travelling one day.

According to tradition,† since the term 'genius' can hardly embrace all the possible higher potentialities of the human mind, the Rosicrucians were supposed to have been of another order of intelligence, elected by co-option. It is, perhaps, truer to say that the Rosicrucian legend lends support to a reality: a permanent secret society of men of exceptional faculties – an open conspiracy, in fact.

* See Part Three of this work: 'That Infinity Called Man . . .'.
† A less reliable translation would suggest that the Rosicrucians were the heirs of civilizations that have disappeared.

28

The Rosicrucian Society probably came naturally into being, consisting of men of superior intelligence seeking similar spirits with whom it would be possible to converse. This suggests an Einstein, who could only be understood by five or six men in the whole world, or a few hundred mathematicians and physicists capable of discussing usefully the implications of the laws governing even numbers.

The Rosicrucians were concerned exclusively with the study of nature; but such a study was illuminating only to minds of a different calibre from that of ordinary men. If such minds are brought to bear on a study of nature, they will attain to a knowledge of all things and perfect wisdom. This new, dynamic idea attracted both Newton and Descartes. Their names have more than once been associated with the Rosicrucians. Does this mean that they were affiliated members? Such a question is meaningless. We are not thinking of an organized society, but of the establishment of the necessary contacts between exceptional minds, and a common language, not secret, but merely inaccessible to ordinary men at a given epoch in time.

If far-reaching discoveries regarding the nature of matter and energy and the laws which govern the Universe have been made and worked on by civilizations that have disappeared, and if some of them have been preserved throughout the ages (which is by no means certain) this could only have been done by people of superior intelligence and in a language necessarily incomprehensible to the ordinary man. If, however, we reject this hypothesis we can nevertheless imagine, from one age to another, a succession of beings of exceptional gifts able to communicate with one another. Such beings are well aware that it is not in their interests to display their powers openly. If Christopher Columbus had been a man of this calibre he would have kept his discovery secret. Obliged as they are to observe some degree of clandestinity, these men can establish satisfactory contacts only with their equals. One has only to think of a discussion between doctors by a patient's bed in a hospital, not a word of which, though clearly audible, can be understood by the sick man; the point of my argument will then be readily grasped without it being necessary to confuse the issue by talking about occultism, initiation, etc. Finally, it is obvious that this intellectual *élite*, being anxious not to attract attention if only to avoid meeting with obstruction, would have something better to do than play at being conspirators. If they form a society it is because they may have no choice in the matter; and if they have a language of their own this is because the ideas expressed in this language are inaccessible to ordinary minds. This is the only sense in which we can accept the idea of a secret society. The other secret societies, the ones that are on record and of which there are many, all more or less powerful and picturesque, are in our opinion, nothing but imitations, like children copying grown-up people.

So long as men cherish the dream of getting something for nothing, money without working, knowledge without study, power without knowledge and virtue without asceticism, so long will pseudo-secret and initiatory societies continue to flourish, with their imitative hierarchies and their mumbo-jumbo that imitates the real secret language, *the language of technicians*.

We have chosen the example of the 1622 Rosicrucians because the genuine members of that sect, according to tradition, did not claim to have derived their knowledge from some mysterious form of initiation, but from the study of the *Liber Mundi*, the Book of the World and of Nature. The Rosicrucian tradition is therefore the same as that of modern science. We are beginning today to understand that a profound and rational study of this book of nature calls for qualities other than mere observation and what we referred to just now as the scientific spirit, and indeed for something other than what we call intelligence. At the stage we have reached in scientific research our minds and intelligence will have to surpass themselves and rise to transcendent heights; the human, all-too-human, will no longer suffice. It is perhaps to a similar conclusion, arrived at centuries ago by men of superior intelligence, that we owe the legend, if not the fact of the Rosicrucian sect. The out-of-date modern is a rationalist. The contemporary of the future is more religiously-minded. Too much modernism separates us from the past; a little futurism brings us nearer to it.

'Among the young atomic scientists', wrote Robert Jungk (in *Brighter Than A Thousand Suns*), 'some looked upon their work as a kind of intellectual exercise of no particular significance and involving no obligations, but for others, their researches seemed like a religious experience.'

Our Rosicrucians in 1622 visited Paris 'invisibly'. What is remarkable today, when police and espionage loom large, is that the great scientists manage to communicate with each other without allowing governments to discover what they are up to. The fate of the world could be discussed openly by ten scientists in the presence of Khruschev and the President of the United States without these gentlemen being able to understand a single word. An international society of research workers who kept aloof from politics would have every chance of being undetected; and the same would apply to a society that confined its interventions to a few very special cases. Even its means of communication might never be traced. The radio might easily have been discovered in the seventeenth century, and rudimentary crystal sets could have been used by initiates. Similarly, modern research on para-psychological media has led to practical applications in the sphere of telecommunications. The American engineer, Victor Enderby, wrote recently that if results had been obtained in this field, they had been kept secret at the express wish of the inventors.

We are again struck by the fact that Rosicrucian tradition makes allusion to certain machines which official science at that date had not been able to produce, such as perpetual lamps, instruments for recording sounds and images, etc. The legend describes apparatus found in the tomb of the symbolic 'Christian Rosenkreutz' which might have been made in 1958, but not in 1622. This shows that the Rosicrucian doctrine was concerned with the domination of the universe through science and technique, and not at all through initiation or mysticism.

In the same way, we can quite well imagine in our own times a society with a secret technology of its own. Political persecution, social restrictions, the growth of a moral sense and the feeling that they bear a terrible responsibility will make it more and more imperative for scientists to work in secret. But this clandestinity will in no way hamper research. It is unthinkable that rockets and enormous machines for splitting the atom will in future be the scientist's only instruments. All the really great discoveries have been made with the simplest of apparatus and the most modest installations. It may well be that there are certain places in the world at this moment where there is a great concentration of intellects and a corresponding degree of this new form of clandestinity. We are entering an epoch that strongly resembles the beginning of the seventeenth century, and a new manifesto, like that of 1622, is perhaps in preparation. Maybe it has already appeared without our noticing it.

What estranges us from this way of thinking is the fact that the ancients always expressed themselves in religious terms. As a result, our approach is exclusively literary, or 'spiritual'. This is where we show that we are 'modern', and not belonging to the future.

Finally, we are impressed by the repeated affirmations of the Rosicrucians and alchemists that the object of the science of transmutations is the transmutation of the human mind itself. This has nothing to do with magic, or with celestial favours; it means that when certain realities have been discovered, the observer will be obliged to look at everything from a different angle. When we remember the very rapid developments in the thinking of the greatest atomic scientists, we begin to understand what the Rosicrucians were trying to say.

We are living at a time when science, at its highest power, has entered the spiritual universe and has transformed the mind of the observer himself, raising it to a plane which is no longer that of scientific intelligence, now proved to be inadequate.

What our atomic scientists have been through is comparable to the experience described in the alchemists' books and in the Rosicrucian tradition. The spiritual language is not the stammering that precedes scientific language, but rather the full consummation of the latter. What is happening to us now may well have happened long ago, on another plane of consciousness, so that the Rosicrucian legend and the realities of today have a common point of contact. We can understand tomorrow better if we look at the ancient world through fresh eyes.

We are no longer living in an age where progress is assessed exclusively in terms of technical and scientific advances. Another factor has to be considered, the same that was envisaged by the

Unknown Élite in olden days who showed that the *Liber Mundi* was concerned with 'something different'. An eminent physicist, Heisenberg, writes today that: 'The space in which man's spiritual being develops is in a different dimension from that in which it was moving in previous centuries.'

Wells died a disappointed man. His whole life had been sustained by his faith in progress. But before he died he saw this progress take on a terrifying aspect. He did not trust it any more. The most formidable methods of destruction had just been invented, and science threatened to destroy the world. In 1946 the ageing Wells wrote, in despair: 'Man has reached the limit of his possibilities.' It was then that this old man, whose genius had anticipated almost everything, ceased to be a contemporary of the future.

We are now beginning to perceive that man has reached the limit of only one of his possibilities; others have been revealed. New paths have been opened up which have been alternately hidden and exposed by the tides of the ocean of time. Wolfgang Pauli, the world-famous mathematician and physicist, used to adopt a narrow scientific approach in the best traditions of the nineteenth century. In 1932, at the Copenhagen Congress, in his icy scepticism and lust for power he seemed like some Faustian Mephistopheles. In 1955 he had so widened his outlook that he became the eloquent advocate of a long neglected method of seeking salvation from within.

This kind of evolution is typical, and has happened to most of the great atomic scientists. It does not mean a revival of a moralistic attitude or a vague religiosity. On the contrary; it signifies an improvement in the observer's approach and a new conception of the nature of knowledge. 'In view of the division of the activities of the human mind into different compartments which have been strictly maintained for centuries,' says Wolfgang Pauli, 'I envisage a method whose aim would be to reconcile contraries in a synthesis incorporating a rational understanding and a mystical experience of their unity. No other objective would be in harmony with the mythology, whether avowed or not, of our epoch.'

II

The prophets of the Apocalypse – A Committee of Despair – A Louis XVI machine-gun – Science is not a Sacred Cow – Monsieur Despotopoulos would like to arrest progress – The legend of the Nine Unknown Men

ON the threshold of modern times, the second half of the nineteenth century, there was in existence a band of violently reactionary thinkers. For them the 'mystique' of social progress was nothing but a swindle; as for scientific and technical progress, this was leading the world to ruin. It was Philippe Lavastine, a new incarnation of the hero of Balzac's *Chef-d'Oeuvre Inconnu* and a disciple of Gurdjieff, who told me about them. At that time, when I was reading René Guénon, chief of the anti-progressists, and was seeing

32

a lot of Lanza del Vasto who had just returned from India, I was inclined to agree with these reactionary thinkers.

The ancients, no doubt, were as wicked as we are, but they knew it. And so they were wise enough to put up protective railings. A Papal Bull condemned the use of the tripod as a means of strengthening the archer's bow; this machine, supplementing the natural force of the archer would make fighting inhuman. This Bull remained in force for two hundred years. Roland de Roncevaux, smitten by the slings of the Saracens, exclaimed: 'Cursed be the coward who invented arms capable of killing from a distance.' Nearer our own times, in 1755, a French engineer named Du Perron, presented the young Louis XVI with a 'military organ' which, when a lever was pulled, discharged twenty-four bullets simultaneously. A memoire was attached to this instrument, the forerunner of the modern machine-gun. The weapon was considered by the King and his ministers, Malesherbes and Turgot, to be so deadly that the offer was refused, and the inventor was deemed to be an enemy of humanity.

In our desire to emancipate everything, we have also emancipated war. Whereas it used to be an occasion for self-sacrifice and salvation for a few, it now spells ruin for all.

These were more or less my views around 1946, and I was thinking of preparing an anthology of 'reactionary thinkers', whose influence at that time was overshadowed by that of the romantic progressists. These 'writers in reverse', these prophets of the Apocalypse crying in the desert, were Blanc de Saint-Bonnet, Emile Montagut, Albert Sorel, Donoso Cortes, etc. Following the same line of revolt as these 'fathers' of the movement I brought out a pamphlet entitled *Le Temps des Assassins*, and my contributors included notably Aldous Huxley and Albert Camus. The American press gave some publicity to this pamphlet which vigorously denounced science, the Army and the politicians, and pleaded for a second Nuremberg to judge all the technicians of destruction.

I feel today that things are not quite so simple, and that a different and higher view must be taken of irreversible history. And yet in the uneasy post-war years around 1946 this line of thought shone like a beacon over the ocean of anxieties that were torturing the intellectuals who had no desire to be either victims nor executioners. And it was true that, after Einstein's telegram, things had got worse. 'What the scientists have got in their brief-cases is terrifying,' said Khruschev in 1960. But a kind of lassitude set in, and after a lot of solemn and useless protests, people turned their attention to other things. Like the condemned man in his cell, they were waiting to know whether they had been reprieved or not. In any case there was a general feeling of revolt against a science which was capable of annihilating the world, and of scepticism as to whether technical progress could do much to save the situation. 'They'll end by blowing up the world.'

Since Aldous Huxley's furious diatribes in *Counterpoint* and *Brave New World*, scientific optimism was at a discount. In 1951

33

the American chemist Anthony Standen published a book called *Science is a Sacred Cow* in which he protested against the tendency to idolize science. In October 1953 a celebrated Professor of Law in Athens, Mr. O. J. Despotopoulos, appealed to UNESCO in a manifesto demanding that scientific research should cease, or at least be kept secret. It ought, he suggested, to be in future entrusted to a council of scientists, elected by a world vote, and consequently having authority to keep silence. Utopian as it may seem, this idea is none the less interesting. It points to something that might, in the future, be possible and, as we shall see presently, re-echoes one of the great themes discussed in bygone civilizations. In a letter I received from Mr. Despotopoulos in 1955, he outlined his ideas as follows:

'Natural science is certainly one of the most meritorious conquests in human history. But the moment it liberates forces capable of destroying the whole human race it ceases from a moral standpoint to be what it used to be. It has become almost impossible to distinguish between pure science and its technological applications. One cannot therefore speak of science *qua* science as being a good thing in itself. Or rather, in some of its more important branches, it has now become a negative value in so far as it no longer conforms to ordinary moral standards and is free to exercise its dangerous activities in order to satisfy the lust for power of the politicians. This adoration of progress and freedom where scientific research is concerned is wholly pernicious. What we propose is this: the codification of the conquests of natural science up to now, and the creation of a Council of World Scientists with powers to prohibit absolutely or partially any progress it may achieve in the future. Such a measure, no doubt, would be tragically severe, even cruel, since the activity it seeks to curtail is one of the noblest human impulses, and it is impossible to underestimate the difficulties inherent in such a solution. But there is no other that could be so efficacious. The objections are easily foreseen: a return to the Middle Ages, to barbarism, etc.; but these do not really carry any weight. Our intention is not to retard intellectual advancement, but to protect it; not to impose restrictions for the benefit of any social class, but in the interests of humanity as a whole. There lies the problem. Anything else can only lead to divisions and time wasted in trying to tackle problems of lesser importance.'

These ideas were favourably received in the British and German press, and dealt with very fully in the bulletin of the atomic scientists in London. They have, in fact, much in common with certain proposals put forward at international conferences on disarmament. There is reason to believe, moreover, that in other civilizations science, though not inexistent, was kept secret. Such would seem to have been the origin of the marvellous legend of the Nine Unknown Men.

This tradition goes back to the time of the Emperor Asoka, who reigned in India from 273 B.C. He was the grandson of Chandragupta who was the first to unify India. Ambitious like his ancestor whose achievements he was anxious to complete, he conquered the region of Kalinga which lay between what is now Calcutta and Madras. The Kalingans resisted and lost 100,000 men in the battle. At the sight of this massacre Asoka was overcome. For ever after he experienced a horror of war. He renounced the idea of trying to integrate the rebellious people, declaring that the only true conquest was to win men's hearts by observance of the laws of duty and piety, because the Sacred Majesty desired that all living creatures should enjoy security, peace and happiness and be free to live as they pleased.

A convert to Buddhism, Asoka, by his own virtuous example, spread this religion throughout India and his entire empire which included Malaya, Ceylon and Indonesia. Later Buddhism penetrated to Nepal, Thibet, China and Mongolia. Asoka nevertheless respected all religious sects. He preached vegetarianism, abolished alcohol and the slaughter of animals. H. G. Wells, in his abridged version of his *Outline of World History* wrote: 'Among the tens of thousands of names of monarchs accumulated in the files of history, the name of Asoka shines almost alone, like a star.'

It is said that the Emperor Asoka, aware of the horrors of war, wished to forbid men ever to put their intelligence to evil uses. During his reign natural science, past and present, was vowed to secrecy. Henceforward, and for the next 2,000 years, all researches, ranging from the structure of matter to the techniques employed in collective psychology, were to be hidden behind the mystical mask of a people commonly believed to be exclusively concerned with ecstasy and supernatural phenomena. Asoka founded the most powerful secret society on earth: that of the Nine Unknown Men.

It is still thought that the great men responsible for the destiny of modern India, and scientists like Bose and Ram believe in the existence of the Nine, and even receive advice and messages from them.

One can imagine the extraordinary importance of secret knowledge in the hands of nine men benefiting directly from experiments, studies and documents accumulated over a period of more than 2,000 years. What can have been the aim of these men? Not to allow methods of destruction to fall into the hands of unqualified persons, and to pursue knowledge which would benefit mankind. Their numbers would be renewed by co-option, so as to preserve the secrecy of techniques handed down from ancient times.

Examples of the Nine Unknown Men making contact with the outer world are rare. There was, however, the extraordinary case of one of the most mysterious figures in Western history: the Pope Sylvester II, known also by the name of Gerbert d'Aurillac. Born in the Auvergne in 920 (*d.* 1003) Gerbert was a Benedictine monk, professor at the University of Rheims, Archbishop of Ravenna and Pope by the grace of Otho III. He is supposed to have spent some time in Spain, after which a mysterious voyage brought him to India where he is reputed to have acquired various kinds of skills which stupefied his entourage. For example, he possessed in his palace a bronze head which answered YES or NO to questions put to it on politics or the general position of Christianity. According to Sylvester II* this was a perfectly simple operation corresponding to a two-figure calculation, and was performed by an automaton similar to our modern binary machines. This 'magic' head was destroyed when Sylvester died, and all the information it imparted carefully concealed. No doubt an authorized research worker would come across some surprising things in the Vatican Library.

In the cybernetics journal, *Computers and Automation* of October 1954, the following comment appeared: 'We must suppose that he (Sylvester) was possessed of extraordinary knowledge and the most remarkable mechanical skill and inventiveness. This speaking head must have been fashioned "under a certain conjunction of stars occurring at the exact moment when all the planets were starting on their courses." Neither the past, nor the present nor the future entered into it, since this invention apparently far exceeded in its scope its rival, the perverse "mirror on the wall" of the Queen, the precursor of our modern electronic brain. Naturally, it was widely asserted that Gerbert was only able to produce such a machine because he was in league with the Devil and had sworn eternal allegiance to him.'

Had other Europeans any contact with this society of the Nine Unknown Men? It was not until the nineteenth century that this mystery was referred to again in the works of the French writer Jacolliot.

Jacolliot was French Consul at Calcutta under the Second Empire. He wrote some quite important prophetic works, comparable, if not superior to those of Jules Verne. He also left several books dealing with the great secrets of the human race. A great many occult writers, prophets and miracle-workers have borrowed from his writings which, completely neglected in France, are well known in Russia.

Jacolliot states categorically that the society of Nine did actually exist. And, to make it all the more intriguing, he refers in this connection to certain techniques, unimaginable in 1860, such as, for example, the liberation of energy, sterilization by radiation and psychological warfare.

Yersin, one of Pasteur and de Roux's closest collaborators, was entrusted, it seems, with certain biological secrets when he visited Madras in 1890, and following the instructions he received was able to prepare a serum against cholera and the plague.

The story of the Nine Unknown Men was popularized for the first time in 1927 in a book by Talbot Mundy who for twenty-five years was a member of the British police force in India. His book is half fiction, half scientific inquiry. The Nine apparently employed a synthetic language, and each of them was in possession of a book that was constantly being rewritten and containing a detailed account of some science.

The first of these books is said to have been devoted to the

* See Vol. CXXXIX of Migne's *Patrologie latine*.

technique of propaganda and psychological warfare. 'The most dangerous of all sciences,' wrote Mundy, 'is that of moulding mass opinion, because it would enable anyone to govern the whole world.'

It must be remembered that Korjybski's *General Semantics* did not appear until 1937 and that it was not until the West had had the experience of the last World War that the techniques of the psychology of language, i.e. propaganda, could be formulated. The first American college of semantics only came into being in 1950. In France almost the only book that is at all well known is Serge Tchocotine's *Le Viol des Foules* which has had a considerable influence in intellectual political circles, although it deals only superficially with the subject.

The second book was on physiology. It explained, among other things, how it is possible to kill a man by touching him, death being caused by a reversal of the nerve-impulse. It is said that Judo is a result of 'leakages' from this book.

The third volume was a study on microbiology, and dealt especially with protective colloids.

The fourth was concerned with the transmutation of metals. There is a legend that in times of drought temples and religious relief organizations received large quantities of fine gold from a secret source.

The fifth volume contains a study of all means of communication, terrestrial and extra-terrestrial.

The sixth expounds the secrets of gravitation.

The seventh contains the most exhaustive cosmogony known to humanity.

The eighth deals with light.

The ninth volume, on sociology, gives the rules for the evolution of societies, and the means of foretelling their decline.

Connected with the Nine Unknown Men is the mystery of the waters of the Ganges. Multitudes of pilgrims, suffering from the most appalling diseases, bathe in them without harming the healthy ones. The sacred waters purify everything. Their strange properties have been attributed to the fact that they contain bacteriophages. But why should these not be formed in the Bramaputra, the Amazon or the Seine? Jacolliot in his book advances the theory of sterilization by radiation, a hundred years before such a thing was thought to be possible. These radiations, he says, probably come from a secret temple hollowed out in the bed of the Ganges.

Avoiding all forms of religious, social or political agitations, deliberately and perfectly concealed from the public eye, the Nine were the incarnation of the ideal man of science, serenely aloof, but conscious of his moral obligations. Having the power to mould the destiny of the human race, but refraining from its exercise, this secret society is the finest tribute imaginable to freedom of the most exalted kind. Looking down from the watch-tower of their hidden glory, these Nine Unknown Men watched civilizations being born,

37

destroyed and re-born again, tolerant rather than indifferent, and
ready to come to the rescue – but always observing that rule of
silence that is the mark of human greatness.

Myth or reality? A magnificent myth, in any case, and one that
has issued from the depths of time – a harbinger, maybe, of the
future?

III

*Fantastic realism again – Past techniques – Further con-
sideration on the necessity for secrecy – We take a voyage
through time – The spirit's continuity – The engineer and the
magician once again – Past and future – The present is
lagging in both directions – Gold from ancient books – A new
vision of the ancient world*

WE are neither materialists nor spiritualists: these distinctions no
longer have any meaning for us. Quite simply, we seek reality while
avoiding the conditioned reflex of the modern man (in our opinion
behind the times) who turns away as soon as this reality takes on
a fantastic air. We have turned ourselves into barbarians again so
as to conquer this reflex, exactly as the painters did in order to tear
away the screen of conventions erected between their vision and
things as they are. Like them, too, we have opted for methods that
may seem elementary, barbaric, even childish at times. We take up a
position *vis-à-vis* the elements and methods of knowledge like
that of Cézanne in front of his apple, or van Gogh in his field of
corn. We refuse to exclude any facts, or aspects of reality on the
grounds that they are not 'respectable', or that they go beyond
the frontiers fixed by current theories.

Gauguin did not hesitate to paint a red horse, nor Manet to
introduce a naked woman among the guests in his *Déjeuner sur
l'herbe*; nor do Max Ernst, Picabia and Dali exclude from their
canvases figures sprung from dreams and the world that lives in the
submerged depths of our mind. Our method will meet with derision,
revolt and sarcasm: *we* shall not be hung in the Academy. What is
now accepted from painters, poets, cineasts and decorators is not
yet acceptable in our domain. Science, psychology and sociology are
beset with taboos. Ideas about sacrosanctity are no sooner got rid
of than they come back in no time, under various disguises. But,
let's face it, science is not a sacred cow: she can quite well be
hustled along to clear the road.

Let us now recapitulate. In this part of our work, entitled *Future
Perfect*, our reasoning has been along these lines:

It may be that what we call esotericism, the keystone of secret
societies and religions, is a remnant, which we find very difficult
to understand or deal with, of a very ancient branch of knowledge,
of a *technical nature*, relating to both mind and matter. This idea
will be expanded later on.

The so-called 'secrets' may not be fables, legends or games, but precise technical systems – keys to open up and reveal the forces contained in man and in things.

Science is not a technique. Contrary to what might be supposed, technique in many cases does not come after science, but precedes it. Technique means doing. Science shows that nothing can be done.

Then the barriers of impossibilities begin to crumble. We do not, of course, pretend that science is useless. The reader will see how highly we value science, and with what wonder and admiration we observe it undergoing a transformation. We simply believe that in the distant past techniques may well have preceded it.

It is possible that techniques used long ago may have endowed men with powers too terrible to be divulged.

There could be two reasons for secrecy:

(*a*) Caution. 'He who knows holds his tongue.' Beware lest the keys fall into evil hands.

(*b*) The fact that the possession and ability to handle techniques and skills of this kind calls for a degree of intellectual acuity above the ordinary, and the exercise of intelligence and a command of language on a different plane, so that there can be no communication at ordinary human level. Thus secrecy results from the nature of the thing kept secret, and is not necessarily imposed by those who know.

A similar state of affairs exists in our modern world. The rapid development of techniques in the world of science makes secrecy not only desirable but essential. Great dangers call for great discretion. As knowledge advances, the more it is surrounded by secrecy. Scientists and technicians form themselves into guilds.

The language of knowledge and power is incomprehensible to the outside world. Physico-mathematical research presupposes a different kind of mental structure. At the highest level, those who, in Einstein's phrase, have 'the power to make far-reaching decisions on good and evil', constitute a real 'cryptocracy' (or secret autocracy).

The vision we have of the knowledge possessed by the ancients owes nothing to 'spiritualist' theories. Our way of looking at the present and the immediate future allows for the possibility of magic in spheres where it is assumed that there is a rationalistic explanation for everything. All we are seeking is illumination of a kind that would enable us to see the whole human adventure in the context of eternity, and we are ready to use any means that will help us to achieve this end.

Basically, in this part of the book, as elsewhere, our theme is the following:

Man no doubt has the possibility of establishing his relationship with the Universe as a whole. You will remember the paradox in Langevin's story about the traveller to the stars. Andromeda is three million light-years from the earth. But a traveller moving at a speed near to that of light would only be a few years older on arriving. According to the unitary theory of Jean Charon, for example, it is not inconceivable that during this journey the Earth, too, would not have grown any older. Thus man would appear to be in contact with the whole of creation, space and time being in reality not what they seem. On the other hand, physico-mathematical research, at the stage where Einstein left it, is an attempt on the part of human intelligence to discover the law governing the whole body of the forces which permeate the Universe (gravitation, electro-magnetism, light and nuclear energy).

An attempt, that is to say, to achieve a unitary vision, an effort of the mind to attain a point where the continuity of things will become apparent. And why should the mind feel this desire, unless it had a presentiment that such a point exists, and that it is capable of reaching this position? 'You would not be looking for me if you had not already found me.'

On another plane, but in the same order of ideas, what we are seeking is a global view revealing the continuity of all the progress made in the sphere of human intelligence and human knowledge. This explains why we shall be passing in rapid succession from magic to progress in technique, from the Rosicrucians to Princeton, from the Maya civilization to the next mutation of man, from the Seal of Solomon to the periodic table of the elements, from civilizations that have disappeared to others still unborn, from Fulcanelli to Oppenheimer, from sorcery to the electronic brain, etc. . . . We shall travel so fast that space and time will burst out from their shells and we shall catch a glimpse of permanent continuity.

There is dream-travel and real travel. We have chosen reality. It is in this sense that this book is not fiction. We have built apparatus – in the shape of demonstrable correspondences, valid comparisons and undisputed analogies. Apparatus that works, rockets that go off. And there have been times when it seemed to us that our minds had reached the point from which it is possible to survey the whole of human endeavour. Civilizations and the high peaks of human knowledge and organization are like rocks in the ocean. We can only catch a glimpse of them as the water strikes them; all we see is the wave as it breaks and the flying spray. But what we are seeking is the place from which it will be possible to contemplate the whole vast ocean in its calm and mighty continuity and harmonious unity.

We must now return to our reflections on techniques, science and magic. They will help to clarify our ideas on secret societies (or rather 'open conspiracies') and prepare the way for future studies, one on Alchemy and the other on Vanished Civilizations.

When a young engineer goes into industry, he quickly distinguishes two separate worlds. On the one hand, the laboratory, with its well defined laws governing experiments that can be repeated and the image it presents of a comprehensible world. On the other hand, there is the 'real' universe where laws do not always apply, and where events cannot always be foreseen, or impossible things happen. If he is strong-minded, our engineer's reaction is one of anger and passion, together with a desire to 'violate this bitch, matter'. Those who adopt this attitude usually have tragic lives.

Think of Edison, Tesla, Armstrong. A demon drives them. Werner von Braun tries out his rockets on London and massacres thousands of people only to be arrested in the end by the Gestapo for having proclaimed: 'After all, I don't care a damn about Germany winning the war; what I want is to conquer the Moon!'* It has been said that the real tragedy today is politics. This is an out-of-date view. The real tragedy is the laboratory. It is to these 'magicians' that we owe technical progress. Technique, in our opinion, has nothing to do with the practical application of science. On the contrary, it is moving against science. The eminent mathematician and astronomer Simon Newcomb demonstrated that a machine heavier than air could never fly. Two bicycle repair-shop men proved him to be wrong. Rutherford and Millikan showed that it would never be possible to make use of the reserves of energy in the nucleus of an atom. The answer was the bomb at Hiroshima. Science teaches that a mass of homogeneous air cannot be separated into hot air and cold air. Hilsch† showed that all that it needed is to drive this mass of air through a specially constructed tube.

Science erects barriers of impossibilities. The engineer, like the magician under the eyes of the Cartesian explorer, passes through these barriers by means of what the physicists call the 'tunnel effect'. He is drawn by a magic attraction. He wants to see behind the wall – go to Mars, capture thunder, manufacture gold. He seeks neither gain nor glory; his aim is to catch out the Universe and expose its mysteries. In the Jungian sense, he is an archetype. Because of the miracles he tries to perform, the fatality which hangs over him and the painful end which so often awaits him, he is the son of the heroes of the Sagas and Greek Tragedy.‡

Like the magician, he cultivates secrecy and obeys that law of similarity that Frazer discovered in his study of magic in *The Golden Bough*. At first, invention is an imitation of natural phenomena. The flying-machine resembles a bird, the automaton is like a man. And yet resemblance to the object, creature or phenomenon whose powers it is designed to capture is almost always useless, and even harmful to the successful working of the inventor's apparatus. Nevertheless, again like the magician, the inventor derives from the resemblance a sense of power and pleasure which acts as an incentive.

It is possible, in many cases, to retrace the transition from magical imitation to scientific technology. Here is an example:

An ancient method of hardening steel practised in the Near East was to plunge a red-hot blade into the body of a prisoner. This is a typical act of magic: the object being to transfer the adversary's

* Walter Dornberger: *The Secret Army of Pennemunde*.
† *Technique mondiale*, Paris, 1957.
‡ Edwin Armstrong: 'The Inventor as Hero' (article in *Harper's Magazine*).

warlike qualities to the sword. This practice was known to the Crusaders in the West, who had noticed that Damascus steel was in fact harder than European steel. As an experiment, steel was dipped into water in which animal skins had been immersed. The same result was obtained. In the nineteenth century it was discovered that these results were due to the presence of organic nitrogen. In the twentieth century, when the problem of liquefying gases had been solved, the method was perfected by immersing steel in liquid nitrogen at a low temperature. In this form nitration has been adopted in our technology.

Another connection between magic and technology can be found in the 'charms' which the old alchemists used to pronounce while engaged in their work. This was probably a method of measuring time in the darkness of the laboratory. Photographers often recite regular incantations while developing their film, and we have heard one of these being recited at the top of the Jungfrau while a film that had been exposed to cosmic rays was being developed.

Finally, there is still another connection, even closer and very striking, between magic and technology, and that is the way in which inventions tend to appear simultaneously. Most countries keep a record of the day, and even the hour when a patent is applied for; and it has often been remarked that inventors working far apart and who do not even know of each other's existence have applied for the same patent at exactly the same time.

This phenomenon can scarcely be explained by a vague idea that 'inventions are in the air', or that 'inventions appear as soon as they are needed'. If this is an example of extra-sensory perception, of communication between minds engaged on the same research, the phenomenon calls for a serious statistical study. Such an inquiry would perhaps help to explain another fact, namely that identical magic techniques are to be found in most ancient civilizations in many different parts of the world. . . .

We are living under the impression that technical inventions are a specifically temporary phenomenon. This is because we never take the trouble to go and consult ancient documents. There is not a single scientific research centre working on the past. Old books are read, if they are read at all, only by a very few scholars whose interests are mainly literary or historical. Consequently they pay scant attention to anything of a scientific or technical nature. Is this lack of interest in the past due to the fact that we are too much taken up with preparing for the future? I am not so sure. French intellectuals seem to be held back by nineteenth century standards. The *avant-garde* writers are not interested in science, and attention generally is still focused on a sociology belonging to the era of the steam-engine and a revolutionary humanism as out-of-date as the musket. The extent to which France is still living in the 1880s is unbelievable. Is her industry more go-ahead?

In 1955 the first world atomic conference was held at Geneva. René Alleau found himself responsible for the distribution throughout France of documents relating to the peaceful uses of atomic energy.

The sixteen volumes containing the experimental results obtained by scientists in every country was the most important publication in the history of science and technology. Five thousand industries with a potential long- or short-term interest in nuclear energy received a letter announcing this publication. Only twenty-five firms replied.

No doubt it will be necessary to wait until the younger generations have reached positions of responsibility before France recovers her mental alertness and flexibility. It is for these generations that this book is written. Those who are really interested in the future should also be interested in the past, and as ready to look for what they are seeking in both directions – backwards as well as forwards.

We know nothing, or next to nothing, about the past. There are unknown treasures still slumbering in libraries. We who pretend to 'love humanity' prefer to think of the progress of knowledge as being discontinuous with hundreds of thousands of years of ignorance to set against a few centuries of wisdom. The idea that there suddenly came a 'century of enlightenment' – an idea which has been accepted with the most disconcerting naïvety – had the effect of plunging into obscurity all other periods in our history. If old books could be studied through fresh eyes, all that would be changed. We should be amazed at the wealth they contain. And still we should have to remind ourselves, as Newton's contemporary, Atterbury, remarked, that 'more old books have been lost than have been preserved'.

To undertake a study of this kind, through fresh eyes, has been the aim of our friend René Alleau, who is both historian and technician. He has outlined a method and obtained some results. Up to the present he does not seem to have been encouraged in any way to pursue this task which is more than one man alone could possibly cope with. In December 1955, at my request, he gave a lecture at a meeting of Automobile Engineers, under the chairman of Jean-Henri Labourdette, of which the gist was as follows:

'What has remained of the thousands of manuscripts in the library at Alexandria founded by Ptolemy Soter, and all those documents on the science of the ancients which can never be replaced? Where are the ashes of the 200,000 volumes in the library at Pergamo? What has become of the Pisistratus collections in Athens, or of the library of the Temple at Jerusalem, or of the one in the sanctuary of Phtah at Memphis? What treasures were contained in the thousands of books which in 213 B.C. were burnt by the Emperor Chou-Hoang-Ti for purely political reasons? As a result of all this the position today with regard to all these ancient books is as if we were looking at an enormous temple of which only a few stones are still standing. But if we examine these fragments and these inscriptions carefully, we shall discover they contain truths far too profound to be attributed merely to the intuition of the ancients.

'In the first place, contrary to what is generally accepted, the methods of rationalism were not invented by Descartes. Take a look at the texts: "He who seeks the truth," wrote Descartes, "must, as far as possible, doubt everything." This saying is well known, and it sounds very new. If, however, we look at the second book of Aristotle's *Metaphysics*, we find this: "He who seeks to acquire knowledge must first know how to doubt, for intellectual doubt helps to establish the truth." Moreover, it is clear that Descartes borrowed not only this striking observation from Aristotle, but nearly all the famous rules for intellectual guidance which are a basis for the experimental method. This proves, in any case, that Descartes had read Aristotle, which is something many of our modern Cartesians have never done. The latter might also be aware that someone wrote: "If I make a mistake, I conclude that I exist; for he who does not exist cannot make a mistake, so that the fact of having made a mistake is proof that I exist." Unfortunately, this was not said by Descartes, but by Saint Augustine.

'As to the scepticism which any observer ought to feel, it is impossible to go further than Democritus who refused to admit the validity of any experiment at which he personally had not been present, and on the results of which he had not set his personal seal as a guarantee of its authenticity. This seems to me to be very far removed from the naïvety with which the Ancients are often reproached. Of course, you will say, the philosophers of antiquity had a genius for pure knowledge and erudition, but, after all, what did they really know about science?

'Contrary, again, to what the modern textbooks say, it was not Democritus or Leucippus or Epicurus who first initiated and formulated atomic theories. Sextus Empiricus informs us that Democritus himself had learnt them from tradition, especially from Moschus the Phoenician who, it seems (an important point to note) had declared that the atom was divisible.

'It will be seen, then, that the earlier theory was also more correct than the views of Democritus and the Greek atomists concerning the indivisibility of atoms. In this particular instance it seems clear that this was a case of some confusion having arisen due to a mis-interpretation of theories of very ancient origin, rather than of new and original discoveries.

'Again, in the sphere of cosmology, it is amazing to reflect that although there were no telescopes in those days, it often happened that the most ancient astronomical observations were the most accurate. For example, in regard to the Milky Way, it was thought by Thales and Anaximenes to be made up of stars, each one of which was a world containing a sun and planets, these worlds being situated in the immensity of space. It is clear that Lucretius was familiar with the theory of the uniformity of the speed of bodies falling in a vacuum, and of an infinite space filled with an infinity of worlds. Pythagoras, before Newton, had formulated the law of the force of attraction varying inversely as the square of the distance between objects. Plutarch, in attempting to explain gravitation,

44

attributed it to a reciprocal attraction between all bodies, thus accounting for the fact that the Earth causes all terrestrial bodies to gravitate towards it, just as the Sun and the Moon draw to their centre everything pertaining to them and by their force of attraction, retain each body in its own particular sphere.

'Galileo and Newton admitted openly their debt to ancient science. Copernicus, also, in the preface to his works addressed to Pope Paul III stated explicitly that it was his reading of ancient authors that gave him the idea of the movement of the Earth. Moreover, the admission of these borrowings does not in any way detract from the glory of Copernicus, Newton or Galileo who all belonged to that species of superior beings whose disinterestedness and generosity have nothing in common with the modern author's self-sufficiency and cult of originality at all costs. A humbler and more profoundly genuine attitude is exemplified in the story of Marie Antoinette's *modiste* exclaiming, as she deftly touched up an ancient hat: "There is nothing new except what has been forgotten."

'The history of inventions, like that of the sciences, is enough to prove the truth of this bright remark. "The fate of most discoveries," wrote Fournier, "is determined by that 'fleeting moment' which the Ancients thought was as unapproachable as a goddess once it had been allowed to escape. Unless the idea that starts a train of thought, or the word that leads to the solution of a problem, or the significant fact are caught on the instant, an invention may have been lost forever or, at all events, delayed for several generations. The only way of ensuring its triumphant return is the chance that a new idea may rescue the old one from oblivion, or else a fortunate plagiarism perpetrated by an inventor at second hand; where inventions are concerned, woe to the first-comer, and glory and profit to the one who comes after." It is reflections such as these that justify the title of my lecture.

'For, in my opinion, it should be possible to a large extent to replace chance by determinism, and the hazards of sporadic periods of invention by the guarantees offered by a vast system of historical documentation based on carefully controlled experiments. With this end in view, I propose to set up an organization, not for the purpose of establishing the priority of patents (which, in any case, ceased in the eighteenth century), but to provide a technological service which will simply study ancient processes and endeavour to adapt them, if possible, to the requirements of modern industry.

'Had such an organization existed before, it might, for example, have drawn attention to a little book, of which no notice was taken when it was published in 1618, entitled *Histoire naturelle de la fontaine qui brûle près de Grenoble* (*The true story of the burning fountain near Grenoble*). Its author was a doctor from Tournon, named Jean Tardin. Had anybody taken the trouble to study this document, gas could have been used for lighting at the beginning of the seventeenth century. For not only did Jean Tardin study the natural gasometer in the fountain; he reproduced in his laboratory the same phenomena he had observed in nature. He put coal into

45

a sealed tube, subjected it to a high temperature, and produced in this way the flames whose origin he was seeking. He explained clearly that the basis of this fire was bitumen which could be broken down into a gas which would give off an "inflammable exhalation". As it turned out, it was not until somewhere round 1797 that the Frenchman Lebon, before the Englishman Winsor, patented his "thermo-lamp". And so, through a failure to re-examine ancient documents, a discovery that might have had considerable industrial and commercial repercussions was forgotten and, therefore, for all practical purposes, lost.

'In the same way, nearly a hundred years before the first optic signals discovered by Claude Chappe in 1793, a letter from Fenelon to Jean Sobieski, secretary to the King of Poland, dated 26th November, 1695, mentions experiments recently carried out, not only in optic telegraphy, but in telephony by means of a loud-speaker.

'In 1636 an unknown author, Schwenter, in his *Délassements physico-mathématiques* was already investigating the principle of the electric telegraph and the possibility of "two persons being able to communicate with one another by means of a magnetic needle". Now, Oersted's experiments in this field date from as late as 1819. Here, again, there was a lapse of nearly two centuries during which the original discovery was forgotten.

'Let me recall briefly a few little known inventions: the diving-bell is described in the manuscript of *Alexander's Romance* in the Royal Print Room in Berlin: date, 1320. The manuscript of the German poem, *Salman und Morolf*, written in 1190 (Stuttgart Library) contains a drawing of an underwater vessel; according to the inscription, the ship was made of leather and navigable in stormy weather. Finding himself one day surrounded by hostile galleys and in danger of being captured, the inventor submerged his vessel and lived for fourteen days at the bottom of the sea, breathing through a tube floating on the surface. In a work written by Ludwig von Hartenstein, *circa* 1510, there is a drawing of a diver's outfit, with two apertures for the eyes covered with glass. At the top there is a long tube with a tap to allow the intake of air from outside. To the right and left of the drawing are shown the indispensable accessories for the descent and return, namely leaden soles and a step-ladder.

'Here is another example of a forgotten discovery: an unknown writer, born at Montebourg, near Coutances, in 1729, published a work entitled *Giphantie*, an anagram of the first part of the author's name, Tiphaigne de le Roche. In it is described not only black-and-white, but colour photography, as follows: "The image is imprinted instantaneously on the exposed sheet (*toile*), which is then at once removed and placed in a dark room. An hour later the prepared surface has dried, and you have a picture all the more precious in that no work of art can imitate its truthfulness." The author adds: "It is first of all necessary to examine the nature of the sticky substance which intercepts and retains the light rays;

secondly, to overcome the difficulty of preparing and employing it; and, thirdly, to study the action of the light and of this dried substance." And yet it was not until a century later, on 7th January, 1839, that Daguerre's discovery was announced by Arago to the French Académie des Sciences. Moreover, it should be mentioned that the properties of certain metallic bodies capable of capturing an image were described in a treatise by Fabricius, *De rebus metallicis*, published in 1566.

'Another example is vaccination, described long ages ago in one of the *Vedas*, the *Sactaya Grantham*. This text was cited by Moreau de Jouet on 16th October, 1826, in his *Mémoire sur la variolide* presented to the Académie des Sciences: "Collect the fluid from the pustules on the point of a lancet and insert it into the arm, so that the fluid mixes with the blood. This will produce fever, but the disease will then be very mild and there will be no cause for alarm." Then follows an exact description of all the symptoms.

'What about anaesthetics? On this subject it would have been possible to study a work by Denis Papin, written in 1681, entitled: *Le Traité des opérations sans douleur*, or else to repeat the old Chinese experiments with Indian hemp, or again to employ for this purpose mandrake wine, well known in the Middle Ages, and completely forgotten in the seventeenth century, the effects of which were studied by a certain Doctor Auriol of Toulouse, in 1823. No one has ever taken the trouble to check the results obtained.

'And penicillin? Here we can mention first an empirical remedy used in the Middle Ages, namely applications of Roquefort cheese; but there is also a record of something still more extraordinary. Ernest Duchesne, a student at the École de Santé Militaire at Lyons, presented on 17th December, 1897, a thesis entitled: *Contribution to a study of hostile influences in micro-organisms – the antagonism between moulds and microbes*. This work describes experiments showing the action of *penicillum glaucum* on bacteria. Yet this thesis attracted no attention. I would stress particularly this flagrant example of a discovery being forgotten so near to our own times when bacteriology was in a flourishing state.

'Examples of this kind are innumerable, and each one could be the subject of a whole lecture. I will take now the case of oxygen, the effects of which were studied in the fifteenth century by an alchemist named Eck de Sulsbach, as Chevreul pointed out in the *Journal de Savants* in October 1849. Moreover, Theophrastus had already stated that a flame is sustained by an ethereal body (*"un corps aériforme"*), an opinion shared by Clement of Alexandria.

'I will pass over the extraordinary anticipations of Roger Bacon, Cyrano de Bergerac and others, because it would be too easy to attribute them to pure imagination. I prefer to stick to facts that can be verified. As regards the automobile, I would point out that in Nuremberg in the seventeenth century a certain Johann Hautch constructed carriages with sprung suspension. In 1645 a vehicle of this type was tested in the grounds of the Temple, but I believe that the Society founded to exploit this invention never came into being. Possibly it met with obstacles like those encountered by the first Parisian Transport Society due, I would remind you, to the initiative of Pascal who caused it to be subsidized and patronized by one of his friends, the Duc de Roannes.

'Even in the case of still more important discoveries than these, we underestimate the influence of data supplied by the Ancients. Christopher Columbus admitted openly how much he owed to the old philosophers, poets and sages. It is not generally known that Columbus copied out twice the chorus in the second act of Seneca's tragedy, *Medea*, in which the author speaks of a world destined to be discovered in future centuries. This copy can be examined in the MS. of *Las profecias* in the Library at Seville. Columbus also remembered Aristotle's observations regarding the roundness of the Earth in his treatise *De Coelo*.

'Joubert was right when he remarked that "nothing makes men so imprudent and conceited as ignorance of the past and a scorn for old books". As Rivarol so well expressed it: "Every State is a mystery ship with its anchor in the sky," so it could also be said, in speaking of time, that the ship of the future has its anchors in the sky of the past. Forgetfulness alone threatens us with the worst shipwrecks.

'An extreme example of this forgetfulness is seen in the story, which would be incredible if it were not true, of the gold-mines in California. In June 1848 Marshall discovered for the first time some nuggets in a water-course near which he was supervising the construction of a mill. Now it happened that Fernando Cortez had already been there when he was looking for some Mexicans who were reported to be in possession of treasure of considerable value. Cortez turned the district upside-down, searched all the huts, but never thought of picking up some sand, while for three centuries bands of Spanish missionaries roamed all over the gold-bearing soil, seeking their Eldorado farther and farther away. And yet, in 1737, more than a hundred years before Marshall's discovery, readers of the *Gazette de Hollande* might have found out that the gold and silver mines of Sonora were workable since their newspaper gave their exact position. Moreover in 1767 a book was on sale in Paris entitled *The Civil and Natural History of California* in which the author, Buriell, described the gold-mines and quoted the evidence of navigators with regard to the nuggets. Nobody paid any attention to this article, or to the work or to these facts which, a century later, were effectively to launch the great "Gold Rush". Nor does anyone read today the records of the old Arab explorers, although they contain valuable information regarding mines.

'This forgetfulness extends to everything. Long research and careful checking have convinced me that Europe and France possess treasures which are hardly exploited at all – namely, the ancient documents in our great libraries. All industrial techniques, however, ought to be organized in three dimensions: experience,

48

science and history. To eliminate or neglect the latter is a sign of pride, or else of naïvety. It also means preferring to run the risk of finding what does not yet exist rather than of trying rationally to adapt what does exist to what one desires to obtain. Before investing large sums, an industrialist should be in possession of all the technological elements relating to his problem. It is obvious, however, that merely seeking for priorities in patents is quite an inadequate way of ascertaining the state of technical proficiency at any given period in history. In point of fact, industries are much older than science; they ought, therefore, to be perfectly acquainted with the history of their technical processes about which they are often less well informed than they think.

'The Ancients, using very simple techniques, obtained results that we can imitate but would often find it difficult to explain, despite all our resources of theoretical knowledge. This simplicity was the most valuable contribution made by ancient science.

'Yes, you will say; but what about nuclear energy? To this I will reply by a quotation which I think should give us serious food for thought. In a very rare book, unknown even to many specialists, that appeared more than eighty years ago under the title *Les Atlantes*, the author, writing under the pseudonym of Roisel, described the results of fifty-six years of research and the study of ancient science. In describing the scientific knowledge with which he credits the inhabitants of Atlantis, Roisel makes the following statement quite astounding when you consider the date at which he was writing: "The consequence of this incessant activity was the appearance of matter, of that other equilibrium whose rupture would also be the cause of violent cosmic phenomena. If, for some unknown reason, our solar system were to disintegrate, its constituent atoms, becoming instantly active on achieving independence, would shine in space with an ineffable light which would announce from afar destruction on a vast scale and the hopes of a new world." This last example, I think, is enough to make us realize the profound truth of Mlle Bertin's remark (quoted above): "There is nothing new except what has been forgotten."

'Let us consider now how far a systematic probing into the past can benefit industry in a practical way. When I suggested that we ought to take the liveliest interest in the achievements of the Ancients, I do not mean for the sake of erudition alone. All we need do, when concrete problems arise in industry, is to examine old scientific and technical documents to find out whether they contain either significant facts that have been overlooked, or technical processes that have been forgotten but are none the less worth studying and directly relevant to the case in point. Thus, plastic materials, which we imagine to have been a recent invention, might have been discovered much earlier if we had repeated certain experiments made by the chemist Berzelius.

'With regard to metallurgy, I would draw your attention to a rather significant fact. When I first began to study certain chemical processes as practised by the Ancients, I was somewhat surprised

49

not to be able to reproduce in the laboratory some metallurgical experiments which seemed to be very clearly described. I tried in vain to understand the reason for my failure, for I had carefully followed the instructions and the proportions indicated. Then, on reflection, I realized that I had none the less made a mistake. I had used a flux (or fusible ?) that was chemically pure, whereas those the Ancients employed were impure, i.e. salts obtained from natural products and consequently capable of provoking catalytic actions. In the event, the experiment proved that this was the case. Specialists will understand what important perspectives are opened up by these observations. Economies in fuel and energy could be achieved by adapting to metallurgy certain processes known to the Ancients, nearly all of which are based on the action of catalysers. In this respect my experiments have been confirmed not only by the work of Dr. Menetrier on the catalytic action of oligo-elements, but by the research carried out by the German, Mittasch, into the part played by catalysis in the chemistry of the Ancients. From different sources similar results have been obtained. This convergence seems to show that in technology the time has come to take into account the fundamental importance of the notion of quality and its role in the production of all observable quantitative phenomena.

'The Ancients were equally familiar with metallurgical processes which seem to have been forgotten, e.g. the immersion of copper in certain organic solutions. They obtained in this way instruments that were extraordinarily hard and penetrating. They were no less skilful in melting this metal, even as an oxide (*"même à l'état d'oxyde"*). I will cite only one example. A friend of mine, a specialist in mine prospecting, discovered, north-west of Agadès in the middle of the Sahara, copper ore bearing traces of fusion, and the dregs of a crucible with some metal remains still in it. This was not a sulphide, but an oxide; that is to say, a body the reduction of which in modern industry raises problems that could not be solved over a simple nomad's fire.

'In the field of alloys, one of the most important in industry today, the Ancients were very well informed. Not only did they know how to produce, directly from a complex of ores, alloys possessing remarkable properties – a process, incidentally, of great interest to Soviet industry at the moment – but they also made use of special alloys such as electrum, which we have never had the curiosity to study seriously, although we know the formulae for its manufacture.

'I will only allude briefly to possible developments in the field of medicine and pharmaceutics, still almost unexplored and open to limitless research. I will merely stress the importance of the question of the treatment of burns, a matter of increasing urgency in view of the frequency of car and aeroplane accidents. Now it is a fact that it was in the Middle Ages, devastated as they were by incessant conflagrations, more than at any other time in history, that the best remedies against burns were discovered, though these recipes have now been completely forgotten. In this connection, it should be known that some of the old pharmaceutical products not only alleviated pain, but even prevented scars from forming and helped to regenerate the injured cells and tissues.

'With regard to dyes and varnishes, there is no need to remind you of the exceedingly high quality of the products prepared according to ancient formulae. The admirable colours used by painters in the Middle Ages have not, as is commonly believed, been lost; I know of at least one manuscript in France which gives the secret of their composition. No one has ever thought of adapting or verifying these formulae. And yet our modern painters, if they were alive in a hundred years time, would not recognize their pictures, because the colours employed today will not last. It would seem, for example, that van Gogh's yellows have already lost their extraordinary and characteristic luminosity.

'On the subject of mines I will merely mention the close connection between medical research and mine prospecting. The use of plants for therapeutic purposes, which we call phytotherapy, was well known to the Ancients and is, in fact, connected with a new science – bio-geo-chemistry. The aim of this discipline is to reveal positive anomalies in respect of traces of metals found in plants which indicate the presence of mineral deposits. In this way it is possible to discover specific affinities in certain plants for certain metals, and these data can then be used for mine prospecting as well as for therapeutic purposes. This is yet another typical example of a fact which in my opinion, is the most important in the history of techniques – namely, *the convergence of the various scientific disciplines*, which implies a need for constant syntheses.

'Among other fields of research having practical results in industry I would mention that of fertilizers – a vast domain in which the chemists of an earlier age obtained results which are for the most part unknown. I am thinking more especially of what they used to call "the essence of fecundity", a product composed of certain salts mixed with digested or distilled manures.

'Glass-making in the ancient world is another matter of which we still know very little. The Romans used glass flooring, for example, and there is no doubt that a study of the processes employed by the old glass-makers might be of great assistance in solving certain ultra-modern problems such as the dissemination of rare soils and of palladium in glass, which would make it possible to obtain fluorescent tubes of black light.

'As regards the textiles industry, despite the triumph of plastics, or rather because of it, the best policy would be to concentrate on the production, for the luxury trade, of tissues of very high quality which might perhaps be dyed after the manner of the Ancients; or else an effort might be made to manufacture that strange material called *Pilema*. This consisted of wool or cotton tissues treated with certain acids, and was not only fire-proof, but could not be cut or pierced by steel. The process was known to the Gauls who used the material for breast-plates.

'The furniture industry, too, owing to the high price of plastic facings, might solve this problem advantageously by adapting certain ancient processes, for example, the soaking of timber in a solution which considerably increased its resistance to various physical and chemical agents. Building contractors, too, would do well to make a study of special cements whose ingredients are described in treatises dating from the fifteenth and sixteenth centuries: in many respects, they are much superior to our modern cements.

'Soviet industrialists have been using recently, in the cutlery trade, ceramics that are harder than metal. This hardening process could also be studied in the light of old methods of tempering steel.

'Finally, though I do not wish to press this point unduly, I would suggest that if research in physics could be directed to a study of the problem of terrestrial magnetic energy, this might have the most far-reaching consequences. There are some very ancient texts dealing with this subject which have never been seriously examined or verified, despite their undoubted interest.

'Whether we are concerned mainly with past experience or future possibilities, I believe that from a profoundly realistic point of view, we should do better to ignore the present. Such a statement may seem paradoxical, but a moment's thought will make it clear that the present is nothing but a point of contact between the lines of past and future. Taking our stand firmly on the experience of our ancestors, we should look forward, rather than down at our feet, and not attach undue importance to that brief interval of disequilibrium during which we are passing through space and time. The fact that we are moving proves this, and we must rely on the lucidity of our vision to keep the balance at all times between what has been and what will be.'

IV

The concealment of knowledge and power – The meaning of revolutionary war – Technology brings back the guilds – A return to the age of the Adepts – A fiction writer's prediction, The Power-House – From monarchy to cryptocracy – The secret society as the government of the future – Intelligence itself a secret society – A knocking at the door

IN a very strange article, but one which I think reflects the views of many French intellectuals, Jean-Paul Sartre refused purely and simply to admit the H-bomb's right to exist. Existence, according to the theory of this philosopher, precedes essence. But here is a phenomenon whose essence he doesn't approve of: therefore he denies its existence. A singular contradiction! 'The H-bomb,' wrote Sartre, 'is against history.'

How can a fact of civilization be 'against history'? What is history? For Sartre, it is the movement that must necessarily bring the masses to power. What is the H-bomb? A reserve of power to which only a few have access. A very narrow society of scientists, technicians and politicians can decide the destiny of humanity. Therefore, so that history can mean what we have said it means, let us abolish the H-bomb. . . . Here is an example of the apostle of social progressism demanding that progress should be halted. A sociology with its roots in the nineteenth century asking to go back to the age in which it was born. Let there be no misunderstanding. For us it is not a question either of approving the fabrication of weapons of destruction or of decrying the thirst for justice that inspires all that is purest in human societies. It is a question of looking at things from a different angle.

(1) It is true that the existence of the 'ultimate weapon' is an appalling danger for humanity. But the fewer the people who control such weapons, the less likely are they to be used. Human society in the modern world survives only because decisions are taken by only a very small number of men.

(2) Nothing can be done with these 'ultimate' weapons except develop them further. In the realm of *avant-garde* operational research the frontiers between good and evil are continually shrinking. Every discovery at the level of basic structures is *at the same time* both positive and negative. Moreover, as techniques progress, they do not become more complicated; on the contrary, they get simpler, moving on to a plane where elementals are involved. The number of operations diminishes, and less equipment is required. In the end men will hold the key to universal forces in the hollow of their hand. A child will be able to make and handle it. The more simplification becomes synonymous with power, the more necessary will it become to hide what is going on behind higher barriers in order to preserve the continuity of life.

(3) This occultation, moreover, happens automatically, as real power passes to the scientists and scholars. The latter have their own language and their own ways of thinking. This is not an artificial barrier. Their language is different because their thought is on a different level. The scientists have convinced the rich that they would be better off, and the ruling classes that they would become more powerful if they invoked their help. And they have rapidly won for themselves a position beyond wealth and beyond governments. How has this been done ? In the first place, by making everything infinitely complicated. When intellectuals wish to gain control they complicate as much as possible the system they wish to destroy so as to render it defenceless, as the spider enmeshes its victim in its web. The so-called 'rulers', the propertied and governing classes, are no longer anything but intermediaries in an epoch which is itself intermediary.

(4) While 'ultimate' weapons are produced in ever greater numbers the character of war is changing. An uninterrupted combat goes on in the form of guerrillas, palace revolutions, ambushes, *maquis*, articles, books and speeches. Instead of ordinary wars there are revolutionary wars. These new forms of war correspond to a change in the aims and aspirations of humanity. Wars used to

be waged for material ends; revolutionary wars are fought to change the conditions in which men live. Formerly men destroyed one another in order to acquire territory, while the spoil was shared between the conquerors. Today, throughout this incessant struggle, resembling nothing so much as a dance of insects interlocking their antennae, it would seem that humanity was seeking some sort of union, a grouping of forces, a unity that would change the face of the Earth. Instead of wanting to enjoy things, today men want to *do* them. The intellectuals, who have not forgotten to prepare for psychological warfare, also have a hand in this profound change of attitude. The revolutionary war corresponds to the birth of a new spirit: the workers' spirit. The spirit of the *'ouvriers de la Terre'*. It is in this sense that history represents a Messianic movement of the masses. This movement coincides with the concentration of knowledge in the hands of a few. This is the phase we are now going through in our campaign for a growing integration of man into the universe as a whole, and a continuous spiritualization of the mind.

Let us descend to concrete cases, and we shall find ourselves once more in the era of secret societies. When we ascend again to consider more important, and consequently less visible facts, we shall see that we are also returning to the age of the Adepts. The Adepts (or Initiates) spread their knowledge among a group of societies organized to keep new techniques secret. It is not impossible to imagine a world run on these lines in the very near future. Except for the fact that history does not repeat itself. Or, rather, if it does pass the same point, it does so on a higher level of the spiral.

Throughout history, the preservation of techniques has always been one of the objects of the secret societies. The Egyptian priests were the jealous guardians of the laws of plane geometry. Recent researches have established the existence at Baghdad of a society that possessed the secret of the electric battery and the monopoly of galvano-plastics two thousand years ago. The Middle Ages saw the formation in France, Germany and Spain of technicians' guilds. Consider the history of alchemy: the secret method of colouring glass red by introducing gold at the moment of fusion; the secret of Greek Fire – a mixture of coagulated linseed oil and gelatine, the forerunner of napalm. Not all the secrets of the Middle Ages have been recovered, e.g. that of a flexible mineral glass, or the simple method of obtaining *'la lumiere froide'*, etc.

We also observe the apparition of groups of technicians preserving secrets of manufacture, either artesan techniques for making such things as harmonicas or glass ball-bearings, or industrial techniques, e.g. for the production of synthetic petrol. In the great American atomic centres the physicists wear badges indicating the level of their qualifications and the extent of their responsibilities, and may only speak to those who wear the same badge as themselves. They form clubs, and friendships and attachments are formed within the same category.

In this way closed circles come into being very similar to the guilds of the Middle Ages, whether the subject of study be jet aeroplanes, cyclotrons or electronics. In 1956 thirty-five Chinese students on leaving the Massachusetts Institute of Technology asked to return to their country. They had not been working on military problems, but it was considered that they knew too much and they were forbidden to leave the country. The Chinese Government, anxious to secure the return of these enlightened young people, proposed in exchange to send back some American airmen who had been detained on charges of espionage.

The safe-keeping of techniques and scientific secrets cannot be entrusted to the police. Or, rather, security officials today are obliged to know something about the sciences and techniques which it is their duty to protect. These specialists are trained to work in nuclear laboratories, and nuclear physicists to be responsible for their security. This leads to the creation of a caste more powerful than governments and political police.

To complete the picture, one has only to think of the groups of experts who are prepared to work for the country that offers the most advantageous terms. These are the new mercenaries, the 'hired men-at-arms' of our civilization in which the *condottiere* wear white overalls. South Africa, the Argentine and India are their best hunting grounds where they win for themselves positions of real authority.

If we turn now to the less visible but more important facts, we shall see that we are witnessing a return to the age of the Adepts. 'Nothing in the universe can resist the cumulative ardour of a sufficiently large number of enlightened minds working together in organized groups': Teilhard de Chardin told this in confidence to George Magloire.

More than fifty years ago John Buchan, who was an important figure in British politics, wrote a short story which was at the same time a message intended for the ears of a few enlightened individuals. In this story, entitled (and not by chance) *The Power-House*, the hero meets a distinguished gentleman who, in the course of a seemingly casual conversation, puts forward some very disturbing ideas:*

'Of course there are many key-points in civilization,' I said, 'and the loss of them would bring ruin. But those keys are strongly held.'

'Not as strongly as you think. Consider how delicate the machinery is growing. As life grows more complex, the machinery grows more intricate, and therefore more vulnerable. Your so-called sanctions become so infinitely numerous that each in itself is frail. In the Dark Ages you had one great power – the terror of God and His Church. Now you have a multiplicity of small things, all

* Extract from *The Power-House*, by John Buchan. Longmans Green & Co.

55

delicate and fragile, and strong only by our tacit agreement not to question them.'

'You forget one thing,' I said, 'the fact that men really are agreed to keep the machine going. That *is* what I call the "goodwill of civilization".'

'You have put your finger on the one thing that matters. Civilization is a conspiracy. What value would your police be if every criminal could find a sanctuary across the Channel, or your law courts, if no other tribunal recognized their decisions? Modern life is the silent compact of comfortable folk to keep up pretences. And it will succeed till the day comes when there is another compact to strip them bare.'

'We won't dispute on the indisputable,' I said. 'But I should have thought that it was in the interest of all the best brains of the world to keep up what you call the conspiracy.'

'I wonder,' he said slowly. 'Do we really get the best brains working on the side of the compact. Take the business of government. When all said is said, we are ruled by amateurs and the second-rate. The methods of our departments would bring any private firm to bankruptcy. The methods of Parliament – pardon me – would disgrace any board of directors. Our rulers pretend to buy expert knowledge, but they never pay the price for it that a business man would pay, and if they get it they have not the courage to use it. Where is the inducement for a man of genius to sell his brains to our insipid governors?

'And yet knowledge is the only power – now as ever. A little mechanical device will wreck your navies. A new chemical combination will upset every rule of war. It is the same with our commerce. One or two minute changes might sink Britain to the level of Ecuador, or give China the key of the world's wealth. And yet we never dream that these things are possible. We think our castles of sand are the ramparts of the universe.'

'I have never had the gift of the gab, but I admire it in others. There is a morbid charm in such talk, a kind of exhilaration, of which one is half ashamed. I found myself interested, and more than a little impressed.

'But surely,' I said, 'the first thing a discoverer does is to make his discovery public. He wants the honour and glory, and he wants money for it. It becomes part of the world's knowledge, and everything is readjusted to meet it. That was what happened with electricity. You call our civilization a machine, but it is something far more flexible. It has the power of adaptation of a living organism.'

'That might be true if the new knowledge really became the world's property. But does it? I read now and then in the papers that some eminent scientist had made a great discovery. He reads a paper before some Academy of Science, and there are leading articles on it and his photograph adorns the magazines. That kind of man is not the danger. He is a bit of the machine, a party to the compact. It is the men who stand outside it that are to be reckoned with, the artists in discovery who will never use their knowledge

56

till they can use it with full effect. Believe me, the biggest brains are without the ring which we call civilization.'

Then his voice seemed to hesitate.

'You may hear people say that submarines have done away with the battleship, and that aircraft have annulled the mastery of the sea. That is what our pessimists say. But do you imagine that the clumsy submarine or the fragile aeroplane is really the last word of science?'

'No doubt they will develop,' I said, 'but by that time the power of the defence will have advanced also.'

He shook his head. 'It is not so. Even now the knowledge which makes possible great engines of destruction is far beyond the capacity of any defence. You see only the productions of second-rate folk who are in a hurry to get wealth and fame. The true knowledge, the deadly knowledge is still kept secret. But, believe me, my friend, it is there.'

He paused for a second; and I saw the faint outline of the smoke from his cigar against the background of the dark. Then he quoted me one or two cases, slowly, as if in some doubt about the wisdom of his words.

It was these cases that startled me. They were of different kinds – a great calamity, a sudden breach between two nations, a blight on a vital crop, a war, a pestilence. I will not repeat them. I do not think I believed in them then, and now I believe less. But they were horribly impressive, as told in that quiet voice in that sombre room on that dark June night. If he was right, these things had not been the work of Nature or accident but of a devilish art. The nameless brains that he spoke of, working silently in the background, now and then showed their power by some cataclysmic revelation. I did not believe him, but, as he put the case, showing with strange clearness the steps in the game, I had no words to protest. At last I found my voice:

'What you describe is super-anarchy, and yet it makes no headway. What is the motive of those diabolical brains?'

He laughed. 'How should I be able to tell you? I am a humble inquirer, and in my researches I come on curious bits of facts. But I cannot pry into motives. I only know of the existence of great extra-social intelligences. Let us say they distrust the machine. They may be idealists and desire to make a new world, or they may simply be artists, loving for its own sake the pursuit of truth. If I were to hazard a guess, I should say that it took both types to bring about results, for the second to find the knowledge and the first the will to use it.'

A souvenir came back to me. It was of a hot upland meadow in Tyrol, where among acres of flowers and beside a leaping stream I was breakfasting after a morning spent in climbing the white crags. I had picked up a German on the way, a small man of the Professor class, who did me the honour to share my sandwiches. He conversed fluently but quaintly in English, and he was, I remember, a Nietzschean and a hot rebel against the established order.

57

'The pity,' he cried, 'is that the reformers do not know, and those who know are too idle to reform. Some day there will come the marriage of knowledge and will, and then the world will march.'

'You draw an awful picture,' I said to my host. 'But if those extra-social brains are so potent, why after all do they effect so little? A dull police officer, with the machine behind him, can afford to laugh at most experiments in anarchy.'

'True,' he said, 'and civilization will win until its enemies learn from it the importance of the machine. The compact must endure until there is a counter-compact. Consider the ways of that form of foolishness which today we call nihilism or anarchy. A few illiterate bandits in a Paris slum defy the world, and in a week they are in jail. Half a dozen crazy Russian intellectuals in Geneva conspire to upset the Romanoffs, and are hunted down by the police of Europe. All the Governments and their not very intelligent police forces join hands, and, hey presto! there is an end of the conspirators. For civilization knows how to use such powers as it has, while the immense potentiality of the unlicensed is dissipated in vapour. Civilization wins because it is a world-wide league; its enemies fail because they are parochial. But supposing. . . .'

Again he stopped and rose from his chair. He found a switch and flooded the room with light. I glanced up, blinking to see my host smiling down on me, a most benevolent and courteous old gentleman.

'I want to hear the end of your prophecies,' I said. 'You were saying . . . ?'

'I said: supposing anarchy learned from civilization and became international. Oh, I don't mean the bands of advertising donkeys who call themselves the International Union of Workers and suchlike rubbish. I mean if the real brain-stuff of the world were internationalized. Suppose that the links in the cordon of civilization were neutralized by other links in a far more potent chain. The Earth is seething with incoherent power and unorganized intelligence. Have you ever reflected on the case of China? There you have millions of quick brains stifled in trumpery crafts. They have no direction, no driving power, so the sum of their efforts is futile, and the world laughs at China. Europe throws her a million or two on loan now and then, and she cynically responds by begging the prayers of Christendom. And yet, I say, supposing . . .'

'It's a horrible idea,' I said, 'and, thank God, I don't believe it possible. Mere destruction is too barren a creed to inspire a new Napoleon, and you can do with nothing short of one.'

'It would scarcely be destruction,' he replied gently. 'Let us call it iconoclasm, the swallowing of formulas, which has always had its full retinue of idealists. And you do not want a Napoleon. All that is needed is direction, which could be given by men of far lower gifts than a Bonaparte. In a word, you want a Power House, and then the age of miracles will begin.'

When one reflects that Buchan wrote these lines about 1910, and

58

then looks back on all the upheavals the world has endured since then and the mass-movements which are sweeping through China, Africa and India, one may well wonder whether, after all, one or more of these power-houses has not been active. This view will only appear romantic to superficial observers, i.e. to historians wedded to the theory that 'facts explain events' which, in the last resort, depends on the way in which you choose your facts.

Elsewhere in this book we shall be describing a power-house which failed, but only after it had plunged the world into a bath of blood and fire: the Fascist power-house. Nor can one doubt the existence of a Communist power-house, or question its prodigious efficiency. 'Nothing in the Universe can resist the cumulative ardour of a sufficiently large number of enlightened minds working together in organized groups.' I repeat my quotation, the truth of which is startling in this context.

Our ideas about secret societies are academic; we take a conventional view of extraordinary facts. If we want to understand the world of the future, we shall have to reconsider and refresh our ideas about secret societies by making a more thorough study of the past and discovering a point of view which will render intelligible the phase of history through which we are now passing.

It is possible, even probable, that the secret society will be the future form of government in the new world of the 'esprit ouvrier'. Let us take a quick glance at the way things have developed. The monarchies claimed to possess supernatural powers. Kings and nobles and ministers and all the other authorities try to appear more than natural, and to arouse astonishment and admiration by their way of dressing, living and behaving. They do everything they can to attract notice; they encourage pomp and ceremony. And they are always on view, infinitely approachable and infinitely different. Remember the French king Henri IV with his: 'Ralliez-vous à mon panache blanc !' And sometimes in summer the king bathed naked in the Seine, in the heart of Paris. Louis XIV was a Sun, but anybody at any time was free to enter the palace and be present at his table. Always exposed to the public view, demi-gods decked in gold and feathers, continually attracting attention and living two lives, one private and the other public. After the Revolution abstract theories prevailed, and governments concealed themselves. The authorities made a point of being 'like everyone else', but at the same time adopted a haughty attitude. On the personal as well as on the factual plane, it became difficult to define exactly what the government consisted of. Modern democracies lend themselves to a thousand and one 'esoteric' interpretations. Some intellectuals assert that America is governed by a handful of industrial tycoons, England by the City bankers, France by the Freemasons, etc. With the advent of governments thrown up by revolutionary wars, power is almost completely hidden. Observers of the Chinese revolution, the war in Indo-China, the Algerian War, the special agents in the Soviet world, are all impressed by the way in which power is submerged in the mystery of the Masses, by the secrecy surrounding the responsible authorities, by the impossibility of knowing 'who is who' and 'who decides what'.

A veritable 'cryptocracy' has taken over. We have no time now to analyse this phenomenon, but a volume might well be written about what we have called the 'cryptocracy'. In a novel by Jean Lartéguy, who took part in the revolution of Azerbaidjan, the war in Palestine and the Korean War, a French captain is taken prisoner after the defeat of Dien-Bien-Phu:

'Glatigny found himself in a tunnel-shaped shelter, long and narrow. He was sitting on the ground, his naked back propped against the earth walls. Opposite him a *nha-quê* squatting on his heels, was smoking some foul tobacco rolled in an old piece of newspaper.

'The *nha-quê* was bare-headed, and wearing a khaki uniform without any badges of rank. He had no sandals, and was wiggling his toes voluptuously in the warm mud. Between puffs he said a few words, and a supple-jointed *bô-doi*, looking like a "boy", leant towards Glatigny:

'"The battalion commander, he ask where is French major commanding post."

'Glatigny's reaction was that of a regular Army officer; he could not believe that this *nha-quê* squatting there smoking stinking tobacco was in command, like himself, of a battalion, and had the same rank and responsibilities. . . . He must, then, have been one of the officers of the 308th Division, the best and the most efficiently staffed in the whole Popular Army. So it was this peasant from the rice plantations who had beaten him – him, Glatigny, descendant of one of the great military dynasties of the West. . . .'

Paul Mousset, the well-known journalist, and a war correspondent in Indo-China and Algeria, once said to me: 'I have always thought that the "boy", or the small shopkeeper were perhaps the ones who wielded the greatest authority. . . . The new world camouflages its leaders, like those insects that resemble twigs or leaves. . . .'

After the downfall of Stalin, the political experts were unable to agree as to the identity of the real ruler of the U.S.S.R. Just as they were telling us at last that it was Beria, the news came of his assassination. No one could possibly name the real rulers of a country with authority over a thousand million souls and extending over half the inhabited areas of the globe. . . .

The threat of war is what reveals the true form of governments. In June 1955 America had planned an operation simulating actual war conditions in the course of which the Government left Washington to carry on 'somewhere in the United States'. In the event of this refuge being destroyed, arrangements had been made for this government to transfer its powers to a 'shadow government' that had been already constituted. This latter consisted of senators, deputies and experts whose names could not be disclosed. Thus the way to a cryptocracy, in one of the most powerful countries on this planet, was officially indicated.

Should war break out, we should no doubt see the regular govern-ments replaced by 'shadow' governments installed, perhaps for the U.S.A. in some caves in Virginia, and for the U.S.S.R. on a floating station in the Arctic. And from that moment it would be treason to disclose the identity of the countries' rulers. Equipped with electronic brains to reduce administrative staff to a minimum, secret societies would organize the gigantic conflict between the two great blocs of humanity. It is even conceivable that these governments might be situated outside our world, in artificial satellites revolving round the Earth.

We are not indulging in philosophy-fiction or history-fiction, but in a fantastic realism. We are sceptical with regard to many points about which others, who are considered to be 'reasonable' men, are less so. We are not in any way trying to focus attention on some empty kind of occultism, or to suggest a semi-crazy, semi-magical interpretation of facts. Nor are we proposing some form of religion. We believe only in human intelligence, and we believe that, at a certain level, intelligence itself is a kind of secret society. We believe that its powers are unlimited when it can develop to its fullest extent, like an oak-tree growing freely in the forest, instead of being dwarfed like a plant in a pot.

It is therefore in the light of the discoveries we have just been making, and of others, still stranger, which we shall soon be con-fronted with, that we should try to reconsider our conception of a secret society. Here, as elsewhere, we have been able only to out-line briefly the general direction of future researches and reflections. And we are well aware that the view we take of things may well seem mad: this is because we are saying rapidly and brutally what we have to say, like a man knocking on a sleeper's door when time is running short.

THE EXAMPLE OF ALCHEMY

I

An alchemist in the Café Procope in 1953 – A conversation about Gurdjieff – A believer in the reality of the philosopher's stone – I change my ideas about the value of progress – What we really think about alchemy: neither a revelation nor a groping in the dark – Some reflections on the 'spiral' and on hope

IT was in March 1953 that I met an alchemist for the first time. It was at the Café Procope in Paris which was then coming into fashion again. A famous poet, while I was writing my book on Gurdjieff, had arranged the meeting, and I was often to see this singular man ˙again, though I never succeeded in penetrating his secrets.

My ideas about alchemy and alchemists were rudimentary and derived from popular literature on the subject, and I had no idea that alchemists still existed. The man seated opposite me at Voltaire's table was young and elegant. After a thorough classical education he had studied chemistry. He was then earning his living in business and knew a lot of artists as well as some society people. I do not keep a regular diary, but sometimes, on important occasions, I jot down my impressions and make comments. That night, when I got home, I wrote as follows:

'How old can he be? He says thirty-five. That seems surprising. He has white, curly hair, trimmed so as to look like a wig. Lots of deep wrinkles in a pink skin and full features. Few gestures, but slow, calculated and effective when he does make them. A calm, keen smile; eyes that laugh, but in a detached sort of way. Everything about him suggests another age. In conversation, highly articulate and completely self-possessed. Something of the sphinx behind that affable, timeless countenance. Incomprehensible. And this is not merely my personal impression. A.B. who sees him nearly every day, tells me he has never, for a second, found him lacking in a "superior degree of objectivity".

'The reasons why he rejects Gurdjieff:

(1) Whoever feels an urge to teach is not living his own doctrine completely and has not attained the heights of initiation.

(2) In Gurdjieff's teaching there is no material point of contact between the pupil who has been convinced of his own insignificance and the energy he must succeed in acquiring in order to become a real being. This energy – this "will to will" as Gurdjieff puts it – the pupil is supposed to find in himself and nowhere else. Now this approach is partially false, and can only lead to despair. This energy exists outside man, and must be captured. The Roman Catholic swallows the host – a ritual way of intercepting this energy. But if you have no faith? In that case,

have a fire – that is all the alchemy is. A real fire. Everything
begins and everything happens through contact with matter.
(3) Gurdjieff did not live alone but always had a crowd round
him. "There are roads in solitude and rivers in the desert", but
there are no roads and no rivers in a man who is always mixed up
with other men.

'I asked him some questions about alchemy which he must have
thought completely foolish. Without showing it, he replied:

' "Matter is everything; contact with matter, working with
matter, working with the hands." He made a great point of this:

' "Are you fond of gardening? That's a good start; alchemy is
like gardening. Do you like fishing? Alchemy has something in
common with fishing. Woman's work and children's games.

' "Alchemy cannot be taught. All the great works of literature
which have come down to us through the centuries contain elements
of this teaching. They are the product of truly adult minds which
have spoken to children, while respecting the laws of adult knowledge. A great work is never wrong as regards basic principles. But
the knowledge of those principles and the road that led to this
knowledge must remain secret. Nevertheless, there is an obligation
on first-degree searchers to help one another."

'Around midnight I asked him about Fulcanelli (author of
Le Mystère des Cathédrales and *Les Demeures philosophales*) and he
gave me to understand that Fulcanelli is not dead: "It is possible
to live infinitely longer than an unawakened man could believe.
And one's appearance can change completely. I know this; my
eyes know it. I also know that there is such a thing as the philosopher's stone. But this is matter on a different level, and not as we
know it. But here, as elsewhere, it is still possible to take measurements. The methods of working and measuring are simple, and do
not require any complicated apparatus: women's work and
children's games. . . ."

'He added: "Patience, hope, work. And whatever the work may
be, one can never work hard enough. As to hope: in alchemy hope
is based on the certainty that there is a goal to attain. I would never
have begun had I not been convinced that this goal exists and can
be attained in this life." '

Such was my first contact with alchemy. If I had begun to study it
in the books of 'magic', I do not think I should have got very far
for lack of time, and because I have little taste for literary erudition.
No sense of vocation either – such as an alchemist (though he does
not know yet that he is one) feels when for the first time he turns
the pages of some old treatise. My vocation is not for doing, but
for understanding; I am a spectator rather than an actor. I think,
like my old friend André Billy, that 'to be able to understand is as
fine a thing as to be able to sing', even if one's understanding is
only of brief duration.*

* In his *Ballad of Reading Gaol* Oscar Wilde makes the discovery that
mental inattention is the worst crime, and that intense mental concen-

63

I am a man in a hurry, like most of my contemporaries. I had the most recent contact imaginable with alchemy: a conversation in a *bistro* at Saint-Germain-des-Près. Later, when I was trying to grasp the real meaning of what that 'young' man had told me, I met Jacques Bergier, who doesn't work in a dusty old garret full of old books, but in places where the life of our century is concentrated – a laboratory and an information bureau. Bergier, too, was seeking something along the lines of alchemy, but not with the idea of making a pilgrimage into the past. This extraordinary little man, completely preoccupied with the secrets of atomic energy, had taken this path as a short cut. I dashed at supersonic speed, hard on his heels, through ancient texts compiled by wise men in love with leisureliness, intoxicated with patience. Bergier enjoyed the confidence of some of those men who still engage in alchemy. He was also in touch with modern scientists.

I soon became convinced, from what he told me, that there is a close connection between traditional alchemy and *avant-garde* science. I saw how intelligence was building a bridge between two worlds. I ventured on to this bridge, and found that it held. This made me very happy and relieved me of my anxieties. Having for a long time taken refuge in anti-progressist thought, along Hindu lines and influence by Gurdjieff, seeing the world of today as a prelude to the Apocalypse, full of despair at the prospect of a disastrous end to everything and not very sure of myself in my proud isolation, suddenly I saw the old past and the future shaking hands. The alchemists' metaphysics, thousands of years old, had concealed a technique which at last, in the twentieth century, had become almost comprehensible. The terrifying modern techniques opened up metaphysical horizons very like those of ancient times. My retreat from reality was nothing but false romanticism. On either side of the bridge, men's immortal souls had kindled the same fires.

In the end I came to believe that in the far distant past men had discovered the secrets of energy and matter. Not only in thought, but by manipulation; not only spiritually but technically.

Now the modern mind, by a different approach and by the methods, which I had long found distasteful, of pure reason and irreligion and by methods which displeased me, was in its turn preparing to discover the same secrets, with a mixture of curiosity, enthusiasm and apprehension. It was face to face with essentials in the spirit of the best tradition.

I then perceived that the opposition between age-old 'wisdom' and contemporary 'madness' was the invention of feeble and backward minds, a compensatory product for intellectuals incapable of keeping up with the times.

There are several ways of gaining access to essential knowledge.

---

tration reveals not only the complete coherence of all the events in a man's life, but also, no doubt, on a vaster scale, the complete concordance and harmony between everything in Creation. And he exclaims: 'Everything understood is good.' I know of no finer saying.

64

Our age has its own methods; older civilizations had theirs. And I am not speaking only of theoretical knowledge.

Finally I realized that, with modern techniques being apparently more efficient than those of yesterday, this essential knowledge that the alchemists (and other wise men before them) no doubt possessed, would reach us with still greater force and weight and would be more dangerous and more demanding. We are getting to the same point as the Ancients, but on a different level. Rather than condemn the modern spirit in the name of the initiatory wisdom of the Ancients, or repudiate this wisdom on the grounds that real knowledge only began with our civilization, we should do better to admire and even venerate the power of the mind which, under different aspects, traverses the same point of light, mounting upwards in a spiral ascent. Instead of condemning, repudiating and choosing, we ought to love. Love is everything: both rest and movement at the same time.

And now for the results of our researches on alchemy. It will only be a brief résumé, naturally, for even if we had the time and the ability (which perhaps we do not possess), it would take us ten or twenty years to make a really conclusive contribution to the subject. Nevertheless, what we have accomplished and the way in which we have done it, are enough to make our little study very different from the works on alchemy that have appeared hitherto.

The reader will find little new information on the history and philosophy of this traditional science; my object has been to throw some new light on some unsuspected links between the dreams of the old 'chemist-philosophers' and the realities of modern physics. Let us, then, sum up our conclusions as follows:

Alchemy, in our view, could be one of the most important relics of a science, a technology and a philosophy belonging to a civilization that has disappeared. What we have discovered in alchemy in the light of contemporary knowledge does not lead us to believe that techniques so subtle, so complicated and so precise can have been the result of a 'divine revelation' fallen from Heaven. Not that we reject altogether the notion of a revelation. But in what we have read about the saints and the great mystics we have never noticed that God spoke to men in technical language: 'Place thy crucible, O my Son, under polarized light! Rinse out the slag in water thrice distilled!'

Nor do we believe that the alchemists developed their techniques by blind gropings, or through the insignificant tinkerings of ignorant amateurs or the fantastic dreams of fanatics, to arrive at what we can only call the disintegration of the atom. Rather we are tempted to believe that alchemy contains the fragments of a science that has been lost, fragments that, in the absence of their context, we find it difficult to understand or to make use of. Progress from this point must necessarily be halting, but in a definite direction. There is also a profusion of technical, moral and religious interpretations. Finally, on those in whose hands these fragments are preserved there is an imperious obligation to maintain secrecy. We believe that our civilization on acquiring in different conditions and with a different approach, knowledge that is perhaps a legacy from a previous civilization, would perhaps have much to gain by a serious study of ancient lore with a view to hastening its own progress.

Finally, we believe that the alchemist, on concluding his operations with matter, feels, as the legend relates, a kind of transmutation taking place within himself. The things that happen in his crucible are also happening in his mind or in his soul. His condition changes.

All the traditional texts stress this phenomenon and evoke the moment when the 'Great Work' is accomplished and the alchemist becomes an 'awakened man'. It would seem that these old texts describe in this way the final stage of all real knowledge of the laws of matter and of energy, including technical knowledge. This is the knowledge towards which our civilization is now heading with all speed. It does not seem to us unreasonable to suppose that men will be called upon, in the near future, to 'change their condition', just as the alchemist, according to the legend, underwent a kind of transmutation. Unless, of course, our civilization should be entirely destroyed on the brink of its reaching its goal as other civilizations before it have perhaps disappeared. Even so, in our last second of lucidity, we should not despair, remembering that if the adventure of the mind repeats itself, it is always one step higher on the spiral. We would then entrust to other epochs the mission of conducting this adventure to its final stage, the centre of immobility, and go down to destruction with hope in our hearts.

II

A hundred thousand books that no one reads – Wanted: a scientific expedition to the land of the alchemists – The inventors – Madness from mercury – A code language – Was there another atomic civilization? – The electric batteries of the museum at Baghdad – Newton and the great Initiates – Helvetius and Spinoza and the philosopher's stone – Alchemy and modern physics – A hydrogen bomb in an oven – Transformation of matter, men and spirits

MORE than a hundred thousand books and manuscripts on alchemy are known to exist. This vast literature, to which the finest minds have contributed and which solemnly affirms its attachment to facts and practical experiments, has never been systematically explored. The current intellectual climate, Catholic in the past, rationalist today, has always maintained in regard to these texts an attitude of ignorance or scorn. A hundred thousand books and manuscripts perhaps contain some of the secrets of energy and matter. If this is not true, they proclaim it nevertheless. Kings and princes and republics have encouraged innumerable expedi-

66

tions to distant lands, and have financed scientific researches of every kind. Never, however, has a team of decoders, historians, linguists and scholars, physicists, chemists, mathematicians and biologists been assembled in an alchemist library with the task of discovering what these old treatises contain that is true and can be put to practical use. It seems inconceivable. The fact that such mental obtuseness is possible and that civilized human societies apparently, like ours, devoid of prejudices of any kind, can forget the presence in their attics of a hundred thousand books and manuscripts labelled 'Treasure' should be enough to convince the most sceptical among us that we are living in a fantastic world.

The scanty research that has been done on alchemy has been carried out either by mystics seeking in texts the confirmation of their spiritual attitudes, or else by historians completely out of touch with science and technology.

The alchemists speak of the necessity of distilling water to be used in the preparation of the elixir many thousands of times. We have heard an expert historian declare such an operation to be completely crazy. He knew nothing whatever about heavy water and the methods employed to convert ordinary water into heavy water. We have heard a learned scientist affirm that since endless repetitions of the process of refining and purifying metals and metalloids do not in any way alter their properties, the recommendations of the alchemists in this connection could only be considered as a kind of mystic lesson in patience, a ritual gesture, like telling the beads of a rosary. And yet it is by just such a refining process and the technique described by the alchemists known today as 'zone fusion', that the germanium and silicon used in transistors is prepared. We know now, thanks to the work done on these transistors, that by purifying a metal very thoroughly and then introducing minute quantities, some millionths of a gramme, of impurities carefully selected, the substance thus treated is endowed with new and revolutionary properties. It is unnecessary to go on citing examples indefinitely, but we wish to stress the desirability of undertaking a really methodical study of alchemist literature. This would be an immense task demanding many years of work and hundreds of research workers drawn from every branch of the sciences. Neither Bergier nor myself have been able even to draft the outline of such a study, but if our book ever inspired some Maecenas to sponsor this undertaking, we shall not have wasted our time completely.

In our brief survey of alchemist texts we observed that they are for the most part 'modern' compared to other occult works of the same date. Moreover, alchemy is the only para-religious activity that has made a real contribution to our knowledge of reality.

Albert le Grand (1193–1280) succeeded in producing *potassium lye*, and was the first to describe the chemical composition of cinnabar, white-lead and minium.

Raymond Lull (1235–1315) prepared bicarbonate of potassium.

Theophrastes Paracelsus (1493–1541) was the first to describe zinc hitherto unknown. He also introduced the use in medicine of chemical compounds.

Giambattista della Porta (1541–1615) produced tin monoxide.

Johann-Baptiste Van Helmont (1577–1644) recognized the existence of gases.

Basil Valentin (whose real identity is still unknown) discovered, in the seventeenth century, sulphuric acid and chloro-hydric acid.

Johann Rudolf Glauber (1604–68) discovered sodium sulphate.

Brandt (*d.* 1692) discovered phosphorus.

Johann Friedrich Boetticher (1682–1719) was the first European to make porcelain.

Blaise Vigenère (1523–96) discovered benzoic acid.

These are some of the alchemist achievements which enriched humanity at a time when chemistry was progressing.* While other sciences were developing, alchemy seems to follow, and sometimes precede this progress. Le Breton, in his *Clefs de la Philosophie Spagyrique* (1722) has some more than ordinarily intelligent things to say about magnetism, and frequently anticipates modern discoveries. Père Castel, in 1728 when ideas about gravitation were beginning to circulate, speaks about this and its relation to light in terms which, two centuries later, seem astonishingly similar to Einstein's ideas:

'I have said that if one took away the Earth's gravity one would take away light at the same time. For indeed, light and sound and all other qualities perceptible to our senses proceed from and are, as it were, a result of the mechanical structure, and consequently the gravity of natural bodies which are luminous or sonorous in proportion to their degree of gravity and buoyancy.'

In the alchemist literature of our own century we often find the latest discoveries in nuclear physics before they have appeared in university publications; and it is probable that the treatises of tomorrow will be dealing with the most advanced and abstract theories in physics and mathematics.

There is a clear distinction between alchemy and the pseudo-sciences, such as radiesthesia which introduces in its publications waves and rays after they have been discovered by 'official' science. There is thus every reason for believing that alchemy is capable of making an important contribution to future knowledge and techniques based on the structure of matter.

We have also noticed in the literature of the alchemists a great many texts that bear the stamp of madness. Attempts have been made to explain this dementia by psychoanalysis.† More often, since alchemy contains a metaphysical doctrine and presupposes a mystical attitude, historians, amateurs and above all the devotees of occultism endeavour to interpret these unbalanced writings as

* cf. *Le Miroir de la Magie*, by Kurt Seligmann, Fasquelle, Paris.
† cf. Jung: *Psychology and Alchemy*, or Herbert Silberer: *Problèmes du Mysticisme*.

being in the nature of supernatural revelations or inspired prophecy. After careful consideration, it seemed reasonable to classify these texts as the work of 'madmen', placing them apart from the other technical and philosophical ones. It also seemed to us that there might be a practical, simple and satisfactory explanation for the madness afflicting some of these practitioners and adepts. The alchemists often used mercury in their experiments; its fumes are toxic, and chronic poisoning induces delirium. Theoretically, the receptacles they employed were hermetically sealed, but not every adept may have known the secret of this method of sealing, and in this way more than one of these 'chemist-philosophers' may have succumbed to madness.

Finally we were impressed by the code-like appearance of alchemist writings. Blaise Vigenère, mentioned above, invented the most perfect codes and the most ingenious methods of cyphering, some of which are still in use today. Now it is probable that Vigenère learned this art while trying to interpret the alchemists' texts.

'To take a clearer example,' writes René Alleau,* 'consider the game of chess, whose rules and principles are relatively simple but permit of an infinite number of combinations. If we look on the whole body of acroamatic treatises on alchemy as so many games annotated in a conventional language, we shall have to confess in all honesty that we know neither the rules of the game nor the cypher employed. Alternatively, we assume that the code language is composed of signs that anyone can understand which is precisely the immediate illusion that a well composed cryptogram should create. We therefore conclude that it would be prudent not to allow ourselves to believe that their meaning is clear, but to study these texts as if they were in an unknown language. Apparently these *messages* are addressed only to other players, other alchemists who, we must assume, already possess, by some other means than written tradition, the necessary key to an exact comprehension of this language.'

Alchemist manuscripts have been found dating from the very earliest times. Nicolas de Valois in the fifteenth century deduced from this that transmutations and the secret techniques of the liberation of energy were known to men before the invention of writing. Architecture preceded writing, and was perhaps a form of writing. And, in fact, there is a very close connection between alchemy and architecture. One of the most significant alchemist texts, by Esprit Gobineau de Montluisant, is entitled: *Explications très curieuses des énigmes et figures hiéroglyphiques qui sont au grand portail de Notre-Dame de Paris*. (*Most curious explanations of the hieroglyphic enigmas and figures on the great West door of Notre-Dame in Paris*.)

The works of Fulcanelli include, notably, *Le Mystère des Cathédrales* and detailed descriptions of *Les Demeures Philosophales*. Certain medieval buildings are believed to be examples of the

* *Aspects de l'Alchimie Traditionnelle*. Ed. de Minuit, Paris.

age-old custom of transmitting through architecture the message of alchemy dating back to the remotest antiquity.

Newton believed in the existence of a chain of Initiates going back to very early times who knew the secrets of transmutations and the disintegration of matter. The English atomic scientist, Da Costa Andrade, in a speech delivered at the Newton Tercentenary Celebrations at Cambridge in July 1946, made it clear that he thought the discoverer of the laws of gravitation perhaps belonged to this chain and had only revealed to the world a small part of his knowledge:

'I cannot hope to convince the sceptical that Newton had some power of prophecy or special vision, had some inkling of atomic power; but I do say that certain passages do not read to me as if all he meant was that the manufacture of gold would upset world trade – "Because the way by which mercury may be so impregnated has been thought fit to be concealed by others that have known it, and therefore may possibly be an inlet to something more noble, not to be communicated without immense danger to the world, if there should be any verity in the Hermetic writings"; – and a little further on – "there being other things beside the transmutation of metals (if those great pretenders brag not) which none but they understand." In pondering what these passages may import, consider the no greater reticence with which he speaks of his optical discoveries. . . .'

To what past age did these great Masters invoked by Newton belong, and from what remote past did they themselves derive their science?

'If I have seen further,' said Newton, 'it is by standing on the shoulders of giants.'

Atterbury, who was a contemporary of Newton's, wrote as follows:

'Modesty teaches us to speak of the Ancients with respect, especially when we are not very familiar with their works. Newton, who knew them practically by heart, had the greatest respect for them, and considered them to be men of genius and superior intelligence who had carried their discoveries in every field much further than we today suspect, judging from what remains of their writings. More ancient writings have been lost than have been preserved, and perhaps our new discoveries are of less value than those that we have lost.'

Fulcanelli believed that alchemy was the connecting link with civilizations that disappeared thousands of years ago and of which the archaeologists know nothing. Of course no archaeologist or historian of high repute will admit that civilizations have existed in the past more advanced than ours in science and techniques. But advanced techniques and scientific knowledge simplify enormously the machinery, and traces of what they accomplished are perhaps staring us in the face without our being able to recognize them for what they are. No serious historian or archaeologist who has not had a very thorough scientific education could carry out the researches and explorations that would be likely to throw any light on these matters. The strict segregation of the various disciplines, necessitated by the fabulous advances in modern science, has perhaps concealed from us other fabulous discoveries of an earlier age.

We know that it was a German engineer, engaged to build sewers for the city of Baghdad, who discovered amongst some bric-à-brac in the local museum, labelled vaguely 'ritual objects', electric batteries – manufactured ten centuries before Volta under the Sassanid Dynasty. So long as archaeology is only practised by archaeologists, we shall never know if the 'mists of antiquity' were luminous or obscure.

'Johann-Friedrich Schweitzer, alias Helvetius, a violent anti-alchemist, relates that on the morning of 27th December, 1666, he was visited by a stranger.* He was a man of honest and serious appearance, dressed in a simple cloak, like a Memnonite. After asking Helvetius whether he believed in the philosopher's stone (to which the famous doctor replied in the negative) the stranger opened a little ivory box "containing three pieces of a substance resembling glass or opal". He then declared that this was the famous stone, and that this very small amount was sufficient to produce twenty tons of gold. Helvetius held a fragment in his hand and, having thanked his visitor for his kindness, begged him to let him have a small piece. The alchemist bluntly refused, adding rather more courteously, that even in exchange for Helvetius's entire fortune he could not part with even the smallest piece of this mineral for a reason he was not permitted to disclose. When asked to prove his statement by performing a transmutation, the stranger replied that he would come back in three weeks' time and would show Helvetius something that would astonish him. He returned punctually on the day specified, but refused to operate, declaring that he was forbidden to reveal his secret. He did, however, condescend to present Helvetius with a small fragment of the stone "no larger than a mustard seed". And when the doctor expressed doubts as to whether so minute a quantity could produce any effect whatever, the alchemist broke the morsel in two, threw away half, and offered him the other half saying: "This is all you need."

'At this the learned doctor was obliged to confess that when the stranger first visited him he had succeeded in appropriating a few particles of the stone and that they had changed some lead, not into gold, but into glass. "You ought to have covered your fragment with some yellow wax," replied the alchemist, "that would have helped it to penetrate the lead and transform it into gold." The man promised to return the next morning at nine o'clock to perform the miracle – but he never came, either that day or the next. Thereupon the wife of Helvetius persuaded him to try the experiment himself:

'Helvetius followed the stranger's instructions. He melted down three drachmas of lead, wrapped the stone in wax and threw it into

* cf. *Le Miroir de la Magie*, by Kurt Seligmann, op. cit.

71

the liquid metal. It turned to gold! "We took it immediately to a goldsmith who declared that he had never seen a finer piece of gold, and offered us fifty florins for an ounce." Helvetius, concluding his report, informed us that he still possessed the ingot of gold, a tangible proof of the transmutation. "May the Holy Angels of God watch over him (the alchemist) as a source of blessings for Christianity. Such is our constant prayer, for him and for us."

'The news travelled like lightning. Spinoza, who can hardly be considered as simple-minded, wished to verify the story in every detail. He went to see the goldsmith who had examined the gold, and the account he gave was more than favourable: during the fusion some silver present in the mixture was also transformed into gold. The goldsmith, named Brechtel, was employed by the Duc d'Orange as his minter, and certainly knew his trade. It seems difficult to believe that he had been the victim of a hoax, or that he had wished to deceive Spinoza. The latter then went to Helvetius who showed him the gold, and the crucible used in the experiment. Some scraps of the precious metal were still adhering to the inside of the receptacle; like the others, Spinoza was convinced that the transmutation really had taken place.'

Transmutation, for the alchemist, is a secondary phenomenon, performed merely as a demonstration. It is difficult to form an opinion as to the reality of these transmutations, although various reports, such as those of Helvetius or van Helmont, for example, are very impressive. It could be argued that the conjurer's art knows no limitations, but is it likely that 4,000 years of research and 100,000 volumes and manuscripts would have been devoted to an imposture? We have another suggestion to make, as will be seen presently. We make it in all diffidence, because the weight of established scientific opinion is formidable. We shall try to describe the work of the alchemist culminating in the fabrication of the 'stone', or 'projection powder', and we shall see that the interpretation of certain operations conflicts with our present knowledge of the structure of matter. But there is nothing to show that our knowledge of nuclear phenomena is complete or definitive. Catalysis, for example, may play an altogether unexpected part in these phenomena.*

It is not impossible that certain natural mixtures produce, under the influence of cosmic rays, nucleo-catalytic reactions on a large scale resulting in a massive transmutation of elements. This may well provide a key to the mystery of alchemy and explain why the alchemist repeats his experiments indefinitely, until the right cosmic conditions are obtained.

To this it will be objected: if transmutations of this kind are possible, what becomes of the energy liberated? If all this were true, the alchemists must often have destroyed the towns they

* Scientists in several countries are now working on the use of particles (produced by powerful accelerators) as catalysing agents in the fusion of hydrogen.

lived in and vast areas of their homeland as well, thus causing appalling catastrophes.

To which the alchemists reply: it is precisely because such catastrophes have occurred in the distant past that we are afraid of the terrible energy contained in matter and therefore keep our science secret. Moreover, the Great Work is only attained through progressive phases, and whoever after scores of years of experimenting and living an austere life learns how to unleash the forces of nuclear energy, learns also what precautions to take to prevent a catastrophe.

Is this argument valid? Perhaps. Physicists today admit that, in certain conditions, the energy of a nuclear transmutation might be absorbed by special particles they call neutrinos, or anti-neutrinos. It would appear that some proofs of the existence of the neutrino have been forthcoming. There are, perhaps, certain types of transmutation which liberate only a small amount of energy, or in which energy is liberated in the form of neutrinos. We shall return to this question later.

M. Eugène Canseliet, a disciple of Fulcanelli and one of the leading specialists on alchemy, was greatly struck by a passage in a study which Jacques Bergier had written as a preface to one of the classics in the *Bibliothèque Mondiale*, an anthology of sixteenth century poetry. In this preface Bergier alluded to the alchemists and their cult of secrecy. This is what he wrote: 'On this particular point it is difficult not to agree with them. If there is a recipe for producing hydrogen bombs on a kitchen stove, it is clearly preferable that this recipe should not be disclosed.'

M. Eugène Canseliet's comment on this was as follows: 'Above all, it is most important that this remark should not be dismissed as a mere pleasantry. You are quite right, and I am in a position to state that it is possible to produce an atomic fission by means of an ore, which is relatively common and cheap, and that this can be done with no other apparatus than a good stove, a coal-fusing oven, some Meker burners and four bottles of butane gas.'

It is, in fact, conceivable that even in nuclear physics important results can be obtained by simple means. This is the direction in which all science and technology are moving today.

'We can do more than we know,' said Roger Bacon. He added, however, a remark that might well be an alchemist's saying: 'Though everything is not permitted, everything is possible.'

For the alchemist, it must never be forgotten that power óver matter and energy is only a secondary reality. The real aim of the alchemist's activities, which are perhaps the remains of a very old science belonging to a civilization long extinct, is the transformation of the alchemist himself, his accession to a higher state of consciousness. The material results are only a pledge of the final result, which is spiritual. Everything is oriented towards the transmutation of man himself, towards his deification, his fusion with the divine energy, the fixed centre from which all material energies emanate. The alchemist's is that science 'with a conscience' of which Rabelais speaks. It is a science which tends to exalt man rather than matter; as Teilhard de Chardin puts it: 'The real aim of physics should be to integrate Man as a totality in a coherent representation of the world.'

'Know, O all ye investigators of this Art,' wrote a master alchemist,* 'that the Spirit is all, and that unless within this Spirit another like Spirit is enclosed, no good will come of anything.'

III

In which a little Jew is seen to prefer honey to sugar – In which an alchemist who might be the mysterious Fulcanelli speaks of the atomic danger in 1937, describes the atomic pile and evokes civilizations now extinct – In which Bergier breaks a safe with a blow-lamp and carries off a bottle of uranium under his arm – In which a nameless American major seeks a Fulcanelli now definitely vanished – In which Oppenheimer echoes a Chinese sage of a thousand years ago

IT was in 1933. The little Jewish student had a pointed nose and wore round spectacles through which shone a pair of cold and lively eyes. His round skull was covered with a thin down of hair. A frightful accent, which was not improved by a stutter, made his speech sound comically like the confused splashing of ducks in a pond. When one got to know him better one had the impression that a hungry, alert, sensitive and incredibly quick intelligence was dancing inside this uncouth little man, full of mischief and as lacking as a child in any kind of *savoir vivre*, like a big, red balloon at the end of a string.

'So you want to become an alchemist?' said the venerable old Professor to the student, Jacques Bergier, who sat, hanging his head, on the edge of his chair, with a brief-case stuffed with papers on his knee. The old Professor was one of France's most distinguished chemists. 'I don't understand you, sir,' said the student, feeling nettled. He had a prodigious memory, and remembered having seen, at the age of six, a German print depicting two alchemists at work amidst a confusion of test-tubes, pliers, crucibles and bellows. One of them, in rags, was tending the fire, open-mouthed, while the other, with his beard and hair awry, was scratching his head and staggering about in a corner of the workshop.

The Professor consulted his files: 'During the last two years of your studies I see that you took a special interest in M. Jean Thibaud's free course of lectures on nuclear physics. This course does not lead to any diploma or certificate, yet you persist in your desire to continue with these studies. Had you been a physicist I could have understood your curiosity. But your subject is chemistry. Are you expecting, by any chance, to learn how to manufacture gold?'

* *La Tourbe des Philosophes*, in *Bibliothèque des Philosophes Chimiques*, 1741.

74

'Sir,' replied the little student raising his hands, 'I believe in the future of nuclear chemistry. I believe that transmutations will be used in industry in the near future.'

'That seems quite crazy to me.'

'But, sir . . .'

Sometimes he stopped at the beginning of a sentence and then went on repeating his opening words like a gramophone that has got stuck, not because he had nothing to say, but because his thoughts were turning to the forbidden realms of poetry. He knew by heart many thousands of lines, and all the poems of Kipling.

'But, sir, even if you do not believe in transmutations, you must surely believe in nuclear energy. The immense potential resources of the nucleus . . .'

'Tut, tut,' said the Professor. 'That's childish and elementary. What the physicists call nuclear energy is an integration constant in their equations. It's a philosophical idea, nothing more. Consciousness is man's chief motive power. But it's not consciousness that drives a locomotive. So all this talk about machines being powered by nuclear energy. . . . No, no, my boy . . .'

The young man swallowed hard.

'Come back to earth and think of your future. What you are obsessed by at the moment, because to me you seem scarcely more than a child, is one of man's oldest dreams – the alchemist's dream. Read Berthelot again. He has given a very good account of this myth of the transmutation of matter. Your studies here have not been particularly brilliant. Let me give you some advice: get yourself a job in industry as soon as possible. What about sugar? Three months in a sugar factory will bring you back to realities, and that's what you need. I'm speaking to you now as a father.'

The unworthy son stammered his thanks and departed, nose in air and hugging his bulging brief-case. He was an obstinate type; he felt he ought to profit from this conversation, but that honey was better than sugar. He would go on studying nuclear problems – and read everything he could about alchemy.

And this is how my friend Jacques Bergier decided to continue with studies that had been dismissed as useless, and with others described as mad. The vicissitudes of life, the war and concentration camps kept him away for a time from nuclear studies, yet he was able to make some contributions that were highly thought of by the specialists. In the course of his researches the dreams of the alchemists and the realities of mathematical physics coincided more than once. But great changes have taken place in the world of science since 1933, and my friend had less and less the impression that he was ploughing a lonely furrow.

From 1934 to 1940 Jacques Bergier worked with André Helbronner, one of the most remarkable men of our time. Helbronner, who was assassinated by the Nazis at Buchenwald in March 1944, had been the first Professor at the Faculty to teach physical-chemistry.

This science, midway between two disciplines, has since given rise to many other sciences: electronic, nuclear and 'stereotronic'.*

Helbronner had been awarded the gold medal of the Franklin Institute for his discoveries on colloidal metals. He was also interested in the liquefaction of gases, aeronautics and ultra-violet rays. In 1934 he devoted himself to the study of nuclear physics and created, with a group of industrialists, a nuclear research laboratory where, up to 1940, some very interesting results were obtained. Helbronner was, in addition, often called upon to advise the judiciary as an expert in all matters pertaining to the transmutation of elements; and it was in this way that Jacques Bergier had an opportunity of meeting a certain number of pseudo-alchemists, impostors or visionaries, and one genuine alchemist of real distinction.

My friend never knew this alchemist's real name and, even if he had, would have been careful not to disclose his identity. The man of whom we are speaking disappeared some time ago without leaving any visible traces, to lead a clandestine existence, having severed all connection between himself and the century in which he lived. Bergier can only guess that he may have been the man who, under the pseudonym of Fulcanelli, wrote, about the year 1920, two strange and admirable books: *Les Demeures Philosophales* and *Le Mystère des Cathédrales*, already referred to. These books were published through the good offices of M. Eugène Canseliet, who never revealed the author's name.† They are certainly among the most important works in the literature of alchemy. They are an expression of the most profound knowledge and wisdom, and several great men of our acquaintance profess the greatest veneration for the legendary name of Fulcanelli.

'Could he,' writes M. Canseliet, 'having attained to the summit of all knowledge, refuse to obey the command of Destiny? No man is a prophet in his own country. This old saying perhaps provides an occult explanation of the upheaval in the solitary and studious life of the philosopher caused by the spark of revelation. Under the action of this divine flame the man as he used to be is entirely consumed. Name, family, country, all illusions, all mistakes, all trivialities crumble into dust. And from these ashes, like the Phoenix of the poets, a new personality is born. This, at least, is what philosophical tradition would have us believe. My master knew it. He disappeared when the fateful hour struck and the sign was accomplished. Who would dare to defy the law? If the same thing that compelled my master to shun all worldly acclaim should happen to me today, despite the anguish of a painful but inevitable separation I should act in exactly the same way.'

* This is an entirely new science concerned with the transformation of energy in solids. One of its applied forms is the transistor.

† These two books have been re-issued by *Omnium Litteraire*, 72 Avenue des Champs-Élysées, Paris. The first edition is dated 1925 and had long been out of print, the rare copies still in circulation being snapped up by collectors at a very high price.

M. Eugène Canseliet wrote those lines in 1925. The man who had entrusted him with the publication of his works was about to change his habits and way of life. One afternoon, in June 1937, Jacques Bergier thought there was good reason to believe that he was in the presence of Fulcanelli.

It was at the request of André Helbronner that my friend met this mysterious personage in the prosaic surroundings of a test laboratory at the offices of the Gas Board in Paris. The following is an exact account of the conversation that then took place:

'M. André Helbronner, whose assistant I believe you are, is carrying out research on nuclear energy. M. Helbronner has been good enough to keep me informed as to the results of some of his experiments, notably the appearance of radio-activity corresponding to plutonium when a bismuth rod is volatilized by an electric discharge in deuterium at high pressure. You are on the brink of success, as indeed are several other of our scientists today. May I be allowed to warn you to be careful? The research in which you and your colleagues are engaged is fraught with terrible dangers, not only for yourselves, but for the whole human race. The liberation of atomic energy is easier than you think, and the radio-activity artificially produced can poison the atmosphere of our planet in the space of a few years. Moreover, atomic explosives can be produced from a few grammes of metal powerful enough to destroy whole cities. I am telling you this as a fact: the alchemists have known it for a very long time.'

Bergier tried to interrupt with a protest. Alchemists and modern physics! He was about to make some sarcastic remarks, when his host interrupted him:

'I know what you are going to say, but it's of no interest. The alchemists were ignorant of the structure of the nucleus, knew nothing about electricity and had no means of detection. Therefore they have never been able to perform any transmutation, still less liberate nuclear energy. I shall not attempt to prove to you what I am now going to say, but I ask you to repeat it to M. Helbronner: certain geometrical arrangements of highly purified materials are enough to release atomic forces without having recourse to either electricity or vacuum techniques. I will merely read to you now a short extract....'

He then picked up Frederick Soddy's *The Interpretation of Radium* and read as follows: 'I believe that there have been civilizations in the past that were familiar with atomic energy, and that by misusing it they were totally destroyed.'

He then continued: 'I would ask you to believe that certain techniques have partially survived. I would also ask you to remember that the alchemists' researches were coloured by moral and religious preoccupations, whereas modern physics was created in the eighteenth century for their amusement by a few aristocrats and wealthy libertines. Science without a conscience. . . . I have thought it my duty to warn a few research workers here and there, but have no hope of seeing this warning prove effective. For that matter, there is no reason why I should have any hope.'

77

Bergier has never been able to forget the sound of that precise incisive voice, speaking with such authority.

He ventured to put another question: 'If you are an alchemist yourself, sir, I cannot believe you spend your time fabricating gold like Dunikovski or Dr. Miethe. For the last year I have been trying to get information about alchemy, and find myself surrounded by imposters or hearing what seem to be fantastic interpretations. Now can you, sir, tell me what is the nature of your researches?'

'You ask me to summarize for you in four minutes four thousand years of philosophy and the efforts of a lifetime. Furthermore, you ask me to translate into ordinary language concepts for which such a language is not intended. All the same, I can tell you this much: you are aware that in the official science of today the role of the observer becomes more and more important. Relativity, the principle of indeterminacy, show the extent to which the observer today intervenes in all these phenomena. The secret of alchemy is this: there is a way of manipulating matter and energy so as to produce what modern scientists call "a field of force". This field acts on the observer and puts him in a privileged position *vis-à-vis* the Universe. From this position he has access to the realities which are ordinarily hidden from us by time and space, matter and energy. This is what we call "The Great Work".'

'But what about the philosopher's stone? The fabrication of gold?'

'These are only applications, particular cases. The essential thing is not the transmutation of metals, but that of the experimenter himself. It's an ancient secret that a few men re-discover once in a century.'

'And what becomes of them then?'

'I shall know, perhaps, one day.'

My friend was never to see this man again – the man who under the name of Fulcanelli has left an indelible trace. All that we know of him is that he survived the war and disappeared completely after the Liberation. Every attempt to find him failed.*

Now the scene changes to a July morning in 1945. Still pale and famished-looking, Jacques Bergier, clad in khaki, is engaged in breaking into a safe with a blow-lamp. Yet another transformation. For the last few years he has been in succession a secret agent, a terrorist and a political deportee. The safe in question stood in a beautiful villa on Lake Constance, the property of the director of a great German business concern. When opened, the safe yielded up its mystery: a bottle containing an extremely heavy powder. The label was inscribed: 'Uranium, for atomic applications.'

* 'The opinion of those who are best qualified to judge is that the man who concealed himself, or is still today hiding behind the famous pseudonym of Fulcanelli, is the most celebrated and without doubt the only genuine (and perhaps the last) alchemist of this century in which the atom is king.' Claude d'Ygé, in the review *Initiation et Science*, No. 44, Paris.

It was the first formal proof of the existence in Germany of a project for an atomic bomb sufficiently advanced to require large quantities of pure uranium. Goebbels was not far wrong when, from his bunker under bombardment, he spread through the streets of a devastated Berlin the rumour that the secret weapon was about to explode in the face of the invaders.

Bergier reported his discovery to the Allied authorities. The Americans were sceptical and gave out that any inquiry into nuclear energy would be pointless. It was a feint: in reality their first bomb had already been exploded secretly at Alamogordo, and an American mission, headed by the physicist Goudsmith, was at that moment in Germany looking for the atomic pile that Professor Heisenberg had constructed before the collapse of the Reich.

In France, nothing was known officially, but there were signs, of which the most significant, in the eyes of those able to read between the lines, was the fact that the Americans were paying fabulous prices for any manuscripts or documents dealing with alchemy.

Bergier reported to the provisional government that research on nuclear explosives was probably being carried on in Germany as well as in the United States. The report was no doubt consigned to the waste-paper basket, but my friend still kept his bottle which he used to show to all and sundry, saying: 'You see that? You need only put a neutron inside to blow up the whole of Paris!' This little man with the comic accent was certainly a joker, and people were amazed that anyone who had just come back from Mauthausen had managed to keep a sense of humour. But the joke did not seem quite so funny after Hiroshima. The telephone in Bergier's room began to ring incessantly, and all sorts of official bodies asked for copies of the report. The American intelligence services begged the owner of the famous bottle to contact urgently a certain Major who refused to give his name. Other authorities insisted that the bottle should be removed to some place outside the Paris area. In vain Bergier explained that the flask certainly did not contain pure uranium 235, and that, even if it did, the uranium was certainly not 'critical'. Otherwise, it would have exploded long ago. However, his toy was taken from him, and he never heard it referred to again. To console him, he was presented with a report from the 'Direction Generale des Études et Recherches', containing all that this organization, a branch of the French Secret Service, knew about nuclear energy. The report was labelled: 'Secret', 'Confidential', and 'Not to be circulated', but all it contained was some clippings from the magazine *Science et Vie*.

To satisfy his curiosity it only remained for him to meet the famous anonymous Major, some of whose adventures had been related by Professor Goudsmith in his book *Alsos*. This mysterious officer endowed with a macabre sense of humour, had camouflaged his unit under the guise of an organization for locating the graves of fallen American soldiers. He was in a state of agitation, and appeared to be harassed by Washington. He wanted first to know everything that Bergier had been able to learn or guess about

German nuclear projects. But, above all, it was essential for the safety of the world, the Allied cause and the promotion of the Major to discover immediately the whereabouts of Eric Edward Dutt and the alchemist known as Fulcanelli.

Dutt, whose antecedents had been looked into by Helbronner, was an Indian who claimed to have had access to some very ancient manuscripts. He declared that he had learned from them certain methods for the transmutation of metals, and that he had, by means of a condenser discharge across a conductor of boride of tungsten, obtained traces of gold in the resulting deposit. Similar results were later to be obtained by the Russians, but this time by using powerful particle accelerators.

Bergier was not able to be of much service to the free world, or to the Allied cause, or to the Major. Eric Edward Dutt, a collaborator, had been shot by the French counter-espionage services in North Africa. As for Fulcanelli, he had definitely disappeared.

Nevertheless, the Major, as a token of his gratitude, showed Bergier the proofs of Professor H. D. Smyth's report *On the Military Uses of Atomic Energy* before publication. This was the first serious document to deal with this question and tended surprisingly to confirm certain affirmations made by the alchemist in 1937.

The atomic pile, an essential instrument for the manufacture of the bomb, was actually 'a geometrical arrangement of highly purified substances'. As Fulcanelli had stated, this instrument used neither electricity nor a vacuum technique. Smyth's report also alluded to radiant poisons and radio-active gases and dust, all highly toxic, which it was relatively easy to prepare in large quantities. The alchemist had spoken of the possibility of poisoning the entire planet.

How had it been possible for an obscure mystic, a solitary investigator to foresee or have knowledge of all these things?

On looking through the proofs of the report my friend remembered this passage in Albert le Grand's *De Alchima:* 'Should you have the misfortune of working for kings and princes, they will never cease asking you: "How is the Great Work progressing? When at last are we going to see something worth while?" And, in their impatience they will call you good-for-nothing and rascal, and make all sorts of trouble for you. And if you are unsuccessful, you will feel the full force of their displeasure. If, on the other hand, you succeed, they will keep you prisoner in perpetual captivity with the intention of making you work for their advantage.'

Was this why Fulcanelli had disappeared and why alchemists throughout the ages had always maintained secrecy about their work?

The advice given first and last in the Harris papyrus was: 'Keep your lips sealed!'

Years after Hiroshima, on 17th January, 1955, Oppenheimer made this statement: 'In a very profound sense and in a way that cannot be lightly dismissed, we scientists have sinned.'

And a thousand years earlier a Chinese alchemist wrote: 'It would be a terrible sin to reveal to the soldiers the secrets of your art. Beware! Do not allow even an insect to be in the room where you are working.'

IV

The modern alchemist and the spirit of research – Description of what an alchemist does in his laboratory – Experiments repeated indefinitely – What is he waiting for? – The preparation of darkness – Electronic gas – Water that dissolves – Is the philosopher's stone energy in suspension? – The transmutation of the alchemist himself – This is where true metaphysics begin

THE modern alchemist is a man who reads treatises on nuclear physics. He is convinced that transmutations and still more extraordinary phenomena can be obtained by manipulations and with the aid of comparatively simple apparatus. It is among contemporary alchemists that the spirit of the isolated seeker is to be found, and the preservation of such a spirit is very important at the present time. For it is generally believed today that no progress in science is possible without large-scale team work, vast apparatus, and considerable financial backing. And yet the fundamental discoveries, such as radio-activity and wave mechanics were made by men working in isolation. America, where everything is done on a big scale, with large teams of workers, is now sending its agents all over the world in search of original minds. The Director of American scientific research, Dr. James Killian, declared in 1958 that it was undesirable to trust entirely in collective research, and that an appeal should be made to solitary workers with original ideas of their own. Rutherford did some of his fundamental work on the structure of matter with old tins and bits of string. Jean Perrin and Mme Curie before the war sent their assistants to the Flea Market on Sundays to look for material. Of course big, well-equipped laboratories are necessary, but it would be advisable to ensure some co-operation between these laboratories and these teams and these solitary workers. The alchemists, however, would refuse the invitation. Their rule is secrecy; their ambition of a spiritual nature. 'There can be no doubt,' wrote René Alleau, 'that the manipulations of the alchemists help to maintain an inner asceticism.' If alchemy contains some science, this science is only a means of gaining access to knowledge. It is consequently most important that it should not be generally known, otherwise it would become an end in itself.

What is the alchemist's working material? The same as that used for high temperature mineral chemistry: furnaces, crucibles, scales, measuring instruments with, in addition, modern apparatus for detecting nuclear radiation – Geiger counters, scintillometers, etc.

Such a stock-in-trade may seem hopelessly inadequate. An orthodox physicist would never admit that it is possible to produce a cathode emitting neutrons with such simple and inexpensive apparatus. If our information is correct, alchemists do in fact succeed in doing this. In the days when the electron was considered to be the fourth state of matter, extremely elaborate and costly machinery was invented to produce electronic currents. Later on, in 1910, Elster and Gaitel showed that it was enough to heat lime in vacuo to a dull red heat.

We do not know all the laws of matter. If alchemy is a more advanced form of knowledge than our own science, it employs simpler methods.

We know several alchemists in France, and two in the United States. There are some in England, in Germany and in Italy. E. J. Holmyard says he met one in Morocco. Three have written to us from Prague. The scientific press in the U.S.S.R. appears to be taking a great interest in alchemy, and is undertaking historical researches.

We are now going to give, for what we believe to be the first time, an accurate description of what an alchemist actually does in his laboratory. We do not claim to reveal every detail of the methods employed, but we believe we can throw some light upon these methods which will not be without interest. Nor do we forget that alchemy's ultimate aim is the transmutation of the alchemist himself, and that his operations are only steps in his slow progress towards 'spiritual liberation'. We are now going to try to give some fresh information about these operations.

The alchemist in the first place spends many years deciphering old texts which to the reader, deprived of any guiding Ariadne's thread, are like a labyrinth where everything has been done deliberately and systematically to throw the uninitiated into a state of inextricable mental confusion. With the help of patience, humility and faith he gradually begins to understand these texts. Having got so far, he is ready to begin actual alchemic operations. These we are going to describe, but there is one thing of which we have no knowledge. We know what happens in an alchemist's laboratory, but we do not know what happens in the alchemist himself, in his mind and heart. It may be that everything is connected. It may be that spiritual energy plays a part in the physical and chemical operations of the alchemist. It may be that a certain method of acquiring, concentrating and directing this spiritual energy is essential to the success of the alchemists' work. This is not certain, but in this rare context it is impossible not to recall Dante's saying: 'I see that you believe these things because I tell you them; but you do not know the reason for them, and therefore, in spite of being believed, their meaning is still hidden.'

Our alchemist begins by preparing in a mortar made of agate a mixture of three ingredients. The first, in a proportion of 95 per cent, is some sort of ore: arseno-pyrites, for example, an iron ore

82

containing among its impurities arsenic and antimony. The second is a metal: iron, lead, silver or mercury. The third is an acid of organic origin, such as tartaric or citric acid. He will continue to grind and mix by hand these ingredients for five or six months. He will then proceed to heat the mixture in a crucible, increasing the temperature by degrees and continuing this operation for ten days or so. He must take precautions, for toxic gases are released: mercury vapour and especially arseno-hydrogen which has killed many an alchemist at the beginning of his experiment.

Finally, he dissolves the contents of the crucible by means of an acid, and it was in their search for a solvent that the old alchemists discovered acetic acid, nitric acid and sulphuric acid.

The dissolution has to be performed under a polarized light, i.e. either weak sunlight reflected in a mirror, or the light of the moon. It is known today that polarized light vibrates in one direction only, whereas ordinary light vibrates in every direction around an axis.

Next the liquid is evaporated and the solid residue re-calcined. The alchemist will repeat this operation thousands of times. Why? We do not know. Perhaps he is waiting for the moment when all the most favourable conditions will be fulfilled: cosmic rays, terrestrial magnetism, etc. Perhaps it is in order to obtain a condition of 'fatigue' in the structure of matter of which we still know nothing. The alchemist speaks of a 'sacred patience' and of the slow condensation of the 'universal spirit'. But behind this para-religious language there is surely something hidden.

This method of working by repeating indefinitely the same operation may seem mad to a modern chemist who has been taught that there is only one satisfactory experimental method – that of Claude Berthelot. This method is based on concomitant variations. The same experiment is carried out thousands of times, but with one different factor every time: the proportions of one of the ingredients, temperature, pressure, a different catalyser, etc. The results obtained are noted, and some of the laws governing the phenomenon deduced therefrom. This is a method that has proved sound, but it is not the only one. The alchemist repeats his operation without any variation until something extraordinary happens. He believes fundamentally in a natural law, somewhat similar to the 'principle of exclusion' formulated by the physicist Pauli, a friend of Jung.

Pauli held that in a given system (the atom and its molecules) there cannot be two particles (electrons, protons, mesons) in the same state. Everything in nature is unique. That is why one goes, without any intermediary, from hydrogen to helium, from helium to lithium and so on as the nuclear physicist is advised in the periodic table of elements. When a particle is added to a system, that particle cannot partake of any of the states existing within the system. It assumes another state, and its combination with the existing particles creates a new and unique system.

For the alchemist, just as there can be no two souls, or no two creatures, or no two plants exactly alike (Pauli would add: no two

83

electrons), so there can be no two experiments exactly the same. If an experiment is repeated thousands of times, something extraordinary will happen in the end. We are not competent to say whether the alchemists are right or wrong. We will merely point out that one modern science – the science of cosmic rays – has adopted a very similar method. This science studies the phenomena caused by the arrival, in a machine designed for their detection, or on a plaque, of particles of enormous energy coming from the stars. These phenomena cannot be obtained at will; they must be waited for. Sometimes an extraordinary phenomenon is recorded. Thus, for example, during the summer of 1957 in the course of some experiments being carried out in the U.S.A. by Professor Bruno Rossi, a particle charged with an immense amount of energy, greater than had ever been recorded, and coming perhaps from some galaxy other than the Milky Way, was recorded on 1,500 Geiger counters simultaneously in a radius of eight square kilometres, creating in its track an enormous shower of atomic debris. It is impossible to imagine a machine capable of producing so much energy. Such a thing had never happened before in living memory, and no one knows if it will ever happen again. It is an exceptional event of this kind, whether cosmic or terrestrial, that our alchemist is apparently waiting for, to see reflected in his crucible. He might perhaps shorten the period of waiting by using more active means than fire – for example, by heating his crucible in an induction furnace by levitation.* Or, again, by adding radioactive isotypes to the mixture. In this way, he could perform his operation over and over again, not several times a week, but several hundreds of thousands of times in a second, thus multiplying his chances of capturing the 'event' necessary for the success of his experiment. But the modern alchemist, like his predecessors, works in secrecy and poverty, and looks upon waiting as a virtue.

To continue our description: after working at the same thing, night and day, for several years, our alchemist finally decides that the first phase is completed. He then adds to his mixture an oxidizing agent, for example, potassium nitrate. His crucible already contains sulphur obtained from pyrites and carbon from the organic acid. Sulphur, carbon and nitrate: it was in performing this operation that the old alchemists discovered gunpowder.

Over and over again he continues this operation of dissolving and then re-heating for months and years without respite, always waiting for a sign. As to the nature of this sign, the books on alchemy differ, but this is perhaps because there are several phenomena that might occur. The sign appears at the moment of melting. For some alchemists it will appear in the form of crystals shaped like stars on the surface of the solution, while in other cases a layer of oxide forms on the surface and then breaks up, revealing the luminous metal in which can be seen a reflection, in miniature, of the Milky Way, perhaps, or some of the constellations. (In

* This method consists of suspending the mixture in a void, so as to have no contact with the furnace wall, by means of a magnetic field.

84

this case melting would be done by a high-frequency current.*)

On receiving this sign, the alchemist removes his mixture from the crucible and allows it to 'ripen', protected from the air and from damp, until the first days of Spring. When he resumes his operations, these will be directed towards what is called in the old texts, 'the preparation of darkness'. Recent research on the history of chemistry has shown that the German monk, Berthold Schwarz (who is generally credited in the West with the invention of gunpowder) never existed. He is a symbolic figure for this 'preparation of darkness'.

The mixture is now placed in a transparent receptacle, made of rock crystal and closed in a special way. Little is known about this method of sealing, generally known as the Hermes method, hence – 'hermetic'. The procedure will now consist of heating the receptacle, regulating the temperatures with the utmost precision. Inside the closed receptacle there is still the same mixture of sulphur, carbon and nitrates, which now has to be brought to a certain degree of incandescence but prevented from exploding. There are many instances of alchemists being seriously burned or killed, for the explosions that occur under these conditions are particularly violent and engender temperatures which logically would seem quite improbable.

The object in view is to procure in the receptacle an 'essence', a 'fluid' which alchemists sometimes call 'raven's wing'.

This calls for some explanation. This operation has no equivalent in modern physics and chemistry, and yet it is not without analogies. When a metal such as copper is dissolved in liquid ammoniac gas it turns a dark blue colour, verging on black in massive concentrations. The same phenomenon occurs if hydrogen under pressure, or organic amines, are dissolved in liquefied ammoniac gas to produce the unstable compound NH which has all the properties of an alcaline metal and is consequently known as 'ammonium'.

There is reason to believe that this blue-black coloration, resembling the fluid the alchemists call 'raven's wing', is the exact colour of electronic gas. What is electronic gas? It is the term applied by modern scientists to the whole body of free electrons which constitute a metal and endow it with all its mechanical, electric and thermal properties. It corresponds in present-day terminology, to what the alchemist calls the 'soul' or the 'essence' of metals. It is this soul or essence which is released in the hermetically sealed receptacle the alchemist has been so patiently tending over his furnace.

He heats it, allows it to cool off, heats it again and continues the process for months or even years, observing through the rock crystal the formation of what is also sometimes called 'the alchemist's egg', i.e. the mixture converted into a blue-black fluid. Finally he opens his receptacle in the dark, lighted only by this kind of fluorescent liquid. On contact with the air, this liquid solidifies and breaks up. In this way he would obtain entirely new

* The American Magazine *Life*, January, 1958, published some excellent photographs of an operation of this kind. Jacques Bergier says he has witnessed this experiment.

substances, unknown in nature and possessing all the properties of pure chemical elements, properties, thať is to say, which cannot be separated by chemical means.

Some modern alchemists claim to have obtained in this way new chemical elements in considerable quantities. Fulcanelli is said to have extracted from a kilogram of iron twenty grammes of an entirely new substance whose chemical and physical properties do not correspond to any known chemical element. The same operation could be applied to all elements, most of which would yield two new elements for each one treated.

Such a statement is likely to shock an orthodox laboratory worker. For modern theory admits only the two following separations of a chemical element: the molecule of an element can assume several states, e.g. ortho-hydrogen and para-hydrogen; or the nucleus of an element can assume a certain number of isotopic states in which the number of neutrons varies. Thus, in lithium 6, the nucleus contains three neutrons, and, in lithium 7, the nucleus contains four.

The techniques for separating the various allotropic states of the molecule and the various isotopic states of the nucleus, necessitate the use of vast and elaborate machinery. By contrast, the alchemist's methods are altogether insignificant: yet he, it seems, would succeed not in altering the state of matter but in creating a new kind of matter; or, at any rate, in decomposing matter and re-composing it differently. All our knowledge of the atom and its nucleus is based on the 'Saturnian' model of Nagasoka and Rutherford: the nucleus and its belt, or ring, of electrons. On the face of it, there seems to be no reason why, in the future, some other theory should not enable us to bring about separations and alterations in the state of chemical elements which today seem inconceivable.

So now our alchemist has opened his crystal receptacle, and obtained, through the cooling on contact with the air of the fluorescent liquid, one or more new elements. Some dregs remain. These he will wash and re-wash for several months with triple-distilled water. Then he will keep this water away from the light and from any variations in temperature.

This water is said to have extraordinary chemical and medical properties. It is the universal solvent, and the elixir of tradition that ensures longevity, the elixir of Faust.*

Here, the alchemic tradition seems to be in harmony with

* Professor Ralph Milne Farley, United States Senator and Professor of Modern Physics at the West Point Military Academy, has drawn attention to the fact that some biologists think that old age is due to the accumulation of heavy water in the organism. The alchemists' elixir of life might then be a substance that eliminates selectively heavy water. Such substances exist in evaporated water. Why, then, should they not be found in liquid water when treated in a certain way? But could so important a discovery be published without danger? Mr. Farley imagines a secret society of immortals, or quasi-immortals, who have existed for centuries and reproduce themselves by co-option. Such a society, keeping aloof from politics and the affairs of men, would have every chance of remaining undetected. . . .

advanced modern science, which takes the view that water is a strongly reactive and highly complex mixture. Researchers who have been studying the question of oligo-elements, notably Dr. Jacques Ménétrier, have observed that all metals are, in fact, soluble in water in the presence of certain catalysers such as glucose, and in certain temperatures. Moreover, water, they suggest, could form actual chemical compounds, hydrates for example, in combination with inert gases such as helium and argon. If it were known which constituent in water was responsible for the formation of hydrates in contact with an inert gas, it would be possible to stimulate the solvent properties of water and in this way to obtain a real universal dissolvent.

The Russian review, *Knowledge and Strength*, a journal of high standing, wrote in 1957 (No. 11) that this result would perhaps be achieved one day by bombarding water with nuclear radiations, and that the alchemist's universal dissolvent would become a reality before the end of the century. It also foresaw a number of possible applications, including the boring of a tunnel by means of a jet of activated water.

Our alchemist, then, is now in possession of a certain number of simple bodies unknown in Nature, and of a few flasks full of an alchemic water capable of prolonging life to a considerable extent by rejuvenating the tissues.

His next step is to try to re-combine the simple elements he has obtained. He mixes them in his mortar, and melts them at low temperatures with the aid of catalysers of which the texts tell us very little. The more one studies the operations of the alchemists, the more difficult to decipher do the texts become. This particular operation will take several years to perform.

In this way, we are told, the alchemist will obtain substances exactly like the metals we know, especially those that are good conductors of heat and electricity. These substances would be alchemic copper, alchemic silver and alchemic gold. Neither the classical texts nor spectroscopy are able to reveal the novelty of these substances, and yet they are supposed to have new and surprising properties, different from those of existing metals. If our information is correct, alchemic copper, which looks very like ordinary copper, yet is in fact very different, has an infinitely feeble resistance to electricity, comparable to that of the super-conductors which the physicists obtain in the neighbourhood of absolute zero. If such a copper could be used, it would revolutionize electro-chemistry.

Other substances obtained by the alchemist's manipulations are, it seems, still more remarkable. One of them is said to be soluble in glass, at low temperature and before the glass has reached melting point. This substance, on touching the half-melted glass, spreads all over it inside, turning it to a ruby red, and giving off a mauve fluorescence in the dark. The powder obtained by grinding the glass thus treated in a mortar of agate is what the alchemists call the 'projection powder', or 'philosopher's stone'.

87

'And thus,' wrote Bernard, Comte de la Marche Trévisane, 'is brought about this precious Stone, excelling all other precious stones, an infinite treasure to the glory of God who lives and reigns for ever.'

Everyone is familiar with the marvellous legends concerning this stone, or powder, which is said to be able to bring about the transmutation of metals in considerable quantities. It is reputed to be capable of transforming certain base metals into gold, silver or platinum, but this is only one aspect of its powers. It might even be a sort of reservoir of nuclear energy, controllable to any degree.

We shall return later to the questions raised by the manipulations of the alchemists to which an enlightened modern man must find an answer; for the moment let us halt where the alchemic texts themselves come to an end. The 'Great Work' is done. The alchemist himself undergoes a transformation which the texts evoke, but which we are unable to describe, having only the vaguest analogies to guide us. This transformation, it seems, would be, as it were, a promise, or foretaste, experienced by a privileged being, of what awaits humanity after attaining the very limits of its knowledge of the earth and its elements: its fusion with the Supreme Being, its concentration on a fixed spiritual goal, and its junction with other centres of intelligence across the cosmic spaces. Gradually, or in a sudden flash of illumination, the alchemist, according to tradition, discovers the meaning of his long labours. The secrets of energy and of matter are revealed to him, and at the same time he glimpses the infinite perspectives of Life. He possesses the key to the mechanics of the Universe. He establishes a new relationship between his own mind, which from now on is *illuminated*, and the universal Mind eternally deepening its concentration. Could it be that certain radiations from the 'projection powder' bring about the transmutation of the psyche?

The manipulation of fire and certain other substances therefore makes possible not only the transmutation of metals, but the transformation of the experimenter himself. The latter, under the influence of forces emitted by the crucible (that is to say, radiations emitted by nuclea undergoing changes in structure) enters himself into a new state. Mutations take place within him. His life is prolonged, his intelligence and his powers of perception are raised to a higher level. The existence of such persons is one of the foundations of the Rosicrucian tradition.

The alchemist passes to another stage of being, attains a higher degree of consciousness. He alone is 'awakened', and to him it seems that all other men are still asleep. He escapes from the rest of humanity – disappears, like Mallory on Everest, having had his moment of truth.

'The philospher's stone thus represents the first rung on the ladder that helps man to ascend towards the Absolute. Beyond, the mystery begins. On this side there is no mystery, no esoterism, no other shadows than those projected by our desires and, above all, by our pride. But just as it is easier to content oneself with ideas and words than to do something with one's hands, in suffering and weariness, in silence and solitude, so is it also more convenient to seek refuge in what is called 'pure' thought than to struggle single-handed against the dead weight and darkness of the world of matter. Alchemy forbids her disciples to indulge in any escapism of this kind, and leaves them face to face with the great Enigma. . . . She guarantees nothing except that, if we fight to the end to deliver ourselves from ignorance, truth itself will fight for us and in the end will conquer everything. This, perhaps, will be the beginning of TRUE metaphysics.'*

V

There is time for everything – There is even a time for the times to come together

THE old alchemic texts affirm that the keys to the secrets of matter are to be found in Saturn. By a strange coincidence, everything we know today in nuclear physics is based on a definition of the 'Saturnian' atom. According to Nagasoka and Rutherford, the atom is 'a central mass exercising an attraction surrounded by rings of revolving electrons'.

It is this 'Saturnian' conception of the atom which is accepted today by scientists all over the world, not as an absolute truth, but as the most fruitful working hypothesis. The physicists of the future, maybe, will consider it absurdly naïve. The quantum theory and wave mechanics both apply to the behaviour of electrons. But no theory or system of mechanics gives a precise account of the laws that govern the nucleus. It is believed that the latter is composed of protons and neutrons, and that is all.

Nothing is known positively about nuclear forces. They are neither electric nor magnetic nor gravitational. The latest accepted hypothesis connects these forces with particles somewhere between the neutron and the proton which are known as mesons. That is only something to go on with until more is known. In two years, or in ten years, other hypotheses will, no doubt, point in a different direction. In any case, it is clear that we are living at a time when scientists have neither the time nor altogether the right to study nuclear physics. All available efforts and material are concentrated on the manufacture of explosives and the production of energy. Fundamental research is relegated to the background. What is urgent is to make the most of what we know already. Power is more important than knowledge. This appetite for power is something that the alchemists have always managed to avoid.

Where, then, do we stand now? Contact with neutrons renders all elements radio-active. Experimental nuclear explosions poison the planet's atmosphere. This poisoning, which follows a geometrical progression, will enormously increase the number of stillborn children, cause cancer and leukaemia, ruin plants, upset the

* René Alleau: Preface to *Les Clés de la philosophie spagyrique*, by M. Le Breton. Editions *Caractères*, Paris.

89

weather, produce monsters, destroy our nerves and finally suffocate us. But governments, whether democratic or totalitarian, will not give up testing – and this for two reasons. The first is that public opinion cannot possibly be consulted, for public opinion is not on the planetary level of understanding that alone would enable it to react. The second reason is that there are no governments, only limited liability companies, with humanity as their capital, whose mission is not to make history, but to express the various aspects of historic fatality.

Now, if we believe in historic fatality, we believe that this is only one of the forms of the spiritual destiny of humanity, and that that destiny is an auspicious one. We therefore do not believe that mankind will perish, even though it may have to suffer a thousand deaths, but that after immense and terrible sufferings it will be born – or re-born – joyfully aware that it is still marching onwards.

Is it true that nuclear physics, used in the interests of power, will, as M. Jean Rostand has said, 'squander the genetic capital of humanity'? Yes, perhaps, for a few years; but it is impossible to believe that science will not find a way of cutting the Gordian knot that it has itself created.

The methods of transmutation known to modern science are powerless to arrest energy and radio-activity. They are transmutations of a strictly limited nature whose harmful effects are nevertheless unlimited. If the alchemists are right, there are simple, economical and safe ways of producing transmutations on a large scale. These means would entail the 'dissolution' of matter and its reconstruction in a different state from what it was originally. No discoveries in modern physics would justify a belief that such a thing is possible. And yet for thousands of years the alchemists have been asserting that it is. The fact is, our ignorance of the nature of nuclear forces and of the structure of the nucleus prevents us from saying that anything is absolutely impossible. If the alchemists' transmutation is really possible, it is because the nucleus has properties of which we know nothing.

The issue is important enough to warrant a really serious study of alchemic literature. Even if such a study does not bring to light irrefutable facts, there is at least a chance that it will suggest a new line of approach. For new ideas are badly needed in nuclear physics in its present state of subjection to power politics, and weighed down as it is by the immensity of the equipment involved.

It is now becoming evident that there are infinitely complex structures in the interior of the neutron and the proton, and that the so-called 'fundamental' laws, such as the principle of parity, do not apply to the nucleus. We are beginning to hear about an 'anti-matter', and of the possible coexistence of several Universes in the midst of our visible Universe, so that anything may be possible in the future, including a vindication of alchemy. It would be fitting and in accordance with the noble traditions of the alchemic language that our salvation should be brought about through the medium of spagyric philosophy. There is time for everything, and there is even a time for the times to come together.

THE VANISHED CIVILIZATIONS

I

In which the authors introduce a fantastic personage – Mr. Fort – The fire at the 'sanatorium of overworked coincidences' – Mr. Fort and universal knowledge – 40,000 notes on a gush of periwinkles, a downpour of frogs and showers of blood – The Book of the Damned – A certain Professor Kreyssler – In praise of 'intermediarism' with some examples – The Hermit of Bronx, or the cosmic Rabelais – Visit of the author to the Cathedral of Saint Elsewhere – Au revoir, Mr. Fort!

IN the year 1910 there lived in New York, in a little bourgeois apartment in the Bronx, a little man, neither old nor young, who looked like a very shy seal. His name was Charles Hoy Fort. His hands were round and plump, his figure paunchy and he had no neck, a big head growing bald, a large Asiatic nose, iron-rimmed spectacles and moustaches *à la* Gurdjieff. He seldom went out, except to go to the Municipal Library where he devoured a quantity of newspapers, reviews and yearbooks of all the different countries and all periods. Round his roll-topped desk were heaped empty shoe boxes and piles of periodicals: the *American Almanach* of 1833; the London *Times* for the years 1880–93; the *Annual Record of Science*; twenty years of the *Philosophical Magazine*, *Les Annales de la Société Entomologique de France*, the *Monthly Weather Review*, *The Observatory*, the *Meteorological Journal*, etc. ... He wore a green eyeshade, and when his wife lighted the gas-stove for dinner he used to go into the kitchen to see that she didn't set the place on fire. That was the only thing that annoyed Mrs. Fort, *née* Anna Filan, whom he had chosen for her complete absence of intellectual curiosity and of whom he was very fond.

Until the age of thirty-four Charles Fort, whose parents had a grocer's shop in Albany, had managed to earn a living, thanks to a mediocre talent for journalism and his skill in embalming butterflies. On the death of his parents he sold the shop, and the slender income he derived from the proceeds enabled him at last to devote himself exclusively to his ruling passion which was the accumulation of notes on improbable and yet well established events.

Red rain over Blankenbergue on 2nd November, 1819; a rain of mud in Tasmania on 14th November, 1902. Snowflakes as big as saucers at Nashville on 24th January, 1891; a rain of frogs in Birmingham on 30th June, 1892. Meteorites. Balls of fire. Footprints of a fabulous animal in Devonshire. Flying disks. Marks of cupping-glasses on mountains. Engines in the sky. Erratic comets. Strange disappearances. Inexplicable catastrophes. Inscriptions on meteorites. Black snow. Blue moons. Green suns. Showers of blood. ...

He collected in this way twenty-five thousand notes, filed in cardboard boxes. Facts, no sooner recorded than forgotten. And yet – facts.

He called this his 'sanatorium of overworked coincidences'. Facts no one would speak about. From his files he could hear a 'noisy silence' escaping. He felt a kind of affection for these incongruous realities, banished from the realms of knowledge, to which he gave shelter in his humble little office in the Bronx and talked to affectionately as he filed them away. 'Little trollops and midgets, humpbacks and buffoons all of you; but the solidity of the procession as a whole: the impressiveness of things that pass and pass and pass and keep on and keep on and keep on coming. . . .'

When he grew tired of passing in review this procession of facts which science had decided to ignore (a flying iceberg fell in fragments on Rouen on 5th July, 1853. Argosies of celestial travellers. Winged beings at a height of 8,000 metres in the sky above Palermo on 30th November, 1880. Luminous wheels in the sea. Rains of sulphur, of flesh. Remains of giants in Scotland. Coffins of little creatures from another world in the cliffs at Edinburgh) . . . when he grew tired, he found relaxation in playing all alone interminable games of super-checkers on a board of his own invention that had 1,600 squares.

And then one day Charles Hoy Fort realized that all this formidable labour amounted to nothing at all. It was useless, of dubious value, nothing but the pastime of a maniac. He perceived that he had only been treading on the threshold of what he was obscurely seeking, and that he had done none of the things that really needed to be done. This wasn't research, only a caricature of the real thing. And this man who was so afraid of fire consigned all his boxes and files to the flames.

He had just discovered his real nature. This maniac with a passion for extraordinary occurrences and facts was really only interested in general ideas. What had he unconsciously been doing during those half wasted years? Ensconced in his den, surrounded by butterflies and old papers, he was in fact attacking one of the most powerful prejudices of this century, namely the civilized man's conviction that he knows everything there is to know about the Universe in which he lives. Why, then, did Mr. Charles Hoy Fort hide himself, as if he had something to be ashamed of?

The truth is that the slightest allusion to the fact that the Universe may contain vast areas of the Great Unknown has a disturbing and disagreeable effect on men's minds. Mr. Charles Fort, in fact, was behaving like an erotomaniac: let us keep our vices secret so that society shall not be furious at discovering that it has been allowing large tracts in the field of sexuality to lie fallow. The next stage was to advance from indulgence in a crazy hobby to a declaration of principles, and from being a crank to becoming a prophet. From now on there was real work to be done – revolutionary work.

Scientific knowledge is not objective. Like civilization, it is a conspiracy. Quantities of facts are rejected because they would upset preconceived ideas. We live under an inquisitional régime where the weapon most frequently employed against non-conformist reality is derision. Under such conditions, then, what can our knowledge amount to? 'In the topography of intellection,' said Fort, 'I should say that what we call knowledge is ignorance surrounded by laughter.' Therefore we shall be obliged to claim another freedom in addition to those guaranteed by the Constitution: freedom to disbelieve science. Freedom to disbelieve in evolution (suppose Darwin's work was only fiction?), in the rotation of the Earth, in the existence of such a thing as the speed of light, in gravitation, etc. To disbelieve everything, in short, except facts. Not carefully selected facts, but facts as they occur – noble or ignoble, bastard or pure-blooded, with all their accompanying oddities and incongruous appendages. Nothing factual must be rejected; the science of the future will discover unknown relationships between facts which seem to us disconnected. Science needs to be galvanized by a spirit of insatiable curiosity; not credulous, but fresh and wild. What the world needs is an encyclopaedia of rejected facts and realities that have been condemned. 'I'm afraid we shall have to give to civilization upon this Earth some new worlds. Places with white frogs in them.'

In the space of eight years our timid little seal-man from the Bronx applied himself to learning all the arts and all the sciences – and to inventing another half-dozen or so as his own contribution. Smitten by an encyclopaedic fever, he devoted himself to the gigantic task, not so much of learning, as of taking cognizance of everything in life. 'I marvelled that anybody could be satisfied to be a novelist, or the head of a steel-trust, or a tailor, or a governor or a street-cleaner.'

Principles, formulae, laws, phenomena of all kinds were devoured and digested at the New York Municipal Library, at the British Museum, and also thanks to an enormous correspondence with all the biggest libraries and bookshops in the world. Result: forty thousand notes divided into thirteen hundred sections, written in pencil on minute scraps of paper in a stenographic language of his own invention. And above all, this wild enterprise was presided over by a man with the gift of being able to consider each subject from the point of view of a superior intelligence confronted with it for the first time. Example: 'Astronomy. And a watchman looking at half a dozen lanterns where a street's been torn up. There are gas lights and kerosene lamps and electric lights in the neighbourhood: matches flaring, fires in stores, bonfires, house afire somewhere; lights of automobiles, illuminated signs – The watchman and his one little system. . . .'

At the same time he resumes his inquiries into facts that have been rejected, but systematically this time, taking care to check and cross-check all his references. He plans his researches under headings covering astronomy, sociology, psychology, morphology, chemistry and magnetism. He no longer collects; he tries to invent a compass for navigating oceans 'on the other side', and to solve the puzzle of other worlds hidden behind this world. He must pluck every trembling leaf from the immense tree of fantasy: screams are heard in the sky over Naples on 22nd November, 1821; fish fall from the clouds over Singapore in 1861; in Indre-et-Loire, on a certain 10th of April there is a cataract of dead leaves; stone hatchets fall on Sumatra in a thunderstorm; living matter descends from the sky; there are kidnappings by supermen from outer space; derelict worlds are floating all round us. . . . 'I am intelligent, as contrasted with the orthodox. I haven't the aristocratic disregard of a New York Curator or an Eskimo medicine-man; I have to dissipate myself in acceptance of a host of other worlds. . . .'

Mrs. Fort was not in the least interested in all this. She did not even see anything strange in it. He never talked about his work, except perhaps to one or two astonished friends, to whom he wrote occasionally. 'I think this is a vice we're writing. I recommend it to those who have hankered for a new sin. At first some of our data were of so frightful or ridiculous mien as to be hated or eye-browed. . . . Then some pity crept in?'

With the strain on his eyes there was a danger of his going blind. He stopped work and meditated for some months, eating nothing but brown bread and cheese. When his eyes were rested he began to expound his own view of the Universe, in which there was no room for dogma, and to arouse the interest of those around him by appealing to their sense of humour. The more he studied the various sciences, the more aware he became of their inadequacies. They needed to be destroyed from the base upwards; the attitude behind them was all wrong. A fresh start would have to be made by re-introducing the rejected facts on which he had assembled a vast documentation. Present them first; explain them afterwards. 'I am not convinced that we make a fetish of the preposterous. I think our feeling is that in first gropings there's no knowing what will afterwards be the acceptable. I think that if an early biologist heard of birds that grow on trees, he should record that he had heard of birds that grow on trees. Then let sorting over of data occur afterwards.'

Let everything be reported, then one day we may have a revelation.

The very structure of our knowledge needs to be revised. Charles Hoy Fort is full of exciting theories, all tinged with an element of the bizarre. He sees science as a highly sophisticated motor-car speeding along on a highway. But on either side of this marvellous track, with its shining asphalt and neon lighting, there are great tracts of wild country, full of prodigies and mystery.

Stop! Explore in every direction! Leave the high road and wander! Even if you have to make wild and clown-like gestures, as people do when they are trying to stop a car, no matter; it's urgent! Mr. Charles Hoy Fort, the hermit of Bronx, feels obliged to go through a number of clownish acts which he considers indispensable as quickly and as energetically as possible.

Convinced of the importance of his mission, and able to dispense now with his documentation, he sets out to assemble all his best explosives in 300 pages.

He writes his first book, *The Book of the Damned* in which he proposes 'a certain number of experiments concerning the structure of knowledge'. This work was published in New York in 1919 and provoked a revolution in intellectual circles. Before the first manifestations of Dadaism and Surrealism, Charles Fort introduced into science what Tzara, Breton and their disciples were going to introduce into art and literature: a defiant refusal to play at a game where everybody cheats, a furious insistence that there is 'something else'. A huge effort, not so much, perhaps, to grasp reality in its entirety, as to prevent reality being conceived in a falsely coherent way. A rupture that had to be. 'I am a horse-fly that stings the scalp of knowledge to prevent it from sleeping.'

The Book of the Damned? 'The crack-pots' *Golden Bough*' – John Winterich. 'One of the monstrosities of literature' – Edmund Pearson. For Ben Hecht, 'Charles Fort is the apostle of the exceptional and the high priest of the improbable.' Martin Gardner, however, admitted that 'his sarcasms are in harmony with the best attested analyses of Einstein and Russell'. John W. Campbell asserted that 'this work contains the germs of at least six new sciences'. 'To read Charles Fort,' wrote Maynard Shipley, 'is like taking a ride on a comet.' While Theodore Dreiser saw in him, 'the greatest literary personality since Edgar Poe'.

It was not until 1955 that *The Book of the Damned* was published in France.* This was done at my instigation but, in spite of an excellent translation and introduction by Robert Benayoun and a message from Tiffany Thayer, President in the U.S.A. of the 'Society of Friends of Charles Fort', this extraordinary work attracted hardly any attention.†

* Editions des Deux-Rives, Paris; collection 'Lumière interdite,' general editor: Louis Pauwels. In 1923 Fort published *New Lands* and afterwards came *Lo!* in 1931 and *Wild Talents* in 1932. These works had a certain vogue in America, England and Australia. I am indebted to Robert Benayoun for much of my information.

† Mr. Tiffany Thayer wrote, among other things, as follows: 'The qualities of Charles Fort greatly impressed a group of American writers who decided to pursue, in his honour, the attack which he had launched against the all-powerful priests of the new god: Science, and against all forms of dogma. It was for this purpose that the Charles Fort Society was founded on 26th January, 1931. The founder-members included Theodore Dreiser, Booth Tarkington, Ben Hecht, Harry Leon Wilson, John Cowper Powys, Alexander Woolcott, Burton Rascoe, Aaron Sussman and the secretary, the undersigned, Tiffany Thayer. Charles Fort died in 1932 shortly before the publication of his fourth book, *Wild Talents*. The innumerable notes he had assembled from libraries throughout the world and from his international correspondence were bequeathed to the Charles Fort Society; today they form the nucleus of the archives of this society, which are swollen every day by contributions from members in forty-nine countries, not counting the U.S.A., Alaska, and Hawaii. The Society publishes a quarterly review: *Doubt*. This is also a sort of clearing-house for all the 'outlawed' facts, i.e. those which

Bergier and I consoled ourselves for this mishap to one of our most cherished idols by imagining with what relish he would be listening, from the bottom of the super-Sargasso Sea where he has doubtless made his home, to the 'noisy silence' reaching him from the country of Descartes.

Our ex-embalmer of butterflies had a horror of anything fixed, or classified or defined. Science isolates phenomena in order to observe them. Charles Fort's great idea was that nothing can be isolated. An isolated object ceases to exist. A swallow-tail butterfly sucks nectar from a flower. Result: a butterfly *plus* nectar; a flower *minus* a butterfly's appetite. Every definition of a thing in itself is a crime against reality. 'In some so-called savage tribes the feeble-minded are held in great respect. It is generally recognized that the definition of an object in terms of itself is a sign of feeble-minded-ness. All scientists begin by using this kind of definition, and in our communities scientists are held in great respect.'

Here we have Charles Hoy Fort, lover of the unusual, recorder of miracles, engaged in the formidable task of reflecting on reflection. What he is attacking is the mental structure of civilized man. He is completely out of sympathy with the two-stroke motor which is the driving power of modern reasoning. Two strokes: Yes and No, Positive and Negative. Modern knowledge and modern intelligence are based on this binary system: right, wrong, open, closed; living, dead, liquid, solid, etc. . . . Where Fort is opposed to Descartes is in his insistence that we should envisage the general from an angle which would allow the particular to be defined in its relation thereto, in such a way that every object or thing would be seen as intermediaries between other things. What he demands is a new mental structure, capable of recognizing as real the intermediate states between the yes and the no, the positive and the negative. In other words, a system of reasoning which is higher than binary and would be, as it were, a third eye for the intelligence.

To express what this third eye perceives, language (which is a binary product, an organized conspiracy and limitation) is not sufficient. Fort was therefore constrained to use double-faced adjectives, Janus-epithets such as 'real-unreal', 'immaterial-material', 'soluble-insoluble', etc.

One day when Bergier and I were lunching with him, a friend of ours invented, out of his head, a grave Austrian Professor, the son of an innkeeper at Magdebourg called Kreyssler. The Herr Professor Kreyssler, he informed us, had undertaken the gigantic task of refashioning the language of the West. Our friend was thinking of publishing in a serious review a study of 'The Verbalism of Kreyssler', which would have been a very fruitful mystification.

---

orthodox science cannot or will not accept, e.g. the flying saucers. In point of fact, the body of information and statistics on this subject which the Society possesses is the oldest, most extensive and the most complete in existence. The review *Doubt* also publishes some of Fort's notes.'

This Kreyssler, then, had tried to lcosen the corset of language so that it would find room for the intermediary states neglected in our present mental structure. Let us take an example: backwardness and progress (*'retard'* and *'avance'*). How am I to define the backwardness of the progress I hoped to make? There is no word for it. Kreyssler proposed: 'atard'. And for my progress in making up for my backwardness? – 'revance'.*

Here we are talking about intermediate degrees in time. Now let us take the plunge into psychological states. Love and hate. If I love in a cowardly way, loving only myself through the other person and thus being on the way to hate, is this love? No; it is only 'lhate'.

If, on the other hand, I hate my enemy, without however losing the thread of unity that binds all creatures, doing my duty as an enemy but reconciling hatred and love, this would be 'hatrove'. And now for the fundamental intermediates. What is dying, and what is living? So many intermediate states that we refuse to recognize! There is 'mouvre' ('delive'), which is not living but merely preventing oneself from dying. And there is 'virir' ('lidie') which is really living despite having to die. Finally, the states of consciousness. For example, our consciousness is suspended between sleeping and waking. How often is my consciousness only 'wakleeping' ('vemir') thinking it is awake when it is allowing itself to sleep! If, on the other hand, knowing its inclination to sleep it tries to keep awake, that would be a state of 'slakefulness' ('doriller').

Our friend had just been reading Fort when he presented us with this farcical but ingenious idea. 'In general metaphysical terms,' said Fort, 'our expression is that, like a purgatory, all that is commonly described as "existence", which we call "Intermediateness", is quasi-existence, neither real nor unreal, but expression of attempt to become real, or to generate for or recruit a real existence.' Such an enterprise is without a parallel in modern times. It foreshadows the great changes in the structure of the mind that are called for today by the discovery of certain physico-mathematical realities. Where the particle is concerned, for example, time moves in two directions at once. Equations are both true and false. Light is continuous and at the same time interrupted.

'But that all that we call "Being" is motion; and that all motion is the expression not of equilibrium, but of equilibrating, or of equilibrium unattained; and that to have what is called being is to be intermediate to Equilibrium and In-equilibrium.' These words were spoken in 1919 and echo the observations of a contemporary biologist and physicist, Jacques Ménétrier, on the inversion of the entropy:

'All phenomena in our intermediary state, or quasi-state of being represent a movement towards organization, harmonization and individualization, in other words, an attempt to attain reality. But all attempts are thwarted by continuity, or by external forces – non-recognized facts side by side with others that are recognized.'

* Possible English equivalents could be: 'slowgress' and 'backforwardness'. – *Translator's note.*

97

This anticipates one of the most abstract operations in quantum physics: the normalization of functions – an operation which consists in determining the function characterizing a physical object in such a way that it is possible to find this object anywhere in the entire Universe.

'We conceive of all things as occupying gradations, or steps in series between realness and unrealness.' That is why it was all the same to Fort whether he started with this fact or that in trying to describe totality. And why choose a rational and reassuring fact rather than a disturbing one? Why exclude? 'One measures a circle, beginning anywhere.' For example, he drew attention to flying objects. There you have a group of facts from which it possible to begin to understand totality. But he hastens to assert that 'gushes of periwinkles would be just as good'.

'We are not realists. We are not idealists. We are intermediatists.' But how is anyone to make himself understood if he attacks the very roots of understanding, the basic principles of the intellect? By an apparent eccentricity, which is the shock-language of the genuine 'centralist' genius: the more far-fetched his images, the surer he is to be able to connect them with the focal point of his profoundest meditations. To a certain extent, Charles Hoy Fort follows Rabelais's example, blending humour and imagery in a chorus loud enough to wake the dead.

'I am a collector of notes upon subjects that have diversity, such as deviations from concentricity in the lunar crater Copernicus and a sudden appearance of purple Englishmen, stationary meteor-radiants; and a reported growth of hair on the bald head of a mummy. But my liveliest interest is not so much in things as in relations of things. I have spent much time thinking about the alleged pseudo-relations that are called coincidences. What if some of them should not be coincidences?'

'In days of yore, when I was an especially bad young one, my punishment was having to go to the store on Saturdays and work. I had to scrape off labels of other dealers' canned goods and paste on my parents' label. ... One time I had pyramids of canned goods containing a variety of fruit and vegetables. But I had used all except peach labels. I pasted the peach labels on peach cans and then came to apricots. Well, aren't apricots peaches? And there are plums that are virtually apricots. I went on either mischievously or scientifically, pasting the peach labels on cans of plums, cherries, string beans and succotash. I can't quite define my motive, because to this day it has not been decided whether I am a scientist or a humorist.'

'If there are no positive differences, it is not possible to say what anything is, as positively distinguished from anything else. What is a house? A barn is a house, if one lives in it. If residence constitutes house-ness because style of architecture does not, then a bird's nest is a house, and human occupancy is not the standard to judge

98

by, because we speak of dogs' houses; nor material, because we speak of snow houses of Eskimos . . . or things seemingly so positively different as the White House at Washington and a shell on the seashore are seen to be continuous.'

'White coral islands in a dark blue sea. Their seeming of distinctness: the seeming of individuality, or of positive difference one from another – but all are only projections from the same sea bottom.
'The difference between sea and land is not positive. In all water there is some earth; in all earth there is some water. So then that all seeming things are not things at all, if all are inter-continuous, any more than is a table-leg a thing in itself, if it is only a projection from something else: that not one of us is a real person if, physically, we are continuous with environment; if, psychically, there is nothing to us but expression of relation to environment. Our general expression has two aspects: conventional monism, or that all things that seem to have identity of their own are only islands that are projections from something underlying, and have no real outlines of their own.'

'By "beauty", I mean that which seems complete. Obversely, that the incomplete, or the mutilated, is the ugly. Venus of Milo: to a child she is ugly. When a mind adjusts to thinking of her as a completeness . . . she is beautiful. A hand, thought of only as a hand, may seem beautiful; found on a battlefield – obviously a part – not beautiful. But everything in our experience is only a part of something else that in turn is only a part of still something else – or that there is nothing beautiful in our experience; only appearances that are intermediate to beauty and ugliness – that only universality is complete; that only the complete is the beautiful: that every attempt to achieve beauty is an attempt to give to the local the attribute of the universal.'

Fort's profound thinking is thus based on the subjacent unity of every thing and of all phenomena. Yet civilized thought at the end of the nineteenth century opened parentheses everywhere, and our binary system of reasoning can only conceive duality. So, then, we see the crazy wise man of Bronx in revolt against the exclusionist science of his day, and also against the very structure of our intelligence. It seems to him another kind of intelligence is needed: an intelligence partly mystical, and awakened to an awareness of the presence of Totality. From these premises he goes on to suggest other methods of knowledge. To prepare us for this he proceeds to tear up, or blow up, our set ways of thinking. 'I'll send you reeling against the doors that open on to "something other".'

And yet Mr. Fort is not an idealist. He militates against our limited realism: we reject reality when it is fantastic. Mr. Fort does not preach a new religion. On the contrary, he endeavours to surround his teaching with a barrier to prevent the feeble-minded from entering. That 'everything is in everything', that the Universe is contained in a grain of sand, he is convinced. But this metaphysical certainty can only be apprehended at the highest level of our reflective intelligence. Brought down to the level of an elementary occultism it would appear ridiculous. It cannot be used to justify the ravings of analogical thinking so dear to those rather suspect esoterics who are continually explaining one thing by something else: the Bible by numbers, the last war by the Great Pyramids, Revolution by cartomancy and my future by the stars – and who see signs everywhere.

'There is probably a connection between a rose and a hippopotamus and yet no young man would ever think of offering his fiancée a bouquet of hippopotami.' Mark Twain, denouncing the same false thinking, declared jokingly that the *Spring Song* can be explained by the Tables of the Law since Moses and Mendelssohn are the same name: you have only to replace '—oses' by '—endelssohn'. And Charles Fort renews the attack with this caricature: 'An elephant can be identified as a sunflower: both have long stems. A camel is indistinguishable from a peanut, if only their humps be considered.' There you have a picture of the man – one who carries his solid learning lightly. Let us see now how his thought can be expanded to cosmic dimensions.

Supposing the Earth itself, as such, were not real? What if it were only something intermediary in the cosmos? Perhaps the Earth has no independent existence, and perhaps life on the Earth is by no means independent of other lives and other existences in space. . . .

Forty thousand notes on all sorts of rains which have fallen on the earth obliged Charles Fort to admit the hypothesis that most of them were not of terrestrial origin. 'I suggest that beyond this earth are other lands from which come things as, from America, float things to Europe. . . .'

It should be made quite clear that Fort is certainly not naïve. He does not believe everything. He only protests against our habit of denying everything *a priori*. He does not point his finger at truths; he hits out with his fists to demolish the scientific set-up of his day, built up of truths so very imperfect as to resemble errors. If he laughs, it is because there seems to be no reason why man's striving after knowledge should not sometimes be accompanied by laughter, which is also human. Does he invent? dream? extrapolate? A cosmic Rabelais? He admits it:

'This book,' he writes, 'is fiction, like *Gulliver's Travels, The Origin of Species*, Newton's *Principia* and every history of the United States.'

'Black rains and black snows, jet-black snowflakes. . . .' 'Slag washed upon the Scottish coast – to have produced so much of it would have required the united output of all the smelting-works in the world.' 'My own notion is of an island near an oceanic trade-route: it might receive débris from passing vessels.' Why not débris or refuse from inter-stellarships?

Sometimes, again, rains contain animal substances, gelatinous matter accompanied by a strong smell of decay 'Will it be admitted that there are vast viscous and gelatinous regions floating about in infinite space?' Could all this be accounted for by food cargoes deposited in the sky by the Great Travellers from other worlds? 'We have a sense of a stationary region overhead in which this Earth's gravitational and meteorological forces are relatively inert, or a region that receives products like this Earth's products, but from external sources.'

What about the rains that contain live animals – fish, frogs, tortoises? If they come from elsewhere, then human beings, too, ancestrally speaking, may also come from 'elsewhere'. . . . Unless they are animals that have been snatched up from the Earth by hurricanes or whirlwinds and deposited in a region in outer space where there is no gravitation, a sort of cold chamber where the objects ravished in this way are indefinitely preserved.

Removed from the Earth, and having crossed the threshold of the gates opening on to 'elsewhere', they are assembled in a kind of super-sea of Sargasso in the skies. 'Objects caught up in hurricanes may enter a region of suspension over this Earth. . . .'

'Those are your data; do with them as you please. . . . Where do the whirlwinds go? Of what do they consist? . . . A super-sea of Sargasso: derelicts, rubbish, old cargoes from inter-planetary wrecks; things cast out into what is called space by convulsions of other planets, things from the times of the Alexanders, Caesars and Napoleons of Mars, or Jupiter, or Neptune. Things raised by this Earth's cyclones: horses and barns and elephants and flies, and dodos, pterodactyls and moas; leaves from modern trees and leaves of the carboniferous era – all, however, tending to disintegrate into homogeneous-looking muds or dusts – red or black or yellow – treasure-troves for the palaeontologists and for the archaeologists – accumulations of centuries, cyclones of Egypt, Greece and Assyria. . . .'

'When lightning is accompanied by thunderbolts, the peasants thought they were meteorites. Scientists exclude meteorites. Peasants believe in "thunderstones"; Scientists exclude thunder-stones. It is useless to argue that peasants are out in the fields and that scientists are shut up in laboratories and lecture rooms. . . .'

Thunderbolts apparently shaped and covered with marks and signs. . . . Could it be that other worlds were trying, in this and other ways, to communicate with us, or at any rate, with some of us? 'With a sect, perhaps, or a secret society, or certain esoteric ones of this Earth's inhabitants.' . . . There are innumerable instances of attempts at this kind of communication. 'Because of our experience with suppression and disregard, we suspect, before we go into the subject at all, that astronomers have seen these pheno-mena; that metereologists and navigators have seen them; that individual scientists and other trained observers have seen them many times; that it is the System that has excluded data of them.'

We would remind readers once again that this was written about 1910. Today the Russians and the Americans are building labora-tories to study signals that might be coming to us from other worlds.

Perhaps we have been visited in the distant past? And supposing the palaeontologists were wrong, and that the great skeletal remains discovered by the exclusionist scientists of the nineteenth century had been arbitrarily assembled? Were they the remains of gigantic beings, occasional visitors to our planet? What really obliges us to believe in the pre-human fauna talked about by the palaeontologists who know no more about it than we do? 'No matter how cheerful and unsuspicious my disposition may be, when I go to the American Museum of Natural History dark cynicisms arise the moment I come to the fossils or old bones that have been found – gigantic things, reconstructed into terrifying but "proper" Dinosaurs. On one of the floors below they have a reconstructed Dodo. It's frankly a fiction . . . but it's been reconstructed so cleverly and so convincingly. . . .'

'Why, if we have been visited, before, are we not visited now? A simple and immediately acceptable answer would be: Would we, if we could, educate and sophisticate pigs, geese, cattle? Would it be wise to establish diplomatic relations with the hen that now functions, satisfied with mere sense of achievement by way of compensation?

'I think we are property. I should say we belong to something; that once upon a time this Earth was no-man's land, that other worlds explored and colonized here and fought among themselves for possession, but that now it's owned by something; that something owns this Earth – all others warned off. Nothing in our own times has ever appeared upon this Earth, from somewhere else so openly as Columbus landed upon San Salvador, or as Hudson sailed up his river. But as to surreptitious visits to this Earth in recent times, or as to emissaries, perhaps, from other worlds, or voyagers who have shown every indication of intent to evade and avoid, we shall have data as convincing as our data of oil, or coal-burning aerial super-constructions. But in this vast subject I shall have to do considerable neglecting or disregarding myself. I do not see how I can in this book take up at all the subject of the possible use of humanity to some other mode of existence, or the flattering notion that we can possibly be worth something. Pigs, geese and cattle. First find out that they are owned. Then find out the whyness of it. I suspect that, after all, we're useful – that among contesting claimants adjustment has occurred, or that something now has a legal right to us, by force, or by having paid out analogues of beads for us to former, more primitive, owners of us – and that all this has been known, perhaps for ages, to certain ones upon this Earth, a cult, or Order, members of which function like bell-wethers to the rest of us, or as superior slaves or overseers, directing in accordance with instructions received – from Somewhere else – in our mysterious usefulness.

'In the past, before proprietorship was established, inhabitants of a host of other worlds have dropped here, hopped here, wafted, sailed, flown, motored – walked here, for all I know – been pulled here, been pushed; have come singly, have come in enormous numbers; have visited occasionally, have visited periodically, for hunting, trading, mining, replenishing harems: have established colonies here, have been lost here; far-advanced peoples, or things, and primitive peoples or whatever they were: – white ones, black ones, yellow ones. . . .'

We are not alone; the Earth is not alone; 'I think we're all bugs and mice, and are only different expressions of an all-inclusive cheese' whose odour of fermentation we dimly perceive. There are other worlds behind ours, other lives behind what we call life. We must do away with the parentheses of exclusionism in exchange for the hypotheses of a fantastic Unity. And no matter if we make mistakes, such as drawing a map of America on which the Hudson is set down as a passage leading to Siberia; what is essential, at a time like this when new methods of knowledge and new ways of thinking are being opened up, is that we should have no doubts at all that maps will have to be altered, that the world is not what we thought it was, and that we ourselves, in the depths of our own consciousness will have to change into something different from what we were before.

Other worlds are in communication with the Earth. Proofs of this exist. Those which we think we can see are not, perhaps, the right ones. But they exist. The marks of cupping-glasses on mountains: do they prove anything? We do not know. At least they stimulate us to look for further signs: '. . . These marks look to me like symbols of communication. But they do not look to me like means of communication between some of the inhabitants of this Earth and other inhabitants of this Earth. My own impression is that some external force has marked, with symbols, rocks of this Earth from far away. I do not think that cup-marks are inscribed communications among different inhabitants of this Earth, because it seems too unacceptable that inhabitants of China, Scotland and America should all have conceived of the same system. Cup-marks are strings of cup-like impressions in rocks. Sometimes there are rings round them, and sometimes they have only semicircles. England, France, America, Algeria, Circassia and Palestine – they are virtually everywhere – except, in the far North, I think. In China cliffs are dotted with them. On a cliff near Lake Como there is a maze of these markings. In Italy, Spain and India they occur in enormous numbers. Given that a force, say, like electric force, could from a distance, mark such a substance as rocks as, from a distance of hundreds of miles, selenium can be marked by tele-photographers. But I am of two minds: the Lost Explorers from Somewhere, and an attempt from Somewhere, to communicate with them: so a frenzy of showering of messages towards this Earth in the hope that some of them would mark rocks near the lost explorers. Or that somewhere upon this Earth, there is an especial rocky surface or receptor or Polar construction, or a steep conical hill upon which for ages have been received messages from some other world; but that, at times, messages go astray and mark substances perhaps thousands of miles from the receptor;

That perhaps forces behind the history of this Earth have left upon the rocks of Palestine, England, China and India records that may some day be deciphered, of their misdirected instructions to certain esoteric ones – Order of the Freemasons, the Jesuits —.'

No image can be too fanciful, no hypothesis too extreme: anything can be used to storm the fortress. There are such things as flying engines and space-explorers. And suppose they pick up *en route*, for examination, a few living organisms from the Earth? ... 'I think that we're fished for. It may be that we are highly esteemed by super-epicures somewhere. It makes me more cheerful when I think that we may be of some use after all. I think that drag-nets have often come down and have been mistaken for whirlwinds and waterspouts. ... I think we're fished for, but this a little expression on the side. ...'

And now we have reached the depths of the inadmissible, murmurs of our strange Mr. Charles Hoy Fort with quiet satisfaction. He takes off his green eyeshade, rubs his big tired eyes, smooths down his seal's moustache and goes off to the kitchen to see whether his good wife Anna, in cooking the haricots for dinner, is not in danger of setting fire to the shed, the folders, the card-index, the museum of coincidences, the conservatory of the improbable, the salon of celestial artists, the office of fallen objects and to that library of other worlds, that Cathedral of Saint Elsewhere, and the fabulous and shining Jester's costume that Wisdom wears.

Anna, my dear, turn off your gas.

Good appetite, Mr. Fort.

II

An hypothesis condemned to the stake – Where a clergyman and a biologist become comic figures – Wanted: a Copernicus in anthropology – Many blank spaces on all the maps – Dr. Fortune's lack of curiosity – The mystery of the melted platinum – Cords used as books – The tree and the telephone – Cultural relativity

As an example of militant action in favour of the greatest possible degree of open-mindedness, and as an initiation into the cosmic consciousness, the works of Charles Fort have been a direct source of inspiration for the greatest poet and champion of the theory of parallel universes, H. P. Lovecraft, the father of what has come to be known as Science-Fiction to which he has contributed some ten or fifteen masterpieces of their kind, a sort of Iliad and Odyssey of a forward-marching civilization. To a certain extent, we too have been inspired in our task by the spirit of Charles Fort. We do not believe everything, but we believe that everything ought to be investigated. Sometimes an inquiry into doubtful facts will throw into their proper perspective facts that are true. Complete results cannot be achieved if anything is omitted. Like Fort, we are trying to repair certain omissions, and are prepared to run the risk of being accused of aberations. We will leave to others the task of discovering which are the right tracks to follow in our jungle.

Fort studied everything which had apparently fallen from the sky. We are studying all the probable, or less probable, traces left on the Earth by civilizations that have long since disappeared. No hypothesis is excluded: an atomic civilization long before what we call the prehistoric era; enlightenment received from the inhabitants of Another World, etc. . . . . Considering that the scientific study of humanity's remote past has scarcely begun and is at present in a state of complete confusion, these hypotheses are no wilder and just as well founded as those which are currently admitted. The important thing, in our opinion, is to throw open the whole question as wide as possible. We are not going to impose upon you a thesis on vanished civilizations, but merely to suggest that you envisage the problem from a new, and non-inquisitorial point of view.

According to the classical method there are two kinds of facts: the 'cursed' ones and the others. For example, the descriptions of flying engines in very ancient sacred texts, the use of para-psychological powers among primitive peoples, or the presence of nickel in coins dating from 235 B.C. are 'cursed' facts.

They are banned; no one will even investigate them. And there are two kinds of hypotheses: the disquieting ones, and the others. The frescoes discovered in the caves at Tassili in the Sahara represent, among other things, human figures wearing helmets with long horns from which project spindles outlined in myriads of little points, or dots. Ears of corn, we are told; the symbol of a pastoral civilization. Possibly; but there is nothing to prove it. And suppose this was a way of representing a magnetic field? Shame! A shocking suggestion! Witchcraft! To the stake!

The following is an extreme example of what the classical, or as we call it the inquisitorial method, may lead to:

An Indian clergyman, the Rev. Pravanananvanda, and an American biologist, a Dr. Strauss of the Johns Hopkins University, have just identified the 'Abominable Snowman' as being none other than the brown Himalayan bear. Neither of these gentlemen has seen the animal. They have stated, however, that 'since our hypothesis is the only one which is not fantastic, it must be the right one'. So it would be a derogation of the scientific spirit to pursue useless researches. All honour to our clergyman and doctor! It only remains for us to inform the Yeti that he is the brown Himalayan bear.

Our method, in keeping with the times we live in, not unlike the Renaissance, is based on the principle of toleration. No more inquisitions. We refuse to exclude facts and reject hypotheses. Sifting lentils is a useful action; gravel is unfit for human consumption. But there is nothing to prove that certain rejected hypotheses and certain 'accursed' facts are not nourishing. We are not working on behalf of the weak and the allergic, but for all those who, as the saying goes, have 'guts'.

We are convinced that the study of past civilizations has been marred by numerous cases of rejected evidence, *a priori* exclusions and inquisitorial executions. The humane sciences have made less progress than physical and chemical science, and the positivist nineteenth century spirit still reigns supreme, and is all the more exacting because it knows it is doomed.

Anthropology is awaiting its Copernicus. Before Copernicus the Earth was the centre of the universe. For the classical anthropologist, our civilization is the centre of all human thought in space and time. Let us pity poor primitive man, engulfed in the darkness of his pre-logical mentality. Five hundred years separate us from the Middle Ages, and we are only just beginning to exonerate this epoch from the charge of obscurantism. The century of Louis XV paved the way for modern Europe, and the recent work of Pierre Gaxotte has done much to demolish the view that this century was a stronghold of egoism erected to arrest the flow of history. Our civilization, like any other, is a conspiracy.

Sir James Frazer's *Golden Bough* is a standard and authoritative work containing a description of the folk-lore of every country. Not for a moment did it enter his head that he was dealing with anything but some touching superstitions and picturesque customs.

Savages suffering from infectious illnesses eat *penicillum notatum* (a kind of mushroom): this must be a form of imitative magic whereby they seek to increase their vigour by consuming this phallic symbol. Their use of digitaline is no doubt another superstition. The science of antibiotics, operations done under hypnosis, creating artificial rain by scattering salts of silver, for example ought to be enough to remove the label of 'naïve' attached to certain primitive practices.

Sir James Frazer, confident of belonging to the only civilization worthy of the name, refuses to envisage the possibility of 'inferior' peoples possessing technical skills which, though different from our own, are none the less real, and his *Golden Bough* is like one of those illuminated maps of the world designed by artists who only knew the Mediterranean and used to fill up the blank spaces with drawings and inscriptions: 'Here is the country of the Dragons', 'Here the Island of Centaurs'. . . . And did not the nineteenth century too, in every domain, make haste to camouflage all the blank spaces everywhere – even on geographical maps? There is in Brazil, between the Rio Tapajos and the Rio Xingu, an unknown land as big as Belgium. No explorer has ever approached El Yafri, the forbidden city of Arabia. A Japanese division under arms in New Guinea disappeared one day in 1943 without leaving any trace. And if the two Great Powers who share the world between them ever reach agreement the real map of the planet will have some surprises in store for us.

Ever since the H-bomb the military have been secretly listing the whereabouts of underground caves: an extraordinary subterranean labyrinth in Sweden; caves beneath the soil of Virginia and Czechoslovakia; a hidden lake under the Balearic Islands. ... Blank spaces on the physical world, blanks on the world of humanity. We do not know everything about man's powers or the resources of his intelligence and psychic make-up, and we have invented Islands of Centaurs and Dragon Lands: pre-logical mentality, superstition, folk-lore, imitative magic.

Hypothesis: some civilizations have gone much further than we have in exploiting parapsychological powers.

Answer: there are no parapsychological powers.

Lavoisier proved that meteorites did not exist by stating: 'It is impossible for stones to fall from the sky because there are no stones in the sky.' Simon Newcomb proved that it would be impossible for aeroplanes to fly since an airship heavier than air was an impossibility.

Dr. Fortune went to New Guinea to study the Dobu tribe. They are a people of magicians, whose peculiarity it is to believe that their magical techniques are valid everywhere and for everyone. When Dr. Fortune went away, one of the natives presented him with a charm which had the power of conferring invisibility, saying: 'I often use it for stealing pork in broad daylight. Follow my instructions carefully, and you will be able to pinch anything you want in the shops in Sydney.' ... 'Naturally,' remarked Dr. Fortune, 'I never tried it out.' Remember the saying of our friend, Charles Fort: 'In the topography of the intelligence, knowledge could be defined as ignorance accompanied by derision.'

Nevertheless, a new school of anthropology is coming into being, and M. Levi-Strauss has aroused indignation by boldly declaring that the Negritos are probably more advanced than we are in psychotherapy. A pioneer of this new school, the American William Seabrook, went to Haiti just after the First World War to study the Voodoo cult. Not to observe it from the outside, but to take an active part in this magic and enter this other world with an open mind. Paul Morand* has written the following magnificent tribute to him:

'Seabrook is perhaps the only white man of our time to have received the baptism of blood. He did so without scepticism and without fanaticism. His attitude towards mystery is that of a man of today. Science in the last ten years has brought us to the brink of the Infinite: there, anything might happen in future – interplanetary travel, discovery of the fourth dimension, radio communication with God. Our superiority over our forefathers must be admitted in so far as from now on we are ready for anything, less credulous and more ready to believe.

'The farther we go back into the origins of the world, and the more closely we study primitive peoples, the more often we discover that their traditional secrets coincide with the present state of scientific research. It is only recently that the Milky Way has been considered as the source and origin of the stellar world:

* Preface to *The Magic Island*, by William Seabrook.

the Aztecs, however, expressly affirmed it, and no one believed them. Savages have preserved what science is rediscovering today. They believed in the unity of matter long before the hydrogen atom was isolated. They believed in tree-men and iron-men long before Sir J. C. Bose measured the sensitivity of plants and poisoned metal with cobras' venom. "Human faith," said Huxley in *Essays of a Biologist*, "has passed from the Spirit to spirits, and then from spirits to gods and from gods to God." It could be added that from God we return to the Spirit.'

But if we are to show that the traditional secrets of the 'primitives' coincide with our present researches, it will be necessary to establish communications between anthropology and recent advances in the physical, chemical and mathematical sciences. The simple traveller, intelligent, full of curiosity and with an historical and literary background, is in danger of missing some of the most important discoveries. Exploration up to now has been only a branch of literature, a subjective activity indulged in as a luxury. When it develops into something else, we shall then perhaps perceive that there have been, in remotest antiquity, civilizations endowed with a technical equipment as important and extensive as ours, though of a different nature.

J. Alden Mason, an eminent and very orthodox anthropologist, asserts and produces reliable evidence to support his claim, that ornaments made of melted platinum have been found on the high plateaus in Peru. Now platinum's melting point is 1,730° C., and to work it, techniques comparable to our own would be required.*

Professor Mason sees the difficulty, and concludes that these ornaments were made from powder obtained by calcination, and not melted. This supposition reveals a real ignorance of metallurgy.

A ten-minute study of Schwarzkopf's *Treatise on Calcinated Powders* (*Traité des Poudres Frittées*) would have shown him that such a hypothesis was inadmissible. Why did he not consult specialists in other branches of science? This is the whole case against anthropology. Professor Mason asserts, equally innocently, that examples have been found, dating from the most ancient Peruvian civilization, of the welding of metals by the use of resin and molten metallic salts. The fact that this technique is the basis

* Further mysteries in the history of techniques include the following: The method of spectral analysis has recently been employed by the Institute of Applied Physics of the Chinese Academy of Science to examine a girdle with openwork ornaments, 1,600 years old, found buried along with a lot of other objects in the tomb of the famous Tsin General, Chou Chou, who lived about A.D. 265–316. It appears that the metal in this girdle was composed of 85 per cent aluminium, 10 per cent copper and 5 per cent manganese. Now, although aluminium is found in many places on the Earth, it is difficult to extract. The only method known today of extracting aluminium from bauxite, namely by electrolysis, has only been in use since 1808. The fact that Chinese technicians were able 1,600 years ago to extract aluminium from such a bauxite is therefore an important discovery in the history of metallurgy. – *Horizons* No. 89, October 1958.

of electronics and is used in conjunction with the most advanced technologies, seems to have escaped his notice. We apologize for seeming to make a display of our knowledge, but it is here that we feel the necessity for the 'concomitant information' so strongly recommended by Charles Fort.

Despite his extremely prudent approach, Professor John Alden Mason, Curator Emeritus of the Museum of American Antiquities of the University of Pennsylvania, does open a door to the realms of fantastic reality when, in his book *The Ancient Civilization of Peru*, he speaks about the *Quipu*. The *Quipu* are cords tied into complicated knots, and are a feature of Inca and pre-Inca civilizations. They appear to be a form of writing, and may have been used to express abstract ideas. One of the best known specialists in the matter, Nordenskjöld, thinks that the *Quipu* were used for mathematical calculations, horoscopes, and various methods of foretelling the future. The problem is a vital one: there may be other means of registering thought than writing.

Let us take the matter further: the knot, on which *Quipu* is based, is considered by modern mathematicians to be one of the greatest mysteries. It is only possible in an *odd* number of dimensions; impossible in dimensions of *even* numbers – 4, 6, 2 – and the topologists have only been able to study the simplest knots. It is therefore not improbable that the *Quipu* may conceal knowledge that we do not yet possess.

Take another example: modern thinking on the nature of knowledge and the structure of the mind might be enriched by a study of the language of the Hopi Indians. This language is better adapted than our own to the exact sciences. It contains words representing not verbs or nouns, but events, and is thus more applicable to the space-time continuum in which we now know that we are living. Furthermore, the 'event-word' has three moods: certitude, probability, imagination. Instead of saying: a man crossed the river in a boat, the Hopi would employ the group: man-river-boat in three different combinations, according to whether the event was observed by the narrator, reported by a third party, or dreamt.

The really 'modern man', in the sense that Paul Morand and we ourselves understand the term, discovers that intelligence is a unity manifested in different structures, just as man's need for shelter is universal, expressed in a thousand different architectural forms.

It is possible that our civilization is the result of a long struggle to obtain from machines the powers that primitive man possessed, enabling him to communicate from a distance, to rise into the air, to liberate the energy of matter, abolish gravitation, etc. It is also possible that we may ultimately discover that these powers can be exercised with an equipment so simple that the word 'machine' will acquire a different meaning. If this happens, we shall have gone from mind to machine and from machine to mind, and certain remote civilizations will appear to us to be less remote.

In his reception address at Oxford University in 1946 Jean Cocteau told the following story: 'My friend Pobers, Professor of parapsychology at the University of Utrecht, was sent on a mission to the West Indies to study the part played there by telepathy, in current use among the simple people. If they want to communicate with their husbands or sons in town, the women speak to a tree, and the men bring back whatever they have been asked for. One day Pobers was present at one of these occasions and asked the peasant woman why she addressed herself to a tree. Her reply was surprising and conducive to solving the whole modern problem of our instincts being atrophied by the machines on which we have come to rely. This, then, was the question: "Why do you address yourself to a tree?" And this the answer: "Because I am poor. If I were rich I should have the telephone." '

Electro-encephalograms of Yogis in a state of ecstasy show curves which do not correspond to any cerebral activities known to us either in states of wakefulness or in sleep. There are plenty of coloured blank spaces on the map of the mind of civilized man: precognition, intuition, telepathy, genius, etc. By the time these regions have been thoroughly explored, and a path opened up through various states of consciousness unknown to our classical psychologists, the study of ancient civilizations and of peoples we call primitive will perhaps reveal the existence of veritable technologies and essential aspects of knowledge. A cultural 'centralism' will be succeeded by a relativism which will throw a new and fantastic light on the history of humanity. Progress does not consist so much in emphasizing parentheses as in multiplying hyphens.

III

In which the authors speculate about the Great Pyramid –
Possibility of 'other' techniques – The example of Hitler –
The Empire of Almanzar – Recurrence of 'ends of the world'
– The impossible Easter Island – The legend of the white man
– The civilizations of America – The mystery of Maya –
From the 'bridge of light' to the strange plain of Nazca

IT has taken humanity 2,200 years, from Aristarchus of Samos to the year 1900, to calculate with sufficient accuracy the distance from the Earth to the Sun: 149,400,000 kilometres. To arrive at the same result it was only necessary to multiply by a thousand million the height of the Pyramid of Cheops, built in 2900 B.C.

We know today that the Pharaohs embodied in the Pyramids the findings of a science of whose origin and methods we know nothing. We find in them the symbol π, the exact calculation of the duration of the solar year and of the radius and weight of the Earth, the law of the precession of the equinoxes, the figure of the degree of longitude, the position of the True North, and perhaps many other data not yet deciphered. Where did this knowledge come from? How was it obtained, or transmitted? And, in the latter case, by whom?

The Abbé Moreux believes that God imparted scientific knowledge to the Ancients. 'Hearken to me, O my son: the number 3.1416 will enable thee to calculate the surface of a circumference!'... According to Piazzi Smyth, God dictated this information to the Egyptians who were too impious and too ignorant to understand what they were inscribing in their stone. And why should God, who is omniscient, be seriously mistaken as to the quality of his pupils? In the opinion of the positivist Egyptologists, the measurements carried out at Gizeh have been faked by explorers too intent on discovering marvels: in fact, they reveal no special science. But the discussion turns on questions of decimals, and the fact remains that the construction of the Pyramids reveals a technique that to us is still totally incomprehensible. Gizeh is a mountain weighing 6,500,000 tons. Blocks of twelve tons are adjusted to a demi-millimetre. The least imaginative idea is the one most generally accepted – namely, that the Pharaohs had a colossal man-power at their disposal. It has never been explained how the problem of dealing with the overcrowding caused by these vast hordes was solved. Nor the reason for such a mad undertaking. How were the blocks of stone extracted from the quarries? Classical Egyptology recognizes no other technique than the use of wedges of wet wood thrust into fissures in the rock. The builders, it seems, had only stone hammers, copper saws and soft metal to work with. This only deepens the mystery. How were these chipped stones weighing 10,000 kg. and more hoisted and put into place? In the nineteenth century we had the greatest difficulty in transporting two obelisks which the Pharaohs used to transport by the dozen. What did the Egyptians use to light the interior of the Pyramids? Until 1890 we ourselves only had lamps that smoked and left a sooty deposit on the ceiling. No trace of smoke, however, has ever been found on the walls of the Pyramids. Did they perhaps intercept the Sun's light and convey it to the interior by some optical contrivance? No traces of a lens of any kind have been found.

Nor has any instrument for scientific calculations, nor any evidence of an advanced technology been discovered. There are two possible explanations. The first is the elementary-mystical theory of God dictating astronomical information to dense but willing stone-masons and lending them a helping hand.

Is it true that there is no scientific knowledge embodied in the Pyramids? The positivists maintain that if there is it is only a coincidence. When coincidences are, as Fort would have said, as exaggerated as in this case, what ought they to be called?

The second alternative is to believe that a few surrealist architects and decorators, in order to satisfy the megalomania of their king, and working to measurements improvised and imagined on the spur of the moment, succeeded in causing the 2,600,000 blocks of the Great Pyramid to be extracted, transported, decorated, hoisted and adjusted to a demi-millimetre by hordes of labourers working with nothing but pieces of wood and saws for cutting cardboard and treading on each other's toes.

All this happened 5,000 years ago, and we know almost nothing about it. What we do know, however, is that research has been in the hands of people for whom the techniques of our modern civilization are the only ones that count. They are therefore obliged to imagine either Divine intervention, or else to look upon the whole thing as a bizarre and colossal task performed by ant-like hordes. It is possible, however, that minds quite different from our own were able to conceive techniques as highly perfected as ours, but also quite different, involving instruments for measuring and methods of manipulating matter unlike anything we know, and leaving no traces that we can see. It may be that a science and a technology of great potency, which provided solutions to these problems very different from anything we can imagine, disappeared completely along with the world of the Pharaohs. It is difficult to believe that a civilization can die and leave no trace. It is still more difficult to believe that it could have been so different from our own that we are unable to recognize it as a civilization. And yet! . . .

When the War in Europe ended on 8th May, 1945, missions of investigation were immediately sent out to visit Germany after her defeat. Their reports have been published; the catalogue alone has 300 pages. Germany had only been separated from the rest of the world since 1933. In twelve years the technical evolution of the Reich developed along strangely divergent lines. Although the Germans were behindhand as regards the atomic bomb, they had perfected giant rockets unmatched by any in America or Russia. They may not have had radar, but they had perfected a system of infra-red ray detectors which were quite as effective. Though they did not invent silicones, they had developed an entirely new organic chemistry, based on the eight-ring carbon chain.

In addition to these radical differences in matters of technique there were still more stupefying differences in the field of philosophy. . . . They had rejected the theory of relativity and tended to neglect the quantum theory. Their cosmogony would have startled astrophysicists in the Allied countries: they believed in the existence of eternal ice and that the planets and the stars were blocks of ice floating in space.* If it has been possible for such wide divergencies to develop in the space of twelve years in our modern world, in spite of the exchange of ideas and mass communications, what view must one take of the civilizations of the past? To what extent are our archaeologists qualified to judge the state of the sciences, techniques, philosophy and knowledge that distinguished, say, the Maya or Khmer civilizations?

We must avoid falling into the trap of paying too much attention to legends: Lemuria or Atlantis. Plato, in the *Critias*, singing the praises of the vanished city, and before him, Homer evoking in the *Odyssey* the fabulous Scheria were perhaps describing Tartessos, the Biblical Tarshish of the Book of Jonah, and the object of the prophet's journey. At the mouth of the Guadalquivir, Tartessos was the richest mining town in the world and represented the

* See Part Two of the present work.

quintessence of a civilization. It flourished for an unknown number of centuries, and had been the seat of wisdom and the depository of many secrets. About the year 500 B.C. it vanished completely, no one knows how or why.*

It may be that Numinor, that mysterious Celtic centre of the fifth century B.C., was not a legend,† but we do not really know. The civilizations of whose existence in the past we can be certain but which are now dead are quite as strange as Lemuria. The Arab civilization of Cordoba and Granada was the cradle of modern science, the founder of experimental research and its practical applications; and among the subjects it studied were chemistry and even jet-propulsion. Arab manuscripts of the twelfth century contain designs for rockets used for bombardment. If the Empire of Almanzar had been as advanced in biology as it was in other spheres, and if the plague had not assisted the Spaniards in its destruction, the Industrial Revolution would perhaps have started in Andalusia in the fifteenth or sixteenth century, and the twentieth would then have been the era of Arab interplanetary adventurers colonizing the Moon, Mars and Venus.

The Empire of Hitler, like that of Almanzar, collapsed in blood and fire. One fine morning in June 1940 the sky over Paris grew dark, the air was filled with petrol fumes, and under this immense cloud that blackened the faces of the population overcome by astonishment, terror and shame, millions of human beings took blindly to flight along roads raked by machine-gun fire. Whoever has lived through that experience, and known also the Twilight of the Gods of the Third Reich, can imagine what the end of Cordoba and Granada was like, and a thousand other ends of the world since time began. The end of the world for the Incas, for the Toltecs, for the Mayas: the whole history of humanity – an endless end. . . .

Easter Island, 3,000 kilometres from the coast of Chile, is about as big as Jersey. When the first European navigator, a Dutchman, landed there in 1722, he thought it was inhabited by giants. Towering over this little piece of volcanic land in Polynesia are 593 enormous statues. Some of them are more than 20 metres high and weigh 50 tons. When were they erected? and how? and for what purpose? Examination of these monuments reveals, it is thought, three levels of civilization, the most advanced one being the oldest. As in Egypt, the enormous blocks of tuff-stone, basalt and lava are adjusted with prodigious skill. The island, however, is hilly, and a few stunted trees could not have provided enough rollers; how, then, were these huge stones transported? Certainly there was no large labour-force available. In the nineteenth century the inhabitants of Easter Island numbered two hundred – three times less than the number of their statues, and there can never

* cf. Sprague de Camp and Willy Ley: *De l'Atlantide à l'Eldorado*; ed. Plon, Paris.
† cf. works of Professor Tolkien of Oxford.

113

have been more than three or four thousand inhabitants on this island where the soil is fertile, but there are no animals. What, then, are we to believe?

As happened in Africa and in South America, the first missionaries to arrive on Easter Island took steps to remove all traces of a dead civilization. At the foot of the statues there were wooden tablets covered with hieroglyphics: these were all burned or dispatched to the Vatican Library which houses many secrets. Was this done to destroy all traces of ancient superstitions, or to remove what could have been evidence of some Unknown Power? A record of the presence on the Earth of other beings – visitors from Elsewhere?

The first Europeans to visit Easter Island discovered that the inhabitants included a race of white men with beards. Where did they come from? The descendants, perhaps, of some degenerate race, in existence for many thousands of years and today completely submerged? There are references in legends to a Master Race of Teachers, of great antiquity, fallen from the skies.

Our friend, the Peruvian explorer and philosopher Daniel Ruzo, went off in 1952 to investigate the desert plateau of Marcahuasi situated at a height of 3,800 metres to the west of the Cordillera of the Andes.*

This plateau, where there is no life of any kind and which can only be approached on mule-back, covers an area of three square kilometres. Ruzo found there animal and human faces carved in the rock and visible only at the summer equinox, thanks to a particular combination of light and shade. He also found there statues of animals belonging to the secondary era such as the stegosaur; also lions, tortoises and camels which are unknown in South America.

One hill was carved in the shape of an old man's head. The negative of the photograph showed a radiant young man. . . . Visible, perhaps, at some initiation rite? It has not been possible to employ carbon 14 to ascertain the date; there are no organic traces on Marcahuasi. The geological indications go back to the remotest antiquity. Ruzo thinks that this plateau may have been the cradle of the Masma civilization, perhaps the oldest in the world.

There is evidence pointing to the existence of white men on another fabulous plateau, Tiahuanaco, at an altitude of 4,000 metres. When the Incas conquered this region round Lade Titicaca, Tiahuanaco was already the heap of gigantic, inexplicable ruins that we see today. When Pizarro arrived there in 1532, the Indians called their conquerors Viracochas: white masters. Their tradition, now more or less extinct, spoke of a master race of huge white men who had come out of space – Sons of the Sun. Many thousands of years ago these men had reigned over them and taught them. Suddenly they disappeared, but will return again. Everywhere in South America, Europeans in quest of gold heard of this tradition of the white man, and benefited by it. Their basest desires for conquest and gain were aided by these mysterious and lofty memories.

* Daniel Ruzo: *La culture Masma*. Revue de la Société d'Ethnographie de Paris, 1956 and 1959.

Modern exploration on the American continent has revealed traces of an extraordinarily advanced civilization. Cortez was amazed to discover that the Aztecs were as civilized as the Spaniards. We know today that they had inherited an even higher culture from the Toltecs. The Toltecs erected the most gigantic monuments in all America. The Pyramids of the Sun at Teotihuacan and Cholula are twice as large as the tomb of Cheops. But the Toltecs were themselves the descendants of an even more perfect civilization, that of the Mayas, the remains of which have been discovered in the jungles of Honduras, Guatemala and Yucatan. Buried under huge forests of dense vegetation are traces of a civilization far older than that of Greece, and some say superior. When and how did this civilization perish? It died a double death, in any case, for here, too, the missionaries made a point of destroying manuscripts, breaking statues, and demolishing altars. Summarizing the results of recent research on vanished civilizations, Raymond Cartier writes as follows:

'In many fields the science of the Mayas surpassed that of the Greeks and Romans. Possessing a profound knowledge of mathematics and astronomy, they had achieved a rare degree of perfection in chronology and everything pertaining to calendar-making. They built observatories whose domes were better orientated than the one erected in Paris in the seventeenth century – notably, the Caracol with its three terraces in their capital of Chichen Itza. They had adopted a sacred year of 260 days, a solar year of 365 days, and a Venusian year of 584 days. The exact duration of the solar year has been fixed at 365·2422 days. The Mayas put it at 365·2420 days – that is to say, within a decimal point of the number we have arrived at after lengthy calculations. It is possible that the Egyptians arrived at the same approximation, but to establish that we should have to believe in the concordances in the Pyramids which have been contested, whereas we actually possess the Maya calendar.

'Other analogies with Egypt are discernible in the admirable art of the Mayas. Their mural paintings and frescoes and decorated vases show a race of men with strongly marked Semitic features, engaged in all sorts of activities: agriculture, fishing, building, politics and religion. Egypt alone has depicted these activities with the same cruel verisimilitude; but the pottery of the Mayas recalls that of the Etruscans; their bas-reliefs remind one of India, and the huge, steep stairways of their pyramidal temples are like those at Angkor. Unless they obtained their models from outside, their brains must have been so constructed that they adopted the same forms of artistic expression as all the other great ancient civilizations of Europe and Asia. Did civilization, then, spring from one particular geographical region and then spread gradually in every direction like a forest fire? Or did it appear spontaneously and separately in various parts of the world? Were some races the teachers and others the pupils, or were they all self-taught? Isolated seeds, or one parent stem giving off shoots in every direction?'

We do not know, and we have no satisfactory explanation of the origins of civilizations such as these – nor of the ways in which they came to an end. According to Bolivian legends recorded in her book on Bolivia by Mme Cynthia Fain, the civilizations of antiquity collapsed after a struggle with a non-human race whose blood was not red. . . .

The high plateaus of Bolivia and Peru give an impression of being on another planet. This is not the Earth, but Mars. The oxygen pressure is 50 per cent less than at sea-level, and yet there are people living there at an altitude of 3,500 metres. They have two or three more pints of blood than we have, eight million red corpuscles instead of five, and their heart beats more slowly. The radio-carbon method of dating reveals the presence of human beings here 9,000 years ago. Certain recent calculations suggest that there may have been human life here 30,000 years ago. It is therefore by no means inconceivable that human beings, skilled in metal-working and possessing observatories and scientific knowledge may have built these giant cities 30,000 years ago. Under whose guidance?

Some of the irrigation works carried out by the pre-Inca peoples could hardly be done today by our electric turbo-drills. And why did men, before the invention of the wheel, construct enormous paved roads?

The American archaeologist Hyatt Verrill devoted thirty years of research to the lost civilizations of Central and South America. In his opinion, these ancient peoples did not use in their great building operations tools for cutting stone, but a kind of radio-active paste which ate into the granite; a sort of etching, in fact, on the scale of the great Pyramids. This radio-active paste, handed down from still more ancient times, Verrill claims to have seen in the hands of the last surviving sorcerers. In his fine novel, *The Bridge of Light*, he describes a pre-Inca city which can be approached only over a 'bridge of light', a bridge of ionized matter that appears and disappears at will, and provides a passage over a rocky gorge that is otherwise inaccessible. Up to the end of his life (he died at the age of eighty-four) Verrill maintained that his book was much more than a legend, and his wife, who has survived him, still makes this claim.

What do the figures at Nazca signify? I refer to the immense geometrical designs traced in the plain of Nazca which can only be seen from a plane or a balloon, and which have only recently been discovered, as a result of aeronautical exploration.

Professor Mason, who, unlike Verrill, can hardly be suspected of fantasy, is at a loss to know what to suggest. The builders could only have been guided by some sort of machine floating in the sky?

Mason rejects this hypothesis, and imagines that these figures were constructed by using a small-scale model or a stencilled plan. Given the level of technique of the pre-Incas, as allowed by classical archaeologists, this seems even more improbable. And what was the purpose of these tracings? Had they a religious

116

significance? That is always the stock explanation – a reference to an unknown religion. People are always more ready to suppose all kinds of strange beliefs rather than admit the possibility of other levels of consciousness and techniques. It is a question of priority: the knowledge we possess today is the only knowledge we recognize. Photographs taken of the plain of Nazca remind one irresistibly of the ground-lighting of an airfield. Sons of the Sun, coming from the sky. . . . Professor Mason is careful not to see any connection with these legends, and has imagined a kind of religion of trigonometry, which must be unique in the history of religious beliefs. Nevertheless, a little later he refers to the pre-Inca mythology according to which the stars are inhabited and the gods have come down from the constellation of the Pleiades.

We do not reject the possibility of visits from the inhabitants of another world, or of atomic civilizations that vanished without leaving a trace, or of stages of knowledge and techniques comparable to those of today, or of remnants of forgotten sciences surviving in various forms of what is known as esoterism, or of factual evidence of what we might call magic. We do not mean that we believe everything, but we shall show in the next chapter that the field of the humane sciences is probably much vaster than is believed. By integrating all facts and excluding none, and being willing to consider all the hypotheses suggested by those facts, without any kind of *a priorism*, a Darwin or a Copernicus of anthropology will create a completely new science, provided they also establish a constant connection between the objective observation of the past and the latest developments in parapsychology, physics, chemistry and mathematics. They will then, perhaps, perceive that the idea of the evolution of intelligence being always slow, and the road to knowledge always long, is not, perhaps, the truth, but rather a taboo that we have set up in order that we may believe ourselves today to be enjoying the benefits of the whole history of mankind.

Why should not the civilizations of the past have experienced sudden periods of enlightenment during which the quasi-totality of all human knowledge was revealed to them? Is there any reason why the moments of illumination, of blinding intuition, and the sudden explosion of genius that occur in the life of a man should not have occurred several times in the life of the human race? Are we not suggesting an entirely false interpretation of such evidence of these moments as has come down to us by talking of mythology, legends and magic? If I am shown an unfaked photograph of a man floating in the air, I do not say: That represents the myth of Icarus, but: That is a snapshot of a high jump or a man diving. Why should there not be similar instantaneous states in the life of civilizations?

We shall be citing other facts, establishing other connections and formulating other hypotheses in due course. Our book, we repeat, will doubtless contain a lot of nonsense, but that is of no importance if it inspires some readers with a sense of vocation and, to a certain extent, opens up new and wider paths for research.

We authors are only a couple of poor stone-breakers; others
will follow and make the road.

IV

*Memory older than us – Metallic birds – A strange map of
the world – Atomic bombardments and interplanetary vessels
in 'sacred texts' – A new view of machines – The cult of the
'cargo' – Another vision of esoterism – The rites of the
intelligence*

DURING the last ten years the exploration of the past has been
facilitated by the discovery of new methods based on radio-activity
and by the progress of cosmology. As a result, two extraordinary
facts have been established:*

(1) The Earth is as old as the Universe: some 4,500 million years.
It was probably formed at the same time as, and perhaps before,
the Sun, by the condensation of particles at low temperature.

(2) Man as we know him, *homo sapiens*, has only existed for
some 75,000 years. This short period saw the transition from
prehistoric man to man. Here we would like to ask two questions:

(*a*) In the course of these 75,000 years have there been other
'technical' civilizations before our own? The specialists, as one
man, answer No. But it is by no means clear that they are able
to distinguish an instrument, or tool, from what is called an
object of worship. In this field research has not even begun.
Nevertheless, there are some disquieting problems to examine.
Most palaeontologists consider eoliths (stones discovered near
Orleans in 1867) to be natural objects. Some, however, believe
them to be man-made. But by what kind of man? Not *homo
sapiens*. Other objects have been found at Ipswich, in Suffolk,
which are believed to indicate the existence in Western Europe
of 'tertiary' man.

(*b*) The experiments of Washburn and Dice prove that the
evolution of man may have been brought about by quite trivial
modifications. For example: a slight alteration in the bones of
the skull.†

Thus, a single mutation, and not, as had hitherto been believed,
a complex combination of mutations, would have been enough to
effect the transition from prehistoric Man to modern Man.

Only one mutation in 4,500 million years? It is possible, but why
should it be a certainty? Why should there not have been several
evolutionary cycles before this period of 75,000 years? It may be
that other forms of humanity, or rather other thinking beings, made
their appearance and disappeared. They may not have left visible
traces, but their memory is preserved in legends. 'The bust outlives
the city': their memory may be perpetuated in power houses, and

* cf. Dr. Bowen: *The Exploration of Time*, London, 1958.
† To prove the correctness of his theory, Washburn changed the skull
formation of rats from a 'Neanderthaloid' to a 'modern' shape.

machines, monuments to their vanished civilizations. Our memory perhaps goes back much farther than our own existence, or even than the existence of our species. What records of an infinitely remote past may not be dissimulated in our genes and chromosomes? *'D'où te vient ceci, âme de l'homme, d'où te vient ceci?'* . . .

In archaeology big changes have already taken place. Our civilization has speeded up communications, and observations carried out all over the globe and then collected and compared bring us to the brink of great mysteries. In June 1958 the Smithsonian Institute published the results obtained by American, Indian and Russian archaeologists.* In the course of excavations carried out in Mongolia, Scandinavia, Ceylon, near Lake Baikal and in the upper reaches of the Lena in Siberia, similar objects in bone and stone were discovered as those found among the Eskimos.

Now the techniques required for the manufacture of these objects do not exist among the Eskimos. The Smithsonian Institute therefore deduced that ten thousand years ago the Eskimos inhabited Central Asia, Ceylon and Mongolia. Later it is assumed that they suddenly emigrated to Greenland. But why? What caused these primitive peoples to decide, all at the same time, to leave these countries and settle in this inhospitable corner of the globe? And how did they get there? To this day they do not know that the Earth is round, and have no idea of geography. And why should they have left Ceylon, that earthly paradise? The Institute does not attempt to answer these questions.

We do not wish to impose our own theory, and only propose it as a kind of exercise in open-mindedness: Ten thousand years ago an enlighted civilization controlled the world. It set up in the Frozen North a zone of deportation. Now what do we find in Eskimo folk-lore? References to tribes being transported to the Frozen North at the beginning of time by giant metallic birds. Nineteenth-century archaeologists have always scoffed at these 'metallic birds'. And what do we think?

No work on objects of a more clearly defined character has as yet been done comparable to that accomplished by the Smithsonian Institute. On lenses, for example. Optical lenses have been found in Irak and Central Australia. The question is: do they come from the same source, the same civilization? No modern optician has yet been asked to give an opinion. All optical glasses for the last twenty years, in our civilization, have been polished with ceria. In a thousand years from now spectroscopic analysis will prove, from an analysis of these glasses, the existence of a single civilization all over the world. And that will be the truth.

A new vision of the ancient world might result from studies of this nature. We can only hope that our book, in spite of being light-weight and poorly documented, may inspire some still naïve young man to embark on a crazy enterprise which will one day provide him with the key to the wisdom of the past.

* cf. *New York Herald Tribune*, 11th June, 1958.

119

There are still other facts to be noted.

Over vast areas in the desert of Gobi patches of vitrified soil have been observed similar to those produced by an atomic explosion.

In the caves of Bohistan inscriptions have been found, accompanied by astronomical maps showing the stars in the positions they occupied thirteen thousand years ago. Lines connect Venus with the Earth.

In the middle of the nineteenth century a Turkish naval officer, Piri Reis, presented the Library of Congress with a set of maps which he had discovered in the East. The most recent date from the time of Christopher Columbus; the oldest from the first century A.D., the former having been copied from the latter. In 1952 Arlington H. Mallery, a well-known expert in cartography, examined these documents.* He noticed, for example, that everything that exists in the Mediterranean had been recorded, but not in the right relationship. Did these people think the Earth was flat? This is not a sufficient explanation. Did they use the projection method in drawing up their maps, taking into account the fact that the Earth is round? Impossible; projective geometry dates from the time of Monge. Mallery then entrusted the study of these maps to an official cartographer, Walters, who compared them with a modern globe map of the World, and found that they were all correct, not only for the Mediterranean, but for all the countries of the world, including the two Americas and the Antarctic. In 1955 Mallery and Walters submitted their work to the Geophysical Year Committee. The Committee passed the file to the Jesuit Father Daniel Lineham, director of the Weston Observatory and in charge of the cartographical department of the American Navy. Father Lineham confirmed that the contours of North America, the location of the lakes and mountains of Canada, the coastal outline of the extreme north of the continent and the contours of the Antarctic (covered with ice and distinguishable only with the greatest difficulty by our modern instruments of measurement) were all correct. Were these copies of still earlier maps? Had they been traced from observations made on board a flying machine or space vessel of some kind? Notes taken by visitors from Beyond?

We shall doubtless be criticized for asking these questions. Yet the *Popul Vuh*, the sacred Book of the Quichés of America speaks of an infinitely ancient civilization which knew about the nebulae and the whole solar system. This is what we read: 'The first race of men were capable of all knowledge. They examined the four corners of the horizon, the four (cardinal) points of the firmament, and the *round surface* of the Earth.'

'Some of the beliefs and legends bequeathed to us by Antiquity are so universally and firmly established that we have become accustomed to consider them as being almost as ancient as humanity

* All this was the subject of a debate at Georgetown University in December 1958. See the study by Ivan T. Sanderson in *Fantastic Universe*, January 1959.

itself. Nevertheless we are tempted to inquire how far the fact that some of these beliefs and legends have so many features in common is due to chance, and whether the similarity between them may not point to the existence of an ancient, totally unknown and unsuspected civilization of which all other traces have disappeared.'

The man who, in 1910, wrote these lines was neither a writer of science-fiction, nor some vague dabbler in the occult. He was one of the pioneers of science, Professor Frederick Soddy, Nobel Prize winner and the discoverer of isotopes and of the laws of transformation in natural radio-activity.*

The University of Oklahoma in 1954 published some records of Indian tribes in Guatemala dating from the sixteenth century. These contained fantastic accounts of apparitions of legendary beings and imaginary descriptions of the private life of their gods. On closer examination it became clear that the Indians were not just spinning yarns, but referring in their own way to their first contacts with the Spanish invaders, whom the Indian 'historians' looked upon as beings of the same order as those that figured in their own mythology. In this way reality is disguised as legend. Indeed, it is highly probable that texts considered as belonging purely to folk-lore or mythology may be based on actual facts that have been wrongly interpreted and integrated with others which are, in fact, imaginary. All this has not yet been sorted out, with the result that while the shelves of our specialized libraries are loaded with a whole literature labelled 'legend', no one has ever thought for a moment that this label may conceal picturesquely presented accounts of events that actually happened.

And yet, with our knowledge of modern science and techniques, we ought to examine this literature with an unprejudiced eye.

The book of Dzyan speaks of 'superior beings of dazzling aspect' who abandoned the Earth, depriving the impure human race of its knowledge, and effacing by disintegration all traces of their passage. They departed in flying chariots, propelled by light, to rejoin their land 'of iron and metal'.

In a recent study published in the *Literaturnava Gazeta* (1959) Professor Agrest, who accepts the hypothesis of the Earth having been visited long ago by interplanetary travellers, relates his discovery among the first texts introduced into the Bible by Jewish priests of references to beings from another world who, like Enoch, disappeared into the heavens in mysterious ark-like vessels. The sacred Hindu texts, such as the *Ramayana* and the *Maha Bharatra*, contain descriptions of airships appearing in the sky at the very beginning of time and looking like 'blueish clouds in the shape of an egg or a luminous globe'.

They could encircle the Earth several times, and were propelled by 'an ethereal force which struck the ground as they rose', or by 'a vibration produced by an invisible force'. They emitted 'sweet and

* Professor at Oxford University, Fellow of the Royal Society. The passage is taken from his book *Radium*.

melodious sounds', and 'a shining light as bright as fire', and their trajectory was not straight, but appeared 'to follow a long and undulating course bringing them alternately nearer to and farther from the Earth'. The material of which these engines were composed is defined, in these texts more than three thousand years old and doubtless based on memories going back infinitely farther into the past, as being a blend of several metals, some white and light, others red.

In the *Mausola Purva* we find this singular description, which must have been incomprehensible to nineteenth-century ethnologists though not to us today: '. . . it was an unknown weapon, an iron thunderbolt, a gigantic messenger of death which reduced to ashes the entire race of the Vrishnis and the Andhakas. The corpses were so burned as to be unrecognizable. Their hair and nails fell out; pottery broke without any apparent cause, and the birds turned white. After a few hours, all food-stuffs were infected. The thunderbolt was reduced to a fine dust.'

And again: 'Cukra, flying on board a high-powered *vimana*, hurled on to the triple city a single projectile charged with all the power of the Universe. An incandescent column of smoke and flame, as bright as ten thousand Suns, rose in all its splendour. . . . When the *vimana* returned to Earth, it looked like a splendid block of antinomy resting on the ground. . . .'

Objection: if you admit the existence of such fabulously advanced civilizations, how do you explain the fact that the innumerable excavations that have been carried out all over the globe have never brought to light a single fragment of any object that could induce us to believe in such civilizations?

Answer: (1) Systematic archaeological exploration has been going on for little more than a century, whereas our atomic civilization is barely twenty years old. No serious exploration has been carried out in South Russia, China, or in Central and South Africa. Vast areas still preserve the secrets of their past.

(2) If a German engineer, Wilhelm König, had not paid a chance visit to the Museum at Baghdad, it might never have been discovered that some flat stones found in Irak, and classified as such, were in reality electric batteries, that had been in use two thousand years before Galvani. The archaeological museums are full of objects classified as 'objects of worship', or 'various', about which nothing is known.

The Russians recently discovered in some caves in the desert of Gobi and in Turkestan semicircular objects made of ceramics or glass ending in a cone containing a drop of mercury. What could these have been? Finally, few archaeologists have any scientific or technical knowledge. Still fewer are capable of realizing that a technical problem can be solved in several different ways, and that there are machines which do not resemble what we call machines – without crankshafts, driving-rods or cogwheels. A few lines traced with special ink on specially prepared paper serve as a receiver for electro-magnetic waves. A simple copper tube acts as a resonator in the production of radar waves. Diamonds are sensitive to nuclear and cosmic radiation. Complicated recordings can be contained in crystals, and may there not be whole libraries enclosed in small cut stones? Suppose that a thousand years hence, after the extinction of our civilization, some future archaeologist discovered, say, some magnetic bands – what would he make of them? And how would he distinguish between a virgin band and one that had been used for a recording?

Today we are on the brink of discovering the secrets of anti-matter and anti-gravitation. Tomorrow we do not know whether the manipulation of these secrets will call for cumbersome or, on the contrary, for surprisingly light machinery. As techniques develop, they do not become more complex; rather, they tend to become simpler, until the apparatus they require shrinks almost to zero. In his book *Magie Chaldéenne* (Chaldean Magic) Lenormand citing a legend which recalls the Orpheus myth, wrote that: 'In olden times the priests of On, by means of sounds, caused high winds to blow and thus raised into the air huge stones to build their temples which a thousand men could not have lifted.'

I quote now from Walter Owen: 'Sound vibrations are forces. . . . Cosmic creation is sustained by vibrations which could equally well bring it to an end.' This theory is not so far removed from modern conceptions. Tomorrow will be fantastic, as everyone knows. Perhaps it will be doubly so if it rids us of the idea that yesterday was banal.

We regard tradition, that is to say, the *corpus* of the most ancient texts known to humanity, entirely from a literary, religious or philosophical point of view. What if it really consisted of immemorial memories, recorded by peoples living long after the events themselves which have since been transposed and embroidered? Immemorial memories of civilizations that were technically and scientifically quite as advanced, and perhaps infinitely more so, than our own?

What has tradition to tell us, if we adopt this view?

In the first place, that science is dangerous. This idea might have seemed surprising to a nineteenth-century man. But we know now that two bombs on Nagasaki and Hiroshima were enough to kill 300,000 people, that these bombs are now completely obsolete, and that one cobalt bomb of 500 tons could destroy all life over the greater part of the globe.

We know, too, that it is possible to make contact with non-terrestrial beings. What was an absurdity in the nineteenth century is no longer one for us. It is not inconceivable that there are Universes parallel with our own with which communication might be established.*

Radio-telescopes receive waves emitted ten thousand million light years ago and modulated in such a way as to resemble messages. The astronomer John Krauss, of the University of Ohio,

* This idea is frequently met with in modern research. See, e.g.: the review *Atomic Industries*, No. 1, 1958, page 17, article by E. C. G. Stuckelberg.

claims to have captured signals coming from Venus on 2nd June, 1956. Other signals from Jupiter, it is alleged, were received at the Princeton Institute.

Finally, tradition asserts that everything that has happened since the beginning of time has left an impression in matter, in space and in all sources of energy, and can be revealed. This is exactly what is asserted by the distinguished scientist Bowen in his book *The Exploration of Time*, and this view is shared today by the majority of investigators.

Another objection: a highly developed technical and scientific civilization does not disappear completely without leaving any trace.

Reply: 'We civilizations know now that we are mortal.' It is precisely the most highly developed techniques that threaten to cause the civilization of which they are a product to disappear completely. Take the case of our own civilization in the near future. All power stations, weapons, transmitting and receiving apparatus in telecommunications, all electric and nuclear instruments – in short, all our technological equipment is based on the same principle of the production of energy. As a result of some chain reaction all these instruments, from the largest to the smallest, might at any time explode. In this way every trace of the material and the greater part of the human potential of a civilization would disappear. All that would remain would be things that threw no light on that civilization, and men who were more or less excluded from it. The survivors would relapse into a state of primitive simplicity. Only memories would remain, unskilfully and in-accurately recorded after the catastrophe: stories of a mythical and legendary character through which might run the theme of expulsion from an earthly paradise and the feeling that there are great dangers and great secrets hidden at the heart of matter. Everything begins again, as in the Book of Revelation: 'The Moon became as blood . . . and the Heaven departed as a scroll when it is rolled together. . . .'

Australian Government patrols exploring in 1946 unknown regions in New Guinea found there tribes in a state of great religious excitement over a new cult – the cult of the 'cargo' – which had just been inaugurated. This arose out of the arrival of various commodities – paraffin lamps, bottles of alcohol, tins of preserves and the like, which had been sent for native consumption. For men still living in the Stone Age, sudden contact with riches of this kind must have been an overwhelming experience. But could the white men have produced all these things themselves? Impossible.

No white men they had ever seen could possible have made anything wonderful with their hands. Let us be clear about this – one can imagine the natives of New Guinea saying to one another – Have you ever seen a white man making anything? No; but they do engage in mysterious activities: they all dress alike, and sometimes they sit in front of a metal box with dials on it and listen to the strange sounds that emerge from it. They also make signs on sheets of white paper. These are magic rites, thanks to which they obtain this 'cargo' from the gods. The natives thereupon tried to copy these 'rites'; they tried to dress in European style, talked into tins of preserves, and put bamboo branches on the roofs of their huts in imitation of wireless antennae. They also constructed false landing-grounds in anticipation of the arrival of the 'cargo'.

Now let us suppose that our ancestors had interpreted in the same sort of way their contacts with superior civilizations? We should still have tradition, i.e. the teaching of 'rites' which were, in reality, perfectly legitimate ways of acting in the presence of knowledge of a different, unfamiliar order. We should have childishly copied attitudes, gestures and practices without understanding them and without connecting them with a whole system of complex realities beyond our comprehension, in the expectation that these gestures and these attitudes would produce for us tangible results. Results that never materialized – a kind of Manna from Heaven produced by means impossible for us to imagine. It is easier to accept a ritual than to gain access to knowledge, easier to invent gods than to understand techniques. Nevertheless, I wish to make it plain that neither Bergier nor myself are trying to equate all spirituality with material ignorance. On the contrary; we believe there is such a thing as a spiritual life. If God is higher than all reality, we shall find God when we know everything that is reality. And if man possesses powers which enable him to understand the whole Universe, God is perhaps the whole Universe, *plus* something else.

Another question now arises: supposing what we call esoterism were in fact only a form of exotericism? What if the most ancient texts known to humanity, sacred in our eyes, were nothing but spurious interpretations, haphazard vulgarizations, third-hand reports of somewhat inaccurate memories of technical realities? We interpret these old sacred texts as if they were unquestionably the expression of spiritual 'truths', philosophical symbols or religious images. This is because, when we read them, we are thinking only of ourselves, preoccupied as we are with our own little private mysteries: I love good and do evil; I am alive and am going to die, etc. Their message is for *us*: all these engines, and thunderbolts and Manna from Heaven and apocalyptic visions represent the world of *our* thoughts and feelings. It's all for *my* benefit, and concerns *me* and *my* affairs. . . . But what if we are only confronted with distant, distorted memories of other worlds which have existed, and of the sojourn on this Earth of other beings who were seeking something, who possessed knowledge and who put their knowledge into practice?

Imagine a time very long ago when messages coming from other intelligent beings in the Universe were intercepted and interpreted when interplanetary visitors had set up a network on the Earth and organized a cosmic traffic. Imagine that hidden in some sanctuary somewhere there are still in existence notes and diagrams and reports that have been deciphered with the greatest difficulty throughout the ages by monks entrusted with these ancient secrets;

incapable of understanding their full significance, but ceaselessly engaged in interpreting and extrapolating their message. Exactly like the witch-doctors of New Guinea trying to understand a sheet of paper containing the time-table of flights between New York and San Francisco. As an extreme example, there is Gurdjieff's book, *Tales of Beelzebub*, full of references to unknown concepts and to a fantastic language.

Gurdjieff claimed to have access to 'sources' – sources which were themselves only deviations. He was translating at a thousand removes, and adding his own ideas; representing symbolically the human psychism: a perfect example of esotericism.

From the prospectus of an internal airline in the U.S.A.: 'You can reserve your seat anywhere. Your application will be recorded by an electronic robot. Another robot will reserve your seat on whatever plane you wish. Your ticket will be issued to you already made out . . . etc.' Now imagine what that would look like, after being translated for the thousandth time, in an Amazonian dialect, by people who have never seen an aeroplane, have no idea what a robot is and who have never heard of the cities mentioned in the guide. Then think of an esoteric studying this text, going back to the sources of ancient wisdom and seeking what message it may contain for the guidance of the human soul. . . .

If there have been in the far distant past civilizations built on a system of specialized knowledge, there must have been textbooks. It is thought that the cathedrals are the textbooks, so to speak, of the science of alchemy. It may well be that some of these textbooks, or fragments of them, have been found and piously preserved and copied over and over again by monks whose duty it was not so much to understand them as to hold them in safe-keeping.

Copied and re-copied indefinitely; illuminated, transposed and interpreted not in terms of this ancient, profound and complex knowledge, but in terms of the relative ignorance of a succeeding age. In the last resort, however, all real scientific or technical knowledge carried to its highest level implies a profound knowledge of the nature of mind and of the resources of the psyche functioning at the highest level of consciousness. If these 'esoteric' texts – even if they are only what we have just been saying – have enabled men to attain this high level of consciousness, then they have, in a sense, provided a link with the splendour of vanished civilizations. It is also conceivable that there were two kinds of 'sacred texts': fragments containing evidence of the existence of a very ancient technology, and fragments of purely religious books, inspired by God

The two have probably been confused in the absence of any references that would help to distinguish one from the other. And in both cases the texts would be equally sacred.

Sacred, too, is the adventure, forever recommencing and yet forever advancing, of intelligence on the Earth, and no less sacred the light in which God looks upon this adventure and by which it is guided.

Part Two

A FEW YEARS IN THE ABSOLUTE ELSEWHERE

I

*All the marbles in the same bag – The historian's despair –
Two amateurs of the unusual – At the bottom of the Devil's
Lake – An empty anti-fascism – The authors in the presence
of the Infinitely Strange – Troy, too, was only a legend – His-
tory lags behind – From visible banality to invisible fantasy
– The fable of the golden beetle – Undercurrents of the future –
There are other things besides soul-less machinery*

DURING the Occupation there lived on the Left Bank in Paris an
eccentric old man who used to dress in seventeenth-century
costume, read nothing but Saint-Simon, dined by candlelight and
played the spinet. He never went out except to buy his bread and
groceries, with a hood over his powdered wig and his nether limbs
encased in black stockings and shoes. The noise and confusion of
the Liberation, the shooting and the crowds disturbed him. Not
knowing what it was all about, but impelled by anger and fear he
came out one morning on his balcony, waving his quill pen, his
costume all awry, and crying in a loud, strange voice: 'Vive Coblenz!'

Nobody understood; the excited neighbours, struck by this
singular behaviour felt instinctively that this queer fellow, living
in another world, was in league with the powers of evil; what he
was shouting sounded German, so into the house they rushed,
broke open his door, felled him to the ground and left him for dead.

That same morning a young Captain in the Resistance who had
just captured the Prefecture, had straw thrown all over the carpet in
the great central office and the firearms arranged in panoplies so that
he could feel he was living in a picture out of his first history book.

At the same time, patrols discovered in the Invalides the table
and thirteen chairs and the standards, robes and cross of the last
assembly of the Knights of the Teutonic Order which had been
suddenly interrupted.

And the first tank of Leclerc's army was just rumbling in through
the Porte d'Orléans, overwhelming proof of the German defeat.
It was driven by Henri Rathenau, whose uncle Walther had been
the Nazis' first victim.

In this way a civilization, at a historic moment, like a man in the
midst of a violent emotional crisis, seems to live again in a thousand
flash-backs from its past, the nature and order of these impressions
being determined by apparently incomprehensible factors.

Giraudoux used to tell the story of how, while dozing for a
moment in a trench before going out to take the place of a comrade
who had been killed while out on reconnaissance, he was awakened

by something tickling his face: the wind had been blowing the dead man's clothes about, had opened his wallet and was scattering his visiting cards; and it was these the poet now felt on his cheek. On this morning of the Liberation of Paris, the visiting cards of the *emigrés* from Coblenz, of the revolutionary students of 1830, of the great German Jewish thinkers and of the Knights of the Crusade, along, no doubt, with many others, were fluttering in the wind which carried with it far and wide the sound of groaning mingled with the strains of countless *Marseillaises*.

When you shake the basket, all the marbles come to the surface in disorder, or rather in obedience to an order and series of movements of an infinitely complicated nature in which, nevertheless, we might discover an infinite number of those strangely illuminating encounters which Jung calls 'significant coincidences'. Jacques Rivière's admirable dictum applies to civilizations and their historic moments: 'A man does not get what he deserves, but what he resembles.' One of Napoleon's school exercise books ends with these words: 'Saint Helena: a small island.'

It is a great pity that the historian thinks that it would be beneath his dignity to record and examine these 'significant coincidences' and chance encounters which mean something and suddenly throw open a door giving on to another side of the Universe where time is no longer linear. His science lags behind science in general, which, in its study of man no less than of matter, shows us that the distances between past, present and future are for ever growing smaller. Thinner and thinner hedges, in the garden of our destiny, separate us from a perfectly preserved Yesterday and a completely formed Tomorrow. Our life, as Alain remarked, 'is on the brink of wide open spaces'.

There is a very delicate and beautiful little flower called the saxifrage. It has also been called 'the despair of painters'. This is no longer true, since photography and many other discoveries have freed artists from having to worry about external resemblances.

Even the least advanced painter does not look at a bunch of flowers in the same way that he used to. His eye sees more than the bunch of flowers; or, rather, he sees in it a model which enables him to express under a coloured surface a reality invisible to an uninitiated eye. He is trying to make creation yield up a secret.

In another age he would have been content to reproduce what the ordinary man sees when he looks at something casually without paying any particular attention. He would have been content to reproduce a reassuring likeness and to connive, as it were in the general conspiracy of deceitfulness with regard to the external aspect of reality. We say a picture is 'the very spit' of its model. But spitting is a sign of illness. It would seem that historians have not developed in the same way as artists have during the last fifty years, and the history we are taught today is as false as a woman's breast, or a kitten or a bunch of flowers used to be under the stereotyped brush of a conformist painter of the 1890s.

'If our generation,' said a young historian, 'wants to form a clear opinion of the past, it will first have to tear off the masks which prevent the real artisans of our history from being given their due. . . . The disinterested efforts of a group of historians in favour of the unvarnished truth are a comparatively recent development.'

Certain things were the 'despair' of the painter of the 1890s. But what about the historian of the present day!

Most contemporary events, like the saxifrage, have become the 'despair of the historian'.

A self-taught madman, surrounded by a handful of megalo-maniacs, rejects Descartes, spurns the whole humanist culture, tramples on reason, invokes Lucifer, conquers Europe, and nearly conquers the world. Marxism is implanted in the only country which Marx himself thought would be impervious to it. London nearly perishes under a rain of rockets designed to reach the Moon. Speculations on the nature of space and time result in the fabrication of a bomb which wipes out 200,000 people in three seconds and threatens to wipe out history itself. Shades of the little saxifrage!

The historian begins to feel anxious and to wonder whether his art is viable. He devotes his talents to deploring the fact that he is unable to exercise them. This can be seen in the arts and sciences in their moments of suffocation: a writer discourses in ten volumes on the impossibility of language; a doctor gives a five-year course of lectures to explain that diseases cure themselves. History is now going through one of these phases.

M. Raymond Aron, turning his back on Thucydides and Marx, comes to the conclusion that neither human passions nor economics are capable of explaining the social adventure. 'The sum-total of causes that determine the sum-total of effects,' he remarks bitterly, 'are beyond human understanding.'

M. Baudin of the Institute confesses: 'History is a blank page that men are free to fill in as they please.'

And M. René Grousset exclaims, almost in despair: 'Is what we call history, by which I mean a succession of empires, political revolutions, and dates for the most part sanguinary, really history?

I confess that I do not think so myself, and that when I look at school textbooks I often feel inclined to delete a good quarter of their contents. . . . 'True history is not a matter of shifting frontiers, but the history of civilization. And civilization means on the one hand technical progress, and on the other progress in the things of the mind. I wonder whether political history is not very largely a parasite of history. True history, from the material standpoint, is the history of techniques obscured by political history which over-shadows it and usurps not only its rightful place but its very name. But true history is even more the history of man's progress in the spiritual world. The function of humanity is to help spiritual man to escape and find himself – to help man, as the Indians have so well expressed it, to become what he is. There is no doubt that history as it appears to us superficially is nothing but a charnel-house. But if history were nothing more than that, the best we could

129

do would be to close the book and hope for oblivion in Nirvana. . . .
But I would like to think that Buddhism has lied and that history
is something more than that.'

The physicist, the biologist, the chemist, the psychologist have all
during the last fifty years had plenty of shocks and come up against
plenty of umbrageous saxifrages, like the others. But today they
do not show the same anxiety. They go on working and advancing.
In fact, the sciences are full of an extraordinary vitality. Compare
the gossamer-like constructions of a Spengler or a Toynbee with the
torrential progress of nuclear physics. History is in a backwater.

There are doubtless several reasons for this, but we incline to
think the following may be the true one: Whereas the physicist or
the psychoanalyst has resolutely given up thinking that reality
is necessarily satisfactory to our reason, and has opted for the
reality of the fantastic, the historian is still a believer in the Cartesian system – an attitude not altogether exempt from a certain
kind of political pusillanimity.

It is said that nations that are happy have no history. But those
that have no historians who are at the same time sharpshooters and
poets are more than unhappy: they are asphyxiated and betrayed.
By turning his back on the fantastic, the historian is sometimes led
into fantastic errors. As a Marxist, he foresees the collapse of the
American economy at a time when the United States is at the
height of its prosperity and power. As a capitalist, he sees
communism spreading through the West only to be confronted
with the revolt of Hungary. In the other sciences, however, fore-
casts as to the future based on present tendencies are more and
more successful.

Starting with a millionth of a gramme of plutonium, the nuclear
physicist plans a gigantic factory which will function exactly as
intended. Starting from a few dreams, Freud brings more light to
bear on the human soul than has ever been brought before. The
fact is that Freud and Einstein in the early stages did immensely
imaginative work. They conceived a 'reality' entirely different from
the generally accepted rational view of the nature of things. Starting
from this imaginative projection they established a body of facts
which experience has proved to be true.

'In the field of science,' said Oppenheimer, 'we learn how vastly
strange the world is.' It is our conviction that history will be
enriched by this admission of strangeness.

We certainly do not claim to have introduced into historical
methods the changes we would like to see. But we think that what
follows now may be of some slight service to future historians,
whether they accept or reject its implications. In choosing as a
subject for investigation an aspect of Hitler's Germany we hope
this may suggest a general line of research that could be used for
other purposes. We have marked the trees in our path with arrows,
but do not claim to have mapped out the whole forest.

We have tried to assemble facts which a 'conventional' historian would reject in anger or in horror. We have turned ourselves for a moment into what Maurice Renard calls: 'Amateurs of the unusual and chroniclers of miracles.' This sort of work is not always very agreeable, but we have consoled ourselves with the reflection that the tetralogy, or study of monsters in which Professor Wolff had distinguished himself, despite the suspicions of the 'rational' scientists, has thrown new light on more than one aspect of biology. We have also been fortified by the example of Charles Fort, the wily American of whom we have already spoken.

Indeed, it is very much in the same spirit as this that we have carried out our researches into the events of recent history, and consequently have thought it worth pointing out that the founder of National-Socialism really believed in the advent of the Superman.

On 25th February, 1957, a frogman was searching for the body of a student drowned in the Devil's Lake in Czechoslovakia. He came to the surface white as a sheet, terrified and unable to utter a word. When he had recovered his speech he declared that he had just seen a phantom array of German soldiers in uniform lying on the bottom of the lake, together with a caravan of chariots and horses in their harness standing upright. . . .

We, too, after a fashion, have plunged into the Devil's Lake. From the records of the Nuremberg Trial, from thousands of books and reviews, and from the testimony of eyewitnesses we have formed a collection of the strangest facts. We have organized our material to fit in with a working hypothesis which, though perhaps scarcely deserving to be termed a theory, has been vividly expressed by a great, but neglected English writer, Arthur Machen: 'There exist in the world around us sacraments for evil as well as for good, and our life and actions are played out in an undreamt of world, full of caverns and shades and twilight beings. . . .'

The human soul loves the light of day. Sometimes it also loves night no less ardently, and such a love can lead men as well as collectivities to perform criminal and disastrous actions in apparent defiance of reason, but which can yet be explained if one looks at them from a certain standpoint. We will enlarge on this later, with a further quotation from Arthur Machen.

In this part of our book our aim has been to provide raw material for an invisible history. We are not the first to do so. John Buchan had already drawn attention to some singular underground currents running beneath historical events. A German entomologist, Margaret Boveri, examining men with the same cold objectivity that she brings to the observation of insects, has written a *History of Treason in the Twentieth Century*, the first volume of which is entitled *Visible History*, and the second *Invisible History*.

But what sort of invisible history is she dealing with? The term is full of pitfalls. The visible side is already so rich and, indeed, up to now so little explored, that one can always find facts that justify any theory; and there are innumerable ways of explaining history in terms of mysterious activities on the part of Jews, Freemasons, Jesuits, or the International Bank. Such explanations seem to us rudimentary. Moreover, we have always been careful not to confuse what we call fantastic realism with occultism, or the secret main-springs of reality with cheap fiction. (We have noticed, however, that reality is often lacking in dignity and sometimes borders on the romantic, so that we have not been able to eliminate facts merely because they seem to belong to the world of fiction.)

We have therefore admitted facts however bizarre, subject to verification later. Sometimes we have preferred to appear to be in search of the sensational or to allow ourselves to be carried away by our love of everything strange, rather than neglect some incident or event however crazy it may seem. Consequently our study in no way resembles the generally accepted picture of Nazi Germany. That is not our fault. What we had to study was a series of fantastic events. It is not customary, but it is logical to think that behind these events may be hidden some very extraordinary realities. Why should history alone among other modern sciences be privileged to explain all phenomena rationally?

Our picture certainly does not conform to generally accepted ideas on the subject, and it is incomplete. We were determined to sacrifice nothing for the sake of coherence. This attitude, moreover, reflects a quite recent tendency in history, and so does the desire for truth: 'There will be lacunae here and there: the reader will have to conclude that the historian of today has abandoned the old idea that the truth would emerge if all the pieces in the puzzle were put together without leaving any gaps or adding anything. He no longer believes that the ideal work of history is like a beautiful mosaic, smooth and complete; rather he conceives it as a kind of excavation site, with all its apparent chaos where are to be found side by side with objects of doubtful value or mildly evocative relics, real works of art, genuine resurrection from the past.'

The physicist knows that it was the abnormal, exceptional pulsation of energy that led to the discovery of uranium fission, thus opening up unlimited fields for the study of radio-activity. The object of our researches has been the pulsations of the extraordinary.

Lord Russell of Liverpool's book, *The Scourge of the Swastika*, published eleven years after the Allied victory, surprised French readers by its extreme sobriety. Usually in matters of this sort indignation takes the place of explanation.

In this book horrible facts speak for themselves, and its readers discovered that they were still unable to understand such depths of villainy. Expressing this attitude, an eminent specialist wrote in *Le Monde*: 'The question that arises is: How was all that possible in the middle of the twentieth century and in countries considered to be the most civilized in the world?'

It is strange that historians should be asking themselves this essential, fundamental question twelve years after having had access to all conceivable archives. But are they in fact asking it? It is by no means certain. In any case, everything suggests that they have been trying to forget it, as soon as it arises, in deference to established public opinion which finds such a question embarrassing. And so we find the modern historian's contribution to the history of our time is to refuse to write that history. No sooner has he written: 'The question that arises is how etc. . . .' than he hastens to prevent it from being asked; by adding immediately: 'This just shows what men will do when they give way to their unbridled and systematically perverted instincts.'

A strange way to explain the Nazi mystery by looking at it from the standpoint of conventional morality! And yet this is the only explanation put forward, as if there were a vast conspiracy in informed circles to reduce one of the most fantastic episodes of contemporary history to the level of an elementary history lesson on evil instincts. It would appear as if pressure were being brought to bear so as to scale history down to fit the extreme timidity of conventional rationalist thought.

As a young philosopher has pointed out: 'Having failed to denounce between the two wars the pagan frenzy by which the enemy was possessed, the anti-fascists could not foresee the odious consequences that would follow Hitler's victory.'

Those who proclaimed that in Germany we were witnessing the substitution of the Swastika for the Cross and the absolute negation of the Gospels were few and far between, and their warning was scarcely heeded.

We do not entirely accept this view of Hitler as the anti-Christ. We do not believe it provides a complete explanation of the facts. But at any rate it is on the right level, so to speak, from which to judge this extraordinary moment in history.

The problem must be faced. We shall never be safe from Nazism, or rather from certain manifestations of the Satanic spirit which, through the Nazis, cast its dark shadow over the world, until we have roused ourselves to a full awareness of the most fantastic aspects of the Hitlerian adventure.

Somewhere between, on the one hand, the Satanic ambition of which Hitlerism was a tragic caricature, and the kind of angelic Christianity which is also caricatured in certain social conventions; between the temptation to become superhuman and take heaven by storm and the temptation to rely on God or on an idea for our human condition to be transcended; between the rejection and acceptance of transcendancy and between a vocation for good and a vocation for evil (both being equally great and profound and secret) – between, in a word, the violently conflicting impulses of the human soul and those, no doubt, of the collective unconsciousness, tragedies are being enacted of which contemporary historians are not, and even, it would seem, do not wish to be fully aware, as if they were afraid to focus attention on certain documents and certain interpretations for fear of depriving large sections of the population of their sleep.

And so the historian dealing with Nazi Germany seems unwilling to know what the defeated enemy was really like. And in this he is supported by public opinion. The fact is that if the Allies had known what kind of an enemy it was they had defeated, their conception of the world and of human destiny would have had to have been in proportion to the magnitude of their victory. Let us hope at least that one result has been to prevent criminals and madmen from doing any more harm, and that in the long run goodness always prevails. They were certainly criminals and madmen, but in a way and to a degree that ordinary serious-minded people do not understand. The conventional anti-fascist attitude seems to have been invented by the victors to cover up their moral emptiness. But Nature abhors a vacuum.

Dr. Anthony Laughton, of the Oceanographic Institute, London, sent a camera down to a depth of 3½ miles off the coast of Ireland. Photographs taken showed very clearly footprints made by some unknown creature. After the Abominable Snowman, we now have to reckon with the mountain creature's brother, the Abominable Seaman, the unknown inhabitant of the ocean depths. History, for investigators like ourselves, is in a sense not unlike 'an ocean which by our soundings is disturbed'.

Investigating invisible history is a very healthy exercise for the mind, and breaks down one's resistance to improbability which, though natural, has so often been an impediment to knowledge.

In every field we have tried to break down this resistance to improbability, whether it is a question of the motives of men's actions, or of their beliefs or of their achievements. Thus, for example, we have studied certain reports of the occult section of the German Intelligence Service – notably a lengthy report on the magical properties of the bells in the belfries of Oxford which were thought to have prevented bombs from falling on the town. It is undeniable that there is an element of aberration here; but the fact that it affected supposedly intelligent and responsible men, thereby illuminating certain aspects of both visible and invisible history, is equally undeniable.

In our view, events often have causes which have no rational explanation, and the power currents in history can be quite as invisible and no less real than those in a magnetic field.

It is possible to go still further. We have ventured into regions where we hope the historians of the future will follow us and have at their disposal better equipment than we possessed. We have sometimes tried to apply to history the principle of 'non-causal liaisons' recently propounded by the physicist Wolfgang Pauli and the psychologist Jung. It was to this principle that I alluded just now in speaking of coincidences. For Pauli and Jung events in no way interconnected may have a causeless relationship that may yet be significant on the human level. These are the 'significant coincidences', the 'signs' in which the two thinkers have detected a phenomenon of 'synchronism' which reveals an unsuspected connection between man, time and space and what Claudel has magnificently described as 'the triumph of hazard'.

A patient is lying on a divan in the consulting-room of the psychoanalyst Dr. Jung. She is suffering from a serious nervous disorder, but the analysis is making no progress. The patient, putting up an extremely realistic and ultra-logical defence, is impenetrable to all the doctor's arguments. Once again Jung tries suggestion, persuasion and commands: 'Relax; do not try to understand, but simply tell me about your dreams.'

'I dreamed about a beetle,' she murmured at last.

At that moment, something tapped softly on the window-pane. Jung opened the window, and in came a handsome golden beetle, rustling its wing-cases. . . . Overcome with amazement, the patient at last relaxed, and the analysis could then begin, and was finally crowned with success.

Jung often cites this incident, which actually happened and which sounds like something out of the *Arabian Nights*. In the history of a man, as in history proper, we are inclined to think there are plenty of golden beetles. . . .

The complex theory of 'synchronism', partly based on the observation of such coincidences as these, might perhaps lead to an entirely new conception of history. Our ambition does not go to such lengths; we seek only to draw attention to the fantastic aspects of reality. In this part of our work we have concentrated on research into, and the interpretation of, certain coincidences which seem to us significant, though they may not seem so to others.

In applying our 'fantastic-reality' theory to history, we have adopted a process of selection. Sometimes we have chosen facts of minor importance, but suggestive of some form of aberration, because, up to a certain point, it was in aberration that we were seeking a clue. An irregularity of a few seconds in the movement of the planet Mercury was enough to demolish Newton's theory and justify Einstein's. Similarly, it has seemed to us that some of the facts which we have discovered might make it necessary to revise the bases of Cartesian philosophy.

Can this method be used to forecast the future? Sometimes we dream about this. In *The Man Who was Thursday*, G. K. Chesterton describes a brigade of political police whose speciality was poetry. A crime is forestalled because a policeman understands the meaning of a sonnet. There is a great deal of truth behind Chesterton's whimsicalities. Trends of thought that escape the notice of the trained observer; writings and works to which the sociologist pays scant attention, together with social phenomena that he considers too insignificant or too 'odd' to worry about, are perhaps a surer indication of events to come than the facts that are there for all to see and the openly expressed opinions and general trend of thinking which cause him serious concern.

The atmosphere of terror under the Nazis, which nobody could foresee, was heralded in the horrible stories of the German writer Hans Heinz Ewers: *The Mandragore* and *In Terror*, who was destined to become the régime's official poet and to write the *Horst Wessel Lied*. It is quite possible that certain books and poems and pictures and statues which are ignored even by critics specializing in these subjects, may give us an exact picture of what the world of tomorrow will be like.

Dante, in the *Divine Comedy*, gives an exact description of the Southern Cross, a constellation which is invisible in the Northern hemisphere and which no traveller in those days could ever have seen.

Swift, in *The Journey to Laputa*, gives the distances and periods of rotation of the two satellites of Mars, unknown at that time.

When the American astronomer, Asaph Hall, discovered them in 1877 and noticed that his calculations corresponded to Swift's indications, he was seized with a sort of panic and named them *Phobos* and *Deimos*: Fear and Terror.*

In 1896, an English author, M. P. Shiel, published a short story in which we read of a band of monstrous criminals ravaging Europe, slaughtering families which they considered were impeding the progress of humanity, and burning their corpses. The story was entitled: *The S.S.*

Goethe said: 'Coming events cast their shadow before', and it may well be that these undercurrents in which the future is reflected may be detected and interpreted, not in events which attract general attention, but in works and human activities which have nothing to do with and are far removed from what we call 'the stream of history'.

There are certain obvious aspects of the fantastic which the historian tries to explain away discreetly and mechanically in the light of cold reason. Germany, when National-Socialism first made its appearance, was the home of the exact sciences. German methods, German logic, and the strictness and integrity of German scientists were universally esteemed. The Herr Professor was occasionally a subject for caricature, but he was generally respected. And yet it was in a society of this kind, rigidly Cartesian, that an incoherent and partially crazy doctrine was introduced and spread like wildfire, starting from quite insignificant premises. In the country of Einstein and Planck there was talk of an 'Aryan physique'; in the

* He was also alarmed because the satellites appeared suddenly; bigger telescopes than his own had failed to notice them the night before. The simple explanation is that he was probably the first to study Mars on that particular night. Since the Sputniks, astronomers today are beginning to think that they were perhaps artificial satellites launched on the day that Hall first observed them. – Robert S. Richardson, of the Mount Palomar Observatory, 1954.

homeland of Humboldt and Haeckel racial problems began to be discussed. Such phenomena cannot, in our view, be explained as being due to economic inflation. This would be altogether the wrong background. It seemed to us far more profitable to seek for an explanation in certain strange cults and discredited cosmogonies hitherto neglected by the historians. This neglect is very strange. The cosmogonies and cults of which we are going to speak have benefited in Germany from official protection and encouragement. They have played moreover a relatively important role in political, spiritual, scientific and social spheres, and it is in this setting that we shall gain a better understanding of the drama to be enacted.

We have restricted ourselves to a particular moment in German history. In order to pin-point the fantastic element in contemporary history we could equally well have shown, for example, how Europe was invaded by Asiatic ideas just at the time when European ideas were opening the eyes of the peoples of Asia. Here we have a phenomenon no less disturbing than non-Euclidian space or the paradoxes of the atomic nucleus. The conventional historian, or 'committed' sociologist, cannot, or refuse to take notice of these profound currents which do not conform to what they call the 'stream of history'. They continue imperturbably to predict and to analyse a kind of future for the human race which has no resemblance either to humanity itself or to the mysterious, but visible signs which men exchange with time, space and destiny.

'Love,' said Jacques Chardonne, 'is much more than love.' In the course of our researches we have acquired the conviction that history is much more than history. This acts like a tonic. In spite of the increasing oppressiveness of social phenomena and the ever-growing threat on all sides to human dignity, we believe that here and there humanity is still lighting torches of knowledge and understanding which show no signs of diminishing. Although the corridors of history are apparently becoming more and more narrow, we are convinced that man has not yet lost in them the thread which links him with the immensity outside. These metaphors are reminiscent of Victor Hugo, but they express very well what we have in mind. We have acquired this conviction and feeling of certainty by immersing ourselves in reality. It is in its deepest strata that reality becomes fantastic, and, in a sense, merciful.

> 'And though the sullen engines swing,
> Be you not much afraid, my friend. . . .
>
> And when the pedants bade us mark
> What cold mechanic happenings
> Must come; our souls said in the dark
> "Belike; but there are likelier things".'*

* G. K. Chesterton: (Preface to *Napoleon of Notting Hill*).

II

In the Tribune des Nations *the Devil and madness are
refused recognition – Yet there are rivalries between deities –
The Germans and Atlantis – Magic socialism – A secret
religion and a secret Order – An expedition to hidden regions
– The first guide will be a poet*

IN an article in the *Tribune des Nations* a French historian gives an
example of the low intellectual standard of most writing about
Hitlerism. In his analysis of the book *Hitler Unmasked*, by Dr. Otto
Dietrich, who was for twelve years the Fuhrer's chief Press officer,
M. Pierre Cazenave writes as follows:

'. . . However, Dr. Dietrich is too easily satisfied with a word he
often repeats and which, in our positivist age, is inadequate to
explain Hitler. "Hitler," he says, "was a demoniac possessed by
nationalist ideas to the point of madness." What does he mean by
"demoniac"? And why "madness"? In the Middle Ages Hitler
would have been described as a man "possessed". But today?
Either the word "demoniac" means nothing, or else it means
possessed by a demon. But what is a demon? Does Dr. Dietrich
believe in the existence of the Devil? We must be clear about this.
I, personally, am not satisfied with the word "demoniac". Nor
with the word "madness", which suggests mental disorder. . . .
That Hitler was a psychopath, even a paranoiac, is not disputed;
but psychopaths and even paranoiacs are to be found everywhere.
But this is hardly the same thing as a more or less recognized form
of madness which, after being diagnosed as such, would lead to the
internment of the afflicted person. In other words: Was Hitler
responsible? In my opinion, Yes. And that is why I reject the word
"madness" just as I cannot accept the term "demoniac", demono-
logy as I see it, having no longer any meaning, apart from being an
historical curiosity.'

We are not satisfied either with Dr. Dietrich's explanation. The
destiny of Hitler and the adventure under his leadership of a great
modern nation could not be wholly accounted for in terms of
madness and demoniac possession. But that does not mean that
we are satisfied with the criticisms voiced by the historian of the
Tribune des Nations. Hitler, he assures us, was not clinically mad.
And the Devil does not exist. Therefore the notion of responsibility
must be retained. True. Our historian, however, seems to attribute
magic properties to this notion of responsibility. No sooner has he
evoked it than the whole fantastic Hitlerian adventure seems quite
clear to him and reduced to the proportions of the positivist age
in which he pretends we are living. Such an approach is quite as
unreasonable as that of Otto Dietrich. The fact is, the term 'responsibility' in our language is a transposition of what the tribunals
of the Middle Ages understood by 'possession by the Devil', as
can be seen in the great political trials of modern times.

138

If Hitler were neither mad nor possessed – which is quite possible – the history of Nazism would still be inexplicable by the standards of a 'positivist age'. Psychology in depth has shown that a man's apparently rational actions are in reality governed by forces of which he himself knows nothing, or which are closely linked with a symbolism having nothing in common with ordinary everyday logic. We know, too, not that the Devil does not exist, but that he is something other than the creature of the medieval man's imagination. In the history of Hitlerism, or rather in certain aspects of this history, everything happens as if the whole conception on which it was based has baffled the ordinary historian so that, if we want to understand, we shall have to abandon our positive way of looking at things and try to enter a Universe where Cartesian reason and reality are no longer valid.

We have been concerned to describe these aspects of Hitlerism because, as M. Marcel Ray pointed out in 1939, the war that Hitler imposed on the world was a 'Manichaean war', or as the Bible says, 'a struggle between gods'. It is not, of course, a question of a struggle between Fascism and Democracy, or between a liberal and an authoritarian conception of society. That is the exoteric side of the conflict; but there is an esoteric side as well.*

This struggle between gods, which has been going on behind visible events, is not yet over on this planet, but the formidable progress in human knowledge made in the last few years is about to give it another form. Now that the gates of knowledge are beginning to open on to the infinite, it is important to understand what this struggle is about. If we consciously want to be men of today, that is to say, the contemporaries of tomorrow, we must have an exact and clear picture of the moment when the fantastic first invaded the realm of reality. This is what we are now going to examine.

'At bottom,' said Rauschning, 'every German has one foot in Atlantis, where he seeks a better Fatherland and a better patrimony. This double nature of the Germans, this faculty they have of splitting their personality which enables them to live in the real world and at the same time to project themselves into an imaginary world, is especially noticeable in Hitler and provides the key to his magic socialism.'

And Rauschning in an attempt to explain the rise to power of this 'high priest of a secret religion', tried to convince himself that several times in history 'whole nations have fallen into a state of

* C. S. Lewis, Professor of Theology at Oxford, announced in 1937, in one of his symbolic novels: *The Silence of the Earth*, the beginning of a war for the possession of the human soul of which a terrible war on the material plane was only the external form. He returned to this idea again in two other works: *Perelandra* and *That Hideous Strength*. Lewis's last book is entitled: *Till We Have Faces*, and it is in this great poetical and prophetic story that we find the admirable phrase: 'The gods will not speak to us face to face until we ourselves have a face.'

inexplicable agitation. They follow the flagellants' procession, or are seized by St. Vitus's Dance. . . . National-Socialism is the St. Vitus's Dance of the twentieth century.'

But where does this strange malady come from? To this question he failed to find a satisfactory answer. 'Its deepest roots are hidden in secret places.'

It is these secret places that we feel we ought to explore. And it is not a historian, but a poet who will be our guide.

III

P. J. Toulet and Arthur Machen – A great neglected genius – A Robinson Crusoe of the soul – The story of the angels at Mons – The life, adventures and misfortunes of Arthur Machen – How we discovered an English secret society – A Nobel Prize-winner in a black mask – The Golden Dawn *and its members*

'Two men who have read Paul-Jean Toulet and who meet (probably in a bar) imagine that that means they belong to an aristocracy.' Toulet himself wrote that. It happens sometimes that important things are suspended on a pin's head. It is thanks to a minor but charming writer, unknown despite the efforts of a few admirers, that I first heard the name of Arthur Machen, practically unknown in France.

After some study, we discovered that Machen's works (there are some thirty volumes in all*) are, from a 'spiritual' point of view, more important than those of H. G. Wells.

Machen himself was conscious of this: 'The Mr. Wells you speak of is certainly a very clever man. I even believed for a time that he was more than that.' – Letter to P. J. Toulet, 1899.

Pursuing our researches on Machen, we discovered an English Society of Initiates with a very distinguished membership. This society, to which Machen was indebted for an experience that had a decisive influence on his inner development and which was a great source of inspiration, is unknown even to specialists. Finally, some of Machen's writings, in particular the text we shall be quoting, throw into clear relief an uncommon notion of the nature of Evil, which is quite indispensable for an understanding of those aspects of contemporary history we are examining in this part of our book. Before entering into the heart of our subject we would therefore like to say a few words about this curious man, beginning with a little literary digression concerning a minor Parisian author,

---

* *The Anatomy of Tobacco* (1884), *The Great God Pan* (1895), *The House of Souls* (1906), *The Hill of Dreams* (1907), *The Great Return* (1915), *The Bowmen* (1915), *The Terror* (1917), *The Secret Glory* (1922), *Strange Roads* (1923), *The London Adventure* (1924), *The Carning Wonder* (1926), *The Green Round* (1933), *Holy Terrors* (1946), and posth. *Tales of Horror and the Supernatural* (1948).

P. J. Toulet, and ending with a vision of a great subterranean gateway behind which lie, still smoking, the remains of the martyrs and the ruins of the Nazi tragedy which disrupted the whole world. The paths of 'fantastic realism', as we shall see once again, do not resemble the ordinary paths of knowledge.

In November 1897 a friend, 'somewhat given to the occult sciences', brought to the notice of Paul-Jean Toulet a novel by an unknown thirty-four-year-old author entitled *The Great God Pan*. This book, which evokes a primitive pagan world, not entirely submerged but still cautiously surviving and occasionally releasing among us its God of Evil and his cloven-hoofed angels, made a profound impression on Toulet and started him on his literary career. He began translating *The Great God Pan* and, borrowing from Machen his nightmarish décor with the Great Pan lurking in the thickets of our countryside, wrote his first novel: *Monsieur du Paur, homme public.*

Monsieur du Paur was published towards the end of 1898, and met with no success. It is not an important work, and might never have been heard of had not M. Henri Martineau, a great Stendhalian and a friend of Toulet, taken it upon himself, twenty years later, to republish the book at his own expense in the *Editions du Divan*. M. Martineau was determined to show that *Monsieur du Paur* was inspired by Machen's book, but was nevertheless an original work, so that it was through him that the attention of a few literary people was drawn to Arthur Machen and his *Great God Pan* and some correspondence between Toulet and Machen was brought to light.*

So far as Machen and his genius was concerned the whole episode was just one of Toulet's early literary attachments.

In February 1899 Toulet, who had been trying for a year to get his translation of *The Great God Pan* published, received from its author the following letter, written in French:

'Dear Colleague,
So there is nothing to be done with *The Great God Pan* in Paris ? If that is the case, I am really disappointed – for the book, of course, but especially on account of my French readers: I had hoped that if they tasted *The Great God Pan* in its French dress and found it to their liking, I should then perhaps have found my public! Here, I can do nothing. I go on writing all the time, but it's absolutely as if I were writing in a monastic scriptorium in the Middle Ages; that is to say, my works remain eternally in the purgatory of the unpublished. I have in my drawer a little volume of short stories which I have called *Ornaments in Jade*. "Your little book is charming," writes a publisher, "but is quite impossible." There is also a novel of some 65,000 words, *The Garden of Avallonius*. "Artistically," says my good

* Henri Martineau: *Arthur Machen et Toulet, correspondance inédite.* *Mercure de France* No. 4, January 1938.

publisher, "it is *sine peccato*, but our British public would find it shocking." At the moment I am working at a book which, I'm sure, will never leave the same Devil's Island! You will, no doubt, my dear colleague, find something very tragic (or, rather, tragi-comical) in these adventures of an English writer; but, as I said, I had high hopes of your translation of my first book.'

In the end, *The Great God Pan* was published in the review *La Plume* in 1901, but attracted no notice at all.*

Maeterlinck alone was impressed by it: 'All my thanks for the revelation of this fine and singular work. It is, I believe, the first time an attempt has been made to combine the traditional, or diabolical brand of Fantasy with the new, scientific kind, and that such a mixture has produced the most disturbing work I have ever come across, for it appeals at the same time to our memories of the past and our hopes in the future.'

Arthur Machen was born in 1863 in the small Welsh village of Caerleon-upon-Usk, which was the seat of King Arthur's court whence the Knights of the Round Table departed in search of the Holy Grail. When one learns that Himmler in the middle of the war organized an expedition to find the Grail (we shall return to this later) and at the same time, with a view to elucidating secret Nazi history, discovers not only a work by Machen, but that he was actually born in this village, the cradle of Wagnerian themes, then once again one can only repeat that, for those with eyes to see, coincidences are clad in shining light.

Machen went to live in London as a young man, and found it terrifying, as did Lovecraft in New York. After working for a few months in a bookshop and later as a schoolmaster, he realized that he could not earn his living in the ordinary way. He started to write in a state of extreme poverty and complete lassitude. For a long time he earned a living by translations: Casanova's *Memoires* in twelve volumes for thirty shillings a week for two years. On the death of his father, a clergyman, he inherited a little money, and, provided with the necessities of life for a short time, continued his work with the growing conviction that 'an immense gulf separated him from other men', and that he would have to enter more and more deeply into this life of a 'Robinson Crusoe of the soul'.

His first fantastic stories were published in 1895. These were *The Great God Pan* and *The Inmost Light*. In them he declares that the Great Pan is not dead, and that the forces of evil, in the magical sense of the word, are always lying in wait for certain individuals, ready to spirit them away to the other side of the world. In the same order of ideas he published the following year *The White Powder*, (considered along with *The Secret Glory*, written when he was sixty, to be his most powerful work).

At the age of thirty-six, after twelve years of happiness, he lost his wife: 'We hadn't spent twelve hours apart during all those years,

* Republished in 1938 by Emile Paul, with a preface by Henri Martineau, it is the only book of Machen's that has appeared in France.

142

so you can imagine how I suffered, and still suffer every day. The only reason why I would like to see my manuscripts in print is so that I could dedicate each one of them to her with these words: *Auctoris Anima ad Dominam.*' But he continues to live in poverty, neglected and broken-hearted.

At the end of three years, at the age of thirty-nine, he gives up literature and becomes a travelling actor.

'You say you haven't much courage,' he wrote to Toulet; 'I haven't any at all. So little that I have given up writing and probably will never write again. I have become an actor, and am now on the stage playing in *Coriolanus.*'

He toured all over England with Sir Frank Benson's Shakespearean company, then joined the St. James's Theatre. Shortly before the 1914 War, having been obliged to give up acting, he took up journalism in order to earn a living.

In the tumult of Fleet Street, among his busy fellow-workers, his strange appearance and slow and polished manners of a man of letters sometimes aroused smiles.

For Machen, as is apparent in all his works, 'man is made of mystery and exists for mysteries and visions.' Reality is the supernatural. The external world can teach us little, unless we look upon it as a reservoir of symbols and hidden meanings. The only works which have some chance of being real and serving some useful purpose are works of imagination produced by a mind in search of eternal verities. As the critic Philip van Doren Stern has pointed out: 'The fantastic stories of Arthur Machen perhaps contain more essential truths than all the graphs and statistics in the world.'

It was a strange adventure that brought Machen back to literature. It made his name famous in a few weeks, and the shock this gave him decided him to devote the rest of his life to writing.

He found journalism irksome, and no longer wanted to write for his own satisfaction. War had just broken out. There was a demand for 'heroic' literature. This was hardly his line. The *Evening News*, however, asked him for a story. He wrote it straight off, but in his own individual style, calling it *The Bowmen.* The newspaper published this story on 29th September, 1914, the day after the retreat from Mons. Machen had imagined an incident in this battle: St. George in shining armour, at the head of his angels in the guise of the old archers of the battle of Agincourt, comes to the rescue of the British Army.

The next thing that happened was that scores of soldiers wrote into the newspaper to say that this Mr. Machen had invented nothing. They had seen with their own eyes on the Mons front the angels of St. George mingling in their ranks. This they could swear to on their honour. Many of these letters were published. England, anxious for a miracle in her hour of peril, was profoundly stirred. Machen had been hurt when no notice was taken of him when he had tried to reveal the secrets of reality. Now, with a cheap kind of fantasy, he had aroused the whole country. Or could it be that hidden forces rose up, in one form or another, summoned by his imagination that had so often been concerned with essential truths and was now, perhaps unconsciously, at work deep down within him? Dozens of times Machen insisted in the Press that his story was pure invention. No one ever believed it. Right up to his death, thirty years later, Machen, now an old man, often reverted in conversation to this fantastic story of the Angels of Mons.

Despite this sudden celebrity, the book he wrote in 1915 had no success. This was *The Great Return*, a meditation on the Grail. Then came, in 1922, *The Secret Glory*, a criticism of the modern world in the light of religious experience. At the age of sixty he began an original autobiography in three volumes.

In 1943 (he was then eighty years old) Bernard Shaw, Max Beerbohm and T. S. Eliot formed a committee to raise funds which would save him from ending his life in a workhouse. He was able to end his days in peace, in a little house in Buckinghamshire, where he died in 1947.* He had always been enchanted by a saying of Murger. In *La Vie de Bohème* Marcel, the painter, did not even possess a bed. 'Then where do you rest?' asked his landlord. 'Sir,' replied Marcel, 'I rest on Providence.'

About the year 1880, in France, in England and in Germany some secret societies of Initiates and members of hermetic orders were founded to which a number of very influential people belonged. The story of this mystical post-romantic crisis has not yet been written. It deserves to be, as it might throw light upon the origin of several important trends of thought which have determined certain political tendencies.

In two letters written by Arthur Machen to Toulet we find the following remarkable passages. In the first, written in 1899, he says: 'When I was writing *Pan* and *The White Powder* I did not believe that such strange things had ever happened in real life, or could ever have happened. Since then, and quite recently, I have had certain experiences in my own life which have entirely changed my point of view in these matters. . . . Henceforward I am quite convinced that nothing is impossible on this Earth. I need scarcely add, I suppose, that none of the experiences I have had has any connection whatever with such impostures as spiritualism or theosophy. But I believe that we are living in a world of the greatest mystery full of unsuspected and quite astonishing things.'

In 1900 he wrote as follows: 'It may amuse you to know that I

* In England Mr. Paul Jordan Smith praised him in a chapter of his book: *On Strange Altars* (London, 1923). Henri Martineau informs us that in America a little coterie of his admirers was formed about 1925, and that a good many articles were written about him at that time. As early as 1918 Mr. Vincent Starett had written a book about him: *Arthur Machen, a Novelist of Ecstasy and Sin* (Chicago). After his death another book, by W. F. Gekle, was published: *Arthur Machen, Weaver of Fantasy* (New York).

sent a copy of my *Great God Pan* to an adept, an advanced "occultist" whom I met in secret, and this is what he wrote me: "The book amply proves that by thought and meditation rather than through reading, you have attained a certain degree of initiation independently of orders or organizations." '

Who was this 'adept'? And what were Machen's 'experiences'?

In another letter, after Toulet had been to London, he wrote: 'Mr. Waite, who likes you very much, asks me to send you his best regards.'

We were interested to learn the name of this friend of Machen and to discover that he was one of the best authorities on alchemy and a Rosicrucian specialist.

We had reached this point in our researches into the intellectual interests of Arthur Machen, when a friend revealed to us the existence in England, at the end of the nineteenth and beginning of the twentieth century, of a secret 'initiatory' society of Rosicrucian inspiration.*

This society was called the *Golden Dawn*, and its members included some of the most brilliant minds in the country. Arthur Machen was himself a member.

The *Golden Dawn*, founded in 1887, was an offshoot of the English Rosicrucian Society created twenty years earlier by Robert Wentworth Little, and consisted largely of leading Freemasons. The latter society had about 144 members, including Bulwer-Lytton, author of *The Last Days of Pompeii*.

The *Golden Dawn*, with a smaller membership, was formed for the practise of ceremonial magic and the acquisition of initiatory knowledge and powers. Its leaders were Woodman, Mathers and Wynn Westcott (the 'occultist' mentioned by Toulet in his letter of 1900).

It was in contact with similar German societies, some of whose members were later associated with Rudolf Steiner's famous anthroposophical movement and other influential sects during the pre-Nazi period. Later on it came under the leadership of Aleister Crowley, an altogether extraordinary man who was certainly one of the greatest exponents of the neo-paganism whose development in Germany we have noted.

S. L. Mathers, after the death of Woodman and the resignation of Westcott, was the Grand Master of the *Golden Dawn*, which he directed for some time from Paris, where he had just married Henri Bergson's daughter.

Mathers was succeeded in his office by the celebrated poet W. B. Yeats, who was later to become a Nobel Prize-winner.

Yeats took the name of '*Frère Démon est Deus Inversus*'. He used to preside over the meetings dressed in a kilt, wearing a black mask and a golden dagger in his belt.

Arthur Machen took the name of '*Filus Aquarti*'. The *Golden Dawn* had one woman member: Florence Farr, Director of the

* See Nos. 2 and 3 of the review *La Tour Saint-Jacques*, 1956: 'L'ordre hermétique de la Golden Dawn' by Pierre Victor.

145

Abbey Theatre and an intimate friend of Bernard Shaw. Other members included: Algernon Blackwood, Bram Stoker (the author of *Dracula*), Sax Rohmer, Peck, the Astronomer Royal of Scotland, the celebrated engineer Allan Bennett, and Sir Gerald Kelly, President of the Royal Academy. It seems that on these exceptional people the *Golden Dawn* exercised a lasting influence, and they themselves admitted that their outlook on the world was changed, while the activities they indulged in never failed to prove both efficacious and uplifting.

IV

A hollow Earth, a frozen world, a New Man – 'We are the enemies of the mind and spirit' – Against Nature and against God – The Vril Society – The race which will supplant us – Haushofer and the Vril – The idea of the mutation of man – The 'Unknown Superman' – Mathers, chief of the Golden Dawn meets the 'Great Terrorists' – Hitler claims to have met them too – An hallucination or a real presence ? – A door opening on to something other – A prophecy of René Guénon – The Nazis' enemy No. 1: Steiner

THE Earth is hollow. We are living inside it. The stars are blocks of ice. Several Moons have already fallen on the Earth. The whole history of humanity is contained in the struggle between ice and fire.

Man is not finished. He is on the brink of a formidable mutation which will confer on him the powers the ancients attributed to the gods. A few specimens of the New Man exist in the world, who have perhaps come here from beyond the frontiers of time and space.

Alliances could be formed with the Master of the World or the King of Fear who reigns over a city hidden somewhere in the East. Those who conclude a pact will change the surface of the Earth and endow the human adventure with a new meaning for many thousands of years.

Such are the 'scientific' theories and 'religious' conceptions on which Nazism was originally based and in which Hitler and the members of his group believed – theories which, to a large extent, have dominated social and political trends in recent history. This may seem extravagant. Any explanation, even partial, of contemporary history based on ideas and beliefs of this kind may seem repugnant. In our view, nothing is repugnant that is in the interests of the truth.

It is well known that the Nazi party was openly, and even flam-boyantly anti-intellectual; that it burnt books and relegated the theoretical physicists among its 'Judaeo-Marxist' enemies. Less is known about the reasons which led it to reject official Western science, and still less with regard to the basic conception of the nature of man on which Nazism was founded – at any rate in the

146

minds of some of its leaders. If we knew this it would be easier to place the last World War within the category of great spiritual conflicts: history animated once again by the spirit of *La Légende des Siècles*.

Hitler used to say: 'We are often abused for being the enemies of the mind and spirit. Well, that is what we are, but in a far deeper sense than bourgeois science, in its idiotic pride, could ever imagine.'

This is very like what Gurdjieff said to his disciple Ouspensky after having condemned science: 'My way is to develop the hidden potentialities of man; a way that is against Nature and against God.'

This idea of the hidden potentialities of Man is fundamental. It often leads to the rejection of science and a disdain for ordinary human beings. On this level very few men really exist. To be, means to be something different. The ordinary man, 'natural' man is nothing but a worm, and the Christians' God nothing but a guardian for worms.

Dr. Willy Ley, one of the world's greatest rocket experts, fled from Germany in 1933. It was from him that we learned of the existence in Berlin shortly before the Nazis came to power, of a little spiritual community that is of great interest to us.

This secret community was founded, literally, on Bulwer Lytton's novel *The Coming Race*. The book describes a race of men psychically far in advance of ours. They have acquired powers over themselves and over things that make them almost godlike. For the moment they are in hiding. They live in caves in the centre of the Earth. Soon they will emerge to reign over us.

This appears to be as much as Dr. Ley could tell us. He added with a smile that the disciples believed they had secret knowledge that would enable them to change their race and become the equals of the men hidden in the bowels of the Earth. Methods of concentration, a whole system of internal gymnastics by which they would be transformed. They began their exercises by staring fixedly at an apple cut in half. . . . We continued our researches.

This Berlin group called itself *The Luminous Lodge*, or *The Vril Society*. The vril* is the enormous energy of which we only use a minute proportion in our daily life, the nerve-centre of our potential divinity. Whoever becomes master of the vril will be the master of himself, of others round him and of the world.

This should be the only object of our desires, and all our efforts should be directed to that end. All the rest belongs to official psychology, morality, and religions and is worthless.

The world will change: the Lords will emerge from the centre of the Earth. Unless we have made an alliance with them and become Lords ourselves, we shall find ourselves among the slaves, on the dung-heap that will nourish the roots of the New Cities that will arise.

The *Luminous Lodge* had associations with the theosophical and

* The notion of the 'vril' is mentioned for the first time in the works of the French writer Jacolliot, French Consul in Calcutta under the Second Empire.

147

Rosicrucian groups. According to Jack Fishman, author of a curious book entitled *The Seven Men of Spandau*, Karl Haushofer was a member of this lodge. We shall have more to say about him later, when it will be seen that his association with this Vril Society helps to explain certain things.

The reader will recall that the writer, Arthur Machen, we discovered was connected with an English society of Initiates, the *Golden Dawn*. This neo-pagan society, which had a distinguished membership, was an offshoot of the English Rosicrucian Society, founded by Wentworth Little in 1867. Little was in contact with the German Rosicrucians. He recruited his followers, to the number of 144, from the ranks of the higher-ranking Freemasons. One of his disciples was Bulwer Lytton.

Bulwer Lytton, a learned man of genius, celebrated throughout the world for his novel *The Last Days of Pompeii*, little thought that one of his books, in some ten years' time, would inspire a mystical pre-Nazi group in Germany. Yet in works like *The Coming Race* or *Zanoni*, he set out to emphasize the realities of the spiritual world, and more especially, the infernal world. He considered himself an Initiate. Through his romantic works of fiction he expressed the conviction that there are beings endowed with superhuman powers. These beings will supplant us and bring about a formidable mutation in the elect of the human race.

We must beware of this notion of a mutation. It crops up again with Hitler, and is not yet extinct today.*

We must also beware of the notion of the 'Unknown Supermen'. It is found in all the 'black' mystical writings both in the West and in the East. Whether they live under the Earth or came from other planets, whether in the form of giants like those which are said to lie encased in cloth of gold in the crypts of Thibetan monasteries, or of shapeless and terrifying beings such as Lovecraft describes, do these 'Unknown Supermen', evoked in pagan and Satanic rites, actually exist? When Machen speaks of the World of Evil, 'full of caverns and crepuscular beings dwelling therein', he is referring, as an adept of the *Golden Dawn*, to that other world in which man comes into contact with the 'Unknown Supermen'. It seems certain that Hitler shared this belief, and even claimed to have been in touch with these 'Supermen'.

We have already mentioned the *Golden Dawn* and the German Vril Society. We shall have something to say later about the *Thule* Group. We are not so foolish as to try to explain history in the light of secret societies. What we shall see, curiously enough,

* Hitler's aim was neither the founding of a race of supermen, nor the conquest of the world; these were only means towards the realization of the great work he dreamed of. His real aim was to perform an act of creation, a divine operation, the goal of a biological mutation which would result in an unprecedented exaltation of the human race and the 'apparition of a new race of heroes and demi-gods and god-men.' (Dr. Achille Delmas.)

148

is that it all 'ties up', and that with the coming of Nazism it was the 'other world' which ruled over us for a number of years. That world has been defeated, but it is not dead, either on the Rhine or elsewhere. And there is nothing alarming about it: only our ignorance is alarming.

We pointed out that Samuel Mathers was the founder of the *Golden Dawn*. Mathers claimed to be in communication with these 'Unknown Supermen' and to have established contact with them in the company of his wife, the sister of Henri Bergson. Here follows a page of the manifesto addressed to 'Members of the Second Order' in 1896:

'As to the Secret Chiefs with whom I am in touch and from whom I have received the wisdom of the Second Order which I communicated to you, I can tell you nothing. I do not even know their Earthly names, and I have very seldom seen them in their physical bodies. . . . They used to meet me physically at a time and place fixed in advance. For my part, I believe they are human beings living on this Earth, but possessed of terrible and superhuman powers. . . . My physical encounters with them have shown me how difficult it is for a mortal, however "advanced", to support their presence. . . . I do not mean that during my rare meetings with them I experienced the same feeling of intense physical depression that accompanies the loss of magnetism. On the contrary, I felt I was in contact with a force so terrible that I can only compare it to the shock one would receive from being near a flash of lightning during a great thunder-storm, experiencing at the same time great difficulty in breathing. . . . The nervous prostration I spoke of was accompanied by cold sweats and bleeding from the nose, mouth and sometimes the ears.'

Hitler was talking one day to Rauschning, the Governor of Danzig, about the problem of a mutation of the human race. Rauschning, not possessing the key to such strange preoccupations, interpreted Hitler's remarks in terms of a stock-breeder interested in the amelioration of German blood.

'But all you can do,' he replied, 'is to assist Nature and shorten the road to be followed! It is Nature herself who must create for you a new species. Up till now the breeder has only rarely succeeded in developing mutations in animals – that is to say, creating himself new characteristics.'

'The new man is living amongst us now! He is here!' exclaimed Hitler, triumphantly. 'Isn't that enough for you? I will tell you a secret. I have seen the new man. He is intrepid and cruel. I was afraid of him.'

'In uttering these words,' added Rauschning, 'Hitler was trembling in a kind of ecstasy.'

It was Rauschning, too, who related the following strange episode, about which Dr. Achille Delmas, a specialist in applied psychology, questioned him in vain: It is true that in a case like this psychology does not apply:

'A person close to Hitler told me that he wakes up in the night screaming and in convulsions. He calls for help, and appears to be half paralysed. He is seized with a panic that makes him tremble until the bed shakes. He utters confused and unintelligible sounds, gasping, as if on the point of suffocation. The same person described to me one of these fits, with details that I would refuse to believe had I not complete confidence in my informant.

'Hitler was standing up in his room, swaying and looking all round him as if he were lost. "It's he, it's he," he groaned; "he's come for me!" His lips were white; he was sweating profusely. Suddenly he uttered a string of meaningless figures, then words and scraps of sentences. It was terrifying. He used strange expressions strung together in bizarre disorder. Then he relapsed again into silence, but his lips still continued to move. He was then given a friction and something to drink. Then suddenly he screamed: "There! there! Over in the corner! He is there!" – all the time stamping with his feet and shouting. To quieten him he was assured that nothing extraordinary had happened, and finally he gradually calmed down. After that he slept for a long time and became normal again. . . .'*

We leave it to the reader to compare the statement of Mathers, head of a small neo-pagan society at the end of the nineteenth century, and the utterances of a man who, at the time Rauschning recorded them, was preparing to launch the world into an adventure which caused the death of twenty million men. We beg him not to ignore this comparison and the lesson to be drawn from it on the grounds that the *Golden Dawn* and Nazism, in the eyes of a 'reasonable' historian, have nothing in common. The historian may be reasonable, but history is not. These two men shared the same beliefs: their fundamental experiences were the same, and they were guided by the same force. They belong to the same trend of thought and to the same religion. This religion has never up to now been seriously studied. Neither the Church nor the Rationalists – that other Church – have ever allowed it. We are now entering an epoch in the history of knowledge when such studies will become possible because now that reality is revealing its fantastic side, ideas and techniques which seem abnormal, contemptible or repellent will be found useful in so far as they enable us to understand a 'reality' that becomes more and more disquieting.

We are not suggesting that the reader should study an affiliation Rosy Cross–Bulwer Lytton–Little–Mathers–Crowley–Hitler, or any similar association which would include also Mme Blavatsky and Gurdjieff. Looking for affiliations is a game, like looking for 'influences' in literature; when the game is over, the problem is still there. In literature it's a question of genius; in history, of power.

The *Golden Dawn* is not enough to explain the *Thule* Group, or the *Luminous Lodge*, the *Ahnenherbe*. Naturally there are cross-

* Hermann Rauschning: *Hitler m'a dit*. Ed. Co-operation, Paris, 1939. Dr. Achille Delmas: *Hitler, essai de biographie psycho-pathologique*. Lib. Marcel Rivimere, Paris, 1946.

currents and secret or apparent links between the various groups, which we shall not fail to point out. Like all 'little' history, that is an absorbing pastime. But our concern is with 'big' history.

We believe that these societies, great or small, related or unrelated, with or without ramifications, are manifestations, more or less apparent and more or less important, of a world other than the one in which we live. Let us call it the world of Evil, in Machen's sense of the word. The truth is, we know just as little about the world of Good. We are living between two worlds, and pretending that this 'no-man's-land' is identical with our whole planet. The rise of Nazism was one of those rare moments in the history of our civilization, when a door was noisily and ostentatiously opened on to something 'Other'. What is strange is that people pretend not to have seen or heard anything apart from the sights and sounds inseparable from war and political strife.

All these movements: the modern Rosy-Cross, *Golden Dawn*, the German Vril Society (which will bring us to the *Thule* Group where we shall find Haushofer, Hess and Hitler) were more or less closely associated with the powerful and well organized Theosophical Society. Theosophy added to neo-pagan magic an oriental setting and a Hindu terminology. Or, rather, it provided a link between a certain oriental Satanism and the West.

Theosophy was the name finally given to the whole vast renaissance in the world of magic that affected many thinkers so profoundly at the beginning of the century.

In his study *Le Théosophisme, histoire d'une pseudo-religion*, published in 1921, the philosopher René Guénon foresaw what was likely to occur. He realized the dangers lurking behind theosophy and the neo-pagan Initiatory groups that were more or less connected with Mme Blavatsky and her sect.

This is what he wrote:

'The false Messiahs we have seen so far have only performed very inferior miracles, and their disciples were probably not very difficult to convert. But who knows what the future has in store? When you reflect that these false Messiahs have never been anything but the more or less unconscious tools of those who conjured them up, and when one thinks more particularly of the series of attempts made in succession by the theosophists, one is forced to the conclusion that these were only trials, experiments as it were, which will be renewed in various forms until success is achieved, and which in the meantime invariably produce a somewhat disquieting effect. Not that we believe that the theosophists, any more than the occultists and the spiritualists, are strong enough by themselves to carry out successfully an enterprise of this nature. But might there not be, behind all these movements, something far more dangerous which their leaders perhaps know nothing about, being themselvs in turn the unconscious tools of a higher power?'

It was at this time, too, that that extraordinary personage, Rudolf Steiner, founded in Switzerland a research society based on the idea that the entire Universe is contained in the human mind, and that this mind is capable of activities outside the scope or range of official psychology. It is a fact that some of Steiner's discoveries in biology (fertilizers that do not harm the soil), medicine (use of metals that affect metabolism) and especially in pedagogy (there are numerous Rudolf Steiner schools in Europe today) have rendered considerable service to humanity. Steiner thought that there are both black and white forms of 'magic', and believed that theosophism and the various neo-pagan societies sprang from the great subterranean world of Evil and heralded the coming of a Satanic, or demoniac age. In his own teaching he was careful to embody a moral doctrine binding the 'initiates' to work only for good. He wanted to create a society of 'do-gooders'.

We are not concerned with the question whether Steiner was right or wrong. What does seem to us very striking is that the Nazis from the beginning seem to have looked upon Steiner as Enemy No. 1.

From the very beginning the Nazis' armed gangs broke up meetings of Steiner's followers by force, threatened his disciples with death, forced them to flee from Germany and, in 1924, burned down the Rudolf Steiner centre at Dornach in Switzerland. The archives were destroyed, Steiner was unable to continue his works and died of grief a year later.

Up till now we have been describing the first signs of the approach of Hitlerism. We are now about to enter into the heart of our subject. Two theories were current in Nazi Germany: the theory of the frozen world, and the theory of the hollow Earth.

These constitute two explanations of the world and humanity which link up with tradition, are in line with mythology and in keeping with some of the 'truths' proclaimed by groups of Initiates, from the theosophists to Gurdjieff. Moreover, these theories have had the backing of important politico-scientific circles, and almost succeeded in banishing from Germany what we call modern science. A great many people came under their influence; they even affected some of Hitler's military decisions, influenced the course of the war and doubtless contributed to the final catastrophe. It was through his enslavement to these theories, and especially the notion of the sacrificial deluge, that Hitler wished to condemn the entire German race to annihilation.

We do not know why these theories, which have been so strongly proclaimed and held by scores of men, including some superior intellects, and which have called for great sacrifices, both human and material, have not yet been studied in our countries and to this day are still unknown.

Here are some of them, together with their origin, history, applications and posterity.

V

ONE summer morning in 1925 the postman delivered a letter to all the scientists of Germany and Austria. No sooner was the letter opened than the notion of a peaceful science was dead, and the laboratories and libraries echoed with the cries and speculations of the accused. The letter was an ultimatum:

'The time has come for you to choose – whether to be with us or against us. While Hitler is cleaning up politics, Hans Horbiger will sweep out of the way the bogus sciences. The doctrine of eternal ice will be a sign of the regeneration of the German people. Beware! Come over to our side before it is too late!'

The man who dared thus to threaten the scientists was sixty-five-year-old Hans Horbiger, a kind of prophet in a rage. He had an immense white beard, and his handwriting would have puzzled the best graphologists. His doctrine was beginning to be universally known under the title of *Wel* (*Welteislehre:* the doctrine of eternal ice). This provided an explanation of the cosmos which was in contradiction with official astronomy and mathematics, but corroborated by ancient mythology. Yet Horbiger considered himself a scientist, but thought that science would have to change its direction and methods. 'Objective science is a pernicious invention', a totem of decadence. He thought, like Hitler, that as a preliminary to any scientific activities it was necessary 'to know who wants to know'. Only prophets should have anything to do with science, since being 'enlightened' persons they have risen to higher level of consciousness. This is what that great initiate Rabelais meant when he wrote: 'Science without conscience is the ruin of the soul.' By this he meant: science without *superior* consciousness. His meaning had been wrongly interpreted in the interests of an elementary, humanistic conscience. When the prophet seeks knowledge, one can then speak of science; but this will be something quite different from what is ordinarily called science. That is why Hans Horbiger could not put up with the slightest expression of doubt, or a hint of contradiction. He would exclaim, in a fury: 'You put your trust in equations but not in me! How long will it be before you understand that mathematics are nothing but lies and are completely useless?'

In a 'Herr Doktor's' Germany, given up to science and

153

technology, Hans Horbiger was noisily and aggressively preparing the way for an 'enlightened' apprehension, an irrational and visionary form of knowledge. In this he was not alone, but it was on him that the limelight was focused. Hitler and Himmler had a private astrologer, but did not announce this to the world. This astrologer's name was Führer. Later on, after they had seized power, and as if to proclaim their determination not only to reign, but to 'change men's lives', they too would dare to challenge the scientists. They would even appoint Führer 'plenipotentiary of mathematics, astronomy and physics' (which is what he actually became).

In the meantime Hans Horbiger set in motion, in intellectual circles, a system comparable to that of political agitators.

He seemed to have considerable funds at his disposal, and operated like a party leader. He launched a campaign, with an information service, recruiting offices, membership subscriptions, and engaged propagandists and volunteers from among the Hitler Youth. The walls were covered with posters, the newspapers filled with announcements, tracts were distributed and meetings organized. When astronomers met in conference their meetings were interrupted by partisans shouting: 'Down with the orthodox scientists!' Professors were molested in the streets; the directors of scientific institutes were bombarded with leaflets: 'When we have won, you and your like will be begging in the gutter.' Business men and heads of firms before engaging an employee made him or her sign a declaration stating: 'I swear that I believe in the theory of eternal ice.'

Horbiger wrote to the big industrialists: 'Either you will learn to believe in me, or you will be treated as an enemy.'

In the space of a few years the movement published three large volumes of theoretical writings, forty books of a popular nature and hundreds of pamphlets. It also issued a monthly magazine which had a large circulation: *The Key to World Events*. The movement had tens of thousands of adherents, and was destined to play a notable part in the history of ideas, as well as in history proper.

At first the scientists protested and published letters and articles demonstrating the impossibilities of Horbiger's system. They became alarmed when the *Wel* assumed the proportions of a vast popular movement. After Hitler took office there was less opposition, although the universities continued to teach orthodox astronomy. Celebrated engineers and scientists subscribed to the doctrine of eternal ice, including such men as, for example, Lenard, who with Roentgen had discovered X-rays; the physicist Oberth, and Stark, whose researches in spectroscopy had made him world-famous.

Hitler openly supported Horbiger and had confidence in him.

'Our Nordic ancestors,' according to a popular *Wel* tract, 'grew strong amidst the ice and snow, and this is why a belief in a world of ice is the natural heritage of Nordic men. It was an Austrian,

154

Hitler, who drove out the Jewish politicians, and another Austrian, Horbiger, will drive out the Jewish scientists. By his own example Hitler has shown that an amateur is better than a professional; it was left to another amateur to give us a thorough understanding of the Universe.'

Hitler and Horbiger, the 'two greatest Austrians', met several times. The Nazi leader listened respectfully to this visionary prophet. Horbiger could not tolerate any interruption when he was speaking and used to tell Hitler to 'Shut up!' He carried to extremes Hitler's conviction that the German people, in its Messianic mission, was being poisoned by Western science, which was narrow, enfeebling and divorced from both the flesh and the spirit. Recent developments, such as psychoanalysis, serology and relativity, were weapons directed against the spirit of Parsifal. The doctrine of eternal ice would provide the necessary antidote. This doctrine destroyed conventional astronomy; the rest of the edifice would then collapse of itself – and it was essential that it should collapse to ensure the re-birth of magic, the only sure, dynamic value. The advocates of National-Socialism and of eternal ice, Rosenberg and Horbiger, used to meet in conference, surrounded by their best disciples.

The history of the human race, as described by Horbiger, with its great floods and successive migrations, its giants and slaves, its sacrifices and adventures, fitted in with the theory of the Aryan race. Himmler, too, was passionately interested in the affinities of Horbiger's theories with the oriental notion, dating from an Antediluvian Age, of the human race going through periods of salvation and periods of punishment. As Horbiger's line of thought became clearer, it was seen to have many points of contact with the visions of Nietzsche and Wagnerian mythology. It seemed to establish firmly the fabulous origin of the Aryan race which descended from mountains inhabited by supermen of another age, and was destined to rule over this planet and the stars. Horbiger's doctrine was closely associated with the 'magic' socialist thinking and mystical activities of the Nazi Party. It also lent strong support to what Jung was later to call 'the libido of unreason', and provided some of these 'vitamins of the soul' contained in myths.

It was in 1913 that a certain Philipp Fauth,* an amateur astronomer specializing in the Moon, published, with the collaboration of a few friends, an enormous book of more than 800 pages: *The Glacial Cosmogony of Horbiger*. The greater part of this work was written by Horbiger himself.

Horbiger at that time had a business of his own which he managed

* Born 19th March, 1867, died 1st April, 1941. Engineer and machine builder, he gained some notoriety for his study of the Moon, of which he made two maps. A double crater to the south of the crater of Copernicus bears his name, as approved by the International Union in 1935. He was appointed Professor in 1939 by a special decree of the National-Socialist Government.

in a casual way. Born in 1860 into an old-established Tyrolean family, he had studied at the Vienna Technological School and also in Budapest. Engaged as a designer by the steam-engine building firm of Alfred Collman, he later joined the firm of Land, in Budapest, as a specialist in steam-rollers. While there, he invented in 1894 a new system of valves for pumps. After the patent had been sold to powerful German and American manufacturers, Horbiger found himself suddenly at the head of a large fortune which was soon to be swallowed up in the war.

Horbiger was especially interested in the astronomical applications of changes in the state of water (liquid, ice, steam), which he had had occasion to study in his profession. He claimed to be able by these means to explain all the problems of cosmography and astrophysics. He used to say that sudden inspirations and lightning flashes of intuition had opened for him the door to a new science which contained all other sciences. He was to become one of the great prophets of Messianic Germany and, as someone described him after his death: 'An inventor of genius blessed by God.'

Horbiger's doctrine was based on a comprehensive vision of history and of the evolution of the Cosmos. It explained the formation of the solar system, the origins of the Earth, of life and of the spirit. It described the whole past history of the Universe, and announced its future transformations. It answered the three fundamental questions: What are we? Where do we come from? and Where are we going? and it answered them triumphantly.

The whole theory was based on the idea of a perpetual struggle, in infinite space, between ice and fire, and between the forces of repulsion and attraction. This struggle, this changing tension between opposing principles, this eternal war in the skies, which is the law of the planets, also governs the Earth and all living matter, and determines human destiny. Horbiger claimed that he could reveal the remotest past and the most distant future of the globe, and put forward the most fantastic theories concerning the evolution of living species. He shattered all our habitual notions about the history of civilizations and the apparition and development of man and society. In this context, he did not envisage a continuous upward movement, but a series of rises and falls. Demi-gods, giants and fabulous civilizations preceded us on this Earth hundreds of thousands, perhaps millions of years ago. What the ancestors of our race were before us, we shall perhaps turn into ourselves, after a succession of extraordinary cataclysms and mutations in the course of a history which, both on Earth and in the Cosmos, will proceed in cycles. For the laws of Heaven are the same as the laws on Earth, and the whole Universe is involved in the same movement and is a living organism in which everything reacts on everything else. Man's adventure is linked with that of the stars; and what happens in the Cosmos happens on the Earth, and vice versa.

As will be seen, this doctrine of cycles and quasi-magical relations between Man and the Universe reinforces some of the most ancient and traditional beliefs of mankind. It reintroduces ancient prophecies, myths and legends, and the old themes of Genesis, the Deluge, giants and Gods.

This doctrine, as will be seen presently, contradicts all the data of 'official' science. But, according to Hitler, 'there is a Nordic and National-Socialist science which is opposed to Jewish-Liberal science'. Official Western science, together with the Judaeo-Christian religion with which it had something in common, was a conspiracy that had to be destroyed. It was directed against the strong man's awareness that he is part of a heroic and magical scheme of things, a vast conspiracy that would exclude humanity from any past or any future outside the brief span of recorded civilizations, cut him off from his origins and fabulous destiny, and prevent him from communing with his gods.

Scientists generally agree that our Universe was created by an explosion some three or four thousand million years ago. But what sort of explosion? The entire Cosmos was perhaps contained in an atom out of which all creation came. It was this atom, perhaps, that exploded and has been constantly expanding ever since. It would have contained all matter and all the forces now active in the world. But this hypothesis would not account for the absolute beginning of the Universe. Those who support the theory of an expanding Universe do not claim to have solved the problems of its origin. In fact, science has nothing more precise to say on this point than has been said in an admirable Hindu poem: 'In the interval between dissolution and creation, Vishnu-Cesha rested in his own substance, glowing with dormant energy, amidst the germs of future lives.'

With regard to the origins of our solar system, the conjectures are equally vague. One theory is that the planets resulted from an explosion in the Sun. A large astral body, it is thought, may in passing too near, have torn off a part of the solar substance which then dispersed into space and became fixed in the form of planets. The large, unknown super-astral body, pursuing its course, then disappeared into infinite space. Another theory is that there may have been an explosion in another Sun, the twin of our own. Professor H. N. Roussel summed up the situation by remarking humorously: 'Until we know how the thing happened, all that we can be sure of is that the solar system did somehow come into being.'

Horbiger, for his part, claimed to know how it did happen, and had a definite explanation which, as he wrote to the engineer Willy Ley, came to him in a flash when he was still a young man. 'It was revealed to me,' he said, 'when as a young engineer I was watching one day some molten steel poured on to wet ground covered with snow: the ground exploded after some delay and with great violence.' That is all. It was on that that Horbiger based his theory that was to be so widely propagated. Another Newton's apple. . . .

Imagine somewhere in space an enormous, intensely hot body, millions of times larger than our Sun. This body collided with a giant planet consisting of an accumulation of cosmic ice. This mass of ice penetrated deeply into the super-Sun. Nothing happened for hundreds of thousands of years. Then suddenly the steam from the melting ice caused a vast explosion. Some fragments were projected to such a distance that they vanished into outer space. Others fell back on to the central mass which had given rise to the explosion. Others, again, were projected into an intermediate zone: these are the planets in our system. They were thirty in number – blocks which gradually became covered with ice. The Moon, Jupiter and Saturn are made of ice, and the canals on Mars are cracks in the ice. Only the Earth is not completely icebound: but is the scene of a perpetual struggle between ice and fire. At a distance three times that of Neptune from the Earth there was, at the time of the explosion, an enormous band of ice. It is still there, and astronomers call it the Milky Way, because some stars resembling our Sun shine through it from outer space. As to the photographs of individual stars which, massed together are supposed to constitute the Milky Way, they are only fakes.

The spots on the Sun which can be observed, and which change their shape and position every eleven years have never been explained by orthodox scientists. They are produced by blocks of ice falling from Jupiter. And Jupiter completes his orbit round the Sun every eleven years.

In the intermediate zone of the explosion, the planets in our system obey two forces: the original force of the explosion which projects them outwards, and the force of gravitation which attracts them to the strongest mass situated in their vicinity.

These two forces are not equal. The force of the initial explosion diminishes, because space is not empty; it contains a tenuous substance consisting of hydrogen and vapour. Moreover, the water that reaches the Sun fills space with ice crystals. Thus the initial force, that of repulsion, is slowed down more and more. On the other hand, gravitation is constant. That is why each planet approaches the planet which is nearest to it and attracts it. It makes its approach by circling round, or rather by describing a spiral which gradually shrinks. In this way, sooner or later, every planet will fall on to its nearest neighbour, and the whole system will end by falling back into the Sun in the form of ice. There will then be another explosion and another beginning.

Ice and fire, repulsion and attraction are in perpetual conflict throughout the Universe. This conflict ensures the life, death and perpetual rebirth of the Cosmos. A German writer, Elmar Brugg, in 1952, wrote a work to the glory of Horbiger, in which the following passage occurs: 'None of the theories about the nature of the Universe has ever been based on the principle of contradiction, of a conflict between two contrary forces; and yet this is what has been going on in the souls of men from time immemorial. The everlasting merit of Horbiger is to have resuscitated so powerfully the intuitive knowledge of our ancestors in regard to the eternal conflict between ice and fire, a theme that recurs in the Icelandic *Edda*. He has made his contemporaries aware of this conflict, and has given a scientific foundation to the grandiose image of a world divided by the dualism of matter and force, of repulsion which disperses, and attraction which brings everything together again.'

It is certain, then, that the Moon will end by falling on to the Earth. Some tens of thousands of years ago the distance from one planet to another seemed fixed. But we shall be able to see that the spiral is shrinking. Gradually, in the course of time, the Moon will draw nearer. The force of gravitation it exercises on the Earth will get stronger and stronger. The water from our oceans will then be drawn together in a permanent high tide, rising higher and higher covering the Earth, drowning the tropics and capping the loftiest mountain peaks. All living creatures will gradually be relieved of their weight. They will increase in size. The cosmic rays will become more powerful; acting on the genes and chromosomes, they will bring about mutations. New species of animals, plants and giant men will make their appearance.

Then, coming still nearer, the Moon will explode, rotating at high speed, and will become an immense ring of rocks, ice, water and gas, rotating at ever-increasing speed. But if any men survive – and they will be the strongest and best, the elect – they will see some strange and terrifying sights. And, perhaps, the final spectacle of all.

After being without a satellite for many millennia, during which time the Earth will have experienced extraordinary immixtures of new and ancient races, civilizations founded by giants, and new beginnings dating from before the Flood and vast cataclysms, Mars, which is smaller than our planet, will end by rejoining it. It will re-enter the Earth's orbit; but it will be too big to be captured and become a satellite like the Moon. It will pass very near the Earth, and even graze it as it goes to fall into the Sun attracted by its fire. Our atmosphere will then be caught up and carried away by the attraction exercised by Mars, and will leave us and be dispersed in space. The oceans will bubble and boil on the surface of the Earth, and the terrestrial crust will explode. Our globe, now dead, will continue on a spiral course and will be overtaken by frozen planetoids drifting in space, after which it will become an enormous ball of ice which, in its turn, will plunge into the Sun. After the collision, there will be a great silence and complete immobility, while the water vapours accumulate, over millions of years, in the interior of the flaming mass. Finally there will be another explosion, giving birth to fresh creations in the eternity of the glowing forces of the Cosmos.

Such will be the fate of our solar system according to the visions of an Austrian engineer whom the Nazi leaders used to call 'The Copernicus of the twentieth century'. We shall now attempt to describe this vision as applied to the past, present and future history of the Earth and of the human race. It is a history which, as seen

through the eyes of the prophet Horbiger, resembles a legend, full
of fabulous revelations and strange happenings.

One day in 1948, at a time when I was a believer in Gurdjieff, one
of his faithful disciples invited me and my family to spend a few
weeks with her in the mountains. This woman was really cultured,
a trained chemist, highly intelligent and a strong character. She
often helped artists and intellectuals. She was not at all the type of
a fanatical disciple, and adopted a strictly rational attitude to the
teaching of Gurdjieff who used sometimes to stay with her.
One day, however, she suddenly, or so I thought at the time,
seemed to be taking leave of her senses. She revealed to me the
depths of her aberration, and I was struck dumb with a feeling of
alarm. It was snowy outside; on a cold and starry night as we
chatted quietly on the balcony of her chalet. We were looking at the
stars, as one does when in the mountains, and experienced a
sensation of absolute solitude which, elsewhere, can be alarming,
but in such surroundings has a purifying effect. Every feature of the
Moon was clearly visible.
'One ought to speak of *a* moon,' said my hostess, '*one* of the
moons. . . .'
'What do you mean?' I said.
'There have been other moons in the sky. This one happens to
be the last. . . .'
'What? Do you mean there have been other moons, apart from
this one?'
'Certainly. M. Gurdjieff knows it, and others besides him.'
'But . . . what do the astronomers say . . . ?'
'Oh! . . . of course, if you trust the scientists . . . !'
Her expression was quite calm, and she had a slightly pitying
smile. From that day on, I felt I was no longer at ease with certain
friends of Gurdjieff whom I had esteemed. I began to see them in a
rather disquieting light, and I felt that one of the threads that bound
me to that family had just been broken. A few years later, on reading
Gurdjieff's book *The Tales of Beelzebub* and discovering the cosmogony of Horbiger, I came to realize that that vision, or rather
that belief, was not merely a fantastic caprice. There was a certain
connection between this bizarre story about the moons and the
philosophy of the superman, the psychology of 'superior states of
consciousness' and the mechanics of mutations. It was, after all, a
traditional belief in the East that men, many thousands of years
ago, had been able to see a sky that was not the same as ours,
different constellations and a different satellite.
Had Gurdjieff merely borrowed from Horbiger, whom he must
have known? Or had he had recourse to ancient founts of knowledge, traditions or legends, that Horbiger had resuscitated, as if
by chance, in the course of his pseudo-scientific flashes of insight?
I did not know, that night on the balcony of the chalet on the
mountainside, that my hostess was giving expression to a belief
that had been held by thousands of men in Hitler's Germany, still

at that time buried under the ruins, bleeding and smoking amidst the debris of her great myths. And my hostess, on that fine, calm night, did not know it either.

And so, according to Horbiger, the Moon, the one that we can see, is only the last, and fourth, of the satellites captured by the Earth. Our globe, in the course of its existence, it seems, had already acquired three others. Three masses of cosmic ice wandering in space had also, we are told, entered our orbit. After spiralling round the Earth, getting nearer and nearer, they finally crashed on us. In the same way, our present Moon will also fall upon the Earth. But this time the catastrophe will be greater still because this last icy satellite is bigger than its predecessors.

The whole history of the globe, the evolution of the species and the whole of human history can be explained by this succession of moons in our sky.

There have been four geological epochs, because there have been four moons. We are in the quaternary. When a moon falls down, it has first exploded and, while turning quicker and quicker, has been transformed into a ring of rocks, ice and gas; and it is this ring that falls on the Earth, covering the terrestrial crust in a circle and fossilizing everything it touches. Buried organisms do not fossilize normally; they decay. They only fossilize when a moon falls. This is why we have been able to determine a primary, secondary and tertiary epoch. However, since a ring is involved, we have only very fragmentary evidence as to the history of life on Earth. Other animal and vegetable species may have come and gone through the ages without leaving any trace in the geological strata. But the theory of a succession of moons makes it possible to imagine changes in living forms that may have occurred in the past. It also makes it possible to predict modifications that may take place in the future.

While the satellite is approaching there is a period of some hundreds of thousands of years during which it revolves round the Earth at a distance of from four to six times the circumference of the Earth – only a stone's throw in comparison with the distance of our present Moon. This entails considerable changes in gravitation. Now it is gravitation that determines the size of living creatures, as this depends on the weight they are able to support. When the satellite is very near there is consequently a period of gigantism.

At the end of the primary epoch: vegetation of enormous size and gigantic insects. At the end of the second: the diplodocus, the iguanodon and animals sixty feet in height. Sudden mutations take place, because the cosmic rays are increasingly strong. Creatures, relieved of their weight, get taller, skulls expand, and animals begin to fly. By the end of the secondary epoch it is possible that giant mammals made their appearance, and also, perhaps the first men, created by mutation. This period could be situated at the end of the secondary epoch when the second moon was close to the Earth, some fifteen million years ago. This was the age of our ancestor, the giant. Mme Blavatsky, who claimed to have seen the *Book of the Dzyans*, supposed to be the most ancient text known to humanity, and to contain the history of the origin of man, also declared that the first humans, a race of giants, appeared during the secondary epoch: 'Secondary man will be discovered one day, and with him his civilizations that have been swallowed up ages ago.'

And so, at an infinitely remote period of time, under a different Moon and in a world peopled by monsters there appeared this first man, of immense size, bearing almost no resemblance to us and possessed of a different kind of intelligence. The first man, and perhaps the first human couple – twins sprung from some animal womb, thanks to miraculous processes of mutation which happen more frequently as the cosmic rays become stronger. *The Book of Genesis* tells us that the descendants of this first ancestor lived to an age of from five to nine hundred years: this is because the diminution in weight decreases the rate of decay of the body. *Genesis* does not mention giants, but this omission is abundantly atoned for in Jewish and Moslem traditions. Moreover, the disciples of Horbiger claim that fossil remains of this secondary man have been discovered in Russia.

What sort of civilization would these giants have had fifteen million years ago? One can imagine them having assemblies and behaving like the giant insects of the primary age of which our insects, still very remarkable creatures, are the degenerate descendants. One can imagine the existence of means of communication at long distance, and of civilizations on the model of those ant communities, veritable power-houses of psychic and material energy, which raise so many disturbing problems in the unexplored domain of the infra-structures – or super-structures – of the intelligence.

And now this second Moon is drawing near, about to break into a ring and descend upon the Earth, which will then enter upon another long period without a satellite. In far-off space a spiral-shaped icy formation will re-enter the orbit of the Earth, which in this way will acquire another Moon. But during this moon-less period only a few specimens will survive of the mutations which occurred at the end of the secondary epoch and which will gradually diminish and become less frequent. There are still giants who adapt themselves to the new conditions. By the time the tertiary moon has appeared ordinary men have made their appearance, smaller and less intelligent. These are our real ancestors. But the giants belonging to the secondary epoch, having survived the cataclysm, still exist, and it is they who will civilize the little men.

The notion that men, starting on the level of savages and wild beasts gradually rose to become civilized, is a recent one. It is a Judaeo-Christian myth that has been imposed on men's minds in order to supplant a more powerful and more revealing myth. When humanity was fresher and nearer to its past, at a time when no well-organized conspiracy had yet effaced this past from men's memory, humans knew that they were descended from gods – kingly giants who had taught them everything. They remembered a Golden Age when superior beings, who had preceded them, had taught them agriculture, metallurgy, the arts and sciences and knowledge of the human soul.

The Greeks evoked the age of Saturn and their ancestors' cult of Hercules. The Egyptians and Mesopotamians referred in their legends to giant rulers who had brought them initiation. Tribes that we now call 'primitive' – the natives of Oceania, for example, have a place in their doubtless corrupted religion for the benevolent giants who flourished when the world was young.

In our own day, when all spiritual and intellectual values have been inverted, those who, by a prodigious effort, have succeeded in emancipating themselves from conventional and accepted habits of thinking, are haunted in their minds by a nostalgia for the happiness that came with the dawn of the ages, for a paradise lost, and by vague memories of a primordial initiation.

From Greece to Polynesia, from Egypt to Mexico and Scandinavia, tradition invariably records that men received their initiation from giants. This was the tertiary Golden Age which lasted for several million years in the course of which moral, spiritual and perhaps technical civilization attained its highest peak in the history of our globe.

> '*Quand les géants étaient encore mêlés aux hommes*
> *Dans les temps où jamais personne ne parla . . .*'

– thus wrote Victor Hugo in a moment of extraordinary illumination.

Now the tertiary Moon, in an ever-narrowing spiral, is approaching the Earth. The waters are rising, attracted by the gravitational pull of the satellite, and the men who inhabited our Earth more than nine hundred thousand years ago, climbed with their rulers, the giants, to the tops of the highest mountains. On these summits, far above the swirling seas which now form a kind of belt encircling the Earth, these men and their Superiors will found a world-wide maritime civilization which, according to Horbiger and his English disciple Bellamy, was the famous civilization of Atlantis.

Bellamy found in the Andes, at an altitude of 12,000 feet, traces of marine sediment covering an area of some 500 miles. The waters that came with the end of the tertiary epoch rose to this height and one of the centres of civilization at this period, it is thought, was Tiahuanaco, near Lake Titicaca. The ruins of Tiahuanaco provide evidence of a civilization many hundreds of thousands of years old, which bears no resemblance to any that have succeeded it.*

Traces left by the giants, according to Horbiger and his school,

* The German archaeologist von Hagen, author of a book published in French under the title: *Au royaume des Incas* (Plon, 1950) has recorded a local Indian tradition, orally handed down, to the effect that 'Tiahuanaco was built before there were stars in the sky'.

are clearly visible together with some of their inexplicable monuments. A stone weighing nine tons, for example, was found hollowed on six sides by mortises ten feet high which architects have been unable to explain, as if their function had been forgotten ever since by all the builders in history. Gateways ten feet high and twelve feet wide have been cut out of a single stone, with doors, false windows and sculptures carved with a chisel, the whole weighing ten tons. Sections of walls, still standing, weigh sixty tons, and are supported by blocks of sandstone weighing a hundred tons embedded in the ground. Among these fabulous ruins there are some gigantic statues, only one of which has been brought down and placed in the garden of the museum at La Paz. It is twenty-five feet high and weighs twenty tons. It is easy for the Horbigerians to conclude that these statues are portraits of giants which they themselves had carved.

'The lines of the face radiate an expression of ineffable goodness and wisdom which touches the heart. An atmosphere of harmony pervades the whole of this colossal figure whose highly stylized torso and hands are modelled with a degree of perfection and equilibrium that have all the attributes of a moral quality. This marvellous monolith creates an impression of peace and tranquillity. If this is a portrait of one of the giant kings who ruled over this people, one cannot help thinking of that saying of Pascal's: "If God were to give us for Masters beings shaped by his own hand . . ." '

If these monoliths were really carved and placed there by giants for the benefit of the men who were their apprentices, and if these sculptures, so highly abstract and so intensely stylized that they leave us dumbfounded were really executed by these Superior Beings, then we need look no further for the origin of the myth which relate that the arts were given to Man by the Gods, and the key to the various mystiques relating to aesthetic inspiration.

These sculptures include certain stylized representations of an animal, the todoxon, whose skeleton remains have been found in the ruins of Tiahuanaco. Now, it is known that the todoxon could only have lived in the tertiary epoch. Finally, in these ruins which date from 100,000 years before the end of the tertiary epoch, embedded in dried mud, there is a portico weighing ten tons bearing inscriptions which were examined by the German archaeologist Kiss, a disciple of Horbiger, between 1928 and 1937. These are believed to be a calendar, based on the observations of tertiary epoch astronomers. This calendar provides data of a strictly scientific nature. It is divided into four parts, separated by the solstices and equinoxes marking the astronomical seasons. Each of these is again divided into three sections, and these twelve subdivisions give the position of the Moon for every hour of the day. Moreover, the satellite's dual movement, its apparent and real movements (taking into account the rotation of the Earth) are shown on this fabulous sculptured portico in a way that suggests that the designers and users of this calendar were in possession of a higher culture than our own.

Tiahuanaco, situated at an altitude of more than 12,000 feet in the Andes, was therefore one of the five great cities of the maritime civilization at the end of the tertiary epoch that were built by the giant race who were the leaders of men at that time. The disciples of Horbiger have found there the remains of a great harbour, with enormous quays, from which the Atlantidians (since the country concerned was probably Atlantis) set out on their wonderful ships to sail round the world on the encircling belt of oceans to call at four other great key-centres: New Guinea, Mexico, Abyssinia and Thibet. Thus this civilization was spread all over the globe which accounts for the resemblance between the oldest traditions known to humanity.

Having attained a high degree of unification and refinement in their knowledge and techniques, this race of men and their giant rulers knew that the spiral course of this third Moon was shrinking, and that the satellite would finally fall on them; but being conscious of the relation between all things in the Cosmos and of the magic ties that bind the individual to the Universe, they doubtless exercised certain powers, certain personal, social, technical and spiritual forces in order to delay the cataclysm and prolong this Atlantidian Age, vague memories of which will continue to haunt men's minds throughout the ages.

When the tertiary Moon falls on the Earth the waters recede, but this civilization will already have been damaged by disturbances that heralded the final cataclysm. As the oceans receded, the five great cities, including this Atlantis of the Andes, disappeared, isolated and asphyxiated by the withdrawal of the seas. The clearest traces are to be found at Tiahuanaco, but the Horbigerians have discovered others elsewhere.

In Mexico the Toltecs left behind them sacred texts which describe the history of the Earth in a way that fits in with Horbiger's theory.

In New Guinea the Malekulas, without knowing why, went on erecting immense sculptured stones more than thirty feet high, representing the 'superior' ancestor; and their oral tradition represents the Moon as the creator of the human race and foretells the satellite's downfall.

The Mediterranean giants are believed to have come down from Abyssinia after the cataclysm, and there is a tradition that this high plateau was the cradle of the Jewish race and the homeland of the Queen of Sheba who knew all the secrets of the ancient sciences. Finally, it is well known that Thibet is a reservoir of very ancient learning, based on psychical experiences.*

Bellamy, an archaeologist who shared Horbiger's views, found all round Lake Titicaca traces of the catastrophes which preceded the fall of the tertiary moon: volcanic ashes and deposits caused by

* An astronomical map, very different from those of today, was found in a cave at Bohistan, at the foot of the Himalayas. Astronomers believe the observations recorded may have been made 13,000 years ago. This map was published in the *National Geographical Magazine* in 1925.

165

sudden inundations. This was the time when the satellite was about to break up and form a ring while rotating rapidly very near the Earth before falling down. Around Tiahuanaco there are ruins which look like workyards that had been hastily abandoned, with tools scattered about everywhere. For some thousands of years the Atlantidian civilization was exposed to the violence of the elements and gradually broke up. Then, 150,000 years ago came the great cataclysm; the Moon fell from the sky and the Earth was shaken by a terrible bombardment. Gravitation ceased, the belt of oceans suddenly retracted and the waters receded. The mountain tops which had been great maritime centres, were turned into swamps and isolated. The air became rarefied, and temperatures fell. Atlantis perished, not by being engulfed in the ocean, but, on the contrary, because the waters left it high and dry. Ships were swept away and destroyed; machines ran down or exploded; food supplies from outside were cut off; myriads of creatures and humans perished; the arts and sciences disappeared and the whole social structure was wiped out. Though the Atlantidian civilization had attained the highest possible degree of social and technical perfection, with a unified and well established hierarchy, it vanished in an astonishingly short space of time, and almost without leaving a trace behind it. One has only to imagine what the collapse of our present civilization would be like in a few hundred years, or perhaps only a few years' time. Apparatus for generating and transmitting energy is becoming simpler every day, and relaying centres are becoming more and more numerous. Each one of us will soon possess a relay of nuclear energy or will have one within easy reach in the form of factories or machines – until one day an accident at the source will cause everything all over the vast network of these relays to disintegrate: men, cities and whole nations. Whatever survives will be precisely the only things that have had no contact with this highly developed technical civilization. And the key-sciences, together with the keys to power, would immediately disappear as a direct result of this high degree of specialization. The greater the civilization, the more rapidly is it engulfed, leaving nothing to posterity.

A disturbing thought, but this is what is likely to happen. Thus, it is probable that the power-houses and relays of psychic energy on which perhaps the tertiary civilization was based, disintegrated all at once, while deserts of mud and slime engulfed the mountain tops, now grown cold, and the air became unbreathable. In a word, this whole maritime civilization, with its Superior Beings, its ships and its commerce, was swallowed up in the cataclysm.

It was still possible for the survivors to descend to the swampy plains, from which the sea had receded, and make their way to the vast steppes of the new continent as yet scarcely free from the retreating waters, bogland on which no useful vegetation would grow for many thousands of years. The reign of the giant kings is over; men have become savages again, and disappear with their fallen gods into the dark, moonless night which henceforth will cover the globe.

The giants who had for millions of years inhabited the Earth, like the gods who, at a much later age, inspired so many of our legends, have now lost their civilization. The men they ruled have become savages again. These dregs of humanity, in the wake of their fallen masters, were scattered far and wide in the deserts of mud. This calamity is said to have happened 150,000 years ago, and Horbiger calculated that our planet remained without a satellite for 138,000 years. During this long period other civilizations came into being under the guidance of the last surviving giant kings. They were established on high plateaus between 40 and 60 degrees latitude North, while the five high summits of the tertiary epoch still retained some relics of the far-off Golden Age. Thus, there may have been two Atlantis: one in the Andes, with its four other centres radiating all over the world, and the other, on a much more modest scale, in the North Atlantic, founded long after the catastrophe by the giants' descendants. This theory of the two Atlantis provides an integrating link between all the ancient traditions and legends. It was of this second Atlantis that Plato spoke.

Some 12,000 years ago the Earth acquired a fourth satellite – our present Moon. Another catastrophe occurred. Our globe swelled out in the region of the tropics; the Northern and Southern seas flowed back to the centre of the Earth, and the glacial epochs set in again in the North over the plains denuded by the withdrawal of water and air caused by the attraction of the new Moon

The second Atlantidian civilization, smaller than the first, disappeared in a single night, engulfed by the waters from the North. This was the Great Flood recorded in our Bible. It was also the Fall remembered by men who had been at the same time driven out of the Earthly Paradise of the Tropics. According to Horbiger and his school, the myths of Genesis and the Deluge are both memories and prophecies, since cosmic events repeat themselves. And the text of the Apocalypse, which has never been explained, would be a faithful representation of the celestial and terrestrial catastrophes observed by mankind throughout the ages which conform to Horbiger's theories.

During this new moon period the giants still living became degenerate. Mythology is full of stories of giants fighting among themselves, and of battles between giants and men. Those who had once been kings and gods, but were now exhausted and crushed by these cataclysms of Nature, became monsters which had to be suppressed.

These were the ogres of legend: Uranus and Saturn devoured their children; David slew Goliath. Hence the allusion in these lines of Victor Hugo to:

'. . . d'affreux géants très bêtes
Vaincus par des nains pleins d'esprit.'

167

This was the death of the gods. When the Hebrews were about to enter the Promised Land they discovered the monumental iron bed of some former giant-king: 'Behold, his bedstead was a bedstead of iron . . . nine cubits was the length thereof, and four cubits the breadth of it.' (Deuteronomy III, 11.)

The frozen astral body that shone by night had been drawn into the Earth's orbit and revolved round it; this was how our Moon began.

For 12,000 years it has always been the object of a vague cult, evoking subconscious memories, and we have never ceased to regard it with a certain amount of apprehension which we should find it difficult to explain. When we gaze upon it we still feel something much greater than ourselves stirring deep down in our subconscious memory. Old Chinese drawings represent the Moon Dragon threatening the Earth. The following passage occurs in the Book of Numbers (XIII, 33): 'And there we saw the giants, the sons of Anak, which come of the giants; and we were in our own sight as grasshoppers, and so we were in their sight.' And Job, too, evokes the destruction of the giants, exclaiming: 'Dead things are formed from under the waters, and the inhabitants thereof.' (XXVI, 5.)

A world has been swallowed up, a world has disappeared, the ancient inhabitants of the Earth have perished and we are beginning our life of solitary men, little men who have been abandoned, while we wait for the mutations and the prodigies and the cataclysms to come, dwelling once more in the dark night of time beneath this new satellite which has come to us out of space where the struggle between ice and fire goes on for ever.

Men everywhere on the globe went on repeating, blindly, the gestures of forgotten civilizations, building without knowing why, gigantic monuments and copying, in a degenerate form, the works of the old masters: for example, the immense megaliths of Malekula, the Celtic menhirs and the statues on Easter Island. Tribes which today we call 'primitive' are merely, no doubt, the degenerate remains of empires that have disappeared, which continue to perform acts which previously were sanctioned by rational laws, without understanding their meaning and distorting their true character.

In a few places – in Egypt, China and, very much later Greece – great human civilizations sprang up, which still, however, bore traces of the influence of the now vanished 'Superior Beings' and the giant Initiate Kings. After four thousand years of culture the Egyptians in the time of Herodotus and Plato continued to assert that the Ancients had achieved greatness because they had learned their arts and sciences directly from the gods.

After a general period of decadence, another civilization arose in the West. A civilization of men cut off from their fabulous past, belonging to a definite time and place, self-sufficing and seeking consolation in mythology, far removed from their origins and un-aware of the immensity of the forces that determine the fate of all living things, forces that are themselves bound up with vast cosmic processes.

This was a human or, rather, a humanist civilization: the Judaeo-Christian. It was small-scale and residual. And yet this relic of a glorious past had limitless possibilities for suffering and understanding. This was the miracle of that civilization. But it is nearing its end. We are approaching another age. There will be mutations; the future will join hands with the most distant past. There will be giants on Earth again; there will be other Great Floods, other Apocalypses, and other races will gain supremacy. 'At first we had a relatively clear recollection of what we had seen. Subsequently this life of ours went up in smoke and quickly blotted everything out, with the exception of a few broad outlines. Now, everything comes back to us more clearly than ever. And in a Universe where everything reacts on everything else, we shall make a deep impression.'

Such was the thesis of Horbiger, and such the spiritual atmosphere it engendered. It is a potent ferment of National-Socialist magic, and we shall be seeing presently the effect it had on events. It threw a new light on the intuitions of Haushofer, it lightened the heavy task of Rosenberg and intensified and prolonged the Führer's visionary dreams.

According to Horbiger, we are now in the fourth cycle. Life on Earth has known three apogees during the three periods of 'low' Moons, marked by sudden mutations and the apparition of giants. During the millennia when there was no Moon the Earth was people by insignificant dwarfs and crawling animals, such as the serpent, which recalled the Fall of Man.

With the 'high' Moons came beings of medium size, the ordinary men no doubt, of the early tertiary epoch, our ancestors. It must also be remembered that the Moons, before their fall, were circling round the Earth, creating different conditions in those parts of the globe that were not immediately under them. This explains why, after several cycles, the Earth presented a very varied appearance with a mixture of races, some decadent, others in progression, and a variety of intermediate beings, some degenerate, others fore-shadowing the future and mutations that were imminent, yet still the slaves of yesterday – dwarfs from the old Dark Ages, and the Lords of tomorrow. '*Il nous faut dégager dans tout cela les routes du soleil d'un oeil aussi implacable qu'est implacable la loi des astres.*'

What happens in the sky determines what happens on the Earth; but there is reciprocity. Just as the secret of the Universe and its ordering are contained in the smallest grain of sand, so, in a sense, is the whole pattern of cosmic events throughout the ages re-produced during our brief sojourn on this globe, so that we experience, both individually and collectively, the same upward and downward progressions that have marked this history of man-kind, and have to prepare for further advances and Apocalypses yet to come. We know that the whole history of the Cosmos has been a struggle between ice and fire, and that this struggle has had powerful repercussions on our Earth. So far as the mind and spirit of man are concerned, when the fires go out the ice takes their place. We know this is true for ourselves and for humanity as a whole, eternally faced with the choice between the deluge or an heroic adventure.

This is the essence of Horbiger's and the Nazis' creed. We shall now examine its full implications.

VI

Horbiger still has a million followers – Waiting for the Messiah – Hitler and political esoterism – Nordic science and magic thinking – A civilization utterly different from our own – Gurdjieff, Horbiger, Hitler and the man responsible for the Cosmos – The cycle of fire – Hitler speaks – The basis of Nazi anti-Semitism – Martians at Nuremberg – The anti-pact – The rockets' summer – Stalingrad, or the fall of the Magi – The prayer on Mount Elbruz – The little man victorious over the superman – The little man opens the gates of Heaven – The Twilight of the Gods – The flooding of the Berlin Underground and the myth of the Deluge – A Chorus by Shelley

THE German engineers responsible for the rockets which launched the first artificial satellites were held up in their work of preparing the V2s by the Nazi leaders themselves. General Walter Dornberger was in charge of the tests carried out at Peenemunde, the cradle of the first tele-guided missiles, but the tests were interrupted while the General's reports were submitted to the authorities who believed in Horbiger's cosmogony. It was, above all, essential to know what the reaction in space would be of the 'eternal ice', and whether the violation of the stratosphere would not expose the Earth to some disaster.

General Dornberger in his *Memoirs* relates that the work was again interrupted for two months a little later. The Führer had dreamt that the V2s would not work, or that they would call down vengeance from Heaven. As this dream occurred during one of Hitler's special 'trances', the Nazi leaders attached more importance to it than to the opinion of the engineers. In the background, behind the façade of a scientific and highly organized Germany, lurked the spirit of the old magicians. And this spirit is still alive. In January 1958 the Swedish engineer Robert Engstrøm, in a memorandum addressed to the New York Academy of Sciences, warned the United States to beware of astronautical experiments. 'Before undertaking these experiments,' he declared, 'the movements of the heavenly bodies should be studied from an entirely new angle.' And he went on to say, as if echoing Horbiger: 'The explosion of an H-bomb on the Moon might cause an appalling deluge on the Earth.'

This singular warning reflects the para-scientific idea of changes in the Moon's gravitation, and the mystical notion of punishment in a Universe where everything reacts upon everything else. These ideas (which, after all, need not be entirely rejected if one wishes to keep open all the doors to knowledge) still exercise a certain fascination. A survey carried out in 1953 by the American Martin Gardner showed that there were more than a million disciples of Horbiger in Germany, England and the United States. In London, H. S. Bellamy has been for the last thirty years working on an anthropological theory which is based on the collapse of the three first moons, and the existence of giants in the secondary and tertiary epochs. It was he who asked the Russians after the War for permission to organize an expedition to Mount Ararat where he expected to find the Ark. *Tass* published a categorical refusal in which the Soviet authorities denounced Bellamy's intellectual approach as 'fascist', such para-scientific movements being, in their view, likely to 'arouse dangerous forces'. In France, M. Denis Saurat, the poet and scholar, acted as Bellamy's mouthpiece, and the success of Welikovsky's work showed that a great many people were still sympathetic to a 'magical' interpretation of the world. Needless to say, the intellectuals who had been influenced by René Guénon and the followers of Gurdjieff aligned themselves with the Horbigerian school of thought.

In 1952 a German writer, Elmar Brugg, published a weighty volume to the glory of 'the Father of eternal ice', 'the Copernicus of our twentieth century'. He wrote as follows:

'The theory of eternal ice is not only a considerable scientific discovery; it is a revelation of the eternal and unchangeable relationship between the Cosmos and everything that happens on Earth. It establishes the connection between cosmic events and the cataclysms attributed to climatic disturbances, disease, death and crime, and thus opens up an entirely fresh approach to a knowledge of the destinies of the human race. The silence on the part of official scientists can only be explained as a conspiracy of mediocre minds.'

The great Austrian novelist, Robert Musil, who has been compared to Proust and Joyce, provides an excellent analysis of the state of mind prevailing in Germany at the time when Horbiger received his 'illumination' and Corporal Hitler was dreaming of redeeming the German people.

'The intellectuals,' he wrote, 'were not satisfied. There was no repose or stability in their thinking, because they were concerned always with that irreducible aspect of things, which is always shifting and can never be reduced to order. And so, in the end they became convinced that the times in which they were living were doomed to intellectual sterility and could only be redeemed by some altogether exceptional event or some altogether exceptional individual.' It was then that the word 'redemption' became fashionable in so-called intellectual circles. It was firmly believed that unless a Messiah came soon, all life would come to an end.

He could, as the case might be, take the form of a Messiah of medicine who would 'save' the art of Aesculapius from being confined to laboratory researches during which men go on suffering and die without being cared for; or he could be a Messiah of poetry capable of writing a play which would draw millions of people to the theatre, and would yet be absolutely original in its spiritual nobility.

Apart from this conviction that there was no department of human activity that could be saved without the intervention of a Messiah, there was also the banal and crude idea of a 'strong man' Messiah who would put everything to rights by force.

In the event it was not just a single Messiah who was going to appear, but, so to speak, a whole society of Messiahs who had appointed Hitler as their chief. Horbiger was one of them, and his para-scientific conception of the laws governing the Cosmos and of an epic history of humanity was to play a preponderant part in the Germany of these 'saviours'. Humanity's origins were more remote and more exalted than was generally believed, and a glorious destiny awaited it.

Hitler, in a constant state of mystical illumination, was conscious of being there in order that this destiny might be accomplished. His ambition, and the mission with which he believed himself to be entrusted, reached far beyond the boundaries of politics and patriotism. As he said himself: 'I had to encourage "national" feelings for reasons of expediency; but I was already aware that the "nation" idea could only have a temporary value. The day will come when even here in Germany what is known as "nationalism" will practically have ceased to exist. What will take its place in the world will be a universal society of masters and overlords.'

Politics are only the outward manifestation, the practical and temporary application of a religious vision of the laws of life on Earth and in the Cosmos. The real destiny of humanity is something that ordinary men could not conceive of and would be unable to stomach if they were given a glimpse of it. That is only possible for a few initiates. 'Politics,' to quote Hitler again, 'are only a practical and fragmentary aspect of this destiny.' In other words, the exoteric side of the doctrine, with its slogans, its social conditions and its wars. But there is also an esoteric side.

What Hitler and his friends were really aiming at while encouraging and supporting Horbiger was to bring about, by scientific or pseudo-scientific means, a return to the beliefs of a bygone age according to which Man, Society and the Universe all obey the same Laws, and there is a close connection between soul-states and the movements of the stars. The struggle between ice and fire which is responsible for the birth, death and rebirth of the planets, has its counterpart in the souls of men.

As Elmar Brugg justly observes: 'The Universe, for Horbiger, is not a piece of dead machinery a single part of which is slowly deteriorating and will eventually succumb, but a living organism in the most prodigious sense of the word – a living being in which every part reacts on every other part, and which hands down from generation to generation its burning force.'

This is the essence of Hitler's creed, as Rauschning has clearly understood: 'It is impossible to understand Hitler's political plans unless one is familiar with his basic beliefs and his conviction that there is a magic relationship between Man and the Universe.'

This conviction, which was shared by wise men in ages past, governs the thinking of what we call 'primitive' peoples and underlies a great deal of Oriental philosophy, is still current in the West today, and it may well be that science itself will give it a fresh lease of life in a most unexpected manner. In the meantime, however, it is to be found in its purest form in the writings of the orthodox Jew, Welikovski, whose book, *Worlds in Collision*, had a world-wide success in 1956-57. For those who, like Welikovski, believe in the theory of 'eternal ice', our actions can have a repercussion in the Universe, and it is quite possible that the sun stood still to favour Joshua. There was a reason for Hitler's having called his private astrologer 'a plenipotentiary of mathematics, astronomy and physics'. To a certain extent, Horbiger and the Nazi esoterists were changing the methods and even the aims of science. They were forcing it to conform to traditional astrology. Everything that happened on the technical plane while the Reich was making a great effort to consolidate its material gains, could, it appears, be carried on independently of these beliefs: the initial impulse had been given, and it was now accepted that all sciences were based on a secret science, a form of magic. As Hitler declared: 'There is a Nordic and National-Socialist Science which is opposed to Judaeo-Liberal Science.'

This 'Nordic science' is a form of esoterism, or rather it is derived from the same source as the whole esoteric movement. It is not merely a coincidence that the *Enneads* of Plotinus were issued in a carefully revised edition in Germany and the occupied countries. The *Enneads* were read during the war in the little mystical societies of pro-German intellectuals, together with the ancient Hindu texts, Nietzsche and the Thibetan seers.

Every line of Plotinus, for example, when he is speaking of astronomy could be matched with a quotation from Horbiger. Plotinus describes the natural and supernatural relations of Man with the Cosmos and of every part of the Universe with all its other parts as follows: 'This Universe is a unique animal that contains within itself all other animals. . . . Without coming into contact, things occur and are bound to produce an effect at a distance. . . . The world is a unique animal, and that is why it must of necessity be in sympathy with itself; there is no such thing as chance in life, but only a harmony and an order that governs everything.' Again: 'Events on the Earth are in sympathetic relationship with celestial things.'

Nearer our own time, William Blake, with his half poetic, half religious visionary insight, sees the whole Universe in a grain of sand. This expresses the notion of the reversibility of the infinitely

173

great and the infinitely small, and the unity of the Universe in all its parts.

According to the Zohar: 'Everything here below happens as it does on high.'

Hermes Trismegistes: 'It is all the same above and below.'

Finally, the old Chinese Law which declares that: 'The stars in their courses are fighting on the side of the just.'

We have now plumbed the depths of the Hitlerian philosophy. In our opinion it is regrettable that this philosophy has never been analysed in this way before. It was not considered necessary to do more than emphasize its outward manifestations, political implications and exoteric aspects. It has obviously not been our intention to revalorise the philosophy of Nazism. But it is inherent in, and has influenced events. It seems to us that it is only when looked at in this light that these events can be really understood. They are still horrible, but viewed from this angle they are seen to be something more than just sufferings inflicted by madmen and evil men on their fellow men. They amplify history, as it were, and establish it on a level where it ceases to be absurd and becomes worth living, despite the suffering entailed, because it is a spiritual level.

The point we are trying to make is that a civilization entirely different from our own made its appearance in Germany and was established there for several years. On reflection, it is not inconceivable that so completely alien a civilization should have been able to establish itself in so short a time. Our own humanist civilization itself is based on a mystery – which is that all sorts of ideas in our world can coexist, and that knowledge acquired from one set of ideas may in the end be used to promote ideas that are quite contrary. Moreover, everything in our civilization helps to make the mind understand that the mind is not everything. An unconscious conspiracy on the part of material powers reduces the risks, keeps the mind within limits from which pride is not excluded, but in which ambition is leavened with a tendency to question whether anything is worth while. As Musil has pointed out: 'If only a single one of the ideas which influence our life were taken really seriously so as to leave no room at all for its opposite, this would be enough to change the whole character of our civilization.' This is what happened in Germany, at any rate in the higher ruling circles of their 'magic' socialist system.

We have a magical relationship with the Universe, but we have forgotten it. The next mutation of the human race will produce beings who will be conscious of this relationship, demi-gods. Already this mutation is having an effect on a few Messianic souls who have established a connection with the distant past and remember the days when the giants could influence the movements of the stars.

Horbiger and his disciples, as we have seen, thought that there were periods during which the human race reached its apogee: for example, the periods of 'low' Moon at the end of the secondary and tertiary epochs. When the satellite threatens to descend upon the Earth and is in close proximity to our planet, it is then that living creatures are at the height of their vital and, no doubt, their spiritual powers. The King-Giant, the Man-God concentrates in himself and directs the psychic forces of the community. He controls this network of radiations in such a way that the stars are maintained on their courses and the catastrophe staved off. This is the essential function of the giant-magician. To a certain extent, he keeps the solar system in its place. He is at the head of a sort of power-house of psychic energy; it is in this that his kingship resides.

This energy is a part of the cosmic energy. Thus, it seems that the monumental calendar of Tiahuanaco, which is supposed to have been drawn up under the guidance of the giants, was not intended to register the passage of time and the movements of the stars, but to create time and maintain these movements. The object is to prolong for as long as possible the period during which the moon is within a certain radius from the Earth; and it may be that, when the giants were in power, all human activities were devoted to creating a concentration of psychic energy in order to preserve the harmony of Earthly and Heavenly events. Human societies, in fact, under the influence of the giants, were a kind of dynamo, producing forces that would contribute to maintaining the equilibrium of the forces in the Universe. In other words, man or, more particularly, the giants and the demi-gods, were responsible for the entire Cosmos.

There is a singular resemblance between this vision and that of Gurdjieff. It is well known that this celebrated thaumaturge claimed to have learned in certain initiation centres in the East a number of secrets relating to the origin of the world and the higher civilizations that disappeared hundreds of thousands of years ago. In his famous work, *All and Everything*, in his familiar picturesque style, he wrote as follows: 'This Committee (of the angels who had created the solar system) having made a survey of all the known facts, came to the conclusion that, although the fragments projected from the planet Earth might maintain for a time their present position, it was possible that in the future, owing to what are known as *tastartoonarian* movements, these satellite fragments might leave their orbits and cause a great number of irreparable catastrophes. The High Commissioners therefore decided to take steps to prevent this, and concluded that the most effective way of doing this would be to ensure that the Earth should constantly send out to its satellites, to keep them in their places, the sacred vibrations called *askokinns*.'

Men, then, are endowed with a special organ for transmitting the psychic forces needed to preserve the equilibrium of the Cosmos. This is what we call, vaguely, the soul, and all our religions, according to this theory, are merely a relic of this forgotten primordial

175

function, namely to play a part in maintaining the equilibrium of the cosmic forces.

Denis Saurat recalls that in prehistoric America the great Initiates used to play a sacred game with rackets and balls: the balls traced in the air the courses of the stars. If an unskilful player dropped or lost a ball he would be the cause of astronomical catastrophes; he would then be killed and his heart torn out.

The souvenir of this primordial function persists in legends and superstitions, from the Pharaoh who, by his magic powers, caused the Nile to rise every year to the prayers of the pagan West that the winds might change or the hailstorms cease, to the incantations of the Polynesian witch-doctors to ensure rainfall.

The origin of all major religions would thus seem to be the obligation, of which the men of past ages and their giant rulers were fully conscious, to maintain what Gurdjieff calls 'the Cosmic movement of Universal harmony'.

In the conflict between ice and fire, which is the key to universal life, Horbiger affirms that cycles occur on the Earth, and that every six thousand years we experience an Ice Age. Floods and major catastrophes occur at the same time. But there is an uprush of fire in human beings every seven hundred years, which means that every seven hundred years Man awakens again to a consciousness of his responsibilities in this cosmic struggle. He becomes once more, in the fullest sense of the word, religious. He renews contact with minds that have long since been buried and forgotten. He prepares for future mutations. His soul expands to the dimensions of the Cosmos. He recaptures the feeling of participating in a Universal and heroic adventure. He is once again capable of distinguishing between the respective spheres of the man-god and the slave-man, and of excluding from humanity whatever belongs to the outcast species. He becomes ruthless again, and spectacular, reverting to the role for which the giants had been preparing him.

We have been unable to understand how Horbiger justified his cycles-theory, or how he reconciled it with the rest of his system. However, like Hitler, Horbiger used to say that to bother about coherence was a deadly vice. The only thing that mattered was to set things in motion. Crime is movement: a crime against the intelligence is a good deed. Moreover, Horbiger learned about his cycles in a vision – a more authoritative source than mere reason. The last uprush of fire occurred at the same time as the apparition of the Teutonic Knights. The most recent coincided with the foundation of the Nazi 'Black Order'.

Rauschning, who did not possess a key to the Führer's way of thinking and had never been anything but a good aristocratic humanist, was alarmed by the things Hitler sometimes allowed himself to say in his presence. 'A theme which constantly recurred in his conversation,' Rauschning relates, 'was what he called the "decisive turning-point in the history of the world". There would be an upheaval on our planet of which we, the uninitiated, would be unable to understand the full implications.'* Hitler spoke like one in a trance. He had built up a biological *mystique* which was the foundation of all his inspirations. He had also invented a personal terminology. 'Taking a wrong turning' meant the abandonment by man of his divine vocation. To acquire a 'magical vision' seemed to him to be the aim of human evolution. He believed that he was himself already on the threshold of this magical knowledge, which was the source of his present and future successes. A contemporary Professor (Horbiger) had written in addition to a certain number of scientific works, some rather strange essays on the primitive world, the formation of legends, the interpretation of dreams among primitive peoples and on the intuitive knowledge these peoples were said to possess, together with a kind of transcendent faculty which enabled them to alter the Laws of Nature. In all this rigmarole there were also references to the single eye of the Cyclops, the eye in his forehead which later became atrophied to form the pineal gland. Hitler was fascinated by these ideas, and loved to immerse himself in them. The only way in which he could explain the miracle of his own destiny was by attributing it to the action of unseen forces – the same forces to which he owed his superhuman vocation of having to preach a new Gospel to humanity.

'The human species,' he used to say, 'has been through a prodigious number of cycles since it made its first appearance. Throughout the ages it has traversed many stages of advancement, and was now coming to the end of its solar period.† Already the first specimens of the superman were beginning to appear. A new race was heralded, which would take precedence over the old. Just as, according to the immortal wisdom of the ancient Nordic peoples, the world continually renewed itself by casting off the past in a series of Twilights of the Gods, and just as the solstices, in ancient mythology, were symbols of the rhythm of life, not developing continuously or in a straight line, but spirally, so did humanity progress in a series of forward and backward leaps.

'When Hitler spoke to me,' continued Rauschning, 'he tried to explain his vocation as the herald of a new humanity in rational and concrete terms. For example: "Creation is not yet completed. Man has reached a definite stage of metamorphosis. The ancient human species is already in a state of decline, just managing to survive. Humanity accomplishes a step up once every seven hundred years, and the ultimate aim is the coming of the Sons of God. All creative forces will be concentrated in a new species. The two varieties will evolve rapidly in different directions. One will disappear, and the other will flourish. It will be infinitely superior to modern man. Do you understand now the profound meaning of

* As the fourth Moon approached the Earth, there would be changes in gravitation. The waters would rise, and humans would enter upon a new era of gigantism. Mutations would be caused by the action of more powerful cosmic rays. The world would enter a new 'Atlantidean' phase.

† The period when the Sun's influence was strongest. The peak periods were when the Moon was nearest the Earth.

177

our National-Socialist movement? Whoever sees in National Socialism nothing but a political movement doesn't know much about it. . . ." '

Rauschning, like other observers, did not connect the racial doctrine with Horbiger's general system. There is, nevertheless, a certain connection. It was a part of the esoteric Nazi philosophy, some other aspects of which we shall be examining shortly.

There was the racialism exploited for propaganda purposes; and it was this that the historians have described and the tribunals, voicing the feeling of the majority, have rightly condemned. But there was another kind of racialism, deeper and no doubt more horrible. This has never been understood either by the historians or the people, and there could be no common language between the exponents of this kind of racialism on the one hand, and their victims and their judges on the other. This, roughly, is their thesis:

The terrestrial and cosmic period in which we are living while waiting for the advent of a new cycle which will bring about mutations on the Earth, a reclassification of species and the return of the giant-magician, the demi-god, is characterized by the coexistence on this globe of forms of life originating in the various phases of the secondary, tertiary and quaternary periods. There have been phases of upward and downward movements. Certain species are degenerating, others are forward-looking and bear within them the seeds of the future. Man is not a unity. Nor are men the descendants of the giants, only their successors, and they, too, were created by mutation. But this intermediate species of humanity is not itself a unity. There is a true race of humans which will come with the next cycle, endowed with the psychic organs that will enable it to assist in maintaining the equilibrium of the cosmic forces, and destined to play its part in a heroic adventure under the guidance of the Unknown Superior Beings of the future. There is also another species of humanity which does not deserve the name and no doubt came into being on the globe during some dark and dismal epoch when, after one of the Moons had descended on the Earth, vast portions of the Earth's surface were nothing but a desolate swamp. It was probably created along with other crawling and hideous creatures, the relics of a baser form of life. The Gypsies, Negroes and Jews are not men, in the true sense of the term. Born after the fall of the tertiary Moon, by a sudden mutation, a kind of unfortunate lapse on the part of an enfeebled creative force, these 'modern' creatures (particularly the Jews) imitate man and are envious of him, but do not belong to the same species. 'They are as far removed from us as animals are from humans,' said Hitler (these were his very words) to a terrified Rauschning who then realized that Hitler's views were crazier even than those of Rosenberg and all the racial theoreticians. 'I do not mean,' Hitler was careful to explain, 'that I look upon Jews as animals; they are much further removed from animals than we are. Therefore, it is not a crime against humanity to exterminate them, since they do not belong to humanity. They are creatures outside nature.'

It is for these reasons that certain sessions of the Nuremberg Trial were meaningless. The judges could not possibly have any kind of communication with those who were really responsible, most of whom, in any case, had disappeared, leaving in the dock only the men who had been their instruments. Two worlds confronted one another, with no means of communication. It was like trying to judge creatures from Mars by the standards of our humanist civilization. They were, indeed, Martians – in the sense that they belonged to a different world from the one we have known for the last six or seven centuries. A civilization totally different from what is generally meant by the word had been established in Germany in the space of a few years, without our having ever properly understood what was going on. Its initiators no longer had any intellectual, moral or spiritual affinities with ourselves in any basic sense; and despite external resemblances, they were as remote from us as the Australian aborigines. The judges at Nuremberg tried to act as if they were not conscious of this appalling state of things. To a certain extent, indeed, there was a case for concealing the truth so that it could be buried and made to vanish, as in a conjuring trick. It was important to keep alive the idea of the permanence and universality of our humanist and Cartesian civilization, and somehow or other it was essential that the accused should be integrated in this system. This was necessary in order not to upset the equilibrium of the Western way of life and conscience. It must not be imagined that we are questioning the benefits that have resulted from the Nuremberg Trial. We merely believe that a world of fantasy was buried there. But this was only right in order to save countless million souls from being corrupted. The exhumation we have been carrying out is only for the benefit of a few amateurs, who have been warned and are equipped with masks.

We find it difficult to admit that Nazi Germany embodied the concepts of a civilization bearing no relationship at all to our own. And yet it was just that, and nothing else, that justified this war, one of the very few known to history in which the cause at stake was really vital. It was essential that one of the two opposing visions of Man, Heaven and Earth, the humanist or the magical, should triumph. Coexistence was out of the question, although one can quite well imagine Marxism and liberalism coexisting, because they are based on the same kind of ideas, and belong to the same Universe. The Universe of Copernicus is not the same as that of Plotinus; they are fundamentally opposed, not only on the theoretical, but also on the social, political, spiritual, intellectual and emotional plane.

What makes it difficult for us to accept this strange vision of another civilization so speedily set up across the Rhine is that the distinction we make between civilized and uncivilized is still a childish one; we still think in terms of feathered helmets, tom-toms and mud-huts. The truth is, of course, that it would be easier to make a civilized person out of a Bantu witch-doctor than to find a place in our humanistic system for a Hitler, a Horbiger or a Haushofer. But this truth was hidden from us by German technology, German science and German organization, comparable, if not superior, to our own. The great innovation of Nazi Germany was to mix magic with science and technology.

Those intellectuals who despise our civilization and turn to the past for their enlightenment, have always been hostile to technical progress. For example, René Guénon or Gurdjieff or all the innumerable devotees of the Hindu way of life. But it was during the Nazi régime that magic was allowed to take control of the wheels of material progress. Lenin used to say that Communism was socialism *plus* electricity. It could also be said that Hitlerism, in a sense, was 'Guénonism' *plus* tanks.

One of the finest poems of our time is entitled *Martian Chronicles*. Its author is an American, a Christian after the manner of Bernanos, and one who dreads a robot civilization. His name: Ray Bradbury. He is not, as is generally believed in France, a writer of 'science-fiction', but a religious artist. His choice of subjects is completely modern, but his object in writing about journeys into space and into the future is to convey something of modern man's ever-increasing and secret anxieties.

At the beginning of *Martian Chronicles* the first great inter-planetary rocket is about to be launched. It will reach Mars and establish for the first time a contact with other intelligent beings. We are in January 1999; a minute ago it was winter in Ohio, with frost and ice everywhere . . . then suddenly the little town is swept by a wave of heat, a rush of burning air as if someone had just opened an oven door. The hot air penetrates into the houses, all over the countryside, and everywhere the ice is melted. . . . *The rocket's summer* . . . the word is passed from mouth to mouth. . . . The frost on the windows is dissolved by the hot desert air, the snow falling from a cold sky is turned into warm rain before it reaches the ground. *The rocket's summer* . . . the inhabitants on their dripping doorsteps watch the sky turn red. . . .

What happened to these people later in Bradbury's poem was sad and tragic, because the author does not believe that spiritual and material progress go together. But, as a prologue, he describes this 'rocket's summer' as if to emphasize one of Man's fundamental dreams: the promise of eternal spring on Earth. When men begin to interfere with the celestial machinery and infuse new motor impulses into it, great changes will take place on the Earth. Everything reacts on everything else. In inter-planetary space, where from now on human intelligence will play a part, chain reactions will occur which will have repercussions on the Earth and bring about changes in temperature. As soon as man conquers, not only the sky, but what lies behind the sky; as soon as a great material and spiritual revolution takes place in the Universe; as soon as civilization ceases to be merely human and becomes cosmic, immediately there will be a kind of compensatory reaction on the Earth. Men will no longer be at the mercy of the elements. The globe will be enveloped forever in warmth and sweetness. Ice, which is a symbol of death, will disappear, and the cold will vanish with it. The promise of an eternal spring will be fulfilled, if humanity accomplishes its divine mission. If it can be integrated with the universal All, an eternally warm and flower-decked Earth will be its reward. The forces of cold, which are the forces of solitude and decadence, will be vanquished by the forces of fire.

The assimilation of fire to spiritual energy is another of Man's archetypal ideas. Whoever possesses this force, possesses fire. Strange as it may seem, Hitler was convinced that wherever he advanced the cold would retreat before him. This mystical belief partly accounts for the way in which he conducted the campaign in Russia.

The Horbigerians, who claimed to be able to predict the weather all over our planet months and even years in advance, had announced a relatively mild winter. But there was another factor: in common with other disciples of the 'eternal ice' theory, Hitler was firmly convinced that he had formed an alliance with the cold, and that the snowy plains of Russia would not be able to delay his advance. Humanity under his leadership was about to enter the new cycle of fire. Winter would retreat before his flame-bearing legions.

Although the Führer usually paid great attention to the material equipment of his troops, the only ridiculously inadequate addition to the outfit of his soldiers in the Russian campaign consisted of a scarf and a pair of gloves.

Then, in December 1941, the thermometer suddenly descended to $-40°$ C. The predictions were false, the elements revolted, the stars in their courses suddenly ceased to work in the interests of the 'just man'. It was the triumph of ice over fire. Automatic weapons ceased to function as the oil froze. In the reservoirs the cold caused the synthetic petrol to separate into two unusable elements. Behind the lines the locomotives were frozen. The soldiers were dying in their greatcoats and army boots. The slightest wound meant death.

Thousands of soldiers died of exposure while performing their natural functions. Hitler refused to believe in this first conflict between mysticism and reality. General Guderian, at the risk of losing his rank and perhaps his life, flew back to Germany to inform Hitler of the situation and to ask him to give the order to retreat.

'As to the cold,' said Hitler, 'I will see to that. Attack.' It was thus that the entire armoured corps that had conquered Poland in eighteen days and France in a month – the armies of Guderian, Reinhardt and Hoeppner, the formidable legion of the conquering heroes whom Hitler called his Immortals – slashed by the wind and scorched by the frost, disappeared in the frozen wastes in order that a mystical idea should be proved truer than reality.

What remained of the Great Army had, in the end, to give in and make at all speed for the south. When, in the following spring, the troops invaded the Caucasus, a strange ceremony took place. Three S.S. mountaineers climbed to the summit of Mount Elbruz, the sacred hill of the Aryan race, the seat of ancient civilizations, the magic peak of the sect of the 'Friends of Lucifer'. There they planted the swastika flag, blessed according to the rites of the Black Order. The blessing of the flag at the top of Mount Elbruz was to mark the beginning of a new era. In future the seasons would be obedient, and fire would triumph over ice for many thousands of years to come.

There had been a serious setback the previous year, but that was only a trial, the last to be overcome before the real spiritual victory. And so, despite the warnings of the official meteorologists who predicted a winter even more severe than the preceding one, and regardless of innumerable threatening indications, the troops turned North again towards Stalingrad in order to cut Russia in two.

It was the 'disciples of reason with their sombre mien' who won the day. It was the practical men, men lacking 'the divine fire', with their courage, their 'Judaeo-liberal' science, and their techniques untainted by religious overtones – it was these men who, aided by the cold and ice, triumphed in the end. They broke the covenant, and won a victory over magic. After Stalingrad Hitler was no longer a prophet. His religion crumbled. Stalingrad was not only a military and political defeat; the balance of spiritual forces was upset, the wheel was turning. German newspapers appeared in heavy mourning, and the descriptions they gave of the disaster were more terrible than those in the Russian communiqués. National mourning was proclaimed. But this mourning was for something more than a nation. 'Do you realize what has happened,' wrote Goebbels; 'It is a whole school of thought, an entire conception of the Universe that have been defeated. Spiritual forces will be crushed, the hour of judgment is at hand.'

Stalingrad was not just the triumph of Communism over Fascism or, rather, it was not only that. Looked at from another angle, at the distance from which the meaning of such vast and far-reaching events can best be judged, it will be seen as a victory of our humanist civilization over a civilization of another kind – a Satanic and magical form of civilization designed, not for Man, but for 'something more than Man'. There are no essential differences in the ultimate aims of two civilizations such as the U.S.S.R. and the U.S.A. The Europe of the eighteenth and nineteenth centuries supplied the motive-power which is still functioning.

The engine does not make exactly the same noise in New York as in Moscow, but that is all. It was not, in reality a mere temporary coalition of basic enemies that went to war with Germany, but a whole world – a single, united world that believes in progress, justice, equality and science. One world having the same vision of the Cosmos, the same understanding of Universal Laws, and one that assigns to man the same place, neither too exalted nor too humble, in the Universe. One world that believes in reason and the reality of things. A world, in a word, which was to have disappeared altogether to leave room for another of which Hitler felt himself to be the prophet.

It was, nevertheless, the 'little men' of the free world, the inhabitants of Moscow, Boston, Limoges and Liège – the little man with his positive and rationalist philosophy, a moralist rather than a religious fanatic, uninterested in metaphysics or the world of fantasy – the type Zarathustra described as an imitation-man, a caricature – it was this little man, a replica of Flaubert's Monsieur Homais, who was to annihilate the Great Army whose mission it was to prepare the way for the Superman, the demi-god, who would reign supreme over the elements, and the stars. And, by a curious freak of justice – or injustice – it was this little man with his limited mentality who, years later, was to launch into space the satellite which was to inaugurate the interplanetary era. Stalingrad and the launching of the first Sputnik were, as the Russians have pointed out, two decisive victories which, incidentally, they celebrated together in 1957 on the anniversary of their Revolution.

A photograph of Goebbels was published in the Russian Press, with the caption: 'He thought we were going to be annihilated. It was necessary for us to win in order to create the interplanetary man.'

The mad, desperate, catastrophic resistance put up by Hitler at a time when it was quite obvious that all was lost can only be explained by his belief in the Horbigerian theory that the world was awaiting a second Deluge. If the situation could not be retrieved by human means, it was still possible to provoke the judgment of the gods. The Deluge would recur as a punishment for the whole human race. Night would cover the Earth, and everything would be submerged under a tempest of water and hail. Hitler, Speer recounts with horror, 'deliberately tried to make everything perish with him. He had reached a state in which, as far as he was concerned, the end of his own life meant the end of the world.' Goebbels, in his last pronouncements, greeted with enthusiasm the enemy bombers which were destroying his country: 'Under the ruins of our demolished cities the accomplishments of the stupid nineteenth century lie buried.' Hitler glorified death: he advocated the total destruction of Germany, caused all prisoners to be put to death, condemned to death his own surgeon, had his brother-in-law executed, passed sentence of death on his defeated soldiers and descended himself into the grave. 'Hitler and Goebbels,' wrote Trevor Roper, 'called upon the German people to destroy their towns and factories, blow up their bridges and dams and demolish the railways and all the rolling-stock, all for the sake of a legend – the Twilight of the Gods.' Hitler called for blood, and sent his last remaining troops out to be sacrificed. 'Our losses never seem to be high enough,' he said.

It was not Germany's enemies who had triumphed, but the

forces of the Universe which had been set in motion to drown the Earth and punish humanity, because humanity had allowed the ice to triumph over fire and the forces of death to prevail over the powers of life and resurrection. The vengeance of Heaven would strike; all that was left for him to do on his deathbed was to summon the Great Flood. Hitler staged a water sacrifice and gave orders that the Berlin Underground should be flooded: 300,000 people who had taken refuge there perished in this way. It was an act of initiative magic: this gesture would be the signal for Apocalyptic events in the Heavens and on the Earth. Goebbels published one last article before putting to death in the Bunker his wife and children and committing suicide himself. He declared that the tragedy that was being enacted was not on an earthly, but on a cosmic plane. 'Our end will be the end of the whole Universe.'

They soared on the wings of their demented imagination into infinite space – and died in a cellar.

They thought they were preparing the way for a demi-god who would command the elements. They believed in a cycle of fire. They would conquer the ice, on Earth and in Heaven, and their soldiers died of exposure in performing their natural functions. They had fantastic ideas about the evolution of the species, and thought that far-reaching mutations would take place. And the last news they received from the world outside came to them from the head keeper of the Berlin Zoo who, from his perch on the branch of a tree, telephoned it to the Bunker.

In the days of their power, ambition and pride, they prophesied:

> *Le grand âge du monde renaît.*
> *Les années d'or reviennent;*
> *La terre, comme un serpent,*
> *Renouvelle ses vêtements usés de l'hiver.'*

But there is, no doubt, a deeper kind of prophesy that condemns the prophets themselves to a more than tragic – a caricatural death. From the depths of their cellar, with the thundering of the tanks growing ever louder in their ears, they ended their tumultuous and evil lives in the agony and supplication which Shelley in his *Hellas*, describes:

> 'Oh, cease! must hate and death return?
> Cease! must men kill and die?
> Cease! drain not to its dregs the urn
> Of bitter prophecy.
> The world is weary of the past,
> Oh, might it die or rest at last!'

VII

A hollow Earth – We are living inside it – The Sun and Moon are in the centre of the Earth – Radar in the service of the Wise Men – Birth of a new religion in America – Its prophet was a German airman – Anti-Einstein – The work of a madman – A hollow Earth, Artificial Satellites and the notion of Infinity – Hitler as arbiter – Beyond coherence

WE are in April 1942. Germany is putting her whole strength into the war. Nothing, it would seem, could distract the technicians, scientists and military chiefs from the performance of their immediate tasks.

Nevertheless, an expedition organized with the approval of Goering, Himmler and Hitler set out from the Reich surrounded by the greatest secrecy. The members of this expedition were some of the greatest experts on radar. Under the direction of Dr. Heinz Fisher, well known for his work on infra-red rays, they disembarked on the island of Rügen in the Baltic. The expedition was equipped with the most up-to-date radar apparatus, despite the fact that these instruments were still rare at that time, and distributed over the principal nerve-centres of the German defence system.

However, the observations to be carried out on the island of Rügen were considered by the Admiralty General Staff as of capital importance for the offensive which Hitler was preparing to launch on every front.

Immediately on arrival at their destination Dr. Fisher aimed his radar at the sky at an angle of 45 degrees. There appeared to be nothing to detect in that particular direction. The other members of the expedition thought that a test was being carried out. They did not know what was expected of them; the object of these experiments would be revealed to them later. To their amazement, the radar remained fixed in the same position for several days. It was then that they learned the reason: Hitler had formed the idea that the Earth is not convex but concave. We are not living on the outside of the globe, but inside it. Our position is comparable to that of flies walking about inside a round bowl. The object of the expedition was to demonstrate this truth scientifically. By the reflection of radar rays travelling in a straight line it would be possible to obtain an image of points situated at a great distance inside the sphere. The expedition also had a second object, namely, to obtain by reflection an image of the British Fleet at Scapa Flow.

Martin Gardner tells the story of this crazy adventure on the island of Rügen in his book *In the Name of Science*. Dr. Fisher himself made some allusion to it after the war. In 1946 Professor Gerard S. Kuiper, of the Mount Palomar Observatory, wrote a series of articles on the theory of a hollow Earth which had inspired this expedition. This is what he wrote in *Popular Astronomy*: 'High officials in the German Admiralty and Air Force believed

185

in the theory of a hollow Earth. They thought this would be useful for locating the whereabouts of the British Fleet, because the concave curvature of the Earth would facilitate long-distance observation by means of infra-red rays, which are less curved than visible rays.' The engineer Willy Ley records the same facts in his essay (May 1947) on 'Pseudo-sciences Under the Nazi Régime'.

All this is extraordinary, but true: high Nazi dignitaries and military experts denied purely and simply what has always appeared self-evident even to a little child in our civilized world – namely, that the Earth is round, and that we are living on its surface. Above us, so the child believes, is an infinite Universe with its myriads of stars and galaxies. Beneath us is a hard rock.

Whether he be English, French, American or Russian, our small boy in all these respects is in agreement with official science, and also with the accepted religions and philosophies. Our moral code, our arts and our techniques are founded on this vision which seems to be confirmed by experience. If we are looking for something that can provide the best guarantee of the unity of our modern civilization, it is in our cosmogony that we shall find it. As regards essentials, that is to say, the situation of man and the Earth in the Universe, we are all agreed, Marxists and non-Marxists alike. Only the Nazis thought differently.

The defenders of the hollow Earth theory, who organized the famous para-scientific expedition to the island of Rügen, believed that we are living inside a globe fixed into a mass of rock extending to infinity, adhering to its concave sides. The sky is in the middle of this globe; it is a mass of bluish gas, with points of brilliant light which we mistake for stars. There are only the Sun and the Moon – both infinitely smaller than the orthodox astronomers think. This is the entire Universe. We are all alone, surrounded by rock.

We shall see how this conception arose – out of legends, intuition and illumination. In the year 1942 a nation engaged in a war in which everything depends on technique expects science to come to the aid of mysticism, and mysticism to increase the efficiency of techniques. Dr. Fisher, a specialist in infra-red rays, is entrusted with the mission of using radar for the benefit of people who believe in magic.

In Paris or London we have our eccentrics, our believers in weird cosmogonies, our prophets who preach all kinds of strange things. They publish pamphlets, frequent old bookshops, address meetings in Hyde Park or the Salle de Geographie in the Boulevard Saint-Germain. In Hitler's Germany we saw people of this kind mobilizing the forces of a nation and the whole technical machinery of an army at war. We saw the influence they had over the High Command, the political leaders and the scientists. This is because such people belonged to a brand-new civilization founded on a contempt for classical culture and reason. In such a civilization intuition, mystical and poetical illumination are elevated to exactly the same level as scientific research and rational learning. 'When I hear anyone speaking of culture I draw my revolver,' said Goering. This terrifying saying has a double meaning: a literal one that shows us a Goering–Ubu demolishing the intellectuals, and a deeper one that is really more harmful to what we call culture which shows Goering firing explosive bullets in the form of Horbiger's cosmogony, the hollow Earth theory or the mystical dogmas of the group known as *Thule.*

The hollow Earth theory was initiated in America at the beginning of the nineteenth century. On 10th April, 1818, all the members of Congress, Heads of Universities and a few leading scientists received the following letter:

Saint-Louis,
Missouri,
N. America.
10th April.

To the whole world:
I declare that the Earth is hollow and habitable in the interior. It contains several solid, concentric spheres, placed one inside the other, and is open to the pole at an angle of from 12 to 16 degrees. I undertake to prove the truth of what I am asserting, and am ready to explore the interior of the Earth if the world agrees to help me in my undertaking.

(*signed*) Jno. Cleves Symnes,
Captain (Retd.) Ohio Infantry.

Sprague de Camp and Willy Ley in their remarkable book, *From Atlantis to Eldorado,* give the following account of the theory and of the adventures of the former Captain:
'Symnes maintained that since everything in the world was hollow, including bones, hair, the stalks of plants, etc., the planets too were hollow; and in the case of the Earth it was possible to distinguish five spheres one inside the other, all of them being habitable both inside and out, and equipped with enormous polar apertures through which the inhabitants of each sphere could go from any one point to another, inside or out, like ants running about on the inside or the outside of a china bowl. . . . Symnes organized lecture tours on the scale of electoral campaigns. He left behind him, after his death, masses of notes and what was probably a little wooden model of the Symnes Globe now in the Academy of Natural Sciences in Philadelphia. His son, Americ Vespucius Symnes, was one of his disciples, who tried, unsuccessfully, to collect his father's notes and present them in a coherent form. He contributed the suggestion that, in the course of time, the Ten Lost Tribes of Israel would be discovered, probably living inside the outermost sphere.'
In 1870 another American, Cyrus Read Teed, proclaimed, in his turn, that the Earth was hollow. Teed was a very learned man, who had specialized in alchemist literature. In 1869, while working in his laboratory and meditating on the Book of Isaiah, he had a vision. He at once understood that we were living, not on the

Earth, but inside it. This vision gave fresh confirmation to ancient legends, so he created a sort of religion and, in order to publicize his teaching founded a small journal entitled *The Sword of Fire*. In 1894 he had a following of more than 4,000 fanatics. His religion was called *Koreshism*. He died in 1908, after announcing that his corpse would not suffer decay. But his disciples were obliged to embalm him after two days.

This idea of a hollow Earth is connected with a tradition which is to be found everywhere throughout the ages. The most ancient religious texts speak of a separate world situated underneath the Earth's crust which was supposed to be the dwelling-place of departed spirits. When Gilgamesh, the legendary hero of the ancient Sumerian and Babylonian epics, went to visit his ancestor Utnapishtim, he descended into the bowels of the Earth; and it was there that Orpheus went to seek the soul of Euridice. Ulysses, having reached the furthermost boundaries of the Western world, offered a sacrifice so that the spirits of the Ancients would rise up from the depths of the Earth and give him advice. Pluto was said to reign over the underworld and over the spirits of the dead. The early Christians used to meet in the catacombs, and believed that the souls of the damned went to live in caverns beneath the Earth. Venus, in some Germanic legends, was banished to the bowels of the Earth. Dante situated his Inferno among the lowest circles. In European folk-lore dragons have their habitat underground, and the Japanese believe that deep down underneath their island dwells a monster whose stirrings are the cause of earthquakes.

We have referred above to a pre-Hitlerian secret society, the Vril which mixed these legends with the theories put forward by the English author Bulwer Lytton in his novel *The Coming Race*. According to the members of this society, beings endowed with psychic powers superior to our own inhabit caverns in the centre of the Earth. One day they will come forth and reign over us.

At the end of the 1914 war a young German airman, Bender, while a prisoner in France, discovered some old copies of Teed's paper *The Sword of Fire* along with some propaganda pamphlets in support of the hollow Earth theory. Attracted by this creed, and having himself received 'enlightenment' on the subject, he developed and formulated this doctrine in precise terms and, on his return to Germany, founded a movement entitled the *Hohl Welt Lehre*. He also continued the work of another American, Marshall B. Gardner, who in 1913 had published a book to prove that the Sun was not above the Earth, but inside it, and that it was the pressure exerted by its rays that kept us attached to the Earth's concave surface.

For Bender, the Earth is a sphere of the same size as in orthodox geography, but hollow; living creatures adhere to its internal surface through the agency of certain solar radiations. All round there is nothing but rock, stretching to infinity. The layer of air inside extends to forty-five miles, after which it rarefies to become a complete vacuum in the centre, where there are three bodies:

the Sun, the Moon, and a Phantom Universe. This consists of a globe of bluish gas pierced by bright, shining points of light which the astronomers call stars. It is night over a part of this concave Earth when the blue mass passes in front of the Sun, and the shadow of this mass on the Moon produces eclipses. We, on the other hand believe in an external Universe, situated outside us, because light-rays do not travel in a straight line but, with the exception of infra-red rays, are curved. This theory of Bender's became popular round about the 1930s. The rulers of Germany and officers of the Admiralty and Air Force High Command believed that the Earth is hollow.

It is quite fantastic that men in charge of a nation's destiny should have shaped their policy to some extent on mystical intuitions and theories which deny the existence of our Universe. It is nevertheless true that for the ordinary German 'man in the street', in the 1930s, crushed by defeat and misery, the idea of a hollow Earth might well have seemed, after all, no crazier than the idea of sources of unlimited energy being contained in a speck of matter, or the notion of a four-dimensional Universe. Since the end of the nineteenth century science has been following a path which seems to run counter to common sense. To a nation of primitive, unhappy and mystically-minded people anything strange seemed admissible, especially if it were something as comprehensible and consoling as the idea of a hollow Earth. Hitler and his cronies, who were men of the 'people' and hostile to any kind of intellectualism, were no doubt more inclined to accept the ideas of a man like Bender than the theories of an Einstein which revealed a Universe of infinite complexity which demanded an infinitely delicate approach. Bender's world was apparently as mad as Einstein's; but represented a more elementary form of madness. Bender's explanation of the Universe, though starting from crazy premisses, was logically developed. The madman had lost everything except his reason.

The *Hohl Welt Lehre*, which considered humanity to be the only intelligence in the Universe, which reduced that Universe to the dimensions of the Earth and gave men the sensation of being enfolded, enclosed and protected, like a foetus in the womb, satisfied certain aspirations of an unhappy people, thrown back on themselves and full of pride and resentment against the outside world. It was, moreover, the only German theory which could be set against the teaching of the Jew Einstein.

Einstein's theory was based on the Michelson–Morley experiment showing that the speed of light travelling in the direction of the Earth's rotation is the same as that of light travelling at right angles to the Earth's orbit. Einstein deduced from this that light is not 'carried' on anything, but is composed of independent particles. From these premisses Einstein saw that light contracts along the path on which it is moving and that it is a condensed form of energy. He then formulated the theory of the relativity of the speed of light. In Bender s system the Earth, being hollow, does not move, so the Michelson theory does not apply. The hollow Earth theory therefore seems to conform to reality just as much as Einstein's. At that time no experiment had yet been made to verify Einstein's thesis, as the atomic bomb had not yet arrived to provide an absolutely conclusive and terrifying proof of its correctness. The German rulers made this a pretext for discrediting the work of the distinguished Jewish scientist, and for launching a campaign against Jewish scientists and official science in general.

Einstein, Teller, Fermi and a number of other eminent scientists were obliged to go into exile. They were welcomed in the United States, and provided with money and well-equipped laboratories. It was from these beginnings that America built up her atomic power. Thus the rise to power of occult forces in Germany had the result of endowing America with nuclear energy.

The most important study centre in the American Army was at Dayton, Ohio. In 1957 it was announced that the laboratory there where work was proceeding on the hydrogen bomb had succeeded in producing a temperature of one million degrees. The scientist who had successfully conducted this astonishing experiment was none other than the Dr. Heinz Fisher who had led the expedition to the island of Rügen to verify the truth of the hollow Earth theory.

Ever since 1945 he had been working freely in the United States. When asked by the American Press about his past, he said: 'The Nazis forced me to do crazy things which hindered me considerably in my researches.' One wonders what would have happened, and how the war would have developed if Dr. Fisher's researches had not been interrupted to further the mystical notions of Bender. . . .

After the Rügen expedition, Bender's prestige, in the eyes of the Nazi leaders, declined, in spite of the protection of Goering who had a great affection for this formerly distinguished airman.

The followers of Horbiger, the believers in the Universe of eternal ice, won the day. Bender was thrown into a concentration camp and died there. He was thus a martyr to the theory of the hollow Earth.

Some time before the crazy expedition, however, the Horbigerians had mocked at Bender and demanded a ban on his writings in support of the hollow Earth theory. Horbiger's system was on the same scale as orthodox cosmology, and it would be impossible to believe at one and the same time in a Cosmos where ice and fire are in eternal conflict, and in a hollow globe surrounded by an infinite expanse of rock. Hitler was asked to decide between them. His answer gives food for thought: 'Our conception of the world need not be coherent. They may both be right.'

The important thing is not coherence and unity in our thinking, but the destruction of systems based on logic and reason, the mystical dynamism and explosive force of intuition.

In the sparkling darkness of the magician's night there is room for more than one spark.

VIII

*Grist for our horrible mill – The last prayer of Dietrich
Eckardt – The legend of Thule – A nursery for mediums –
Haushofer the magician – Hess's silence – The swastika and
the mysteries of the house of Ipatiev – The seven men who
wanted to change life – A Thibetan colony – Exterminations
and ritual – It is darker than you thought*

IN Kiel, after the war, there lived a worthy doctor, a *bon vivant*
specializing in National Health Insurance, named Fritz Sawade.
Towards the end of 1959 a mysterious voice warned the doctor
that he was going to be arrested. He ran away, wandered about
for a week and then surrendered. He was in reality the *Ober-
sturmbannführer* S.S. Werner Heyde. Professor Heyde had been
the doctor responsible for the scheme for euthanasia which from
1940 to 1941 caused the death of 200,000 Germans and prepared
the way for the extermination of foreigners in the concentration
camps.

With reference to this arrest, a French journalist who has made a
special study of Hitler's Germany (M. Nobecourt) wrote as follows
in *Carrefour* on 6th January, 1960:

'The case of Heyde, like many others, can be compared to an
iceberg, of which the part that is visible is the least important. . . .
Euthanasia of the weak, and mass extermination of all communities
liable to "contaminate the purity of German blood" were carried
out with a pathological degree of ruthlessness and an almost
religious conviction that bordered on madness. To such an extent,
indeed, that many observers who followed the post-war trials –
scientific or medical authorities who would be most unlikely to
accept any explanation of a mystical nature – were forced in the end
to the conclusion that the motive could not have been merely
political passions, but that there must have been a kind of mystical
bond between all those, chiefs and subordinates alike, who acted
in this way – between Himmler, in fact, and the lowest-ranking
guard in a concentration camp.

'The hypothesis of a community of Initiates beneath the cloak
of National-Socialism gradually came to be accepted. This must
have been a truly Satanic community, obeying secret dogmas far
more elaborate than the elementary precepts of *Mein Kampf* or the
Twentieth Century Myth, and practising rites single instances of
which would not attract attention although the experts on Nazi
pathology (who, as we said before, were trained scientists and
doctors) had no doubt whatever that they existed.' More grist for
our horrible mill!

We do not, however, believe that there was only one well
organized and widely diffused secret society, or only one dogma
or even an organically constituted ritual system. On the contrary;

191

plurality and incoherence seem to be most typical of this subterranean Germany we are trying to describe. To a Westerner, brought up in a positivist and Cartesian Society, unity and cohesion seem indispensable conditions in any undertaking, even if it is of a mystical nature. But here we are no longer in the presence of Western ways of thought, but are confronted, rather, with a multiform cult, a state of super (or sub) awareness that absorbs various rites and beliefs having little in common. What is important is to keep the sacred fire burning and alive; anything will serve for fuel.

For this mentality nothing is impossible. Natural laws are suspended, the world becomes fluid. Some S.S. leaders declared that the English Channel was much narrower than is marked on the maps. For them, as for the Hindu sages two thousand years ago and for Bishop Berkeley in the eighteenth century, the Universe was only an illusion, and its structure could be altered by an effort of will on the part of the Initiates. . . .

The probable explanation for all this in our opinion is the existence of a magic 'puzzle', a powerful and Satanic mystical current such as we have tried to describe in the course of the preceding chapters. This could explain a great many terrible facts in a more realistic way than that of the conventional historians who are ready to attribute so many cruel and irrational acts to the megalomania of a syphilitic, the sadism of a handful of nevropaths and the servile obedience of a pack of cowards.

Pursuing our method of research, we shall now present the reader with some information about other neglected aspects of this 'magic socialism', such as, for example, the Thule Society, the Black Order and the Ahnenerbe Society. We have assembled a considerable volume of documentation, about a thousand pages, on this subject, although this would all have to be carefully checked and considerably supplemented if we wanted to write a complete and convincing study of these questions. For the moment we are not equipped to do this. Moreover, we are anxious not to overload this book which only deals with contemporary history in so far as it illustrates our thesis of 'fantastic realism'. A brief summary follows of some facts which may be found illuminating.

In the autumn of 1923 the death took place in Munich of a singular personage – poet, playwright, journalist and Bohemian – named Dietrich Eckardt. With his lungs injured by mustard-gas, he addressed a prayer of a very personal nature, before he died, to a black meteorite which he used to call his 'Mecca Stone' and had left in his will to Professor Oberth, one of the pioneers of astronautics. He had just sent a lengthy manuscript to his friend Haushofer. After his death the Thule Society (such was his prayer) would continue to exist and would soon change the world and all life upon it.

In 1920 Dietrich Eckardt and another member of the Thule Society, the architect Alfred Rosenberg, had made the acquaintance of Hitler. Their first meeting took place in Wagner's house at

Bayreuth, and for the next three years they were to be the constant companions of the little Reichswehr corporal, dominating all his thoughts and acts. Konrad Heiden (in his *Adolph Hitler*) wrote that 'Eckardt undertook the spiritual formation of Adolph Hitler'. He also taught him to write and speak. His instruction was given on two levels: one being concerned with the 'secret' doctrine, and the other with the doctrine of propaganda.

He has related some of his conversations with Hitler, at the second level, in a curious pamphlet entitled: *Bolshevism from Moses to Lenin*. In July 1923 Eckardt became one of the seven founder-members of the National-Socialist Party.

Seven: a sacred figure. In the autumn, before he died, he told his colleagues: Follow Hitler. He will dance, but it is I who called the tune. We have given him the means of communicating with Them. Do not mourn for me: I shall have influenced history more than any other German. . . .'

The legend of Thule is as old as the Germanic race. It was supposed to be an island that had disappeared somewhere in the extreme North. Off Greenland? or Labrador? Like Atlantis, Thule was thought to have been the magic centre of a vanished civilization. Eckardt and his friends believed that not all the secrets of Thule had perished. Beings intermediate between Man and other intelligent beings from Beyond, would place at the disposal of the Initiates a reservoir of forces which could be drawn on to enable Germany to dominate the world again and be the cradle of the coming race of Supermen which would result from mutations of the human species. One day her legions would set out to annihilate everything that had stood in the way of the spiritual destiny of the Earth, and their leaders would be men who knew everything, deriving their strength from the very fountain-head of energy and guided by the Great Ones of the Ancient World. Such were the myths on which the Aryan doctrine of Eckardt and Rosenberg was founded and which these prophets of a 'magic' form of socialism had instilled into the mediumistic mind of Hitler. But the Thule Society was at that time, no doubt, nothing more than a fairly powerful little machine for confounding fact and fiction. Under other influences and in the hands of other persons it was soon to become a much stranger instrument – an instrument capable of changing the very nature of reality. It would seem that it was under influence of Karl Haushofer that the group took on its true character of a society of Initiates in communion with the Invisible, and became the magic centre of the Nazi movement.

Hitler was born at Braunau-am-Inn, on 20th April, 1889, at 5.30 p.m. at No. 219, Salzburger Vorstadt. As an Austro-Bavarian frontier town, where two great German States met, it became for Hitler in later life a symbolic city. It enjoyed the singular reputation of being the birthplace of a number of mediums, notably of Willy and Rudy Schneider whose psychic experiments created a sensation some thirty years ago. Hitler had the same wet-nurse as Willy Schneider. Jean de Pange wrote, in 1940: 'Braunau is a centre for mediums. One of the best known is Mme Stokhammes who, in 1920, married in Vienna Prince Joachim of Prussia. It was also from Braunau that the Munich spiritualist, Baron Schrenk-Notzing, recruited his subjects, one of whom was in fact a cousin of Hitlers.'

Occultism teaches that, after concluding a pact with hidden forces, the members of the Group cannot evoke these forces save through the intermediary of a magician who, in turn, can do nothing without a medium. It would seem, therefore, that Hitler must have been the medium, and Haushofer the magician.

Rauschning, in describing the Führer, wrote as follows: 'One cannot help thinking of him as a medium. For most of the time mediums are ordinary, insignificant people. Suddenly they are endowed with what seem to be supernatural powers which set them apart from the rest of humanity. These powers are something that is outside their true personality – visitors, as it were, from another planet. The medium is possessed. Once the crisis is past, they fall back again into mediocrity. It was in this way, beyond any doubt, that Hitler was possessed by forces outside himself – almost demoniacal forces of which the individual named Hitler was only the temporary vehicle. This mixture of the banal and the supernatural created that insupportable duality of which one was conscious in his presence. This was a Being who might have been invented by Dostoievsky. It was like looking at a bizarre face whose expression seems to reflect an unbalanced state of mind coupled with a disquieting impression of hidden power.'

According to Strasser: 'Listening to Hitler one suddenly has a vision of one who will lead mankind to glory . . . A light appears in a dark window. A gentleman with a comic little moustache turns into an archangel. . . . Then the archangel flies away . . . and there is Hitler sitting down, bathed in sweat with glassy eyes. . . .'

Bouchez said: 'I looked into his eyes – the eyes of a medium in a trance. . . . Sometimes there seemed to be a sort of ectoplasm; the speaker's body seemed to be inhabited by something . . . fluid. Afterwards he shrank again to insignificance, looking small and even vulgar. He seemed exhausted, his batteries run down.'

François-Poncet records: 'He entered into a sort of mediumistic trance; the expression on his face was ecstatic.'

The medium represented, no doubt, not just one man, but a group, a collectivity of forces, a sort of magic power-house. What seems to us certain is that Hitler was animated by something other than what he was preaching: by forces and doctrines badly co-ordinated, no doubt, but infinitely more dangerous than the mere theory of National-Socialism – an idea far greater than anything he had thought of himself, which was more than he could grasp and of which he could only convey to his people and his collaborators in a much vulgarized and fragmentary form. In the words of Dr. Delmas:

'A powerful resonator, Hitler had always been the "sounding-board" he claimed to be at the Munich Trial, and remained so until the end. Nevertheless, he only retained and used what at any given moment could satisfy his ambition and lust for power, his dreams of conquering the world and his crazy obsession: the biological selection of a species that would be half man, half god.

Another of his dreams, which was also an obsession, was to change life on Earth everywhere. He sometimes alluded to it or, rather, was unable to prevent what he was thinking from escaping now and then in some casual remark. He once said to Rauschning: 'Our revolution is a new stage or, rather, the final stage in an evolution which will end by abolishing history. . . .' Or, again: 'You know nothing about me; my party comrades have no conception of the dreams which haunt me or of the grandiose edifice of which the foundations, at least, will have been laid before I die. . . . The world has reached a turning point; we are now at a critical moment in time. . . . The planet will undergo an upheaval which you uninitiated people cannot understand. . . . What is happening is something more than the advent of a new religion. . . .'

Rudolf Hess had been Haushofer's assistant when the latter was a professor at the University of Munich. It was he who had brought Haushofer and Hitler together. (His flight to England during the war was the result of Haushofer having told him that he had seen him in a dream flying to England in an aeroplane. In one of the rare moments of lucidity which his inexplicable malady allowed him the prisoner Hess, the last survivor of the *Thule* Group, is said to have stated formally that Haushofer was the magician, the secret Master.)*

After his abortive rising, Hitler was confined to prison at Landshurt. Introduced by Hess, General Karl Haushofer visited Hitler every day and spent hours with him expounding his theories and deducing from them every possible argument in favour of political conquest. Left alone with Hess, Hitler amalgamated, for the purposes of propaganda, the theories of Haushofer and the projects of Rosenberg which form the basis of *Mein Kampf*.

Karl Haushofer was born in 1869. He paid several visits to India and the Far East, and was sent to Japan, where he learned the language. He believed that the German people originated in Central Asia, and that it was the Indo-Germanic race which guaranteed the permanence, nobility and greatness of the world. While in Japan, Haushofer is said to have been initiated into one of the most important secret Buddhist societies and to have sworn, if he failed in his 'mission', to commit suicide in accordance with the time-honoured ceremonial.

In 1914 Haushofer, then a youthful General, was known for his extraordinary gift of being able to predict events before they occurred: the hour when the enemy would attack, the places where shells would fall, storms and political changes in countries about which he knew nothing. Did Hitler also possess this gift of clairvoyance, or was it Haushofer who communicated to him his own visions?

Hitler predicted exactly the date of the entry of his troops into

* See Jack Fishman: *The Seven Men of Spandau*.

Paris, the date of the arrival at Bordeaux of the first blockade raisers. When he decided to reoccupy the Rhineland in 1935, all the experts in Europe, including the Germans, were convinced that France and England would resist. Hitler predicted that they would not. He also announced the date of the death of Roosevelt.

After the First World War, Haushofer returned to his studies and seems to have specialized exclusively in political geography. He founded the *Geo-Political Review*, and published a number of books. Curiously enough, these works appear to be founded on a strictly materialist form of political realism. The care which all the members of the Group took to employ a purely materialistic exoteric language, and to exteriorize their pseudo-scientific conceptions, was a perpetual source of mystification.

Behind the Geo-Politician there was another personality – a disciple of Schopenhauer who had taken up Buddhism, an admirer of Ignatius de Loyola who wanted to govern men, a mystic in search of hidden realities, a man of great culture and intense psychic sensitivity. It seems that it was Haushofer who actually chose the swastika as an emblem.

In Europe, as in Asia, the swastika has always been considered a magic sign. It has been taken as a symbol of the Sun, source of life and fecundity, or of thunder, a manifestation of divine wrath which has to be appeased. In contrast to the cross, the triangle, the circle or the crescent, the swastika is not a primitive sign which could have been invented and re-invented at any time in the history of humanity or at any place on the globe, with a different symbolic meaning every time. It is in fact the first sign traced with a definite intention. The study of migrations raises the problem of the common origins from the earliest times of the various religions and of the prehistoric relations between Europe, Asia and America. The earliest known specimen of the swastika is supposed to have been found in Transylvania, dating from the end of the polished Stone Age. It is found on hundreds of spindles as far back as 1400 B.C., and in the remains of Troy. It appears in India in the fourth century B.C., and in China in the fifth century A.D. A century later it is found in Japan at the time of the introduction of Buddhism which adopted it as an emblem. Of capital importance is the fact that it is entirely unknown, or only occurs accidentally, in all Semitic regions such as Egypt, Chaldea, Assyria and Phoenicia. It is an exclusively Aryan symbol.* In 1891 Ernest Krauss drew the attention of the Germanic public to this fact: Guido List, in 1908, described the swastika in his popular science books as a symbol of racial purity, and at the same time, a sign of esoteric knowledge revealed by the deciphering of the Icelandic epic poem known as the *Edda*. At the Russian Court the swastika was introduced by the Empress Alexandra Feodorovna. Was this due to

---

* R. Petitfrère: *La mystique de la croix gammée.*

196

the influence of the theosophists ? Or of the medium Badmaiev, a strange character who had been brought up at Lhasa and had since been closely connected with Thibet ? Now, Thibet is one of the countries in the world where the swastika, turned either to the right or to the left, is most commonly met with.

In Berlin there was a Thibetan monk, nicknamed 'the man with the green gloves', who had correctly foretold in the Press, on three occasions, the number of Hitlerian deputies elected to the Reichstag, and who was regularly visited by Hitler. He was said by the Initiates to 'possess the keys to the Kingdom of Agarthi'.

This brings us back again to Thule. At the same time as *Mein Kampf*, the Russian, Ossendovski, published a book entitled *Men, Beasts and Gods*, in which appeared, for the first time in public, the names Schamballah and Agarthi – names which will be heard again from the lips of those responsible for the *Ahnenerbe* at the Nuremberg Trial. The year is 1925.*

The National-Socialist Party was beginning an active recruiting campaign. Horst Wessel, Horbiger's right-hand man, was organizing shock troops. The following year, he was shot down by the Communists. To commemorate him, the poet Ewers composed a song which was to become the Party's sacred Hymn. Ewers, who was a 'Lovecraft' German, was an enthusiastic member of the Party because he saw in it, at the beginning, 'the strongest expression of the Powers of Darkness'.

The seven founders of the movement, who dreamed of 'changing life on the Earth', were physically and spiritually certain that they were being sustained by these Powers. If our information is correct, the oath which bound them, and the myth to which they looked for strength, confidence and luck, were both derived from a Thibetan legend. Thirty or forty centuries ago in the region of Gobi there was a highly developed civilization. As the result of a catastrophe, possibly of an atomic nature, Gobi was transformed into a desert, and the survivors emigrated, some going to the extreme North of Europe, and others towards the Caucasus. The Scandinavian god Thor is supposed to have been one of the heroes of this migration.

* In 1931, in his book *Le symbolisme de la Croix*, René Guénon has the following note: 'We read recently, in an article in the *Journal des Débats* of 22nd January, 1929, the following news item which shows that the old traditions are not as dead as people think: "In 1925 the Cuna Indians rose in revolt, slaughtered the gendarmes from Panama who lived on their territory, and founded the independent Republic of Thule, whose flag is a swastika on an orange ground with a red border. This republic exists to this day." Of special interest is the association of the swastika with the name of Thule, which is one of the oldest designations of that supreme spiritual centre, which has since been applied to some of its lesser branches.'

The 'Initiates' of the Thule Group were convinced that these survivors were Aryans, members of the original race from which all humanity had sprung. Haushofer proclaimed the necessity of 'a return to the sources' of the human race – in other words, that it was necessary to conquer the whole of Eastern Europe, Turkestan, Pamir, Gobi and Thibet These countries constituted, in his opinion, the central core, and whoever had control of them controlled the whole world.

According to the legend with which Haushofer no doubt became acquainted in 1905, and the version which René Guénon gave of it in his *Le Roi du Monde*, after the cataclysm of Gobi the lords and masters of this great centre of civilization, the All-Knowing, the sons of Intelligences from Beyond, took up their abode in a vast underground encampment under the Himalayas. There, in the heart of these caves, they divided into two groups, one following the 'Right Hand Way', and the other the 'Left Hand Way'. The first of these had its centre at Agarthi, a place of meditation, a hidden city of Goodness, a temple of non-participation in the things of this world.

The second went to Schamballah, a city of violence and power whose forces command the elements and the masses of humanity, and hasten the arrival of the human race at the 'turning-point of time'. The Wise Men, leaders of the peoples of the world, would be able to conclude a pact with Schamballah, which would be sealed with solemn oaths and sacrifices.

In Austria, the group *Edelweiss* announced in 1928 the coming of a new Messiah. In England, Sir Oswald Mosley and Bellamy gave out that Germany had been touched by the 'Light'. In America, the 'Silver Roads' of Colonel Ballard made their appearance. A number of important persons in England tried to warn the people against this movement in which they discerned a threat to spiritual life and the advent of a Satanic religion. Kipling gave orders that the swastika should be removed from the covers of his books. Lord Tweedsmuir, who wrote as John Buchan, published two *romans à clé*: *The Judgment of Dawn* and *A Prince in Captivity* which contained a description of the dangers to which Western civilization could be exposed through the action of a 'power station' of intellectual, spiritual and magical forces working in the interests of Evil. Saint George Saunders, in his *Seven Sleepers* and *The Hidden Kingdom* denounced the dark menace of Nazi esotericism and its 'Thibetan' sources of inspiration.

It was in 1926 that a small Hindu and Thibetan colony settled in Berlin and Munich. When the Russians entered Berlin, they found among the corpses a thousand volunteers for death in German uniform, without any papers or badges, of Himalayan origin. As soon as the movement began to acquire extensive funds, it organized a number of expeditions to Thibet which succeeded one another practically without interruption until 1943.

The members of the Thule Group were going to be masters of the world, protected against all dangers, and their reign would last for a thousand years, until the next Deluge. They undertook to commit suicide if they ever did anything to break their pact, and to perform human sacrifices. There seem to have been only 'magic' reasons for the extermination of the Gypsies (750,000 dead).

Wolfram Sievers was appointed official executioner, a kind of ritualistic, sacrificial butcher. We shall return to this later, but it is as well to bring as much light as possible at this juncture to bear on one aspect of the terrifying problem raised for all thinking people today by these exterminations. Those responsible looked upon them as a means of overcoming the indifference of the 'Powers' and attracting their attention. From the Mayas to the Nazis, this was the magic significance of human sacrifices.

At the Nuremberg Trial the indifference shown by the worst assassins often astonished those present. A terrible remark made by one of Merritt's heroes in his novel *Les Habitants du Mirage* may help to make this attitude clear: 'I had forgotten, as I always do, the victims of the sacrifice in the sombre excitement of the rite.'

On 14th March, 1946, Karl Haushofer killed his wife Martha and committed suicide, Japanese fashion. His grave is not marked by any stone or cross. He had learned, some time after the event, of the execution at the Moabit camp, of his son Albrecht, who had been arrested with the organizers of the plot against Hitler and the abortive attempt on his life on 20th July, 1944. In the pocket of Albrecht's blood-stained coat they found a poem in MS.:

'For my father destiny had spoken . . .
Once again the demon had to be repulsed
and shut up in his jail . . .
My father broke the seal –
He did not feel the Evil One's breath,
But set him free to roam the world . . .'

All the foregoing may seem to be only a bundle of coincidences, signs, cross-checkings and presumptions. Admittedly the facts we have assembled, according to our method, do not absolutely exclude a rational explanation of the Hitlerian phenomenon in terms of politics or economics. It is also true, of course, that not everything in the conscious, or even subconscious minds of the men of whom we have been speaking, was governed by beliefs of this nature. Nevertheless, their minds were haunted, at one time or another, by the crazy notions we have been describing, whether they recognized them as such, or mistook them for realities; that much, at least, seems certain.

It is a fact, however, that deep down in ourselves our dreams are never completely effaced, any more than the stars are when daylight returns. They continue to shine, as it were, behind our feelings, our thoughts and our acts. There are facts, and beneath them a substratum of other facts: this is the region we are exploring.

Or rather, on the strength of what we have been able to discover, we are suggesting that this region needs exploring. All we can say is that in these depths it is darker than you think.

IX

Himmler and the other side of the problem – 1934 a turning-point – The Black Order in power – The death's-head warrior monks – Initiation in the Burgs – Sievers' last prayer – The strange doings of the Ahnenerbe – The High-Priest Frederick Hielscher – A forgotten note of Jünger's – Impressions of war and victory

IT was during the grim winter of 1942. Germany's best troops and the flower of the S.S., for the first time, were no longer advancing, suddenly bogged down in the Russian steppes. England was obstinately preparing for future struggles, and America was on the verge of entering the fray. One morning during that winter portly Dr. Kersten found his patient, Reichsführer Himmler, depressed and discouraged. 'My dear Doctor, I'm in a terrible predicament. . . .'

Was it that he was beginning to doubt the possibility of victory? No, it was not that. As he lay on the couch, while the doctor massaged his stomach, he began to talk, his eyes fixed on the ceiling. He explained that the Führer had become convinced that there could be no peace on Earth so long as a single Jew was left alive. . . . 'And so,' continued Himmler, 'he has ordered me to liquidate immediately all the Jews in our possession.' His long, desiccate hands lay on the divan inert, as if frozen. He remained silent.

Kersten, taken aback, thought he discerned in the Master of the Black Order signs of pity and revulsion, and his alarm at the news was tempered by a gleam of hope:

'Yes, Yes; I understand; your conscience forbids you to approve of this atrocity. . . . I understand your deep distress.'

'—But, not at all! It isn't that!' cried Himmler, starting up. 'You don't understand!'

Hitler had summoned him and asked him to exterminate immediately from five to six million Jews. This was a very big job, and Himmler was very tired; besides, he had a lot of work on hand at the moment. It was really inhuman to expect him to undertake the new assignment in the near future. Really too bad. He had said as much to his beloved chief, and the beloved chief had not been pleased and had flown into a rage. So now Himmler was feeling depressed because he had acted selfishly and given way to a moment of weakness.*

How can one possibly understand such an astonishing reversal of values? It cannot be explained as being simply a sign of madness. We have to imagine a Universe parallel to our own, the laws and structure of which are radically different. The physicist George Gamow has conceived of a parallel Universe in which, for example, a billiard ball can go into two holes at the same time. The Universe in which people like Himmler live is at least as far removed from ours as Gamow's. A real man, a Thule 'initiate', is in communication with the Powers, and all his energies are directed towards changing life on Earth. What happens if the 'medium' asks such a man to liquidate a few million 'false' men? Very good, but the order comes at an awkward time. Must it absolutely be done immediately? All right, then; let us make an extra effort of self-sacrifice. . . .

On 20th May, 1945, some British soldiers arrested on the Berweverde bridge, twenty-five miles west of Luneberg, a tall man with a round head and narrow shoulders, carrying papers in the name of Hitzinger, in civilian dress with a bandage over his right eye. He was taken to the Military Police station where, for three days, the British officers tried to discover his true identity. Finally, worn out by this questioning, he removed his bandage and said: 'My name is Heinrich Himmler.' They did not believe him. He insisted. To test him he was made to strip naked. He was then offered a choice between American clothes and a blanket. He wrapped himself in the blanket. He was then searched to make sure he was concealing nothing on his body, and asked to open his mouth. At that moment the prisoner crushed a phial of cyanide concealed in a tooth, and fell dead. Three days later an officer and three N.C.O.s took delivery of the body. They went to a nearby forest, dug a trench there, threw in the corpse and carefully replaced the soil. No one knows exactly where Himmler is buried, or under the branches of what bird-frequented tree lies decomposing the flesh of one who claimed to be the reincarnation of the Emperor Henry I, known as the 'Bird-catcher'.

Had Himmler lived to stand his trial at Nuremberg, what could he have pleaded in his defence? He had no common language with the members of the jury. He did not inhabit the same world; he belonged to an entirely different order of things, with a different mentality. He was like a kind of fighting monk from another planet. 'No one has ever been able to explain satisfactorily,' said the *rapporteur* Poetel, 'the psychological complexes which led to Auschwitz and everything that word stands for. For the Nuremberg Trial did not really throw any light on this phenomenon, and the issue was only confused by all the psychoanalytical explanations which

* cf. Kersten's *Memoirs*, and Joseph Kessel's: *Les Mains du Miracle*. Ed. Gallimard.

bluntly declared that it was possible for whole nations to lose their mental balance in the same way as single individuals. No one knows, in fact, what took place in the brain of people like Himmler when they issued their orders of extermination.' . . . If we place ourselves at the level of what we call 'fantastic realism', we may perhaps begin to understand.

Denis de Rougemont said of Hitler: 'Some people think, from having experienced in his presence a feeling of horror and an impression of some supernatural power that he is the seat of "Thrones, Dominations and Powers", by which St. Paul meant those secondary spirits which can descend into any ordinary man and occupy him like a garrison. I have heard him pronounce one of his great speeches. Where do the superhuman powers he shows on these occasions come from ? It is quite obvious that a force of this kind does not belong to the individual, and indeed could not even manifest itself unless the individual were of no importance except as the vehicle of a force for which our psychology has no explanation. What I am saying would be the cheapest sort of romantic nonsense were it not that what has been accomplished by this man – or rather by the forces working through him – is a reality that is one of the wonders of the century.'

In point of fact, during his rise to power Hitler, who had received instruction from Eckardt and Haushofer, seems to have used the Powers placed at his disposal or, rather possessing him, to satisfy what were, after all, rather narrow political and nationalist ambitions. He was fundamentally an insignificant little man with strong patriotic feelings and a passion for social reforms. He functioned on a low level, and there were limits to his dreams.

Suddenly, as if by a miracle, he surged to the front and was successful in everything he undertook. But the medium who is possessed by outside forces is not necessarily conscious of their strength, nor of the direction in which they are leading him. He dances to a tune which is not his own. Until 1934 he thought he was doing all the correct steps. But he was not keeping strict time. He thought that all he had to do was to make full use of his 'Powers'. But one cannot use such Powers; one can only serve them. This is the meaning (or one of the meanings) of the fundamental changes which occurred during and immediately after the Purge of June 1934. The movement, which Hitler himself thought would be National and Socialist and nothing more, became what it was destined to become and adhered more closely to the secret doctrine. Hitler never dared to inquire into the reasons for the 'suicide' of Strasser, and he was made to sign the order which elevated the S.S. to the rank of an autonomous organization, above the Party. Joachim Gunthe wrote in a German journal after the débâcle: 'The vital idea which inspired the S.A. was replaced on 30th June, 1934, by an idea that was purely Satanic – the S.S.'

'It is difficult to say exactly when Hitler began to dream of biological mutations,' says Dr. Delmas. This idea is only one aspect of the esoteric apparatus to which the Nazi Movement became better adjusted from this time onwards when the medium became not, as Rauschning believed, a complete lunatic, but a more pliable instrument and the bandleader of an infinitely more ambitious kind of march than the march to power of a party or a nation, or even of a race.

It was Himmler who was entrusted with the task of organizing the S.S., not as a police force, but as a real religious order with a regular hierarchy ranging from the lay brother to the Father Superior. Among the highest ranking officials were those in charge of a Black Order, whose existence, moreover, was never officially recognized by the National-Socialist Government. Within the Party reference was made to those who were members of 'the inner circle', but they never received any official recognition. It seems certain that the doctrine, never fully defined, was based on an absolute belief in powers that surpassed ordinary human powers. In religion theology, which is considered a science, is distinguished from mysticism which is intuitive and incommunicable. The Ahnenerbe Society, of which we shall have something to say later, represented the theological, and the Black Order the mystical aspect of the religion of the Lords of Thule.

Above all, it must not be forgotten that from the moment when a change in the early methods and policy of the Hitler Party began to be apparent, or rather, as soon as it was made to conform more closely to the secret doctrine which hitherto had only been incompletely understood and obeyed by the 'medium' in charge of propaganda, we are no longer in the presence of a national and political movement. The immediate objectives, generally speaking, remained unchanged or rather continued to be presented to the public in the same exoteric language, but they only served as a cover for other, hidden, aims.

'The only thing that mattered now was the tireless pursuit of a fantastic dream. From now on, if Hitler had had at his command a people better fitted than the German people to serve him and help him to realize his supreme ambition, he would not have hesitated to sacrifice the German people.' Not 'his supreme ambition', but the supreme ambition of a magic group acting through his person. Brasillach admits that 'he would sacrifice the happiness of the whole human race, his own and that of his fellow-countrymen included, if ordered to do so by the mysterious Force whose commands he obeyed.'

'I will tell you a secret,' said Hitler to Rauschning; 'I am founding an Order.' He spoke of the Burgs where the first initiation would take place, saying: 'It is from there that the second stage will emerge – the stage of the Man-God, when Man will be the measure and centre of the world. The Man-God, that splendid Being, will be an object of worship. . . . But there are other stages about which I am not permitted to speak. . . .'

A power-house built round the central generating station, the

Black Order isolates its members from the world, no matter to what degree of initiation they belong. 'Naturally,' writes Poetel, 'it was only a very small circle of high-ranking officials and superior S.S. officers who were familiar with the theories and essential demands of the Order. The members of the various "preparatory" formations were only instructed in these when they had, before marrying, to obtain the permission of their chiefs, or when they were placed under a special jurisdiction which was extremely severe, but gave them protection against any action on the part of the civil authorities. It was then clear to them that outside the Laws of the Order, they had no other duties, and no longer any private life of their own.'

The fighting monks (*monos* – alone), the Death's Head S.S. (not to be confused with other groups, such as the *Waffen S.S.* consisting of the lay brothers or tertiary members of the Order, or of human machines modelled on the genuine S.S. men) received their first instruction in the Burgs, after passing through the *Napola* seminaries. When inaugurating one of the *Napola*, or preparatory schools, Himmler reduced the doctrine to its lowest common measure: 'Believe, obey, fight; that's all.' These were schools in which, as stated in the *Schwarze Korps* of 26th November, 1942, 'pupils learn how to kill and how to die'. Later on, if they proved worthy, the cadets admitted to the Burgs were given to understand that 'to die' could be interpreted as 'the death of the self'. If, however, they were not worthy, they would meet with physical death on the battlefields. 'The tragedy of greatness is to have to trample on corpses.' So what? Not all men are really alive, and there is a hierarchy of existence ranging from the pseudo-man to the Great Magician. No sooner has he emerged from nothingness than the cadet returns there having caught a glimpse, for his salvation, of the road that leads to the splendid figure of the Being. . . .

It was in these Burgs that they pronounced their vows and embarked on an 'irreversible, superhuman destiny'. The Black Order carried out in practice the threats uttered by Dr. Ley: 'He who shall be deemed by the Party to be unworthy of the Brown Shirt – and every one of us ought to know this – shall not only be deprived of his office, but destroyed in his own person, and in the persons of his family, his wife and his children. Such are the harsh and pitiless laws of our Order.'

We are no longer in this world. It is no longer a question of Germany the immortal or of a National-Socialist State, but of a magical preparation for the coming of a Man-God, the New Man whom the Powers will establish on the Earth when we have altered the balance of the spiritual powers. The ceremony of admission to the ranks of the S.S. must have been similar to that which Reinhold Schneider describes when he speaks of the members of the Teutonic Order, in the great hall of the Remter at Marienburg, taking the oath which transformed them into a Church Militant: 'They came from many different countries, having lived adventurous lives. As they entered the austere precincts of this castle, they abandoned their personal shields engraved with arms which had been borne by at least four ancestors. Now their emblem would be the Cross which bound them to wage the sternest battle of all and ensured for them eternal life.' Those who know do not talk; there is no description in existence of the initiatory ceremony in the Burgs, but it is known that such a ceremony took place. It was called 'the ceremony of the Stifling Air' (*'l'Air Epais'*) the allusion being to the extraordinarily tense atmosphere which prevailed until the vows had been pronounced. Some occultists, such as Lewis Spence, believe that the ceremony included a Black Mass in the purest Satanic tradition. On the other hand, Willi Frieschauer, in his study of Himmler, interprets the 'Stifling Air' as the moment when the participants were overcome by complete stupor. Between these two theories there is room for a more realistic, and therefore a more fantastic interpretation.

An irreversible destiny: plans were drawn up to isolate the Death's Head S.S. men from the world of 'pseudo-men' for the rest of their lives. There was a scheme to create cities and colonies of veterans all over the world who would be responsible only to the administration and authority of the Order. But Himmler and his 'brothers' had conceived a still vaster project. The world would have for its model a sovereign S.S. State. 'At the Peace Conference,' said Himmler in March 1943, 'the world will be apprised of the resurrection of the old province of Burgundy, formerly the land of the arts and sciences, which France has reduced to the role of an appendix preserved in spirits of wine. The sovereign State of Burgundy with its own army, its own laws and currency and postal system, will be the model S.S. State. It will comprise French Switzerland, Picardy, Champagne, the Franche-Comté, the Hainaut and Luxembourg. The official language, naturally, will be German. The National-Socialist Party will have no jurisdiction over it. It will be governed by the S.S. alone, and the world will be astonished by and full of admiration for this State in which the ideals of the S.S. will be embodied.'

The true-blooded S.S. man, one of the 'initiates', is in his own estimation, above good and evil. 'Himmler's organization does not count on the fanatical assistance of sadists seeking pleasure in murder: it relies on "new men".' Outside the 'inner circle', consisting of the 'Death's-Heads', their leaders, having access, according to their rank, to the sacred doctrine and owing allegiance to Thule, the Holy of Holies, there was the ordinary rank-and-file S.S. man who was only a soul-less machine, a working robot. He was mass-produced, chosen for his 'negative' qualities. Here there was no question of doctrine, only of training. 'We do not want to do away with inequalities between men,' said Hitler, 'but, on the contrary, to increase them and make them into a principle protected by impenetrable barriers. What will the social order of the future be like? Comrades, I will tell you: there will be a class of overlords, and after them the rank and file of Party Members in hierarchical order, and then the great mass of anonymous followers, servants and workers in perpetuity, and beneath them, again all the conquered foreign races, the modern slaves. And over and above all these there will reign a new and exalted nobility of whom I cannot speak. . . . But of all these plans the ordinary militant members will know nothing. . . .'

The world is matter to be transformed to liberate the concentrated energy of the Wise Men – a psychic energy capable of attracting the Powers from Beyond, the Superior Unknown Beings, the Lords of the Cosmos. The institution of the Black Order had no political or military significance; its *raison d'être* was purely magical. The concentration camps were a form of imitative magic: they were a symbolic act, a model for the social order of the future. All the peoples of the world will be uprooted and turned into an immense nomad population, a kind of raw material which can be exploited and out of which will emerge the flower: Man in contact with the Gods. It is the plaster mould (as Barbey d'Aurévilly used to say: Hell is the mould for Heaven) of our planet transformed into a field of operations for the magicians of the Black Order.

In the instruction given in the Burgs, a part of the secret doctrine is imparted in the following formula: 'The only living being that exists is the Cosmos, or Universe. Everything else, and all other beings, including Man, are only the various forms, which have been multiplied through the ages, of the living Universe.' We ourselves are not alive until we have taken cognizance of this Being which surrounds us, and encloses us and uses us to prepare new forms. Creation is not yet completed; the Spirit of the Cosmos is not at rest; so let us be ready to execute its orders which are transmitted by Gods to us here below – we, the dauntless wonder-workers, shaping to our will the blind and bleeding human masses! The gas-ovens of Auschwitz? Merely ritual.

The S.S. Colonel Wolfram Sievers, who had put up a purely rational defence asked, before his execution, to be allowed for the last time to celebrate his rites and say mysterious prayers. He then calmly went to the gallows unperturbed.

He had been the General Manager of the Ahnenerbe, and it was for this that he was condemned to death at Nuremberg. The Society for the Study of Ancestral Heritages, the Ahnenerbe, was founded privately by Sievers' spiritual teacher Frederick Hielscher, the mystic and friend of the Swedish explorer Sven Hedin who was himself closely associated with Haushofer.

Sven Hedin, an expert on the Far East, had lived for a long time in Thibet and played an important part in establishing the Nazis' esoteric doctrines. Frederick Hielscher was never a Nazi, and was even friendly with the Jewish philosopher Martin Buber. But his profound theories had something in common with the 'magic' doctrines of the Grand Masters of National-Socialism. Himmler, in 1935, two years after its foundation, turned the Ahnenerbe into an official organization, attached to the Black Order. Its declared aims were: 'To make researches into the localization, general characteristics, achievements and inheritance of the Indo-Germanic race, and to communicate to the people the results of this research. This mission must be accomplished through the use of strictly scientific methods.' In other words, the whole machinery of German rational organization was to be employed in the interests of irrationality.

In January 1939 the Ahnenerbe was purely and simply incorporated into the S.S., and its leaders absorbed into Himmler's personal staff. At that time it had fifty branches under the direction of Professor Wurst, an expert on ancient sacred texts who had taught Sanskrit at Munich University.

It seems that Germany spent more on the Ahnenerbe's researches than America did on its preparations for the first atomic bomb. These researches ranged from strictly scientific activities to the practice of occultism, and from vivisection practised on prisoners to espionage on behalf of the secret societies. Negotiations were entered into with Skorzeny with a view to stealing the Holy Grail, and Himmler created a special section for the collection of information 'in the sphere of the supernatural'.

One is astounded at the list of reports drawn up at enormous cost by the Ahnenerbe on such subjects as: the strength of the Rosicrucian confraternity; the symbolism of the suppression of the Irish harp in Ulster; the occult significance of Gothic towers and of the Etonian top-hat, etc. . . . When the German troops were evacuating Naples, Himmler gave repeated orders that they should not forget to take away with them the enormous tombstone of the last Hohenstoffen Emperor. In 1943 after the fall of Mussolini, the Reichsführer summoned to a villa in the outskirts of Berlin the six greatest experts in Germany on occultism to discover the place where the Duce was being held prisoner. Meetings of the General Staff began with Yoga concentration exercises. In Thibet, acting on orders from Sievers, Dr. Scheffer was in contact with a number of lamas in various monastries, and he brought back with him to Munich, for scientific examination, some 'Aryan' horses, and 'Aryan' bees, whose honey had special qualities.

During the war, Sievers organized in the camps for deportees the horrible experiments which have since been the subject of several 'black' books. The Ahnenerbe was 'enriched' by an *Institute of scientific research for national defence* equipped with 'all the facilities available at Dachau'. Professor Hirt, who was in charge of these Institutes, formed a collection of typically Jewish skeletons. Sievers ordered the army in Russia to bring back a number of skulls of Jewish commissaires. When reminded of these crimes at Nuremberg, Sievers betrayed no signs of normal human feeling or pity. He was elsewhere. He was listening to other voices.

Hielscher had no doubt played an important part in the drafting of the secret doctrine. Except in relation to this doctrine, the behaviour of Sievers, as of the other principal instigators of these crimes, remains incomprehensible. The expressions 'moral monstruosity', 'mental cruelty' or madness explain nothing. Little is known about Sievers' spiritual mentor. Ernest Jünger, however, speaks of him in the diary which he kept during the Occupation in Paris. On 14th October, 1943, Jünger wrote in his diary: 'In the evening, a visit from Bogo. (As a precaution Jünger, refers to all important personages by a pseudonym "Bogo" was Hielscher; "Kniebolo", Hitler.) At a time when strong personalities are so scarce, although he is one of the people I have thought a lot about, I do not seem able to form an opinion about him. I thought once that he would make his mark in the history of our time as one of those people who are little known but are exceptionally intelligent. I think now he will play a more important role. Most of the young intellectuals of the generation which has grown up since the last war have come under his influence, and often been through his school. . . . He has confirmed a suspicion I have had for a long time that he has founded a Church. He has now gone beyond dogma, and is mainly concerned with liturgy. He has shown me a series of songs and festivities to celebrate the "pagan year", involving a whole system of gods, and colours and animals, food, and stones and plants. I noticed that the "consecration of light" would take place on 2nd February.'

And Jünger adds, confirming our theory: I have noticed in Bogo a fundamental change that is characteristic of all our *élite*: he is throwing himself into metaphysics with all the enthusiasm of a mind brought up on rationalist lines. The same thing had struck me in the case of Spengler, and seems to be a propitious sign. It could be said, roughly, that while the nineteenth century was the century of reason, the twentieth is the century of cults. Kniebolo (Hitler) lives on them which accounts for the total incapacity of liberally-minded people to see even where he stands.'

Hielscher, who had not been disturbed, came to give evidence on Sievers' behalf at Nuremberg. He confined himself at the trial to political matters and to intentionally absurd statements about races and ancestral tribes. He asked as a favour to be allowed to accompany Sievers to the gallows, and it was with him that the condemned man said the prayers peculiar to a cult which was never mentioned throughout the trial. He then returned to obscurity.

They wanted to change life and mix it with death in another way. They were preparing the way for the coming of the Unknown Higher Being. They had a magical conception of the world and of man, to which they had sacrificed all the youth of their country and offered to the gods an ocean of human blood. They had done everything in their power to conciliate the Powers. They hated modern Western civilization, both bourgeois and working-class – the insipid humanism of the former, and the narrow materialism of the latter. They were bound to win, because they bore within them a flame which their capitalist or Marxist enemies had long since allowed to be extinguished, lulling themselves to sleep with their

208

dull and timid ideas about their destiny. They would be the Masters for a thousand years, for they were in the camp of the miracle-workers, the High-Priests and the demi-gods. . . . And now, there they were, defeated, crushed, condemned, humiliated by ordinary common men, chewers of gum and drinkers of vodka; men devoid of any sacred flame with narrow beliefs and limited, Earthbound aims.

Superficial, worldly people – postivist, rational, moral – ordinary humans. Millions of insignificant little men of goodwill had defied the Will of the Knights of the Powers of Darkness! In the East a lot of mechanized simpletons, in the West a bunch of spineless Puritans had been able to turn out superior quantities of tanks, aeroplanes and guns. And they possessed the atomic bomb – without knowing anything about the great hidden forces! And now, like snails after a shower, having escaped the storm of iron, here they all were – monocled judges, Professors of human rights and horizontal virtues, Doctors of mediocrity, baritones of the Salvation Army, stretcher-bearers from the Red Cross, all naïvely babbling about 'brighter tomorrows' – assembled here in Nuremberg to preach elementary sermons to the Great Ones of this Earth, the militant monks who had signed a pact with the Powers; to the Sacrificers who could read in the mirror of Darkness; to the Allies of Shamballah, the heirs of the Holy Grail! And they actually sent them to the gallows, and treated them like criminals or raving lunatics!

What the Nuremberg prisoners and their leaders who committed suicide could not understand was that the civilization that had just triumphed was also, and far more certainly, a spiritual civilization, a formidable movement which, from Chicago to Tashkent, was impelling humanity towards a higher destiny. What they had done was to dethrone Reason and put Magic in its place. It is true that Cartesian reason does not cover the whole of Man or the whole of his knowledge. So they had put it to sleep. But when Reason sleeps, it brings forth monsters. What had happened here was that Reason, which had not been put to sleep, but pushed to its extreme limits, was operating on a higher level, linking up with the mysteries of the mind and spirit, the secrets of energy and universal harmony. Rationalism pushed to extremes breeds the Fantastic, of which the monsters engendered by Reason when asleep are only a sinister caricature. But the Nuremberg judges, the spokesmen for the civilization that had triumphed, did not know themselves that this war had been a spiritual war. They did not have a lofty enough conception of their own world; they only believed that Good would triumph over Evil, without having realized how black was the evil that had been defeated or how glorious the good that had triumphed.

The mystical German and Japanese warriors thought they were better magicians than they were in reality. The civilized nations who had beaten them had not been aware of the higher magical significance of their own world. They talked of Reason, Justice, Liberty, Respect for Human Life, etc., on a level which no longer

209

has a place in this second half of the twentieth century when knowledge is being transformed and the transition to *another state* of human consciousness is already apparent.

It is true that the Nazis would have won if the modern world had only been what most of us still think it is: a legacy, purely and simply, from the materialist and scientific nineteenth century, when the man in the street looked upon the Earth as a place to be exploited for his enjoyment. There are two Devils: one that changes the divine Order into disorder, and one that changes order into another kind of order, which is not divine. The Black Order should have triumphed over a civilization which it considered had sunk to the level of 'satisfying' purely material appetites hypocritically disguised as moral values. But it was something more than that. It presented a new face to the world, while suffering the martyrdom inflicted on it by the Nazis, like the apparition of the Face on the Holy Shroud. At every level, from that of popular education to nuclear physics, from advanced psychological exploration to interplanetary rockets, a sort of alchemy was at work, raising hopes for a transmutation of humanity and the prospect of a better life. This was, perhaps, not very apparent on the surface, and some people of only medium intelligence regretted the far-off days of ancient spiritual traditions, thus finding themselves in their deepest convictions on the side of the enemy, resolutely hostile as they were to this world in which they saw only the menace of an ever-increasing mechanization. Yet at the same time there were men, like Teilhard de Chardin for example, who saw more clearly. The eyes of the highest intelligence and the eyes of love discover the same things on different planes. The people's thirst for liberty, the martyrs' hymn of faith, contained in them the seeds of this great transcendent hope. This civilization, criticized no less from the outside by the mystical worshippers of the past than on the inside by the naïve believers in progress, had to be saved.

Diamonds cut glass. But borazon, a synthetic crystal, cuts diamonds. The structure of the diamond is more regular than that of glass. The Nazis might have won. But an awakened intelligence can create, as it develops, figures of a purer order than those which shine in the dark.

'When someone smites me on the cheek, I do not turn the other cheek, nor do I put up my fists; I strike with a thunderbolt.' It was necessary that this struggle between the Lords of the underworld and the little men above, between the Powers of Darkness and humanity on the march to progress, should be decided at Hiroshima by a clear sign from the Power which admits of no discussion.

Part Three

THAT INFINITY CALLED MAN . . .

I

A NEW KIND OF INTUITION

*The Fantastic in fire and blood – The barriers of incredulity –
The first rocket – Bourgeois and 'Workers of the Earth' –
False facts and true fiction – Inhabited worlds – Visitors
from Beyond – The great lines of communication – Modern
myths – Fantastic realism in psychology – Towards an
exploration of the fantastic within – The method described –
Another conception of liberty*

WHEN I came out of the cellar, Juvisy, my home town, had disappeared. A thick, yellow fog covered a mass of rubble out of which came cries for help and groans. The world of my games and friendships and loves and nearly everything that I had known all my life lay there buried under all this desolation looking like the surface of the Moon. A little later, when the rescue operations were under way, the birds, deceived by the searchlights, came back and began to sing in the dust-covered branches.

Another memory: one summer morning three days before the Liberation, I was with ten of my friends in a private house near the Bois de Boulogne. We had met there by chance, having all come from different Youth Camps to this final Training School where they were still teaching us imperturbably, while everything outside was changing amidst the noise of war, how to make marionettes, and to act and sing. That morning, standing in the pseudo-Gothic hall, we were singing under the direction of a romantic choir-leader, a folk-tune: '*Donnez-moi de l'eau, donnez-moi de l'eau, de l'eau, de l'eau pour mes deux seaux. . . .*'

We were interrupted by the telephone ringing. A few minutes later our singing-master made us all go into a garage. Other youths, with Sten-guns, guarded the approaches. There, among the old cars and barrels of oil, lay the bodies of some young men, riddled with bullets and finished off with grenades: this was the group of Resistance workers who had been tortured by the Germans at the *Cascade* in the Bois. Somehow their bodies had been recovered.

Their coffins were there; their families had been informed by messenger. We had to wash these corpses, wipe up the blood, button up again their jackets and trousers split open by the grenades, and put white paper in their coffins to cover up these murdered boys whose eyes and mouths and wounds seemed to cry out in terror. We had somehow to make these faces and bodies look decent in death, and with our sponges and our brushes in our

211

hands and the stink of this butchery in our nostrils, we were indeed 'giving water, water, water . . .' as in the song. . . .

Pierre MacOrlan, before this war, used to travel in search of the fantastic in social life which he found in the picturesqueness of the great ports: in the little bistros of Hamburg in the rain, on the banks of the Thames or in the slums of Antwerp. How charmingly out of date! The fantastic had ceased to be the prerogative of artists to become, to the accompaniment of blood and fire, part of everyday life in the civilized world. Your local grocer would appear one morning in his doorway wearing a yellow star, while your concierge's son would be receiving surrealist messages from London and wear an invisible captain's uniform. In the villages you would see corpses hanging from the balconies, victims of some secret partisan war.

Several violently contrasted Universes were superposed; the merest chance could send you from one to another.

Bergier gave me the following account of his experiences:

'In the camp at Mauthausen we were labelled N.N. – night and fog. None of us expected to survive. On 5th May, 1945, when the first American jeep came up the hill, a Russian deportee, who had been in charge of the anti-religious campaign in the Ukraine and was lying by my side, raised himself on his elbow and cried: "God be praised." All fit men were repatriated in a flying fortress, and this was how I found myself a few days later on the airfield at Heinz, in Austria. The plane had come from Burma. "It's a world war, isn't it?" said the wireless operator, who sent a message for me to Allied Headquarters in Rheims and then showed me his radar equipment. There were all sorts of apparatus which I had never thought would be possible before the year 2000. At Mauthausen the American doctors had spoken to me of penicillin.

'In two years the sciences had jumped a century. A mad idea came into my head. "And what about atomic energy?" I asked. "It's being talked about," said the operator. "It's still hush-hush, but one hears rumours. . . ."

'A few hours later I was on the Boulevard de la Madeleine in my striped uniform. Was this Paris? Was it a dream? People clustered round me, asking questions. I took refuge in the Métro, and telephoned my parents to say I was on my way. But I came out again; there was something more important than anything else: I had to go to what had been my favourite haunt before the war: Brentano's, the American bookshop in the Avenue de l'Opéra. I was recognized immediately . . . soon my arms were full of newspapers and Reviews. Seated on a bench in the Tuileries I tried to reconcile the Universe I was in now with what I had known recently. . . . Mussolini had been hung; Hitler incinerated. There were German troops in the Ile d'Oléron and the Atlantic ports. So the war in France was not yet over? The technical reviews were full of the most astonishing things. Penicillin had been discovered by Sir Alexander Fleming: so it was really true? There were new discoveries in chemistry – silicones, an intermediary between organic and mineral substances. Helicopters, which had been proved impracticable in 1940, were being mass-produced. Fantastic progress was being made in electronics. Television would soon be as universal as the telephone. I had entered a world in which all my dreams about the year 2000 were coming true. Certain references, however, were incomprehensible. Who was this Marshal Tito? And the United Nations? And what was D.D.T.?

'Suddenly I realized that I was no longer a prisoner, neither in body nor soul; that I was not condemned to death, and that I had plenty of time and was entirely free to understand and act. To begin with, I had all tonight, if I wanted. . . . I must have turned very pale. A woman came up to me and wanted to take me to a doctor. I escaped, and ran home to my parents, whom I found in tears. On the table in the dining-room were messages brought by cyclists, and military and civil telegrams. Lyons was to name a street after me; I was promoted Captain; decorated by various countries, and an American expedition going to look for secret weapons in Germany asked me to help them. About midnight my father sent me off to bed. As I was falling asleep, two Latin words were running through my brain, for no apparent reason: *magna, mater*. The next morning when I woke I realized what they meant. In ancient Rome candidates for admission to the secret cult of *magna mater* had to pass through a bath of blood. If they survived, they would be born again.'

In this war all the channels of communication between the different worlds were opened wide, and let in a powerful draught. Then came the atomic bomb to project us into the Atomic Age. A moment later, the rockets ushered in the cosmic era. Everything became possible. The barriers of incredulity, so firmly planted in the nineteenth century, had been severely shaken by the war. Now they were about to collapse altogether.

In March 1954 Mr. Charles Wilson, United States Secretary for War, declared: 'The United States and Russia from now on have the power to annihilate the entire world.' People began to think seriously about the end of time. Cut off from the past, suspicious of the future, men looked upon the present as an absolute value, seeing in this frail frontier a promise of eternity. Like despairing travellers, they embarked in solitude on a raft on the seas of eternity, the Noahs of some future Flood, living on planckton and flying-fish.

At the same time reports began to flow in from every country on the apparition of the 'flying saucers'. The skies were peopled by Intelligences from Beyond. A little sandwich-seller named Adamsky, who had his shop at the foot of the giant telescope on Mount Palomar in California, calling himself a Professor, announced that he had been visited by travellers from Venus, told the story of his encounters in a book that became a best-seller, and settled down in the role of a Rasputin at the Court of Holland. In a world where the strange and the tragic are equally mixed, one wonders what people are made of who have neither faith nor any desire to have a good time.

When anyone spoke to Chesterton about the end of the world, he would say: 'Why should I worry? It has already happened several times.' During the million years or so that men have lived on this Earth they have probably experienced more than one Apocalypse. Intelligence has been extinguished and relit more than once. A man seen walking in the distance at night, carrying a lantern, is alternatively shadow and light. There is every reason to believe that the end of the world has happened again, and that we are serving a new apprenticeship in the sphere of intelligence in a new world – a world of mass movements, nuclear energy, the electronic brain and interplanetary rockets. Perhaps we shall need a different mind and a different soul for this different Earth.

On 16th September, 1959, at 10.2 p.m. radio stations all over the world announced that for the first time a rocket launched from the Earth had landed on the Moon. I was listening to Radio-Luxembourg. The announcer gave the news and went straight on to present a variety show broadcast every Sunday at this time called 'The Open Door. . . .' I went out into the garden to look at the shining Moon, with its Lake of Serenity on which the débris of the rocket were now lying. The gardener was out, too. 'It's as beautiful as the Gospels, isn't it, sir?' he said. Instinctively he saw the event in its right perspective. I felt really near this man, and all the simple men who at this moment were gazing into the sky, full of wonder and emotion. 'Happy the man who loses his head; he will find it again in Heaven!' At the same time, I felt very remote from people of my sort – all those writers and philosophers and artists who refuse to give way to enthusiasms of this kind because it is important to keep a clear head and defend the humanistic outlook.

My friend Jean Dutourd, for example, a remarkable writer and a great admirer of Stendhal, had said to me only a few days previously: 'Come now; let's keep our feet on the Earth and not let ourselves be distracted by these electric trains for grown-ups.' Another dear friend, Jean Giono, whom I had been to see at Manosque, told me that he had seen the captain of the gendarmerie and the curé one Sunday morning at Colmar-les-Alpes, bowling hoops.

'As long as there are curés and gendarmes who will play with hoops, there's room for happiness here on Earth; and we shall be better off here than on the Moon. . . .' So all my friends were little bourgeois, still lingering on in a world in which men, lured by the prospect of vast projects on a cosmic scale, were beginning to feel themselves 'Workers of the Earth'. 'Let's stick to the Earth,' they cried. They were reacting in the same way as the old silk-weavers of Lyons when the loom was first invented; they were afraid of losing their jobs. In the era which we are about to enter, my writer friends feel that all the social, moral, political, philosophical standards of humanistic literature and of the psychological novel will soon seem insignificant. The main result of so-called modern literature is that it prevents us from being really modern. It is no good their thinking that they are writing for the masses. They feel that the time is coming when the masses will be attracted by a new mythology and by the prospect of terrific adventures, and that, by continuing to write their little 'human' stories, they will be deceiving people with false facts, instead of regaling them with true fiction.

When on that evening of 16th September, 1959, I went into the garden and gazed, with my tired and eager eyes – the eyes of a grown man – at the Moon in the sky – a Moon that from now on would bear a human imprint – my emotion was twofold, because I was thinking of my father. I gazed upwards, as he used to do and asked myself the question that he, too, often asked: 'Are we, the inhabitants of this Earth, the only living beings?' My father asked this question because he was broadminded, and also because he had read books on spiritualism of a rather spurious and elementary kind. I asked it, because I read *Pravda* and works of pure science, and move in intellectual circles. But there, under the stars, with upturned face, I shared with my father the same curiosity, accompanied by a sense of infinite exhilaration.

I referred just now to the origin of the myth of the flying saucers. It was a significant social phenomenon. But it is obvious that no credence can be attached to those space-ships from which little men descended to gossip with railway-men or sandwich-sellers.

Martians, Saturnians or Jupiterians are improbable. Charles-Noël Martin, however, summarizing serious scientific opinion on this question, writes as follows: 'There are so many possible habitats in the Galaxies, especially our own, that it seems almost certain that they contain exceedingly numerous forms of life.' On any planet of another sun, even several hundred light-years distant from the Earth, provided its mass and atmosphere are identical, there must be beings like ourselves. Now, it has been calculated that there may be, in our galaxy alone, some ten or fifteen million planets more or less similar to the Earth. Harlow Shapley, in his *Stars and Men*, reckons that there are in the known Universe ten probable sisters of our Earth. There is every reason to believe, in fact, that there are other inhabited worlds, and other living beings that haunt our Universe. At the end of 1959 new laboratories were built at the Cornell University in the United States, where, under the direction of Professors Coccioni and Morrison, pioneers in space communications, observers are on the look-out for signals that are perhaps being sent to us by other living beings in the Cosmos.

More than the landing of rockets on the nearer astral bodies, for men to make contact with other intelligent beings and, perhaps, other psychisms, could well be the most staggering event in the whole of our history.

If there are in existence other intelligent beings elsewhere, do they know of our existence? Do they receive, and can they decipher the far-off echo of our radio and television waves? Can they see, with the aid of apparatus, the perturbations on our Sun caused by the giant planets Jupiter and Saturn? Do they send space-ships into our Galaxy? Our solar system may frequently have been traversed by observer-rockets without our ever knowing anything about it. At the time of writing, we are even unable to trace our Lunik III whose transmitter is out of order; we do not know what is happening in our own domain.

Have we already been visited by the inhabitants of Elsewhere? It is highly probable that some planets have been visited. Why especially the Earth? There are billions of astral bodies scattered in the field of light-years. Are we the nearest, or the most interesting?

Yet it is quite legitimate to imagine that 'Strangers from Beyond' have been to inspect our globe, and have even landed and stayed there for a time. There has been life on the Earth for at least a thousand million years, and our memories go back for scarcely more than four thousand years. What do we know? It is possible that prehistoric monsters long ago may have raised their long necks when some space-ship passed over; if so, no traces remain of such a fabulous event. . . .

Dr. Ralph Stair, of the American N.B.S., when analysing some strange hyaline rocks scattered in the region of the Lebanon known as *tektites*, admitted that these might have come from a planet now extinct situated between Mars and Jupiter. These *tektites* have been found to contain radio-active isotopes of aluminium and beryllium.

Several eminent scientists think that Phobos, the satellite of Mars, may be hollow, and may be an artificial asteroid put into orbit round Mars by intelligent beings outside the Earth. This was the conclusion arrived at in a serious article in the review *Discovery* in November 1959 and the same hypothesis has been put forward by the Soviet Professor Chtlovski, an expert on radio-astronomy.

In a sensational article in the Moscow *Literary Gazette* of February 1960, Professor Agrest, Doctor of physical-mathematics, declared that the *tektites*, which could only have been formed at an extremely high temperature and under the action of powerful nuclear radiation, are perhaps the traces left by missiles dispatched from the outer Cosmos. A million years ago the Earth may have had visitors from Beyond. Professor Agrest (who, in this article, did not shrink from propounding this fantastic theory, thereby showing that science, within the framework of positivist philosophy, could and should reserve as generous a place as possible for creative imagination and bold hypotheses) believes that Sodom and Gomorrah were destroyed by a thermo-nuclear explosion set off by space-travellers either wantonly, or because they considered it necessary to destroy their depots of energy before leaving for the Cosmos.

The Dead Sea scrolls contain the following description: 'A column of smoke and dust rose into the air like a column of smoke issuing from the bowels of the Earth. It rained sulphur and fire on Sodom and Gomorrah, and destroyed the town and the whole plain and all the inhabitants and every growing plant. And Lot's wife looked back and was turned into a pillar of salt. And Lot lived at Isoar, but afterwards went to the mountains because he was afraid to remain at Isoar. The people were warned that they must go away from the place of the future explosion and not stay in exposed places; nor should they look at the explosion but hide beneath the ground. . . . Those fugitives who looked back were blinded and died. . . .'

In this same region round Lebanon, one of the most mysterious monuments is the 'terrace of Baalbeck'. This is a platform made of blocks of stone, some of which are nearly sixty feet long and weigh two thousand tons. It has never been explained why, or how, or by whom this platform was built. In Professor Agrest's opinion it is not inconceivable that it may be the remains of a landing-ground constructed by astronauts arriving from the Cosmos.

Finally, it is suggested in the reports of the Moscow Academy of Sciences on the explosion of 30th June, 1908, that this may have been caused by the disintegration of an inter-stellar space-ship.

On this day, at seven o'clock in the morning, a pillar of fire rose up over the Siberian *taiga* to a height of fifty miles. The forest was burnt to the ground over an area of twenty-five miles after a gigantic ball of fire had hit the Earth. For several weeks strange clouds, flecked with gold, drifted over Russia, Western Europe and North Africa, reflecting at night the light of the Sun. In London photographs were taken of people reading their newspapers in the streets at one o'clock in the morning. To this day the vegetation has never grown again in this region of Siberia. Measurements taken in 1960 by a Russian scientific expedition revealed that the level of radio-activity on the spot was three times above normal.

If we have been visited, did these fabulous explorers ever walk about among us? Common sense replies: if so, we should certainly have seen them. Nothing is less certain. The first rule of ethology is not to disturb the animals one is observing. Zimanski, the German scientist from Tubingen and a pupil of the brilliant Conrad Lorenz, spent three years studying snails, becoming so familiar with their language and behaviour that they actually looked upon him as one of themselves. Our visitors could do the same with human beings. The idea is revolting: it is nevertheless plausible.

Is it possible that well-intentioned explorers arrived on the Earth before anything was known of the history of the human race? An Indian legend tells of the Lords of Dzyan who came from Beyond to bring fire and the bow to dwellers on the Earth. Did life itself begin on the Earth, or was it introduced there by travellers from space?*

* The majority of astonomers and theologians think that life on the Earth began on the Earth. Not so, says the Cornell astonomer, Thomas Gold. In a paper he read at Los Angeles at the Congress of space scientists in January 1960, Gold suggested that life may have existed elsewhere in

217

'Did we come from Elsewhere?' asks the biologist Loren Eiseley; 'did we come from Elsewhere, and are we now preparing to go back to where we came from, with the help of our modern apparatus?...'

A further word about the skies: stellar dynamics show that a star cannot annex to itself another star. Therefore, the double or triple stars that have been observed ought to have the same age. Spectroscopy, however, reveals differences in age between members of these double or triple sets. Thus, for example, a white dwarf star 10,000 million years old may accompany a red giant only 3,000 million years old.

It is impossible, yet it is a fact. We have questioned many astronomers and physicists about this. Some of them, and not the least eminent, do not exclude the hypothesis that these groups of abnormal stars may have been placed there by Intelligences or Powers able to displace the stars and reassemble them artificially, thereby proclaiming to the Universe that life exists in this or that region of the skies.

Foreseeing with astonishing clairvoyance the advent of a new kind of spirituality, Blanc de Saint-Bonnet* wrote the following: 'Religion will be revealed to us through absurdities. We shall no longer listen to neglected doctrines or the voice of conscience that nobody heeds. Facts will speak in a loud voice. Truth will no longer reside in lofty words, but will be present in the bread we eat. Our light will be fire!'

In addition to the theory that human intelligence is perhaps not the only living and active intelligence in the Universe, we must now get used to the idea that our intelligence is capable of penetrating to worlds that are different from our own and of understanding their

---

the Universe for countless millions of years before taking root on the Earth. How did life reach the Earth and begin its long ascent culminating in Man? Perhaps it was brought here by space-ships. As Gold pointed out, life has existed on the Earth for about a hundred thousand years. It began in the simplest forms, of microscopic size. At the end of this time according to Gold, the planet may have developed creatures sufficiently intelligent to have travelled farther into space, visiting other planets, fertile but still virgin, and implanting in them adaptable microbes. This sort of contamination, in fact, is probably the normal way in which life begins on any planet, including the Earth.

'Space travellers,' said Gold, 'may have visited the Earth a thousand million years ago, and the residuary forms of life they abandoned there proliferated until the microbes soon had another agent (human space-travellers) capable of dispersing them over a still wider field.' What happened to the other galaxies floating in space far beyond the boundaries of the Milky Way? Astronomer Gold believes in the theory of a fixed Universe. When, then, did life begin? The fixed Universe theory postulates that space is boundless and time is without a beginning or an end. If life is handed down from the old galaxies to the new, its history may go back in time to eternity; it has neither a beginning nor an end.

* 1815-80, little-known French philosopher, author of *L'Unité Spirituelle*.

laws – that it can, as it were, traverse the mirror and continue to function on the other side. This fantastic penetration has been made possible by the genius of mathematics.

It is our lack of curiosity and knowledge that has made us think that the enrichment of poetic experience since Rimbaud has been the salient feature of the intellectual revolution in the modern world. The outstanding event has been the spectacular achievements in mathematics, as Valéry understood very well. Henceforward man is confronted by his own mathematical genius as he would be by a visitor from Beyond. Modern mathematical entities live, and grow and multiply in inaccessible worlds, remote from all human experience. In *Men Like Gods* H. G. Wells imagined that there are as many Universes as there are pages in a thick volume. We only live in one of these pages. But mathematical genius ranges over them all, from one end to another, it alone represents the real and unlimited powers of the human brain. For traversing as it does other Universes, it returns from these explorations equipped with the tools necessary for the transformation of the world we live in. It is both being and doing. The mathematician, for example, studies the space theories which necessitate two complete turns before returning to the point of departure. Now, it is work of this kind which has no connection with any sort of activity in our own sphere of existence, which makes it possible to discover the properties governing the elementary particles in microscopic space, thus contributing to the progress of nuclear physics which is transforming our civilization. The mathematician's intuition, which opens a path to other Universes, substantially alters our own. Mathematical genius, so akin to musical genius, is at the same time the one that has the greatest effect on matter. For out of the 'Absolute Elsewhere' is born the 'Absolute Weapon'.

Finally, in raising mathematical thought to its highest degree of abstraction, Man perceives that such thought is not perhaps his exclusive property. He discovers that insects, for example, seem to possess a spatial sense which we lack, that there is, perhaps, such a thing as a universal mathematical intelligence, and that out of the totality of all living things emerges a Voice which is the Voice of the Supreme Master-Mind. . . .

In this world where, for Man, nothing any longer is sure – neither himself nor the world as defined by laws and facts hitherto accepted, a mythology very quickly takes over. Cybernetics has encouraged the idea that human intelligence has been superseded by the electronic brain, and to the 'man in the street' the green eye of the 'machine that thinks' is as much an object of awe and wonder as the Sphinx was to the ancient Egyptians. The atom is throned on Olympus, brandishing its thunderbolts. Work on the atomic station at Marcoule in France had hardly begun before the local inhabitants were saying that their tomatoes were shrivelling up. The bomb upsets the weather, and causes monsters to be born. The *Odyssey* of our century is contained in the pages of so-called 'science-fiction', more widely read than books on psychology, with its stories of Martians and 'Mutants', and that metaphysical Ulysses who comes home after vanquishing space and time.

To the question: 'Are we alone?' must be added the question: 'Are we the last?' Did evolution stop at Man? Is the Superman not already being formed? Is he not already among us? And are we to think of this Superman, or Superior Being, as an individual, or as a collective entity, humanity *en masse* in a state of fermentation and coagulation being impelled towards a realization of its unity and high destiny?

Under mass-rule the individual dies; but his death is the salvation of the spiritual tradition that man must die in order to be born again. His psychological consciousness is superseded by a cosmic consciousness. He is subjected to terrific pressure: he must either die resisting it, or die in yielding to it. Resistance refusal, means total death. Obedience means death, but only as a stage on the way to total life; for now it is a question of conditioning the masses with a view to creating a universal psychism embracing an awareness of Time and Space and an appetite for Discovery.

It must be admitted that all this reflects more accurately the basic thoughts and anxieties of modern Man than the analytical neo-naturalist novel, or politico-sociological studies; this will soon become apparent, when those false witnesses who look at a new world through old eyes are annihilated by the truth.

At every step he takes in this world on the threshold of strangeness, Man is confronted with question-marks as enormous as the animals and vegetables of prehistoric times. They are out of proportion to his size – on a different scale. But what is the scale of Man? Sociology and psychology have developed much less quickly than physics and mathematics; nineteenth-century Man suddenly finds himself in another world. But is the sociological and psychological Man of the nineteenth century the real Man? Nothing is less certain. After the intellectual revolution that followed the *Discours de la Méthode*, the scientific revival and the new encyclopaedic approach and the far-reaching effects of nineteenth-century rationalism and optimistic scientific thinking, we have reached a stage where the immensity and complexity of the new realities that have just been revealed were bound to alter the views we have hitherto held as to the nature of human knowledge and revolutionize the ideas now current as to Man's relationship to his own intelligence; in other words, an attitude of mind very different from what only yesterday we were still calling the 'modern' attitude, is now called for. If we are to be invaded by the Fantastic in the world outside us, we ought to explore the Fantastic that is within us. Does this exist? And is it not probable that what Man has achieved is a projection of what he is, or will become?

We shall now, accordingly, proceed to explore the fantastic that is within us; or, at least, try to show that this exploration is necessary, and outline a method.

Naturally, we have had neither time nor the means of carrying out the experiments and other measures we considered desirable, but which will perhaps be attempted by others better qualified than ourselves. But it was not really our intention to measure and carry out experiments but, here as elsewhere in this extensive study, to assemble facts and relations between facts that official science sometimes ignores, or whose existence it refuses to recognize. This method of working may seem unusual and even suspect. And yet it has often led to important discoveries.

Darwin, for example, always worked on these lines, collecting and comparing information to which no one had ever paid any attention before. The theory of evolution was the outcome of this apparently haphazard collecting of information. Similarly, if on a humbler scale, we have evolved in the course of our work a theory of what constitutes Man's real inner self in the light of total intelligence and an awakened consciousness.

To complete our task we should have needed another ten years. Moreover, we have merely summarized our findings, or rather presented them in the form of a sketch in order not to put the reader off; for we are relying on his having an open mind, having always tried to be in that state ourselves.

Total intelligence and an awakened conscience – we feel that man is aiming at these essential conquests in a world in the throes of a new birth which seems to be urging him, to begin with, to renounce his freedom. 'But freedom to do what?' asked Lenin.

It is true that he is gradually being deprived of his freedom to be merely what he has always been. The only freedom that will soon be granted him is freedom to become something other, to rise to a higher degree of intelligence and consciousness. Freedom of this kind is not basically psychological, but mystical – according to ancient standards, at least, and in the terminology of yesterday. In a certain sense, we believe that civilization makes it possible for this mystical approach, on this Earth of ours teeming with factories and rockets, to extend to humanity as a whole. It will be seen that such an approach is practical, and that it is, in a sense, the 'second wind' which will enable men to keep pace with the ever-increasing speed at which the Earth is advancing towards its destiny.

'God has created us as little as possible. Liberty, which gives us power to be the cause of things and opportunity for merit, demands of Man that he should re-create himself.'

THE FANTASTIC WITHIN

*Some pioneers: Balzac, Hugo, Flammarion – Jules Romains
and the 'Great Question' – The end of positivism – What is
parapsychology? – Some extraordinary facts and experiences – The example of the* Titanic *– Clairvoyance –
Precognition and dreams – Parapsychology and psychoanalysis – We reject occultism and the pseudo-sciences – In quest
of machinery for sounding the depths*

THE literary critic and philosopher Albert Béguin thought that
Balzac was a visionary rather than an observer, and I think he was
right. In an admirable story entitled *Le Requisitionnaire* Balzac
foresaw the beginnings of parapsychology which will make its
appearance in the second half of the twentieth century and seek to
establish as an exact science the study of Man's 'psychic powers':
'At the exact hour when Mme de Dey died at Carentan, her son
was shot in the Morbihan region. We can see a connection between
this tragic event and what we know about the sympathetic currents
which take no account of the laws of space; documents assembled
in a spirit of learned curiosity by a few solitary men which one day
will help to lay the foundations of a new science which up to now
has lacked a man of genius.'

In 1891 Camille Flammarion, in an article in *Le Figaro Illustré*
(November 1891) declared: 'Our *fin de siècle* is rather like that of
the preceding century. Our minds are tired of the affirmations of
so-called positivist philosophy. One has the impression that it
may be wrong. . . . "Know thyself," said Socrates. For thousands
of years we have been learning an immense amount about all sorts
of things except the one that interests us most. It would seem that
the present tendency among thinking men is at last to obey the
advice of Socrates.'

Conan Doyle used to come from London every month to visit
Flammarion at his observatory at Juvisy and study with him
phenomena of clairvoyance, apparitions and materializations –
mostly of a questionable nature. Flammarion believed in ghosts,
and Conan Doyle collected photographs of 'fairies'. The 'new
science' foreseen by Balzac was not yet born; but the need for it
was apparent.

Victor Hugo, in a magnificent passage of his astonishing study
on William Shakespeare, wrote as follows: 'Every man has within
him his own Pathmos. He is free to venture, or not to venture,
upon that terrifying promontory of thought from which one can
see into the shadows. If he refrains from doing so, he continues to
live an ordinary life, with ordinary thoughts, ordinary virtues,
ordinary beliefs and ordinary doubts – and it is well that he should.
It is clearly best for his internal peace of mind. For if he ventures
on to this summit, he is lost. He will have glimpsed the mighty
waves of the Marvellous – and no one can look upon that ocean
with impunity. . . . He persists in contemplating this alluring abyss,

in exploring the unexplored, in remaining detached from life on the Earth, and in his efforts to penetrate a forbidden world, to touch the untouchable, to gaze on the invisible he returns again and again to the edge of the precipice, leans over, takes one step down and then another – and that is how one penetrates the impenetrable and loses oneself in a limitless extension of infinity.'

In my own case, it was in 1939 that I had an exact vision of a science that, by bringing irrefutable evidence to bear on the inner self, would soon inevitably lead to a fresh evaluation of the Nature of Knowledge and eventually to a revision of the methods of all scientific research in every field. I was then nineteen years old, and the war had claimed me just as I had decided to devote my life to establishing a psychology and a physiology of mystical experience. It was then that I read in the *Nouvelle Revue Française* an essay by Jules Romains under the title: *Answer to the Greatest Question of All*, which most unexpectedly strengthened my position This essay was also prophetic, for after the war there arose a new psychic science, parapsychology, which is today flourishing, while at the same time there was a change in direction, as it were, even in 'official' sciences such as mathematics or physics.

'I believe,' wrote Jules Romains, 'that the principal difficulty for the human mind is not so much to reach correct conclusions in a certain order or in certain directions, as to discover the means of co-ordinating the conclusions it arrives at when working on different levels of reality, or in different directions which vary according to the period or epoch concerned. It is, for example, very difficult for it to harmonize the ideas, in themselves very precise, to which it has been introduced by modern science working on physical phenomena with the ideas, perhaps equally valid, which it had acquired at a time when it was more concerned with spiritual or psychic realities and which are still an inspiration to those who, today, are devoting themselves to research into spiritual or psychic, as distinct from physical, phenomena. I am not at all of the opinion that modern science, which is often accused of being materialistic, is threatened by a revolution which would ruin the results of which it can be sure (the only threat could be to hypotheses, either premature or of too general a nature, of which it is not sure). Yet it may one day be confronted with results, achieved by methods vaguely termed "psychic", that are so coherent and conclusive that they cannot possibly be dismissed as null and void. When this happens, many people think that there will be nothing to prevent so-called "positive" science from continuing peacefully as before, while tolerating the development outside its own frontiers of an entirely different kind of knowledge which at present it either dismisses as pure superstition, or relegates to the realm of the "unknowable" or of what it contemptuously describes as metaphysics. But it will not be as easy as all that. Some of the most important results obtained through psychic experiments, as soon as they are confirmed (if they have to be) and officially recognized as "true" will represent a threat to positive science *within its own frontiers*; and the human mind which up to now, shrinking from its responsibilities, has pretended to ignore the conflict will then be obliged to arbitrate. This will create a serious crisis – no less serious than that provoked by the application to industrial techniques of discoveries made in the realm of physics. It may even change the whole of human life. I believe this crisis is not only possible but probable, and may even be with us very soon.'

One winter morning I accompanied a friend to the clinic where he was to undergo an immediate operation. It was scarcely light, and we were walking in the rain, anxiously on the look-out for a taxi.

Suddenly my friend, who was trembling from fever, pointed to a playing-card lying on the pavement covered with mud. 'If it's a Joker,' he said, 'all will be well.'

I picked up the card. It was a Joker.

Parapsychology attempts to systematize the study of facts of this nature by the accumulation of experiments. Are normal men endowed with powers which they scarcely ever use merely because, so it would seem, they have been persuaded that they do not possess them? Strictly scientific experiments seem definitely to have eliminated the notion of chance. At the international congress of parapsychology which I attended in 1955 in the company, notably, of Aldous Huxley, I was able to study the work of the American, Swedish and German doctors and psychologists engaged in this research. There can be no question but that their work was conducted on strictly scientific lines. If the attitude of scientists towards poetry were not tinged with a certain legitimate distrust, it would be possible to find an excellent definition of parapsychology in these lines of Guillaume Apollinaire:

> Tout le monde est prophète, mon cher André Billy,
> Mais il y a si longtemps qu'on fait croire aux gens
> Qu'ils n'ont aucun avenir et qu'ils sont ignorants à jamais
> Et idiots de naissance
> Qu'on en a pris son parti et que nul n'a même idée
> De se demander s'il connaît l'avenir ou non.
> Il n'y a pas d'esprit religieux dans tout cela,
> Ni dans les superstitions ni dans les prophéties
> Ni dans tout ce que l'on nomme occultisme
> Il y a avant tout une façon d'observer la nature
> Et d'interpréter la nature
> Qui est très légitime – (Calligrammes).

Parapsychological experiments seem to prove that between Man and the Universe there exist means of communication other than those provided by the five senses. Every normal human being could perceive objects at a distance, or through a wall; could influence the movement of objects without touching them; could project his thoughts and feelings into the nervous system of another human being, and finally have an exact knowledge of events that have not yet taken place.

Rider Haggard, the English writer who died in 1925, gave, in his novel *Maiwa's Revenge*, a detailed description of the escape of Alan Quatermain, his hero. The latter is captured by savages just as he was climbing over a wall of rock. His pursuers held him by the foot; he freed himself by shooting them with his revolver held parallel to his right leg. Some years after the book was published, an English explorer came to call on Haggard. He had come specially to London to ask the author how he had learned of his adventure in all its details, because he had never spoken of it to anyone and had hoped to conceal the killing.

In the library of the Austrian writer, Karl Hans Strobl, who died in 1946, his friend Willy Schrodter made the following discovery: 'I opened some of his own books arranged on a shelf, and found between the pages a number of Press-cuttings. They were not, as I had first supposed, reviews, but news items. It gave me a shock when I realized that they recorded events that Strobl had described long before they happened.'

In 1898 an American science-fiction writer, Morgan Robertson, described the shipwreck of a giant ship. This imaginary ship of 70,000 tons, was 800 feet long and carried 3,000 passengers. Its engines were equipped with three propellers. One night in April, when on its first voyage, it encountered in the fog an iceberg, and sank. Its name was: *The Titan.*

The *Titanic,* which was wrecked in similar circumstances years later, displaced 66,000 tons, was 828½ feet long, carried 3,000 passengers and had three propellers. The catastrophe happened on a night in April.

Those are the facts. Here are some experiments carried out by parapsychologists:

In Durham, U.S.A., the experimenter holds in his hand a pack of five special cards. He shuffles them, then draws one after another. At the same moment at Zagreb in Yugoslavia, another experimenter tries to guess in what order the cards are drawn. This is repeated a thousand times. The proportion of correct guesses is shown to be higher than could be attributed to chance.

In London, in a closed room, the mathematician J. S. Soal draws cards from a similar pack. Behind a solid partition, a student tries to guess the cards. On checking, it is revealed that the student, here too, every time in a proportion too great to be attributable to chance, has guessed the card that was to be drawn in the next operation.

In Stockholm, an engineer has built a machine which automatically throws dice into the air and films them as they fall. The spectators, members of the University, try by an effort of willpower to ensure the fall of a particular number. They are successful to a degree which cannot only be due to chance.

While studying the phenomena of precognition during sleep, the Englishman J. W. Dunne has proved scientifically that certain dreams can foretell even distant future events,* and two German

* *An Experiment with Time.* Dunne dreamed in 1901 that the town of Lowestoft, on the East coast of England, was bombarded by foreign warships. The bombardment actually took place in 1914, and happened exactly as Dunne had described it in 1901. The same writer saw in a dream the newspaper headlines announcing the eruption of Mount Pelé several months before the event.

research workers, Moufang and Stevens, in a work entitled *The Mystery of Dreams* have cited a number of cases, which have been carefully checked, in which dreams revealed future events and led to important scientific discoveries.

The celebrated atomic scientist, Niels Bohr, when he was a student, had a strange dream. He saw himself on a Sun consisting of burning gas. Planets whizzed by, whistling as they passed. They were attached to the Sun by thin filaments, and revolved round it. Suddenly the gas solidified and the Sun and planets crumbled away. Niels Bohr then woke up and realized that he had just discovered the model of the atom, so long sought after. The 'Sun' was the fixed centre round which the electrons revolve. The whole of modern atomic physics and its applications have come out of this dream.

The chemist Auguste Kékulé tells the following story: 'One summer's evening I was on the platform of my bus, on my way home, and went to sleep. I saw clearly and distinctly how, on every side, the atoms united in couples which were then merged in larger groups which, in their turn, were attracted by others still more powerful; and all these corpuscles were spinning round in a frenzied dance. I spent part of that night transcribing what I had seen in my dream. I had hit upon the theory of atomic structure.'

After reading in the newspapers accounts of the bombardment of London, an engineer of the American Bell telephone company had a dream one night in the Autumn of 1940 in which he saw himself drawing the plan of an apparatus which would enable an anti-aircraft gun to be aimed at the exact spot where an aeroplane whose speed and trajectory were known, would pass. On awakening he traced the blueprint 'from memory'. A study of this apparatus, which was to use radar for the first time, was undertaken by the eminent scientist Norbert Wiener, and Wiener's report on this machine resulted in the birth of cybernetics.

'One certainly ought not to underestimate,' wrote Lovecraft (in *Beyond the Walls of Sleep*) 'the gigantic importance of dreams.' Nor will it be possible in the future to dismiss as negligible the phenomena of precognition, whether in dreams or in a state of wakefulness. Thus, exceeding the bounds of 'official psychology', the American Atomic Energy Commission proposed in 1958 that 'clairvoyants' should be employed in an attempt to foresee where Russian bombs would fall in the event of war. (31st August, 1958, Report of the Rand Commission.)

In the field of 'paranormal cures', i.e. cures obtained by psychological treatment, whether by a 'healer' who possesses the 'fluid', or by a psychoanalyst (a clear distinction being made between the two methods) the parapsychologists have reached some very interesting conclusions. They have introduced a new conception: that of the doctor-patient couple. The success of the treatment will depend on whether or not telepathic communication exists between the practitioner and his patient. If so – and this relationship resembles an amorous one – it produces the same hyper-lucidity and hyper-receptivity that can be observed in a pair of lovers; a cure is then possible. Otherwise both healer and patient are wasting their time.

The notion of a 'fluid" is replaced by the image of 'the couple'. No doubt it would be possible to obtain a picture of the inner psychological make-up of both practitioner and patient. Certain tests would reveal the true nature of their intelligence and sensibility and the kind of relationship that could exist between them. The analyst could then compare his own and his patient's picture and decide from the beginning whether his treatment would be effective or not.

A psychoanalyst in New York one day broke the key of a cabinet in which he kept his files. He managed to get a locksmith to make him a new key on the spot, and told no one of the incident. A few days later, during a *seance* with a patient, the latter saw in a waking dream a key, and gave a description of it. It was broken, and bore the same number as the doctor's key: a good example of the phenomenon of osmosis.

The celebrated American psychoanalyst Dr. Lindner relates in his book, *The Fifty-Minute Hour*, that in 1953 he had as a patient a well-known atomic scientist. This man had lost interest in his work, his family and everything else. He confessed to Lindner that he had escaped to another world; in his thoughts he was continually travelling on another planet where science was more advanced and he himself was playing a leading part. He had a very clear vision of this world and of its laws and customs and culture. The extraordinary thing is that Lindner felt himself being gradually infected by his patient's madness, imagined that he was sharing his experiences in this other world, and began partially to lose his reason. It was then that the sick man began to detach himself from his vision and gradually became normal again. A few weeks later Lindner was also cured; he had just had a personal experience of the immemorial advice addressed to healers that they should 'take upon themselves' the troubles of others and atone for their sins.

Parapsychology has absolutely no connection with occultism or the pseudo-sciences: on the contrary, its object is to eliminate the element of mystification in this field. Notwithstanding, the scientists, propagandists and philosophers who denounce it think that it may encourage quackery. This is false, although it is true that the times we live in are more favourable than ever before to the development of these pseudo-sciences which 'seem to be everything but are in reality nothing'. We are convinced that there are unexplored regions in Man. Parapsychology offers us a method of exploring them. In the following pages we shall also suggest a method. This exploration has scarcely begun; in our opinion it will be one of the great tasks of the civilization that is to come. Natural forces still undreamed of will no doubt be revealed and studied and mastered so that Man can fulfil his destiny in a world that will be completely transformed. Of this we are convinced. But we are equally sure that the fact that occultism and the pseudo-sciences are at present in such high favour with an enormous public is an unhealthy symptom. It is not cracked mirrors that bring bad luck, but cracked brains.

There are now in the United States more than 30,000 astrologers, and 20 magazines exclusively devoted to astrology, one of which has a circulation of 500,000.

More than 2,000 newspapers have an astrological column. In 1943 five million Americans followed the advice of these prophets and spent 200 million dollars a year to learn what the future had in store. In France alone there are 40,000 'healers', and more than 50,000 practising occultists. It has been reliably estimated* that the fees paid to prophets, soothsayers, clairvoyants, healers, radio-esthetists, etc. amounted, in Paris alone, to Frs. 50 thousand million. The over-all 'magic' budget for France is in the neighbour-hood of 300 thousand million francs a year – far more than the budget for scientific research.

'If a fortune-teller trades in truth,' said Chesterton in *Father Brown*, 'then I think he is trading with the enemy.'

It is essential, if only to clean up the field of investigation, that this invasion should be repulsed. But this must be done in order to further the progress of knowledge. There can be no question, however, of reverting to the positivism which Flammarion already considered outdated in 1891, nor to a narrow 'conventional' scientific position, since science itself is now inviting us to approach from a fresh angle the problem of the structure of the mind. If Man possesses powers that have hitherto been neglected or ignored, and if there is such a thing, as we are inclined to believe, as a higher state of consciousness, then we must certainly not reject any hypothesis that could be tested experimentally, or any undisputed fact or illuminating comparison in our campaign against this invasion of occultism and the pseudo-sciences. There is an English saying: 'When you empty the bath, be careful not to throw away the baby with the bath-water.'

Even Soviet scientists admit that 'we don't know everything, but no particular domain is taboo and there are no permanently inaccessible regions'. Specialists in the Pavlov Institute and the Chinese scientists working on the higher nervous system, are studying Yoga. According to the science newspaper reporter Saparine, writing in the Review *Strength and Knowledge* ('Force et Savoir') 'the phenomena presented by the Yogis are at present inexplicable, but no doubt an explanation will be found one day. Such phenomena are extremely interesting because they are a revelation of the extraordinary possibilities of the human machine.'

The study of extra-sensory perception, which American investigators call 'psionic', by analogy with electronic and nucleonic, may well, indeed, lead to practical applications on a large scale. Recent work, for example, on the sense of direction in animals reveals the

* Statistics cited by François Le Lionnais in his study: *Une Maladie des Civilizations: Les Fausses Sciences: La Nef*, No. 6, June 1954.

228

existence of extra-sensory faculties. The migrating bird, the cat that travels 1,000 miles to find its home, the butterfly that can sense the female at a distance of ten miles all seem to possess the same faculty of perception and action at a distance. If we could discover the nature of this phenomenon and learn to make use of it we should acquire new methods of communication and orientation. We should, in fact, have a perfect human radar at our disposal.

The direct communication of emotions, such as appears to take place in the doctor-patient relationship, might have valuable medical possibilities. Human consciousness is like an iceberg floating on the ocean: the greater part is underneath the water.

Sometimes the iceberg tilts over, revealing an enormous mass we knew nothing about; we then say: this man is mad. If it were possible, in the doctor-patient couple, to establish direct communication between the submerged regions by means of some sort of 'psionic amplifier', mental disorders might disappear altogether.

Modern science teaches us that it is limited by the extreme perfection of experimental techniques. For example, a sufficiently powerful microscope would employ a source of light so strong that it would displace the electron under observation, thus making it impossible to observe. We cannot discover what a nucleus contains by bombarding it, because this changes it. But it is possible that an unknown extension of human intelligence may make it possible to perceive directly the ultimate structures of matter and the harmony of the Universe. We may, perhaps, one day have 'psionic' microscopes and 'psionic' telescopes that will tell us directly what there is in the interior of a distant star or an atomic nucleus.

There may be a region in the interior of Man from which it will be possible to perceive reality as a whole. Such an hypothesis seems crazy. Auguste Comte declared that we should never know the chemical composition of a star. The following year Bunsen invented the spectroscope. We are now, perhaps, on the verge of discovering an ensemble of methods which would enable us to develop systematically our extra-sensory faculties and to make use of powerful mechanisms hidden within us. It is with this perspective in view that I and Bergier have worked knowing, like our master, Chesterton, that 'the humbug is not the man who dives into mystery but the one who refuses to come out of it'.

III

TOWARDS A PSYCHOLOGICAL REVOLUTION

The mind's 'second wind' – Wanted: an Einstein for psychology – A renaissance of religion – Our society is at death's door – Jaurès and the 'tree buzzing with flies' – We see little because we are little

'AN Earth of smoking factories. An Earth teeming with industries. An Earth vibrating with a hundred new radiations. This great organism only lives for the sake of and thanks to a new soul. As the age changes, so does thought. Where, then, is to be sought or situated that subtle and rejuvenating change that, without appreciably altering our bodies, has made new beings of us? Nowhere else but in a new kind of intuition that is changing the whole physiognomy of the Universe we inhabit – in other words, an awakening.'

Thus, for Teilhard de Chardin, the mutation of the human species has begun: a new soul is being born. This mutation is taking place in the profoundest regions of the intelligence and, thanks to this 'rejuvenating change', a vision, and a totally different vision of the Universe as a whole is there before our eyes. Our waking consciousness has been replaced by a higher state compared to which the former was no more than sleep. The time for a true awakening has come.

We would now ask our readers to reflect upon the nature of this awakening. I have told, at the beginning of this book, how my childhood and adolescence were permeated with feelings similar to those which have inspired Teilhard. When I look back at all that I have done or written or sought for I can see clearly that the motive impulse behind it all was the conviction, which my father had held so strongly and so passionately that human consciousness has got to advance another step and find its 'second wind', and that the time for this has come. Indeed, this book has no other purpose than to proclaim this conviction as forcibly as possible.

Psychology lags considerably behind science. So-called modern psychology studies a Man who still conforms to the conception of him current in a nineteenth century given over to militant positivism. Genuinely modern science sets out to prospect a Universe which is found to be more and more surprising and less and less adjusted to the officially accepted view of the structure of the mind and the nature of knowledge. The psychology of states of consciousness presupposes a complete and static Man: *homo sapiens* of 'the century of light'. Physics unveils a world which operates on several levels at the same time and has many doors opening on to infinity. . . . The exact sciences border on the fantastic. The humane sciences are still hedged about with positivist superstitions. The notion of 'becoming', of evolution, dominates scientific thinking.

Psychology is still based on a vision of a 'finished' Man, whose mental functions have been catalogued and classified in hierarchic order once and for all. Now, it seems to us, on the contrary, that Man is by no means in his final state; we believe it is possible to discern, through the formidable upheavals that are changing the face of the world, vertically in the sphere of knowledge, horizontally as a result of mass groupings, the first signs of a new trend in human consciousness, a 'rejuvenating change' in the interior of Man himself. Consequently a psychology adapted to the times we live in, if it is to be effective, ought, so we believe, to be based, not on what Man *is* (or rather appears to be), but on what he may *become* – that is to say, on his possible evolution. This is the research on which we are now engaged.

All traditional teaching is based on the notion that Man is not a 'complete' being and has not yet reached his final stage, and the earliest psychologists studied the conditions that would determine the changes, alterations and transmutations that would enable Man to attain his real fulfilment. It is our belief, in accordance with a certain trend in contemporary thinking which we interpret in our own way, that Man perhaps possesses faculties which he does not exploit to the full; the machinery is there, but is never used. As we said before: a knowledge of the external world, pushed to its extreme limits, can only end in a reassessment of the very nature of knowledge, and of the structure of our intelligence and powers of perception. We also stated that the next revolution would be in the field of psychology. We are not alone in thinking this: this view is shared by many contemporary observers, from Oppenheimer to Costa de Beauregard, from Wolfgang Pauli to Heisenberg, from Charles-Noël Martin to Jacques Ménétrier.

Nevertheless, it is true that the lofty, quasi-religious ideas by which those investigating these problems are inspired are not shared by 'the man in the street', and have made no impression whatever on the general public. Everything has changed inside the brains of a few thinkers; nothing has changed since the nineteenth century in the general conception of the nature of Man and Human Society. In an unpublished article on God, Jaurès at the end of his life expressed this thought in the following fine words:

'All we wish to say today is that religious ideas, having suffered a temporary eclipse, may return to our minds and consciousness because the conclusions of modern science make it easier for us to accept them. Today already there is, so to speak, a religion ready and waiting for us; and if it fails under present conditions to penetrate deeply into our society – if the middle classes are either prosaically spiritualistic or foolishly positivist – if the proletariat is torn between slavish superstition and crude materialism – this is because the present social régime is a régime of degradation and hatred, and therefore irreligious. It is not, as is often proclaimed by loud-mouthed critics and thoughtless moralists, because our society is materialistic that it is irreligious. On the contrary, there is something religious about Man's conquest of Nature and in the adaptation of the forces in the Universe to the needs of humanity. No, what is really irreligious is the fact that Man conquers Nature only by enslaving his fellowmen. It is not their concern with material progress that prevents men from having lofty thoughts and meditating on the things of the spirit; it is the inhuman labour to which the majority of men are subjected that deprives them of the strength to think or even to be conscious of their life, that is to say, of God. It is also the agitation provoked by evil passions, by jealousy and pride, that saps the energy of even the strongest and happiest men by forcing them to engage in godless strife. Exposed on the one side to hunger and on the other to hate, how can humanity be thinking of the infinite ? Humanity is like a great tree, a-buzz with angry flies under a stormy sky; and under this clamour of hate the deep and divine voice of the Universe is no longer heard.'

It was not without emotion that I discovered this text of Jaurès. It corresponded to the sentiments of a long message my father had sent him, to which he had waited in vain for a reply. A reply which reached me, in the form of this unpublished paper fifty years later.

It is true that Man's knowledge of himself is not on a par with his knowledge of his *actions* – by which I mean everything that science, which is the supreme reward of his obscure labours, discovers about the Universe – its mysteries, its forces and its harmony. And the reason for this being so is that the organization of our society, based on obsolete ideas, deprives him of hope, of leisure and of peace. How could a man deprived of life in the fullest sense of the word ever discover its infinite potentialities ? There is every reason to believe, however, that all this will very soon be changed; the emancipation of the masses, the irresistible pressure of new discoveries and techniques, the diffusion of ideas in really responsible circles and contact with intelligences from outside will make a clean sweep of the old principles which paralyse modern life, after which Man, coming into his own again after traversing all the stages from alienation to revolt, and from revolt to acceptance, will be conscious of the growth within himself of that 'new soul' of which Teilhard speaks, and will discover, in freedom, that ability to be 'the cause of things' which is a bond between being and doing.

That Man possesses certain powers: precognition, telepathy, etc., is now an accepted fact; these phenomena can be observed. Up till now, however, such phenomena have been presented as so-called 'proofs' of the 'reality of the soul', or of the 'intelligence of the dead'.

To cite the extraordinary as proof of the improbable is an absurdity. We have, therefore, in our work, rejected any explanation in terms of the occult or of magic. This does not mean that we should neglect the whole ensemble of facts and documents in this field.

The only progress made in psychology has been the attempt to explore the deep-lying zones of the subconscious. We believe there are also summits to be explored – a super-conscious zone. Or, rather, our researches and investigations incline us to admit as a hypothesis the existence of a superior equipment in the brain that has scarcely as yet been investigated. In the ordinary waking state of consciousness, only a tenth of the brain is actively functioning.

What is happening in the other, apparently dormant, nine-tenths ? And is there not a state in which the brain as a whole is fully engaged. All the facts we are now about to record and study can be ascribed to the excitation of zones in the brain that are normally

232

asleep. No branch of psychology deals specifically with this phenomenon.

We shall have to wait, no doubt, for further progress to be made in neuro-physiology before a 'summit-psychology' can be developed. Without waiting for this new physiology to be formulated, and with no wish to prejudge its results, we desire simply to call attention to this domain. It may be that its exploration will prove to be as important as the exploration of the atom or of outer space.

Until now interest has been focused entirely on the subconscious, while consciousness itself, in modern theory, has always been considered as a phenomenon originating in some lower region: sex, for Freud; conditioned reflexes for Pavlov, etc. . . . Consequently all psychological literature – the modern novel, for example – is an illustration of what Chesterton meant when he referred to those people 'who cannot talk about the sea without talking about sea-sickness'. But Chesterton was a Catholic: he took a higher consciousness for granted because he admitted the existence of God. Psychology, like any other science, had to break away from theology; all we are saying is that the break-away is not yet complete, and that it can be liberated from above, by the methodical study of phenomena that are above consciousness, and of an intelligence vibrating at a higher rate of frequency.

The spectrum of light is composed as follows: on the left, a wide band of Hertzian and infra-red waves; in the centre, a narrow band of visible light; on the right, an infinite band ranging from ultra-violet, X and gamma rays to the unknown. . . .

And what if there were a comparable spectrum of intelligence, of human light? On the left, the infra, or subconscious; in the centre the narrow band of consciousness, on the right the infinite band of the ultra-conscious. Until now, only the conscious and subconscious have been studied. The vast domain of the ultra-conscious seems only to have been explored by mystics and magicians: secret explorations, evidence that can only be deciphered with difficulty. From the scanty information available, we tend to explain certain undeniable phenomena, such as intuition and genius, corresponding to the beginning of the right-hand band, as being manifestations of the subconscious, corresponding to the end of the left-hand band.

From what we know about the subconscious we try to explain the little we know about the super-conscious state. One cannot, however, explain the right-hand portion of the light-spectrum in terms of the left-hand portion – the gamma rays cannot be compared to the Hertzian waves: their properties are not the same. Therefore, we think that, if there is a state above and beyond that of our waking consciousness, the properties of the intelligence in that sphere will be totally different, and it will be necessary to devise other methods for their exploration than those employed in ordinary psychology.

What are the conditions necessary for the mind to attain this 'other' state? What properties will it then possess, and into what realms of knowledge will it be able to penetrate? The vast strides made in knowledge generally have brought us to the point where the mind knows that it must change in order to see what is to be seen, and to do what has to be done. 'We see little because we are little.' But are we only what we think we are?

IV

THE MAGIC MIND REDISCOVERED

The green eye of the Vatican – The 'other' intelligence – The story of the 'relavote' – Is Nature playing a double game? – The starting-handle of the super-machine – New cathedrals and new slang – The last door – Existence as an instrument – A new view of symbols – All is not everything

To decipher certain manuscripts found on the shores of the Black Sea, all the knowledge of the best linguists in the world was not enough. An electronic calculating machine was then set up in the Vatican and presented with an appalling scrawl, the débris of a parchment dating from time immemorial covered in every direction with indecipherable signs. The machine was being asked to do what hundreds and hundreds of brains, working for hundreds and hundreds of years could not have done: to compare the sign-traces; reconstruct all the possible series of similar signs; choose between all the possible probabilities; discover a common factor of resemblance between all imaginable terms of comparison; and finally having exhausted the infinite number of possible combinations, constitute an alphabet from the one acceptable similitude, recreate a language, restore and translate it. The machine, cold and motionless, opened its green and glassy eye; began to hum and click; its electronic brain was traversed by innumerable rapid waves; and at last from this poor rotting scrap of parchment a message emerged, a voice from an ancient world that vanished long ago. The machine translated. Those shadowy letters on that dusty parchment came to life again, reunited and refecundated; and from this shapeless carcass of what had once been the Word there issued a voice full of promise. The machine said: 'And in this desert we will trace a road that will lead to God.'

We know the difference between arithmetic and mathematics. Mathematical thought, since Evariste Gallois, has discovered a world which is alien to Man and has nothing in common with human experience or with the Universe as apprehended by our normal waking consciousness. In that world our ordinary Yes-or-No logic is replaced by super-logic operating on a basis of Yes *and* No. This super-logic stems not from reason, but from intuition. It is in this sense that intuition, which is an 'untamed' faculty, an 'unusual' property of the mind, 'is now a governing principle in the work of a considerable body of mathematicians'.*

How does the brain normally work? It functions like an arith-

* Charles-Noël Martin: *Les Vingt Sens de l'Homme.*

metical machine – a binary machine: Yes, No, Agreed, Not agreed, True, False, I like, I don't like, Good, Bad. In the binary field our brain is unbeatable. Some great human calculators have succeeded in beating electronic machines.

What is an arithmetical electronic machine? It is a machine which with extraordinary rapidity, classifies, accepts, rejects and arranges various factors in series. In other words, it is a machine which introduces order into the Universe. . . . It imitates the way in which our brains work. Man classifies; it's his privilege. All sciences depend on some system of classification.

Yes, but there are now electronic machines which function, not only arithmetically, but by analogy. For example: if you want to study *all* the conditions which could affect the resistance of the dam you are building, you make a model of the dam. On this model you carry out every possible kind of test. You then provide the machine with the result of all your observations. It co-ordinates and compares these data with inhuman speed, establishes *all* the possible connections between a thousand and one points of detail and then tells you: 'Unless you reinforce the props of the third pier on the right, it will collapse in 1984.'

The analogical machine has grasped, with its fixed and infallible eye, all the possible reactions of the dam, envisaged every aspect of its existence, and then assimilated this existence and deduced from it the necessary laws. It has *seen* the present in all its aspects as a whole, while establishing, at a speed which causes time to shrink, all the possible connections between every separate factor; and at the same time, it has seen into the future. In a word it has advanced from know-how to knowledge.

We believe that the human brain also can, in certain circumstances, function like an analogical machine. That is to say, it should be able:

(*a*) to assemble everything possible that can be observed about a thing;

(*b*) Draw up a list of constant relationships between the manifold aspects of an object;

(*c*) Become, in a sense, the thing itself; assimilate its essence and discover everything about its future destiny.

All this, it goes without saying, at electronic speed, tens of thousands of connections being established in a flash, as if time had been atomized. This fabulous series of exact mathematical operations is what we sometimes call, when the mechanism is triggered off by accident, an 'illumination'.

If the brain can function like an analogical machine, it can also, like the machine, work not on the thing itself but on a model of the thing. Not on God Himself, but on an idol. Not on eternity, but on an hour. Not on the Earth, but on a grain of sand. In other words it should be able, as the connections are grasped at a speed exceeding that of the most rapid binary reasoning, to see in an image serving as a model, in the words of Blake: 'The Universe in a grain of sand, and eternity in an hour.'

If that could happen; if the process of making comparisons, classifications, deductions could be enormously accelerated; if our intelligence, in certain cases, behaved like a particle in the cyclotron, then all magic would be explained. After observing a star with the naked eye, a Maya priest would have been able to recompose in his brain the whole solar system and discover Uranus and Pluto without a telescope (as certain bas-reliefs would seem to suggest).

From his observation of a phenomenon in his crucible an alchemist might have obtained an exact picture of the most complex atom, and have discovered the secret of matter. We should have an explanation of the formula: '*Ce qui est en haut est comme ce qui est en bas.*'

In the cruder sphere of imitative magic, we should understand how the Cromagnon magician looking in his cave at a picture of a ceremonial bison was able to comprehend the laws that governed the bison world and announce to his tribe the date and place and weather conditions that would be most favourable for their next hunt.

The cybernetics technicians have perfected electronic machines which function first arithmetically and then analogically. These machines are used to decipher codes. But scientists generally are so constituted that they refuse to believe that *what Man has made he can also be*. Strange humility!

If we admit the following hypothesis: Man is endowed with powers at least equal, if not superior, to any technically realizable machinery, and intended to achieve the same results as any other technique – namely the ability to understand and control Universal forces: why, then, should he not possess a sort of analogical electronic machine in the deepest recesses of his brain? We know today that nine-tenths of a man's brain are unused in his ordinary conscious life, and Dr. Warren Penfield has demonstrated the existence within us of this vast silent domain. But what if this vast silent domain were a kind of immense engine-room, full of machinery in perfect working order and only waiting to be set in motion? If that were the case, then magic would be vindicated.

We have a Post Office: hormone secretions travel all over our bodies, provoking reactions in the various centres.

We have a Telephone: our nervous system; if you pinch me, I cry out; if I am ashamed, I blush, etc. . . .

Why should we not possess a radio? The brain perhaps emits waves of high velocity moving inside a myeline sheath, in the same way that V.H.F. waves are passed through hollow conductors. If that were so, we should then possess an unknown system of communications and connections. Our brain is perhaps continually emitting waves of this kind, but the receiving apparatus is not in use, or else only works on rare occasions, as when a wireless set that is out of order comes to life for a moment as a result of some sudden shock.

236

I was seven years old. I was in the kitchen with my mother who was at the sink washing up. My mother took up a dish-mop [*lavette*] to scour the plates and as she did so the thought flashed through her mind that her friend Raymonde called this instrument a 'relavote'. I was only just beginning to talk, but in that same second I said: 'Raymonde calls that a "relavote" ', and then I went on chattering. I should not have remembered this incident had not my mother, on whom it made a great impression at the time, often reminded me of it, as if a great mystery had been revealed to her in that moment, making her feel, in a sudden uprush of joy, that I was a part of her, and that this was a more than human proof of my love. Later on, when I had caused her to suffer in any way, she used to recall this moment of 'contact' as if to convince herself that something deeper then her blood had been transmitted from herself to me.

I know what to think about coincidences – even those privileged coincidences that Jung calls 'significant'; but after having experienced the same kind of thing with a very dear friend or a woman with whom one was very much in love, it seems to me that the notion of a coincidence is not enough, and that one might go so far as to seek an explanation for these things in magic. All we have to do is to decide what we mean by 'magic'.

What really happened in that kitchen that evening when I was seven years old? I believe that as a result of an imperceptible shock, a minute vibration such as is enough sometimes to cause an object that has been delicately balanced for a long time to fall suddenly for no apparent reason, some mechanism inside me, made infinitely sensitive by repeated bursts of love – the simple, violent, exclusive love of a child – without my being aware of it, was suddenly set in motion. This brand-new machine, all ready to function in the silent recesses of my brain, like a kind of cybernetic Sleeping Beauty, 'looked at' my mother. She saw it; she made an amalgam of all her thoughts and feelings and moods and sensations; she became my mother; she took cognizance of her essential being and her destiny up to that moment. At a speed greater than that of light she arranged under their proper headings all the feelings and associations of ideas my mother had had ever since she was born, and came to the very latest association – the dish-mop, Raymonde and the 'relavote'. It was I who then expressed the result of the work of this machine which had been done with such fantastic speed that its meaning went through me without leaving any trace, like the Cosmic waves which go through our bodies without our feeling them. I said: 'Raymonde calls that a "relavote".' Then the machine stopped working, or else I ceased to be receptive, after having been so for a thousand-millionth of a second, and went on with what I had been saying before. Before time stopped or, if you like, before it was speeded up in every direction – past, present, future: it makes no difference.

I have had experience, in other circumstances, of similar coincidences. I think they can be interpreted in the same way. It may be that the machine is working all the time, but that we can only be receptive on occasions. In any case, this receptivity can only be extremely rare; in some people, no doubt, it is non-existent. This is why some people are 'lucky', and others unlucky. The lucky ones would be those who sometimes receive a message from the machine: it has analysed all the elements of the situation – classified, selected, compared all possible causes and effects and, having thus discovered the most auspicious course to take, delivers its opinion like an oracle which is accepted without the person concerned having been conscious in the slightest degree of all this prodigious activity. These are indeed the people whom the gods love. From time to time they are connected with their inner power-station. In my own case, I am what is known as 'lucky'. I have every reason to believe that the phenomena on which this luck depends are of the same order as those which were responsible for the story of the 'relavote'.

And so we are beginning to see that the magical conception of man's relations with other men and with things and space and time is not altogether foreign to our own ideas about modern science and techniques. It is their modernity which makes it possible for us to believe in magic. It is the electronic machines which make us take seriously the Cromagnon sorcerer and the Maya High Priest.

If ultra-rapid connections operate in the silent regions of the brain, and if, in certain circumstances, the result of these operations penetrates our consciousness, we should then have to consider as real manifestations of the mind in a state of wakefulness certain procedures of imitative magic, certain prophetic revelations, certain poetic or mystical illuminations and certain divinations we now attribute to madness or to chance.

Yet we have known for some years now that Nature is not reasonable. She does not conform to the ordinary rules which govern the working of our intelligence. For that part of our brain which is normally in use, every operation is binary: black or white, Yes or No, continuous or discontinuous. Our understanding machine, on the other hand, is arithmetical. It classifies and compares. The *Discours de la Méthode* is entirely based on this system. So is the whole principle of Ying and Yang in Chinese philosophy (and the *Book of Mutations*, the only oracular book the rules of which have come down to us from antiquity, is composed of graphic figures: three continuous lines, and three discontinuous in every possible order). But, as Einstein said at the end of his life: 'I wonder whether Nature always plays the same game.' It would seem, in fact, that Nature is not a slave to the binary system which governs the working of our brain in its normal state.

Since Louis de Broglie's discovery, we are forced to admit that light is *at one and the same time* continuous *and* broken. But no human brain is capable of imagining such a phenomenon or of really knowing or understanding what it implies. We accept it. We know it is a fact, but the thing itself we cannot *know*. Now

238

suppose that a brain, contemplating some representation of light (religious literature and iconography are full of evocations of light) passes in a flash of illumination from the arithmetical to the analogical state. It *becomes* light. It *sees* the incomprehensible phenomenon. It is born with it. It knows it. It reaches a point where the sublime intelligence of de Broglie cannot penetrate. Then it falls back; it has lost contact with the transcendent machines that function in the vast secret recesses of the brain. Its memory only retains scraps of the knowledge it has just acquired. And there is no language in which to describe those scraps. It may be that some mystics have *known* in this way natural phenomena which our intelligence has been able to discover and to accept, but not to integrate.

'And when I asked her how, and what sort of thing she saw, and whether what she saw had bodily form, she answered thus: "I saw a plenitude, a great light which filled me so completely that I have no words to describe it and know not to what it could be compared. . . ." '

This passage from Angèle de Foligno's statement to her confessor is highly significant.

The electronic calculator on a mathematical model of a dam or an aeroplane functions analogically. To a certain extent it *becomes* this dam or this aeroplane, and discovers every possible aspect of their existence. If the brain can act in the same way* we begin to understand why the witch-doctor makes an image to represent the enemy he wishes to destroy, or draws a picture of the bison he is going to hunt. In the presence of these models he waits for his intelligence to switch from the binary to the analogical stage, and for his ordinary state of consciousness to pass to a higher plane. In fact, he is waiting for the machine to start working analogically and for the the propagation in the silent recesses of his brain of those ultra-rapid connections which will reveal to him the total reality of the object represented. He waits, but not passively. What is he doing? He has chosen the time and place in obedience to ancestral instructions and traditions which are perhaps the result of countless experiments in the past. A particular hour on a particular night, for example, is better than some other time on some other night, perhaps because of the disposition of the stars, or the Cosmic rays or certain magnetic fields. He stands in a certain position, makes certain gestures – perhaps performs a special dance – utters certain words or noises, breathes in a particular way, etc. No one has yet suggested that these may all be special techniques (however rudimentary and tentative) designed to set in motion the ultra-rapid machines contained in the dormant part of our brain. The rites are perhaps merely a complicated pattern of rhythmic exercises calculated to stimulate the higher faculties of the brain, rather like

* Of course our comparison with the electronic machine is not absolute. Like any other comparison, it is only a starting point, and is itself only the suggestion of an idea.

cranking up a motor-car. There is every reason to believe that the setting in motion of these higher faculties, these analogical electronic brains, calls for adjustments a thousand times more complicated and subtle than those which take place during the transition from a sleeping to a waking state.

Thanks to the work of von Frisch it is known that bees have a language: they trace in the air infinitely complicated mathematical figures during their flight, and transmit in this way instructions necessary to the life of the hive. It is highly probable that Man, in order to establish contact with his highest faculties, must set in motion a series of impulses at least as complex and substantial, and no less remote from what normally determines his intellectual activities.

Thus prayers and rites performed in front of religious symbolic figures could be ways of trying to capture and direct subtle magnetic, cosmic or rhythmic forces with a view to arousing that analogical intelligence which will enable Man to *know* the divinity who is being thus invoked.

If that were so; if there be techniques for increasing the brain's efficiency and output so as to produce results far in advance of anything that could be obtained from even the greatest binary intelligence; and if it be true that these techniques have up till now only been employed by the occultists – then it is easy to understand why most of the important practical and scientific discoveries prior to the nineteenth century were made by them.

Our language, like our thought, is conditioned by the arithmetical, binary way in which our brain functions. We classify everything under Yes or No, positive or negative; we make comparisons and deductions. If language helps us to introduce order into our thought, which itself is wholly occupied with putting things in their places, it is obviously not an external creative element or a divine attribute. It does not add thoughts to our thought. When I speak or write, I am slowing down my machine. I can only describe it if I can observe it in slow motion. Therefore I am only expressing my binary awareness of the world – and, what is more, only at a time when it has ceased to function at its normal speed. My language therefore only reflects a slow-motion picture of the world – a picture, moreover, which is itself limited to binary dimensions. This inadequacy of language is only too evident and a matter for regret. But what can be said about the inadequacy of a binary intelligence? The inner existence, the essence of things are beyond its grasp. It can make the discovery that light is both continuous and discontinuous at the same time, or that the molecule of benzene establishes between six atoms a double, yet mutually exclusive relationship; it can accept these facts, but cannot understand them; it cannot integrate into its own system the reality of the profound structures which it studies. To be able to do this, it would have to change its condition; other machinery than that normally in use would have to be started up in the brain, whose binary system of reasoning would have to be replaced by an analogical consciousness which would assume the form, and assimilate the inconceivable rhythms of these profound structures. No doubt that happens already in scientific intuition, poetic illumination, religious ecstasy and in other cases of which we know nothing. Recourse to an *awakened* consciousness – that is to say, to a state different from that of ordinary wakefulness – is the *Leit-motiv* of all the ancient philosophies. It is also the *Leit-motiv* of the greatest modern physicists and mathematicians, who hold the view that 'something has to happen in human consciousness for it to be able to progress from knowing to knowledge'.

It is therefore not surprising that language which can only reflect the world as it appears to our consciousness in its normal waking state becomes obscure as soon as it has to express those profound structures or anything to do with light, eternity, time, energy, the essence of Man, etc. Nevertheless we can distinguish two kinds of obscurity.

One is due to the fact that language is the vehicle of an intelligence that endeavours to examine these structures without ever being able to assimilate them. It is the vehicle of one kind of Nature that is in conflict with another kind of Nature. At best, it can only demonstrate an impossibility and convey an impression of frustration and isolation. Its obscurity is real and positive; in fact, it is nothing but obscurity.

The other kind of obscurity occurs when the man who is trying to express himself has had, by a flash of intuition, a brief glimpse of another state of consciousness. He has *lived* for an instant in the intimacy of those profound structures. He has *known* them. I am thinking of mystics like St. John of the Cross, or intuitional scientists like Einstein, or inspired poets like William Blake, or enraptured mathematicians like Galois, or visionary philosophers like Meyrink.

On returning to Earth, the 'seer' fails to communicate what he has experienced. But in doing so he expresses the certitude that the Universe could be controlled and manipulated if Man succeeded in establishing as close an association as possible between his ordinary waking state and a state of hyper-wakefulness. Such a language could be really efficient, a sovereign instrument. Fulcanelli, speaking of the mystery of the Cathedrals; Wiener on the structure of Time, are obscure; but this is not real obscurity, but a sign that something is shining elsewhere.

The language of modern mathematics is the only one, no doubt, that can give some account of certain results of analogical thinking. There exist in mathematical physics regions of the 'Absolute Elsewhere' and of '*continus de mesure nulle*', that is to say measurements applied to Universes that are inconceivable and yet real. We may wonder why it is that the poets have not yet turned to this science to catch an echo of the music of those spheres of fantastic reality – unless it be for fear of having to accept this evidence –

241

that the magic art lives and flourishes outside their study walls.*

This mathematical language which is proof of the existence of a Universe beyond the grasp of a normally waking consciousness, is the only one that is in a state of constant ferment and activity.†

Mathematical 'entities', i.e. the expressions, the signs which symbolize the life and the laws of the invisible world – of the *unthinkable* world – develop and fertilize other 'entities'. This language is, strictly speaking, the 'slang' of the present age.

Yes; it is true that we find this 'slang', in the original sense of the word as it was in the Middle Ages (and not in the degenerate form favoured by writers who like to think of themselves as 'emancipated') in the *avant-garde* science of mathematical physics which is, if we look at it closely, a challenge to what is generally meant by intelligence – a rupture, a kind of 'second sight'.

What is Gothic art, to which we owe the Cathedrals? Fulcanelli, in his book *Le Mystère des Cathédrales*, expressed the opinion that 'Gothic art ("*art gothique*") is only an orthographic distortion of the word *argotique*, in accordance with the law of phonetics which governs, in all languages regardless of orthography, the traditional cabal.' The cathedral, then, is a work of Gothic art (*Art got*) or *Argot*.

And what is the cathedral of today, which teaches men the structures of the Creation, but the *equation* that has taken the place of the rosette, or rose-window? Let us cease to pay a useless homage to the past, so that we can understand it better. The modern cathedral is not to be found in a large building made of glass and cement. The cathedral of the Middle Ages was the book of mysteries for the use of the men of yesterday. Today the book of mysteries is the work of mathematical physicists who compose it with 'mathematical entities' enshrined, like rose-windows, in such constructions as interplanetary rockets, atomic piles or the cyclotron. This is true continuity, the real link with tradition.

The *argotiers* of the Middle Ages, spiritual descendants of the Argonauts who knew the road to the Garden of the Hesperides,

* Cantor: 'The essence of mathematics is liberty.' Mittag-Leffler (on the work of Abel): 'They are real lyrical poems of sublime beauty; the perfection of their form allows the grandeur of thought to appear and fills the mind with images of a world more remote from the banal semblances of life, and a more direct expression of the soul than the finest creation of the finest poet in the ordinary sense of the word.' Dedekind: 'We are a divine race, and possess the power to create.'

† 'Here, everything is open: the techniques of thought, logical processes and "ensembles" – all this is alive and constantly renewed, while the strangest and most transparent conceptions are formed in the mind, one leading to another and being transformed, like the movements of a symphony; we are in the divine domain of the imagination. But an abstract imagination, so to speak, for these images arising out of mathematical techniques have nothing in common with those pertaining to the illusory world in which we are bogged down, *although they contain the key which can unlock the latters' hidden meaning*.' Georges Buraud: *Mathématique et Civilization*, La Table Ronde, April 1959.

242

wrote in stone their hermetic message. Signs incomprehensible to men whose consciousness has not undergone transmutations and whose brains have not been subjected to that terrific acceleration thanks to which the inconceivable becomes real and can be felt and manipulated. These men were not secretive because they loved secrecy, but simply because their discoveries about the Laws of Energy, of matter and of the mind had been made in another state of consciousness and so could not be communicated directly. They observed secrecy because 'being' meant for them 'being different'.

As if in memory of so lofty an example, our modern slang is a kind of special dialect for the use of rebels, those who are hungry for liberty, outlaws, nomads and all who live outside the law and conventions.

But we shall find the tradition unimpaired if we realize that this *art got* is today the art of the 'mathematical entities' and integrals of Lebesgue, and of the numbers beyond infinity; the art of the mathematical physicists who build in unwonted curves, in 'forbidden lights', in thunder and in flames, the cathedrals in which our Masses will in future be celebrated.

It is possible that religious readers may find these remarks shocking. They are intended to be so. We believe that the potentialities of the human brain are infinite. This view conflicts with that of the official scientists and psychologists whose 'belief in man' depends on his remaining within the boundaries traced for him by the nineteenth-century rationalists. But it should not be considered as being incompatible with the spirit of religion – at any rate with religion in its purest and loftiest forms.

Man can have access to a secret world – *see* the Light, *see* Eternity, comprehend the Laws of Energy, integrate within himself the rhythm of the destiny of the Universe, consciously apprehend the ultimate concentration of forces and, like Teilhard de Chardin, live the incomprehensible life that starts from 'Point Omega', in which the whole of creation, at the end of terrestrial time, will find its accomplishment, consummation and exaltation. Man is capable of anything. His intelligence, equipped from the very beginning, no doubt with a capacity for infinite knowledge, can in certain conditions apprehend the whole mechanism of life. The powers of the human intelligence, if developed to their fullest extent, could probably cope with anything in the whole Universe. But these powers stop short at the point where the intelligence, having reached the end of its mission, senses that there is still 'something other' beyond the confines of the Universe. Here it is quite possible for an analogical consciousness to function. There are no models in the Universe of what may exist outside the Universe. This door through which none may pass is the gateway to the Kingdom of Heaven. We can accept this expression if written thus: 'Kingdom of Heaven'.

As a result of trying to outstrip the Universe by imagining a

243

number greater than anything that could be conceived within the Universe, and trying to formulate a concept whose conditions the Universe could not satisfy, the great mathematician Cantor went mad. There is ultimately a door which no analogical intelligence can open.

To return to our initial proposition. We do not say: there is, in the vast silent portion of the brain, an analogical electronic machine. What we say is this: since arithmetical and analogical machines exist, is it not possible to imagine an intelligence functioning on a higher plane, beyond the level on which it normally works? That intelligence may possess powers similar to those of the analogical machine? Our comparison must not be taken literally. It is only a point from which to start, a launching ramp aimed at untouched and still unexplored regions of the intelligence. In those regions it may be that intelligence begins to glow suddenly and to throw light on things that are normally hidden in the Universe. How does it succeed in attaining those regions where its own existence becomes a prodigy? How is this change in condition operated? We maintain that there are in magic and religious rites and in the vast literature both ancient and modern, devoted to unique and fantastic moments in the life of the mind, thousands and thousands of fragmentary descriptions which ought to be brought together and compared, and which perhaps point to a method that has been lost, or possibly to one that has still to be found.

It may be that the intelligence sometimes, as if by chance, comes up against the frontier protecting these untried regions and sets in motion, for a fraction of a second, the super-machinery whose sound it vaguely perceives. This is what happened in my story of the 'relavote'; it is an example of all those so-called 'parapsychological' phenomena which we find so disturbing – those extraordinary flashes of illumination which most sensitive people experience on rare occasions in the course of their lives, especially in childhood. They leave no trace, scarcely a memory.

Crossing this frontier (or as the traditional texts phrase it, 'entering a state of enlightenment') is infinitely more rewarding and would seem to be not altogether a matter of chance. There is every reason to believe that this transit cannot be effected without an enormous concentration of external and internal forces. It is only reasonable to suppose that these forces are there for us to make use of, if we knew how. But until quite recently we did not know how to liberate nuclear energy. Nevertheless, these forces are probably available to us only if we are prepared to stake our whole existence on capturing them.

The great ascetics and saints, the wonder-workers and seers, the poets and inspired scientists all say the same thing. And this is what the contemporary American poet, William Temple, meant when he wrote: 'No individual revelation is possible unless the whole of existence is itself an instrument of revelation.'

To revert to our comparison. It was during the Second World

War that what is known as 'operational research' came into being involving methods which became necessary as problems arose which seemed to defy common sense and ordinary human experience. The tacticians therefore had recourse to the mathematicians: 'When a situation arises which, owing to the complexity of its apparent structure and visible evolution, cannot be dealt with by ordinary methods, scientists are called in to deal with this situation in the same way that, in their own special field, they treat natural phenomena, and are asked to formulate a theory. To theorize about a situation or an object means that an abstract model has to be imagined whose properties are similar to those of the object in question. Such a model is always mathematical. By its intermediary, concrete questions are translated into mathematical terms.'

Here we are concerned with the 'model' of an object or a situation too new or too complex to be grasped in its totality by the intelligence. 'In fundamental operational research it is therefore advisable to construct an analogical electronic machine in order to obtain this model. It is then possible, by manipulating the control levers and watching the machine operating, to find the answers to all the questions the model was designed to deal with.'

These definitions are taken from a technical bulletin: *Bulletin de Liaison des Cercles de Politique Economique*, March 1959. They are more important as a contribution to our conception of a man in a state of 'enlightenment', or to our understanding of the spirit of 'magic' than the majority of books in the literature of occultism. If we translate 'model' by 'idol' or 'symbol', and analogical machine by a state of hyper-lucidity, or sudden flash of illumination in the brain, we shall see that the most mysterious road to human knowledge – and one that the heirs to the nineteenth century positivist tradition refuse to admit – is a true and royal road. And it is modern technical methods which encourage us to look upon it as such.

'The presence of symbols and enigmatic signs with mysterious connotations in religious tradition, in works of art and in the legends and customs of folk-lore attests the existence of a language universally current in the East as in the West whose trans-historic significance seems to lie at the very roots of our existence, our knowledge and our values.'* But are not symbols the model, in abstract, of a reality, a structure that the human intelligence cannot altogether grasp but about which it can 'theorize'?

'The symbol reveals certain aspects of reality – the most profound – which it is impossible to know.'†

Like the 'model' which the mathematician constructs out of a situation or object defying common sense or ordinary human experience, the properties of a symbol simulate the properties of the object or situation thus abstractly represented, but whose real, fundamental aspect remains hidden. The next step would be to set an analogical electronic machine to work on this model, so that the symbol may reveal the reality it contains and supply the

* René Alleau: *De la Nature des Symboles.* Ed. Flammarion.
† Mircea Eliade: *Images et Symboles.*

answers to all the questions the model was designed to deal with. We believe the equivalent of such a machine exists in Man. Certain mental or physical attitudes, of which at present little is known, might serve to set it in motion. All the techniques of asceticism, religion and magic seem designed to obtain this result; and this, no doubt, according to age-old tradition, is the 'state of enlightenment' which wise men have always striven to attain.

And so symbols are perhaps the abstract models established since men first began to think which could reveal to us secrets of the profound structure of the Universe. But here we must be careful.

Symbols do not represent the thing itself, the actual phenomenon. It would also be wrong to think that they are purely and simply schematic formulae. In operational research the model is not a small-scale or simplified model of a known object; it is a possible approach to, or means of getting to know this object. And it is outside reality, in the mathematical Universe. The next requirement is that the analogical machine constructed on this model should enter into an electronic trance so that it can give *practical* answers. This is why all the usual occultist explanations of symbols are useless. They look upon symbols as if they were schemas that can be interpreted by the intelligence at its normal level and so lead immediately to an apprehension of reality. For centuries they have been treating in this way the St. Andrew's Cross, the swastika and the Star of Solomon, but have contributed nothing to a study of the profound structure of the Universe.

Einstein, with his sublime intelligence, was able, in a flash of illumination, to catch a glimpse of the space-time relationship, but without completely understanding or integrating it into his scheme of things. To communicate his discovery at a communicable and intelligible level, and to help him to recapture his own illuminating vision, he drew the sign λ representing the trihedral angle. This sign is not a schema of reality and means nothing to the mass of mankind. It is a signal, a rallying cry to all workers in the field of mathematical physics. And yet all the progress made in this field by the greatest intellects will only succeed in discovering what this trihedral symbol evokes, but will not be able to penetrate the Universe where the law of which this symbol is an expression actually operates. At least, at the end of this forward march, we shall know that this other Universe exists.

All symbols are perhaps of the same nature. The inverse swastika, whose origin is lost in the mists of time, is perhaps the 'model' of the law that governs all destruction. Whenever there is destruction, whether material or spiritual, the movement of these forces conforms, perhaps, to this model, just as the space-time relationship conforms to the trihedron

Similarly, the spiral, so we are told by the mathematician Eric Temple Bell, is perhaps the 'model' of the profound structure of all forms of evolution (energy, life, consciousness). It may be that the brain, in its 'enlightened' state can function like the analogical machine, using an established model and that it can in this way penetrate, through the swastika, the universal structure of destruction, and through the spiral, the universal structure of evolution.

Thus, signs and symbols are perhaps models designed for the use of the higher-level mechanism in our minds to enable our intelligence to function in another 'state'.

Our intelligence, in its ordinary state, is perhaps engaged in tracing with its finest pen, models by means of which, in a higher state, it could assimilate and absorb the ultimate reality of things.

When Teilhard de Chardin conceived his 'Point Omega', he was establishing in this way the 'model' of the final stage of evolution. But in order to *feel* the reality of this point and to assimilate so unimaginable a reality into the depths of one's being and absorb it completely into one's consciousness – in order, in a word, that one's consciousness may itself become the Point Omega and apprehend all that may be apprehended at such a point – namely the ultimate meaning of earthly life, the cosmic destiny of the perfected Mind beyond the end of terrestrial time; in order that the gap between Ideas and Knowledge may thus be bridged, it is essential that another form of intelligence be set in motion. An analogical intelligence, if you like; or mystical illumination, or a state of absolute contemplation.

And so the ideas of Eternity, of the 'Transfinite' and of God, etc., are perhaps models we have set up in the hope that, in another region of our intelligence which normally lies dormant, they will be able to supply the answers to the questions they were designed to deal with.

It is important to realize that the sublimest idea is perhaps the equivalent of the Cromagnon witch-doctor's drawing of a bison. It is only a sketch. The next step is for the analogical machines to start working on this model in the secret zone of the brain. The sorcerer in a trance is transported into the world of bisons, discovers everything there is to be known about them in a flash and can then announce the time and place for the next bison hunt. This is magic at its lowest degree. At its highest, the model is not a drawing or a statuette, or even a symbol. It is an idea; the finest product of the finest possible binary intelligence. This idea has been conceived only with a view to attaining another stage in the quest: the analogical stage, the second phase in all operational research.

It now seems clear that the highest and most intense activity of the human mind consists in establishing 'models' designed to stimulate another kind of mental activity about which little is known, and which moreover cannot easily be set in motion. It is in this sense that we can say: everything is a symbol, everything is a sign, everything is an evocation of another reality.

This opens for us a door on to the infinite potentialities of Man. It does not, however – contrary to what the symbologists believe – supply the key to everything. Whether it be an idea, such as that of the Trinity or the Transfinite or an image like the statuette into which the village sorcerer sticks pins, or a symbol such as the Cross, the Swastika, a stained-glass window, a cathedral, the Virgin Mary, mathematical entities, numbers, etc., all these things are models, 'sketches' of something that exists in a different Universe from that in which the model itself has been conceived. But these 'models' are not interchangeable: a mathematical model of a dam fed into an electronic machine is not comparable with a model of a supersonic rocket.

All is not in everything. The spiral is not in the Cross. The image of the bison is not in the photograph studied by a medium; the Père Teilhard's 'Point Omega' is not in Dante's *Inferno*; the menhir is not in a cathedral; Cantor's numbers are not among the figures of the Apocalypse. If everything has its 'maquette', all 'maquettes' are not like a nest of tables and do not form a whole which can be taken to pieces to reveal the secret of the Universe.

If the most potent models available to an intelligence in a state of super-consciousness are non-dimensional – in other words, ideas – we must abandon any hope of finding the model of the Universe in the Great Pyramid or the West Door of Notre Dame. If a model of the whole Universe exists at all, this can only be in the human brain at the extreme point of the most sublime intelligence. But surely the Universe has other resources than Man? If Man is an infinity, then would not the Universe be infinity plus . . . ?

Nevertheless, to have discovered that everything is a 'maquette', a model, sign or symbol helps us to find a key. Not one that opens the door of the inscrutable mystery – for no such key exists – or, if it does, is in the hands of God. I mean a key to an attitude, not to a certainty. What we want to do is to set in motion that 'other' intelligence for whose use these models have been prepared. It is therefore a question of passing from our ordinary waking state to a higher state of wakefulness. An 'awakened' state. All is not in everything. But it is all-important to keep awake.

V

THE NOTION OF AN 'AWAKENED STATE'

After the fashion of theologians, scientists, magicians and children – Salute to an expert at putting spokes in wheels – The conflict between spiritualism and materialism: the story of an allergy – The legend of tea – Could it be a natural faculty? – Thought as a means of travel on the ground or in the air – A supplement to the Rights of Man – Some reflections on the 'awakened' Man – Ourselves as honest savages

I ONCE wrote a book describing a group of intellectuals who sought, under the guidance of the wonder-worker Gurdjieff, to attain an 'awakened' state. I still think that there is nothing more important than this quest. Gurdjieff used to say that the modern spirit, born

248

on a dunghill would return to a dunghill, and he taught men to despise the times we live in. It is true, indeed, that the modern mentality is compounded of forgetfulness and ignorance of the necessity for such a quest. But Gurdjieff, who was a man of old ideas, confused the modern spirit with the narrow Cartesianism of the nineteenth century. To the really modern mind Cartesianism is no longer a panacea, and the very nature of intelligence is something that has to be reconsidered. Consequently, it is on the contrary a spirit of extreme modernity that is likely to lead men to meditate profitably on the possible existence of another state of consciousness: a state of 'awakened' consciousness. Here the mathematicians and physicists of today join hands with the mystics of yesterday. Gurdjieff's contempt (like that of René Guénon, another partisan, but a purely theoretical one, of the 'awakened' state) is therefore out of date. And I believe that if Gurdjieff had been completely 'enlightened' himself, he would not have mistaken the climate of the times we live in. For an intelligence convinced of the absolute necessity for a transmutation, it should be clear that this is not the time to despise, but rather to love this century.

Up to the present time the 'awakened' state has been evoked in religious, esoteric or poetic terms. Gurdjieff's outstanding contribution was to show that there could be a psychology and a physiology pertaining to this state. But his language was wilfully obscure and he kept his disciples in a state of isolation. We are trying to speak the language of men of the second half of the twentieth century using terms that all can understand.

For daring to approach such a subject in this way we shall, of course, be looked upon as barbarians by the 'experts'. And perhaps that is just what we are, to some extent. We are conscious in the world of today that a new spirit is abroad to meet the challenge of a new era in the history of the world. Our method of establishing the probable existence of an 'awakened' state will not be exclusively religious, or esoteric, or poetic or scientific, but will be a blend of all these and in contradiction to all the disciplines. That is what we call a Renaissance: a soup containing a mixture of the methods of theologians, scientists, magicians and children.

One morning in August 1957 a crowd of journalists had assembled on the quay as a liner was about to sail from the London Docks for India. They had come to see the famous biologist J. B. S. Haldane who, accompanied by his wife, was about to leave England for good.

'I've had enough of this country and of a lot of things in it,' he said quietly, 'especially the Americanization which is spreading everywhere. I'm going in search of new ideas, to work freely in a new country.'

Thus began a new stage in the career of one of the most extraordinary men of our time. J. B. S. Haldane had taken part in the defence of Madrid, gun in hand, against the troops of Franco. He had been a member of the British Communist Party, but after the

Lysenko affair he tore up his card. And now he was off to seek the truth in India.

For some thirty years people had found his grim sense of humour somewhat disconcerting. To a newspaper questionnaire on the subject of the decapitation of King Charles I, which had revived old controversies he had replied: 'If Charles I had been a geranium the two halves would have survived.'

After making a violent speech at the Atheists' Club, he had received a letter from an English Roman Catholic informing him that 'His Holiness the Pope did not agree with him'. Adopting this respectful formula, he then wrote to the Minister for War addressing him as 'Your Ferocity', to the Air Minister, as 'Your Velocity', and to the Chairman of the Rationalist Society as 'Your Impiety'.

On that August morning his 'Leftist' colleagues were also, no doubt, quite pleased to see him go, For, while defending Marxist biology, Haldane nevertheless was in favour of extending the field of science and of observing phenomena which did not conform to rationalist ideas. In reply to criticism, he answered coolly: 'I study whatever is really strange in physical chemistry, but I do not neglect anything in any other field.'

He had been urging for a long time that science should make a systematic study of the notion of an 'awakened state'. As early as 1930, in his books *The Inequality of Man* and *Possible Worlds*, in spite of his official position in the world of science, he had declared that the Universe was certainly stranger than was generally thought, and that poetic or religious testimony relating to a state of super-consciousness ought to be a subject for scientific research.

It was inevitable that such a man would one day go off to India; and it would not be surprising if his future works treated such subjects as: 'Electro-Encephalography and Mysticism', or 'The Fourth State of Consciousness and the metabolism of carbonic gas'. This could be expected of a man whose works already include a *Study of the application of 18-dimensional space to essential problems of genetics.*

Our official psychologists admit the existence of two states of consciousness: sleep and waking. But from the earliest times down to the present day there is abundant evidence as to the existence of states of consciousness superior to our normal waking consciousness. Haldane was probably the first modern scientist to examine objectively this state of super-consciousness.

It was only logical, in the period of transition in which we are living, that this Man should have been considered by his spiritualist enemies no less than by his materialist friends as an expert in the art of putting spokes in wheels.

Like Haldane, we ought to remain entirely aloof from the old controversy between spiritualists and materialists. That is the really 'modern' attitude. It is not a question of being 'above' the dispute, because there is no 'above' and no 'below'; in fact there is no sense in it at all.

The spiritualists believe in the possibility of a super-consciousness, and see in it an attribute of the immortal soul.

The materialists are up in arms against the very idea, and brandish Descartes. Neither side is willing to approach the subject with an open mind or give it serious study. There must be another way of considering this problem; a realistic way, in the sense in which we understand the term, implying an integral realism which takes into account the fantastic aspects of reality.

It may well be, too, that this old controversy is not philosophical at all, except on the surface. It may be nothing but a dispute between people who, according to their natures, react differently towards natural phenomena – just as one person may revel in the wind, and another detest it. A conflict between two human types is not likely to lead to any illumination! If this were really so, how much time would be wasted in abstract discussions, and how right we should be to withdraw from the debate in order to approach the whole question from a 'barbarian' point of view!

We may proceed on the following hypothesis:

The passage from sleep to a waking state produces a certain number of changes in the body. For example: the arterial tension is different, and there are variations in the nervous impulses. If, as we think, there is another state, which we may call one of super-wakefulness, or super-consciousness, the passage from our normal waking to this super-state must also be attended by transformations of various kinds.

Now, it is well known that for some people the process of waking up is painful, or at any rate extremely disagreeable. Modern medicine is aware of this phenomenon, and distinguishes two types of human beings according to their reaction to the process of waking up.

What is this state of super-consciousness, of a really 'awakened' consciousness? Men who have experienced it have difficulty, on their return to normality, in describing it. It cannot be expressed in ordinary language. We know that it is possible to attain this state voluntarily; and the mystics' exercises are all directed to this end. We also know that it is possible, as Vivekananda says, that 'a man who is not versed in this science (mystical exercises) may attain this state by chance'.

There are a great many instances in the poetry of every nation of sudden illuminations of this kind. And how many people, who are neither poets nor mystics, have not felt for a fraction of a second that they were on the brink of such an experience?

Now let us compare this singular and exceptional state with another exceptional state. Doctors and psychologists are beginning to study, for military reasons, the behaviour of human beings in a state of weightlessness. Beyond a certain degree of acceleration, weight is abolished. A passenger in an experimental plane travelling at such a speed floats for a few seconds. For some the sensation is one of extreme well-being, for others one of extreme anguish and horror.

Similarly, it may well be that the passage from the ordinary

251

waking state to one of super-consciousness (illuminative, magic) is attended by certain subtle changes in the organism, disagreeable for some, and agreeable for others. The study of the physiology of states of consciousness is still at a rudimentary stage. Some progress has already been made in connection with hibernation. The physiology of a state of super-consciousness has not, with a few exceptions, attracted the attention of scientists. If our hypothesis is valid, we can readily conceive the existence of a positivist, rationalist human type who, in self-defence, becomes aggressive as soon as there is any question, whether in literature philosophy or science, of going outside the sphere in which consciousness normally functions. We can equally well imagine the spiritualist type in whom any allusion to a state beyond reason produces the sensation of a lost paradise. May not the basis of a fundamental scholastic dispute prove to be, in the last resort, a question of: 'I like, or I don't like'? But what is it in us that likes or does not like? In point of fact, it is never 'I'; merely: 'something in me likes, or does not like', and that is all. Let us therefore get rid altogether of the false 'spiritualism *versus* materialism' problem, which is perhaps nothing but a question of allergies. What is essential is to know whether Man possesses in unexplored regions of his being, superior instruments, enormous amplifiers, as it were, of his intelligence – a whole equipment to enable him to conquer and comprehend the Universe, to conquer and comprehend himself, and to shoulder his whole destiny.

Bodhidarma, the founder of Zen Buddhism, one day while he was meditating, fell asleep (i.e. he allowed himself inadvertently to relapse into what is for most men their normal state of consciousness). This failing seemed to him so horrible that he cut off his eyelids.

According to the legend, the eyelids fell to the ground and there gave birth to the first tea plant. Tea, which is a protection against sleep, is the flower that symbolizes the desire of wise men to keep awake; and that is why so it is said, 'The taste of tea and the taste of Zen are much alike.'

This notion of an 'awakened state' seems to be as old as humanity It is the key to the most ancient religious texts, and perhaps the Cromagnon man already sought to enter that state. The radio-carbon method of dating has shown that six thousand years ago the Indians to the south-east of Mexico used to absorb certain mushrooms to induce a state of hyper-lucidity. It is always a question of getting the 'third eye' to open and of escaping from the ordinary level of consciousness where everything is illusion, a prolongation of the dreams belonging to deep sleep. 'Sleeper awake!' In the Gospels as in fairy-tales, it is always the same admonition.

Mankind has sought this 'awakened state' in all sorts of rites, in dancing and song, by mortification of the flesh, fasting, torture and various drugs. As soon as modern Man realizes the importance of what is at stake – which must be very soon – other means will certainly be found. The American scientist J. B. Olds has imagined an electronic stimulation of the brain.*

The English astronomer Fred Hoyle† suggests the projection of luminous images on a television screen. Already H. G. Wells, in *In the Days of the Comet*, had imagined that after colliding with a comet, the atmosphere of the Earth was impregnated with a gas that induced a state of hyper-lucidity. At last men could cross the frontier that separates truth from illusion. They were awakened to eternal realities. Of a sudden, all problems – practical, moral, spiritual, found their solution.

This state of an 'awakened consciousness' seems to have been sought until now only by mystics. If it is possible, to what is it to be attributed? Religious persons speak of 'divine grace'; the occultists of 'magical initiation'. But what if it were a natural faculty?

According to the latest scientific discoveries, considerable portions of the brain are still *terra incognita*. Are they the seat of powers we do not know how to use? Machines of whose purpose we are ignorant. Instruments in reserve with a view to future mutations?

We also know that normally a man, even for the most complicated intellectual operations, uses only nine-tenths of his brain. The greater part of our faculties therefore is still virgin soil. The immemorial myth of the 'hidden treasure' has no other meaning.

This is what the English scientist, Dr. Gray Walter, says in one of the most essential books of our time: *The Living Brain*. In a second work, *Farther Outlook*, in which anticipation and observation, philosophy and poetry are mixed, Walter affirms that there are doubtless no limits to the possibilities of the human brain, and that in our thought we shall one day explore Time, as we now explore Space. He shares this vision with the mathematician Eric Temple Bell who endows the hero of his novel *The Waves of Time* with the power of voyaging through the entire history of the Cosmos.‡

* *The centres of pleasure in the brain: Scientific American*, October 1956.
† In his novel, *The Black Cloud*. Black clouds in space, between the stars, are higher forms of life. These super-intelligences propose to arouse the inhabitants of the Earth by sending luminous images which produce in the brain a state of awakened consciousness'.
‡ 'I discovered by means which I only imperfectly understand, the secret of going backwards through history. It is like swimming. Once one has learned the stroke, one never forgets it. But to learn it calls for constant practice, and a certain involuntary tightening of the mind and muscles. One thing I am sure of: no one knows exactly how, the first time, he overcame the difficulty of swimming; and doubtless even the most expert *clairvoyants* would be unable to explain to others the secret of voyaging backwards through the waves of time.' Like Fred Hoyle, and many other British scientists, Eric Temple Bell writes fantastic stories and essays (under the pseudonym of John Taine). Only the most naïve reader would imagine that these merely represent a relaxation for great minds. It is the only way to disseminate certain truths that are inacceptable to official philosophy. As in every pre-revolutionary period, all advanced thinking is published in disguise. The 'jacket' of a work of space-fiction is the cloak of the 1960s.

Let us stick to the facts. The phenomenon of the super-conscious state can be attributed to the existence of an immortal soul. This notion has been advanced for thousands of years without ever having done much towards solving the problem. But if, so as to keep within the facts, we confine ourselves to saying that the notion of an 'awakened state' is one of humanity's constant aspirations, that is not enough. It is an aspiration, but it is something else as well.

Resistance to torture, the mathematician's moments of inspiration, the observations recorded by the Yogis' electro-encephalogram and other instances as well, oblige us to admit that man can enter a state other than his normal waking state. As to the nature of that state, every man is free to propose whatever hypothesis he chooses – the Grace of God, or the awakening of the Immortal Self. He can also be a 'barbarian' and seek a scientific explanation.

Note that we are not pretending to be scientists. We are simply determined to neglect nothing that is of our own age in order to explore what belongs to every age.

Our hypothesis is as follows:

Communications with the brain are effected normally through nervous impulses. It is a slow-motion process: a few metres per second on the nerves' surface. It may be that in certain circumstances another, but much more rapid form of communication is established by an electro-magnetic wave travelling at the speed of light. We should then obtain the extreme rapidity in the recording and transmission of information that is peculiar to electronic machines. There is no Law of Nature that would exclude the existence of such a phenomenon. Waves of this kind would not be detectable outside the brain. This is the hypothesis we put forward in the preceding chapter.

If this 'awakened state' exists, how is it made manifest? The descriptions given by Hindu, Arab and Christian mystics have never been systematically collected and studied. It is extraordinary that among the very numerous anthologies of every kind published in this age of catalogues and classification, there is not a single anthology devoted to the 'awakened state'. The descriptions that exist are convincing, but not at all clear. And yet, if we want to evoke in modern terms what is the outward sign of such a state, this is what we should have to do:

Normally, thought travels at a walking pace, as Emile Meyerson has clearly shown. Most of the achievements of thought are, after all, the fruit of a very slow advance towards something that later appears self-evident. The most admirable discoveries in mathematics are nothing but equalities – unexpected, perhaps, but still equalities. The great Leonard Euler thought that the sublime summit of all mathematical thought was expressed in the equation: $e^{i\pi} + 1 = 0$.

This relation, which joins the real to the imaginary and is the basis of natural logarithms, is an 'evidence'. As soon as it is explained to an advanced student, he invariably declares that it is, of course, glaringly obvious. Why did it require so much thought for so many years to arrive at something so patently self-evident?

In physics, the discovery of the wave-mechanism in particles is the key that has opened up the modern era. Here, too, something self-evident is involved. Einstein had declared that energy $= mc^2$, when m $=$ mass, and c $=$ the speed of light. That was in 1905. In 1900 Planck stated: energy $=$ hf, when h is a constant, and f the frequency of vibrations. But it was not until 1923 that Louis de Broglie, a man of exceptional genius, thought of combining the two equations and writing: hf $= mc^2$.

Thought moves at a snail's pace, even in the greatest minds. It does not dominate the subject.

One last example: since the end of the eighteenth century it has been taught that mass figured both in the formula of kinetic energy (e : $\frac{1}{2}mv^2$) and in Newton's Law of Gravity (masses attract one another with a force varying . . . inversely as the square of their distances apart).

Why was it left to Einstein to comprehend that the word mass has the same meaning in the two classic formulae? The whole theory of relativity can immediately be deduced from it. Why did one mind alone in the whole history of human intelligence see that? And why not immediately instead of after ten long years of intensive research? Because our thought travels along a winding path on one level which often turns back on itself. And no doubt ideas disappear and reappear periodically, and inventions are forgotten and then rediscovered again.

And yet it seems possible that the mind can rise above this path and no longer have to plod along – that it can have an over-all view and speed from point to point like a bird or an aeroplane. That is what the mystics call an 'awakened state'.

But are there one or more such states? There is every reason to believe that there are several, just as there are several altitudes at which one can fly. 'The first stage is called genius. The others are unknown to the masses and thought to be only a legend. Troy also was a legend, before the excavations revealed that it really had existed.'

If men have in them the physical possibility of attaining one or other of these states, the quest for the best means of doing so ought to be the principal aim of their lives. If my brain is equipped with the necessary machinery – if all this does not belong exclusively to the domain of religion or mythology – if it is not all a question of divine 'grace' or 'magical initiation' but depends on certain techniques and certain internal and external attitudes capable of setting this machinery in motion – then I am satisfied that my only ambition and most urgent duty ought to be to reach this 'awakened state' and attain these heights at which the mind can soar.

It is not because they are 'frivolous' or 'wicked' that men do not concentrate all their efforts on this research. It is not a question of morals. And in an affair of this kind a little goodwill and a few attempts here and there are quite useless. Perhaps the superior instruments in our brain can only be brought into use if our whole life (individual and collective) is itself an instrument to be lived and looked upon exclusively as a means of establishing a connection and switching on the current that will put this machinery in motion.

The reason why men are not exclusively concerned with attaining this 'awakened' state is because the difficulties of social life and the necessity of earning a living leave them no leisure for such pursuits. Men do not live by bread alone; but up till now our civilization has been unable to provide everyone with this necessity.

In proportion as technical progress will gradually allow men time to breathe, so will the quest for the 'third state' of awareness and lucidity take precedence over all other aspirations. The possibility of taking part in this research will finally be recognized as one of the 'Rights of Man'. The next revolution will be a psychological one.

Let us imagine a Neanderthal man miraculously transported to the Institute of Advanced Studies at Princeton. In the presence of Dr. Oppenheimer he would be in a situation comparable to that in which we should find ourselves when face to face with a really 'awakened' man, whose thoughts no longer plod, but can range at will through three, four or n dimensions.

Physically, it would seem that we could become such a man. There are enough cells in our brain, and enough possible interconnections. But it is difficult for us to imagine what such an intelligence could see and understand.

The alchemists claimed that manipulation of matter in their crucibles could provoke what the moderns would call radiation, or a field of force. This radiation would transmute all the cells in the operator's body and turn him into a truly 'awakened' man – a man who would be alive, both here and on the 'other side'.

Let us now accept this hypothesis, this superbly non-Euclidean psychology. Let us suppose that one day in 1962 a man like ourselves, while manipulating matter and energy in a certain way, suddenly becomes entirely changed – in other words, 'awakened'.

In 1955 Professor Singleton showed to some friends during an atomic conference in Geneva some carnations which he had grown in the radio-active field of the great nuclear reactor at Brookhaven. They had been white; now they were a purply-red, a hitherto unknown species. All their cells had been modified, and they would, whether by grafting or reproduction, continue in their new state.

So it would be with our new man. He is now superior to us; his thought no longer plods – it flies. By integrating in a different way what all of us know in our various specialities, or by simply establishing all possible connections between the scientific facts contained in textbooks and University manuals, he could form concepts which would seem as strange to us as chromosomes would have been to Voltaire, or the neutrino to Leibnitz. Such a man would have absolutely no interest in trying to communicate with us, nor would he seek to dazzle us by trying to explain the enigmas of light, or the secret of genes. Valéry did not publish his thoughts in *La Semaine de Suzette*. This man would be above and beyond humanity. He could only communicate to advantage with minds like his own. There is substance here for meditation.

It is conceivable that the various traditions connected with 'initiation' have resulted from contact with minds on other planets. It may be that, for an 'awakened' man, time and space present no barriers, and that communication is possible with intelligences on other inhabited worlds; this, incidentally, would explain why we have never been visited.

We can dream about these things – on condition, as Haldane reminds us, that we do not forget that dreams of this kind are probably always less fantastic than reality.

Now follow three true stories. They will serve as illustrations. Illustrations are not proofs, but these three stories oblige us to believe that there are other states of consciousness than those recognized in official psychology. Even the vague notion we have of genius is not enough. We have not chosen these illustrations from the lives or works of mystics, although this would have been easier, and perhaps more efficacious. But we maintain our claim to approach these matters in a spirit of complete freedom and as honest 'barbarians'.

VI
THREE TRUE STORIES AS ILLUSTRATION
The story of a great mathematician 'in the raw' – The story of the most wonderful clairvoyant – The story of a scientist of the future who lived in 1750

1. RAMANUJAN

ONE day, early in 1887, a Brahmin from the province of Madras went into the Temple of the Goddess Namagiri. The Brahmin had seen his daughter married many months before, but the couple were still childless. He prayed that the Goddess Namagiri might make their union fertile. His prayer was answered: on 22nd December a son was born and given the names of Srinivasa Ramanujan Alyangar. On the eve of his birth, the goddess had appeared to the mother to announce that her son would be extraordinary.

He was put to school at the age of five. From the first his intelligence was astonishing. He won a scholarship to the college of Kumbakonan where he aroused the admiration of his fellow pupils and of his teachers. He was now fifteen. One of his friends procured for him from the local library a work entitled: *A Synopsis of Elementary Results in Pure and Applied Mathematics*. This work published in two volumes, was a handbook edited by Professor George Shoobridge, of Cambridge. It contained the terms and *résumés*, without any argument, of some 6,000 theorems. The impression it made on the young Hindu was fantastic. Ramanujan's brain began suddenly to function in a way that is incomprehensible to us. He demonstrated all the formulae. After coming to the end of geometry, he applied himself to algebra. Ramanujan said later that the Goddess Namagiri had helped him to solve the most complicated problems. At sixteen, he failed in his examinations, because his English was still weak, and was deprived of his grant.

He continued, alone, without any documents, to pursue his mathematical researches. He had soon caught up with everything that was known or had been discovered in this field up to the year 1880. He had no further use for Professor Shoobridge's work; he had gone far beyond that. Alone and single-handed he had mastered and outstripped the mathematical achievements of a whole civilization – starting from a mere *aide-memoire* that was not even complete. There is nothing like it in the whole history of human thought. Even Galois himself had not worked alone. He had studied at the École Polytechnique, which was at that time the leading mathematical centre in the world. He had had access to thousands of books, and was in contact with the best brains. There is no other example of the human intelligence reaching such heights unaided.

In 1909, after years of solitary toil and poverty, Ramanujan married. He had to look for a job. He was given an introduction to a local tax-collector, a keen amateur mathematician. This man has given the following account of the meeting: 'A little man, dirty and unshaven, but with eyes such as I had never seen, came into my room, with an old notebook under his arm. He spoke to me of marvellous discoveries which were completely beyond my powers of comprehension. I asked him what I could do for him. He replied that all he wanted was just enough to live on so that he could continue his researches.'

Ramachandra Rao offered him a very modest wage; but Ramanujan was too proud to stay. Finally a situation was found for him – a mediocre clerkship in an office in Madras.

In 1913 he was persuaded to enter into a correspondence with the great English mathematician G. H. Hardy, of Cambridge University. He wrote to him and sent by the same post 120 theorems of geometry which he had just demonstrated. Hardy wrote later: 'These notes could only have been written by a mathematician of the very first order. No borrower of other men's ideas, however brilliant, would have been capable of comprehending such lofty abstractions.'

Hardy immediately invited Ramanujan to come to Cambridge. But his mother was against it, on religious grounds. Once again the goddess Namagiri came to the rescue. She appeared to the old lady and assured her that her son could go to Europe without endangering his soul, and showed her in a dream Ramanujan seated in the great amphitheatre at Cambridge among his English admirers.

At the end of 1913 Ramanujan sailed for England. For five years he worked hard and made great advances in mathematics.

He was elected a Fellow of the Royal Society, and to a Fellowship at Trinity College, Cambridge. In 1918 he fell ill. Tuberculosis set in, and he went back to India to die there at the age of thirty-two.

On all who came in contact with him he made an extraordinary impression. He lived in a world of numbers. Hardy went to see him in hospital and told him he had taken a taxi. Ramanujan asked what its number was: 1729. 'What a wonderful number,' he exclaimed; 'it is the lowest number that can be expressed in two ways as the sum of two cubes!'

For it is a fact that 1729 equals $10^3 + 9^3$, and also $12^3 + 1^3$. It took Hardy six months to demonstrate this; and the same problem has not yet been solved at the fourth power.

The story of Ramanujan is one that is almost incredible. But it is strictly true. It is impossible to express in simple terms the nature of Ramanujan's discoveries, which had to do with the most mysterious properties of numbers, especially 'prime' numbers.

It is not known whether Ramanujan had any interests apart from mathematics. He cared little for art or literature. But he had a passion for anything strange. While at Cambridge he had formed a small library and a card-index of all sorts of phenomena that did not admit of a rational explanation.

2. CAYCE

EDGAR CAYCE died on 5th January, 1945, taking with him to the grave a secret that he himself had never solved and that had terrified him all his life. The doctors and psychologists at the Edgar Cayce Foundation at Virginia Beach are still studying the files of his case.

Since 1958 the study of clairvoyance in America has been subsidized by the State, bearing in mind the fact that valuable services could be rendered in the military field by men capable of telepathy and precognition. Of all known cases of clairvoyance, that of Cayce is the purest, the best attested and the most extraordinary.*

Young Edgar Cayce was very ill. The country doctor was at his bedside. There was nothing he could do to rouse the little boy from his coma. Suddenly Edgar spoke in a clear and steady voice. And yet he was fast asleep. 'I will tell you what is the matter with me, I was hit by a ball at baseball on the spine. You must make a special cataplasm and apply it to the base of the neck.' In the same quiet voice, the boy then dictated the list of plants that had to be mixed and prepared. 'Hurry up; otherwise the brain may be affected.'

They decided to chance it and carried out these instructions. That evening the boy's temperature dropped, and the next day he awoke fresh as a daisy. He remembered nothing. He had never even heard of most of the plants he had mentioned.

* cf. Joseph Millard's *Cayce*: copyright Cayce Foundation; John W. Campbell's study in *Astounding Science-Fiction*, March 1957; and Thomas Sugrue: *Edgar Cayce* Dell Books).

This was the beginning of one of the most astonishing stories in the history of medicine. Cayce, an ignorant peasant from Kentucky and most reluctant to use his strange gift and continually complaining about 'not being like everyone else', was to treat and heal, during his hypnotic trances more than 15,000 sick people, all the cases being duly attested.

Starting as a labourer on his uncle's farm, then becoming an assistant in a bookshop at Hopkinsville, and finally the proprietor of a little photographer's shop where he hoped to end his days in peace, it was against his inclination that he performed his miracles. An old friend, Al Layne, and his fiancée had to beg him to use his powers, not for his personal ambition, but because he had no right to refuse to help the sick. Layne was a weakling whose health was always bad. Cayce agreed to go into a trance; diagnosed the nature of the illness and dictated the remedies. When he woke up, he exclaimed: 'But it's impossible! I don't know half the words you have noted down. Don't take these drugs – it's dangerous! I don't know anything about it – all that's just magic!' He refused to see his friends, and shut himself up in his shop. A week later Layne came to see him; he had never been so well in his life. The little town was all agog: everyone wanted a consultation. Protesting: 'It's not because I talk in my sleep that I'm going to start healing people,' Cayce finally agreed – but only on condition that he never saw his patients for fear that, if he knew them personally, he might be influenced. He also insisted that a doctor should always be present at his *séances*, and that he should receive no payment for them at all, not even the smallest present.

His diagnoses and prescriptions, while under hypnosis, were so accurate and showed such insight that the doctors were convinced that he was really one of them, disguised as a healer. Though he limited his *séances* to two a day Cayce was not afraid of overtaxing himself; he was completely relaxed when he came out of his trances. But he wanted to go on being a photographer; he had no desire to acquire any medical knowledge, never read a book, and remained a practically uneducated peasant all his life. And he continued to protest against his strange gift. Only whenever he decided to give it up, he lost his voice.

An American railway magnate, James Andrews, came to consult him. Cayce, under hypnosis, prescribed a series of drugs including a certain preparation made from the plant *clary*. This remedy could not be traced anywhere. Andrews advertised in medical journals, without success. In the course of another *séance* Cayce dictated the exact composition of this preparation, and one day Andrews received a communication from a young Parisian doctor whose father, also a doctor, had patented this medicine, but had withdrawn it from the trade half a century ago. Its composition was identical with what the little photographer had seen in a 'dream'.

The secretary of the local medical syndicate, John Blackburn, was greatly interested in the Cayce phenomenon, and formed a committee of three members who attended all the *séances* and were astounded by what they saw. The General Syndicate recognized Cayce's extraordinary faculties, and authorized him to give 'psychical consultations'.

Cayce eventually married. When his son was eight years old he was playing with matches one day, and accidentally caused an explosion in a depot of magnesium. The specialists predicted that the boy would become totally blind, and recommended the removal of one eye. Cayce, terrified, went into a trance and while unconscious opposed the idea of an operation and prescribed the application of bandages soaked in tannic acid. This seemed madness to the specialists, but Cayce, in a great state of agitation, dared not disobey his voices. Two weeks later his son was cured.

One day after a consultation he stayed asleep and dictated one after another four very detailed prescriptions. It was not known at the time for whom they were intended; they were forty-eight hours in advance of the four persons who were going to come for treatment.

Once during a *séance* he prescribed a drug called Codiron, and gave the address of the laboratory in Chicago where it was prepared. To a telephone inquiry the answer came: 'How could you have heard of Codiron? It is not yet on sale. We have only just found the formula and given it a name.'

Cayce, who suffered from an incurable disease which he alone knew about, died on the day and the hour he had predicted: 'On the evening of the fifth I shall be definitely healed.' Healed from being 'something different'.

On being questioned during a trance as to how he operated, he declared (though remembering nothing about it, as usual on waking) that he was able to enter into contact with any human brain and use the information contained in that brain, or brains, for the diagnosis and treatment of the cases brought to him. It was perhaps a 'different' intelligence that inhabited Cayce at these times and used all the knowledge available to the whole of humanity in the way that one uses a library, but almost instantaneously – or at any rate, at the speed of light or electro-magnetic waves. But we cannot really explain the phenomenon of Edgar Cayce in this, or any other way. All that is known, beyond any doubt, is that a humble village photographer, incurious and uncultured, was able at will to enter a state in which his mind operated like that of the most brilliant medical genius – or, rather, like the minds of all the most brilliant medical geniuses acting together.

3. BOSCOVITCH

A THEME for science-fiction: if the relativists are right, if we are living in a four-dimensional Universe and if we were capable of being aware of this, then that would be the end of common sense.

Some 'anticipation authors' try to *think* in terms of the space-time continuum. Their efforts resemble those, on a higher plane of research and expressed in theoretical language, of the great mathematical physicists. But is it possible for a man to think in four dimensions ? For this he would require a special mental structure. Will these structures be available to the Man of the future, the product of the next mutation? And is this Man of the future already among us? Some fiction-writers have made this claim. But neither Van Vogt, in his book of phantasy *The Slans*, nor Sturgeon in his description of the *More than Humans* have dared to imagine a personage as fabulous as Roger Boscovitch. A Mutant? A Time-Traveller? An inhabitant from another planet disguised as this mysterious Serbian?

Boscovitch, it would seem, was born in 1711 at Dubrovnik: at any rate that is what he declared when enrolling at the age of fourteen as an independent student at the Jesuit College of Rome. There he studied mathematics, astronomy and theology. In 1728, having finished his novitiate, he entered the Order of the Jesuits. In 1736 he published a paper on the spots in the Sun. In 1740 he taught mathematics at the Collegium Romanum, and then became scientific adviser to the Papacy. He created an observatory, drained the Pontine Marshes, repaired the dome of St. Peter's, measured the meridian between Rome and Rimini on two degrees of latitude. He then explored various regions in Europe and Asia, and started excavations on the very site on which Schliemann subsequently discovered the remains of Troy. He was elected a Fellow of the Royal Society in England on 26th June, 1760, and published on that occasion a long poem in Latin on the visible features of the Sun and Moon, which caused his contemporaries to exclaim: 'This is Newton speaking through the mouth of Vergil.' He was entertained by all the most learned men in Europe, and carried on an important correspondence with, among others, Dr. Johnson and Voltaire. In 1763 he was offered French nationality. He was then appointed head of the department of optical instruments of the Royal Navy in Paris, where he lived until 1783. Lalande considered him to be the greatest living scientist. D'Alembert and Laplace were alarmed by his advanced ideas. In 1785 he retired to Bassano, and devoted himself to the publication of his complete works. He died in Milan in 1787.

It is only recently, at the instigation of the Yugoslav Government, that the works of Boscovitch have been re-examined – notably his *Theory of Natural Philosophy* (*Theoria philosophiae naturalis redacta ad unicam legem virium in natura existentium*) published in Vienna in 1758. The results of this study have caused general astonishment. Allan Lindsay Mackay, describing this treatise in an article in the *New Scientist* of 6th March, 1958, expressed the opinion that this was a case of a twentieth century mind being forced to live and work in the eighteenth century.

It seems that Boscovitch was in advance, not only of the science of his time, but of our own. He proposed a unitary theory of the Universe, a single general and unique equation governing mechanics,. physics, chemistry, biology and even psychology. According to this theory, matter, time and space are not infinitely divisible but composed of points, or grains. This recalls the recent work of Jean Charon and of Heisenberg whom Boscovitch seems to have surpassed. He succeeded in giving an account not only of light, but of magnetism, electricity and all the chemical phenomena known at the time, discovered since, or which are yet to be discovered. We find in his works the quanta, the wave mechanics and the atom formed of nucleons. The scientific historian, L. L. Whyte, assures us that Boscovitch was at least two centuries ahead of his times, and that we shall only really be able to understand him when the junction between relativity and quantum physics has finally been effected. It is estimated that in 1987, on the 200th anniversary of his birth, his work will be appreciated at its true value.

No explanation has as yet been put forward to account for this phenomenon. Two complete editions of his works, one in Serb and the other in English, are now in preparation. In the correspondence already published (Bestermann collection) between Boscovitch and Voltaire the following modern ideas are to be found:

The creation of an international geo-physical year;

The transmission of malaria by mosquitos;

Possible applications of rubber (ideas put into practice by Boscovitch's Jesuit friend, La Condamine);

The existence of planets in orbit round stars other than our own Sun;

The impossibility of localizing 'psychism' in a particular part of the body;

The conservation of the 'quantity grain' of movement in the world: this is Planck's constant, enunciated in 1958.

Boscovitch attached considerable importance to alchemy, and has provided clear and scientific translations of the alchemists' language. For him, for example, the four elements Earth, Water, Fire and Air are only distinguishable by the particular way in which the particles, without mass or weight, of which they are composed are arranged. Clearly an anticipation of the most advanced work being done now on the Universal equation.

Another no less fantastic anticipation in the work of Boscovitch is to be found in his study of accidents in Nature. This contains already the statistical mechanics theory of the American scientist Willard Gibbs, formulated at the end of the nineteenth century but not accepted until the twentieth. It also provides a modern explanation of radio-activity (completely unknown in the seventeenth century) as one of a series of exceptions to natural laws: what is called today 'statistical penetrations of the barriers of potentiality'.

Why is it that the works of this extraordinary man have had no influence on modern thought? Because the German philosophers and scientists who led the field in research up to the 1914–18 War believed in the 'continuous structure' theory, whereas the work of Boscovitch was essentially based on the idea of discontinuity. Also, because library research and historical investigations concerning Boscovitch, who travelled extensively and whose works are widely dispersed, and who, moreover, came from a country liable to

263

constant upheavals, were only systematically undertaken long after his death. When his complete works have been published, and the testimony of his contemporaries collected and classified, we shall see what a strange, disquieting and altogether astounding personality he was.

VII

THE 'AWAKENED' MAN: SOME PARADOXES AND HYPOTHESES

Why our three stories may have disappointed some readers – We know very little about levitation, immortality, etc. – Yet Man has the gift of ubiquity, has long sight, etc. – How do you define a machine? – How the first 'awakened' Man could have been born – A fabulous, yet reasonable dream about vanished civilizations – The fable of the panther – The writing of God

THESE three cases are clear and positive. Yet to some they may not seem conclusive. This is because most men prefer images to facts. Walking on the water is an image of dominating movement; stopping the Sun, a triumph over time. These things could perhaps be realities in a changed state of consciousness within a powerfully accelerated intelligence. And they could no doubt lead to all kinds of tangible results in techniques, science and the arts.

Most men, however, when the question arises of there being such a thing as 'another' state of consciousness, at once want to see people walking on water, stopping the Sun, going through brick walls or looking twenty at the age of eighty. In order to begin to believe in the infinite possibilities of an 'awakened' state they must first satisfy and find a justification for the childish part of their intelligence which believes in images and legends.

Furthermore, when confronted with cases like those of Ramanujan, Cayce or Boscovitch, people refuse to believe that their minds were really 'different'. At most they would admit the possibility that minds like ours were privileged to 'rise to unusual heights' and that 'up there' they acquired some special knowledge. As if somewhere in the Universe there was a kind of storehouse of things connected with medicine, mathematics, poetry or physics for the benefit of a few super-intelligences able to climb up there. This absurd vision is found to be reassuring.

It seems to us, on the contrary, that Cayce, Ramanujan and Boscovitch were on our level (where else could they be?), but that their minds worked at an extraordinary speed. It is not a question of a different level, but of a different speed. The same applies to the greatest mystics. The miracles, in nuclear physics as well as in psychology, are to be found in acceleration. And it is from this standpoint, we believe, that the third state of consciousness, the 'awakened' state, should be studied.

And yet, if such a state is possible – if it is not a gift from Heaven, or some God-sent favour, but is, in fact, a part of the equipment of our brain and body – could not this equipment, once it starts functioning, affect faculties in us other than our intelligence? If the 'awakened' state is a property of some higher nervous system, this activation should be capable of affecting the whole body and endowing it with strange powers.

In all the traditions, the 'awakened' state is associated with special powers: immortality, levitation, telekinesis, etc. But are not all these powers merely images of what the mind, in its transformed state, can do in the sphere of knowledge? Or are they actual facts? There have been some probable cases of levitation.*

As regards immortality, the case of Fulcanelli has not yet been elucidated. That is all that can be said on that subject. We have no valid proofs. Nor, we must admit, does this question interest us very much. We are not concerned with the bizarre, but with the fantastic. Moreover, this question of para-normal powers ought really to be approached from another angle. Not from the point of view of Cartesian logic (which Descartes, if he were alive today, would repudiate) but from the standpoint of the open-minded science of today. Let us look for a moment at things through the eyes of a visitor from 'Beyond' who has landed on our planet: levitation exists, so does long-distance vision; Man has the gift of ubiquity and has harnessed the energy of the Universe. The aeroplane, the radio-telescope, television, and the atomic pile exist. They are not natural products, but creations of the human mind. This observation may seem puerile, but it is a vivifying thought. What is puerile is to reduce everything to the level of an individual man. A man alone, in isolation, has not the gift of ubiquity; or of levitation, or of long-distance vision, etc. For it is human society as a whole, and not the individual, which possesses these powers. The notion of an individual by himself is perhaps puerile, for it may be that tradition, with its accompanying legends, is the voice of humanity as a whole, an expression of the phenomenon of Man. . . .

'You are not serious! You talk to us about machines!' That is what we shall hear from the Cartesian rationalists and the occultists who rely on 'tradition'. But what is meant by machines? That is another question that needs to be clarified.

A few lines traced in ink on parchment: is that a machine? The technique of printed circuits currently employed in modern electronics makes it possible to use a wave receiver composed of lines traced with different inks, one containing graphite and the other copper.

Is a precious stone a machine? By general consensus: No. And yet the crystalline structure of a precious stone is a complex machine, and the diamond is used to detect atomic radiations. Artificial crystals, or transistors, have replaced electronic lamps, transformers,

* cf. *La Lévitation*, by R. P. Olivier Leroy. Ed. du Cerf, Paris.

265

and electric revolving machines of the commuter type to increase voltage, etc.

The human mind, in its most subtle and most efficient technical creations uses more and more simple means.

'You are juggling with words!' exclaims the occultist. 'I am talking about manifestations of the human spirit without any kind of intermediary.'

It is he who is juggling with words.

No one has ever registered a manifestation of the human spirit without the aid of a machine of some sort. This notion of a 'self-contained spirit' is a pernicious fallacy. The human mind in action uses a most complex machine that it has taken 300,000 years of evolution to perfect: the human body. And this body is never alone, and does not exist alone: it is bound to the Earth and to the whole Cosmos by thousands of material and energy-producing links.

We do not know everything about the body. We do not know everything about its relations with the Universe. No one could say what are the limits of the human machine, or how it could be used by a mind able to exploit all its possibilities to their fullest extent.

We do not know everything about the forces that are active deep down within ourselves and all around us, on the Earth, and round the Earth throughout the whole vast Cosmos. No one knows what simple, natural forces of which we know nothing but which are within our grasp could be made use of by a man endowed with an 'awakened' consciousness having a more direct and immediate apprehension of Nature than our linear intelligence could ever have.

Simple, natural forces. Let us once more look at things through the lucid, 'barbarian' eyes of a visitor from 'Beyond': nothing is simpler or more easily realized than an electric transformer. The ancient Egyptians could quite well have built one if they had been familiar with the theory of electro-magnetics.

Nothing is easier than the liberation of atomic energy. All that is necessary is to dissolve salts of pure uranium in heavy water; and heavy water can be obtained by re-distilling ordinary water over a period of anything from twenty-five to a hundred years.

Lord Kelvin's machine for predicting the tides (1893), which was the precursor of our analogical calculators and of the whole of our system of cybernetics, was made with pulleys and bits of string. The Sumerians would have been able to make one.

If we look at things in this way, the problem of the vanished civilizations takes on a new dimension. If in the past there have been men who attained the state of an 'awakened' consciousness, and supposing they applied their powers not only in the sphere of religion, philosophy, or mysticism, but also to problems of technique and practical knowledge, it is perfectly natural, rational and reasonable to admit that they may have been able to work 'miracles', even with the simplest apparatus.*

* Although the majority of archaeologists categorically deny the existence in the past of advanced civilizations with powerful material

Jorge Luis Borges relates that once upon a time there was a wise man who devoted his whole life to seeking, among the innumerable signs in Nature, the ineffable name of God, the key to the Great Secret. After a life of tribulations, he was arrested on the orders of a Prince, and condemned to be devoured by a panther. While waiting in the cell into which he had been thrown, he observed through the bars the wild beast who was waiting to devour him. Gazing at the spots on its skin, he discovered in the pattern and rhythm of the design the number, the Name that he had been seeking for so long and in so many places. He knew then why he had to die, and that he would die only after his great wish had been fulfilled – and that that would not be death.

The Universe devours us, or else it yields up its secrets to us; that depends on whether or not we know how to observe it. It is highly probable that the most subtle and profound Laws of Life and of the destiny of all created things are clearly inscribed on the material world by which we are encompassed; that God has left his handwriting everywhere, as the wise man discovered on the panther's skin; and that we only have to look at things in a certain way. . . . The man who can do this is the 'awakened' Man. . . .

---

means at their disposal, the possibility of the existence at every epoch of a small percentage of 'awakened' beings utilizing natural forces with improvised means, can scarcely be denied. We even believe that a methodical examination of archaelogical and historical data would confirm this hypothesis. How could this 'awakening' have started? Of course it is possible to imagine interventions from 'Beyond'; alternatively one may seek a purely materialist and rationalist explanation. This is what we would suggest. Physicists dealing with cosmic rays have recently discovered what they call extraordinary 'events'. In cosmic physics, an 'event' is the collusion between a particle from space and terrestrial matter. In 1957, as we stated in our study of alchemy, scientists detected an exceptional particle of fantastic energy (an energy of 10^{18} electron-volts, whereas the fission of uranium produces only 2×10^8.) Let us assume that *only once* in the history of the human race, such a particle came into contact with a human brain. Who knows if the enormous energy resulting therefrom might not have produced an activation inducing for the first time an 'awakened' state in Man? This Man might have discovered and might have applied techniques for inducing this 'awakened state'. In various forms these techniques may have been preserved down to our times, and the alchemists' Great Work, the Initiation, could be something more than a legend. Our hypothesis is, of course, only a hypothesis. It would be difficult to test it experimentally, for it is impossible even to imagine an artificial accelerator producing such a fabulous and fantastic amount of energy. All we can do is to recall that the great English scientist, Sir James Jeans, once wrote: 'It was perhaps cosmic radiation which turned the Monkey into Man.' (cf. *The Mysterious Universe.*) We are now only carrying on these ideas, with modern data at our disposal which Sir James Jeans did not have and which enable us to state: 'It was perhaps exceptional cosmic "events" releasing fantastic energy, which turned Man into super-Man.'

VIII

SOME DOCUMENTS ON THE 'AWAKENED STATE'

Wanted: an anthology – The sayings of Gurdjieff – When I was at the school for 'awakening' – Raymond Abellio's story – A striking extract from the works of Gustav Meyrinck a neglected genius

IF there is such a thing as an 'awakened state', there is a chapter missing in the history of psychology. Here follow four documents, all contemporary. We have not selected them specially, not having had time to make a thorough investigation. There is room for an anthology of testimonies and studies on the 'awakened' state.

It would be most useful, as it would put us in touch again with tradition, and show how essential values have been preserved in our century; it might also indicate new paths that could be followed in the future. Writers would find in it a key; to natural scientists it would be a source of stimulation; intellectuals everywhere would find in it the thread that runs through all the great adventures of the mind, and would feel less isolated. It goes without saying that in assembling these documents which lay ready to hand we are making no such far-reaching claims.

We wish only to give some brief examples of a possible psychological approach to the question of the 'awakened state' in its elementary forms. These consist of:

1. Extracts from the sayings of Georg Ivanovitch Gurdjieff, recorded by the philosopher Ouspensky;

2. My own account of the attempts I made to enter the path of the 'awakened state' under the guidance of instructors of the Gurdjieff school;

3. The story of a personal experience, by the writer and philosopher Raymond Abellio;

4. The finest of all documents, in our opinion, in the whole of modern literature dealing with this subject; an extract from a little known novel by the German poet and philosopher Gustav Meyrinck, whose works rise to the highest peaks of mystical intuition.

1. SOME SAYINGS OF GURDJIEFF

'IN order to understand what the difference between states of consciousness is, let us return to the first state of consciousness which is sleep. This is an entirely subjective state of consciousness. A man is immersed in dreams, whether he remembers them or not does not matter. Even if some real impressions reach him, such as sounds, voices, warmth, cold, the sensation of his own body, they arouse in him only fantastic subjective images. Then a man wakes up. At first glance this is a quite different state of consciousness.

He can move, he can talk with other people, he can make calculations ahead, he can see danger and avoid it, and so on. It stands to reason that he is in a better position than when he was asleep. But if we go a little more deeply into things, if we take a look into his inner world, into his thoughts, into the causes of his actions, we shall see that he is in almost the same state as when he is asleep. And it is even worse, because in sleep he is passive, that is, he cannot do anything. In the waking state, however, he can do something all the time and the results of all his actions will be reflected upon him or upon those around him. And yet he does not remember himself. He is a machine, everything with him happens. He cannot stop the flow of his thoughts, he cannot control his imagination, his emotions, his attention. He lives in a subjective world of 'I love', "I do not love", "I like', "I do not like", "I want", "I do not want", that is, of what he thinks he likes, of what he thinks he does not like, of what he thinks he wants, of what he thinks he does not want. He does not see the real world. The real world is hidden from him by the wall of imagination. He lives in sleep. He is asleep. What is called "clear consciousness" is sleep and a far more dangerous sleep than sleep at night in bed.

'Let us take some event in the life of humanity. For instance, war. There is a war going on at the present moment. What does it signify? It signifies that several millions of sleeping people are trying to destroy several millions of other sleeping people. They would not do this, of course, if they were to wake up. Everything that takes place is owing to this sleep.

'Both states of consciousness, sleep and the waking state, are equally subjective. Only by beginning to remember himself does a Man really awaken. And then all surrounding life acquires for him a different aspect and a different meaning. He sees that it is the life of sleeping people, a life in sleep. All that men say, all that they do, they say and do in sleep. All this can have no value whatever. Only awakening and what leads to awakening has a value in reality.

'How many times have I been asked here whether wars can be stopped? Certainly they can. For this it is only necessary that people should awaken. It seems a small thing. It is, however, the most difficult thing there can be because this sleep is induced and maintained by the whole of surrounding life, by all surrounding conditions.

'How can one awaken? How can one escape this sleep? These questions are the most important, the most vital that can ever confront a man. But before this it is necessary to be convinced of the very fact of sleep. But it is possible to be convinced of this only by trying to awaken. When a man understands that he does not remember himself and that to remember himself means to awaken to some extent, and when at the same time he sees by experience how difficult it is to remember himself, he will understand that he cannot awaken simply by having the desire to do so. It can be said still more precisely that a man cannot awaken by himself. But if, let us say, twenty people make an agreement that whoever of them awakens first shall wake the rest, they already have some chance. Even this, however, is insufficient because all the twenty can go to sleep at the same time and dream that they are waking up. Therefore more still is necessary. They must be looked after by a man who is not asleep or who does not fall asleep as easily as they do, or who goes to sleep consciously when this is possible, when it will do no harm either to himself or to others. They must find such a man and hire him to wake them and not allow them to fall asleep again. Without this it is impossible to awaken. This is what must be understood.

'It is possible to think for a thousand years; it is possible to write whole libraries of books, to create theories by the million, and all this in sleep, without any possibility of awakening. On the contrary, these books and these theories, written and created in sleep, will merely send other people to sleep, and so on.

'There is nothing new in the idea of sleep. People have been told almost since the creation of the world that they are asleep and that they must awaken. How many times is this said in the Gospels, for instance? "Awake", "watch", "sleep not". Christ's disciples even slept when he was praying in the Garden of Gethsemane for the last time. It is all there. But do men understand it? Men take it simply as a form of speech, as an expression, as a metaphor. They completely fail to understand that it must be taken literally. And again it is easy to understand why. In order to understand this literally it is necessary to awaken a little, or at least to try and awaken. I tell you seriously that I have been asked several times why nothing is said about sleep in the Gospels. Although it is there spoken of almost on every page. This simply shows that people read the Gospels in sleep.

'Speaking in general, what is necessary to awake a sleeping man? A good shock is necessary. But when a man is fast asleep one shock is not enough. A long period of continual shocks is needed. Consequently there must be somebody to administer these shocks. I have said before that if a man wants to awaken he must hire somebody who will keep on shaking him for a long time. But whom can he hire if everyone is asleep? A man will hire somebody to wake him up but this one also falls asleep. What is the use of such a man? And a man who can really keep awake will probably refuse to waste his time in waking others up: he may have his own much more important work to do.

'There is also the possibility of being awakened by mechanical means. A man may be awakened by an alarm clock. But the trouble is that a man gets accustomed to the alarm clock far too quickly, he ceases to hear it. Many alarm clocks are necessary and always new ones. Otherwise a man must surround himself with alarm clocks which will prevent him sleeping. But here again there are certain difficulties. Alarm clocks must be wound up, in order to wind them up one must remember about them; in order to remember one must wake up often. But what is still worse, a man gets used to all alarm clocks and after a certain time he only sleeps the better for them. Therefore alarm clocks must be constantly changed, new ones must be continually invented. In the course of time this may help a man to awaken. But there is very little chance of a man doing all the work of winding up, inventing, and changing clocks all by himself, without outside help. It is much more likely that he will begin his work and that it will afterwards pass into sleep, and in sleep he will dream of inventing alarm clocks, of winding them up and changing them, and simply sleep all the sounder for it.

'Therefore, in order to awaken, a combination of efforts is needed. It is necessary that somebody should wake the man up; it is necessary that somebody should look after the man who wakes him; it is necessary to have alarm clocks and it is also necessary continually to invent new alarm clocks.

'But in order to achieve all this and to obtain results a certain number of people must work together.

'One man can do nothing.

'Before anything else he needs help. But help cannot come to one man alone. Those who are able to help put a great value on their time. And, of course, they would prefer to help, say, twenty or thirty people who want to awake rather than one man. Moreover, as has been said earlier, one man can easily deceive himself about his awakening and take for awakening simply a new dream. If several people decide to struggle together against sleep, they will wake each other. It may often happen that twenty of them will sleep but the twenty-first will be awake and he will wake up the rest. It is exactly the same thing with alarm clocks. One man will invent one alarm clock, another man will invent another, afterwards they can make an exchange. Altogether they can be of very great help one to another, and without this help no one can attain anything.

'Therefore a man who wants to awake must look for other people who also want to awake and work together with them. This, however, is easier said than done because to start such work and to organize it requires a knowledge which an ordinary man cannot possess. The work must be organized and it must have a leader. Only then can it produce the results expected of it. Without these conditions no efforts can result in anything whatever. Men may torture themselves but these tortures will not make them awake. This is the most difficult of all for certain people to understand. By themselves and on their own initiative they may be capable of great efforts and great sacrifices. But because their first effort and their first sacrifice ought to be obedience nothing on Earth will induce them to obey another. And they do not want to reconcile themselves to the thought that all their efforts and all their sacrifices are useless.

'Work must be organized. And it can be organized only by a man who knows its problems and its aims, who knows its methods; by a man who has in his time passed through such organized work himself.'

2. My First Encounter with the Gurdjieff School

'Take a watch,' we were told, 'and look at the big hand while trying to remain conscious of yourself and concentrate on the thought: "I am Louis Pauwels, and I am here now, at this moment." Try to think of nothing else but that; simply follow the movement of the big hand and go on being conscious of yourself, your name, your existence and the place where you are now.'

At first this seemed simple, and rather ridiculous. Of course I could concentrate on the idea that my name was Louis Pauwels and that I was there, at that moment, watching the big hand of my watch moving slowly round. Soon I had to admit that this idea did not remain stable within me for long; it began to take on a thousand shapes and to flow about in every direction, like those objects that Dali paints in mud. But I had to remember, too, that I had not been asked to keep alive and fixed in my mind an idea, but a perception. I had not only to think that I existed, but to know it and to have an absolute knowledge of that fact. I felt that that would be possible, and that it could happen in me and bring me something new and important. I discovered, however, that I was perpetually being distracted by a thousand more or less vague thoughts, sensations, images and associations of ideas that had nothing to do with the object of my efforts, and indeed prevented me from pursuing it. Sometimes it was the watch-hand that absorbed all my attention, and while gazing at it I lost sight of myself. Sometimes it was my body – a twitching muscle in my leg, a sensation in my stomach that took my attention away from both the watch and myself. Sometimes, again, I thought I had closed down my little internal cinema and eliminated the external world; but I soon found then that I had sunk into a kind of sleep in which the watch-hand as well as myself had disappeared, while images, sensations and ideas continued to be mixed up in my mind behind a kind of veil, as if in a dream unfolding itself independently of me while I slept. Sometimes, for a fraction of a second, while looking at the watch-hand, I was totally and completely conscious that I was I. But in the same fraction of a second, I was congratulating myself on having achieved this state; my mind, so to speak, was applauding, whereupon my intelligence, by expressing satisfaction at my success, ruined it irremediably. Finally, disappointed, but above all thoroughly exhausted, I gave up the experiment, because it seemed to me that I had just been through the most difficult few minutes in the whole of my existence and deprived of air to a degree that had taxed my endurance to its extreme limits. How interminable it had seemed! And yet it had lasted scarcely more than a couple of minutes; and in those two minutes I had only had a real perception of myself in three or four imperceptible flashes. I was then forced to admit that we are practically never conscious of ourselves, and that we are hardly ever conscious of the difficulty of being conscious.

The state of consciousness, we were told, is at first the state of a

Man who, having at last discovered that he is hardly ever conscious then begins gradually to learn what, in himself, are the obstacles to what he is trying to do. In the light of this little experiment one knows now that a Man may, for example, read a book, approve or be bored by it, protest or be enthusiastic, without ever being conscious for a moment of the fact that He himself 'is' and that consequently nothing of what he has read has really impinged on the Man he 'is'. His reading is another dream added to his own dreams – a flux in the perpetual flux of the unconscious. For our real consciousness may be – and almost always is – completely absent from everything we do, think, desire or imagine.

I understood then that there is very little difference between our normal waking and sleeping states. Our dreams when we are awake have become invisible, as it were, like the stars in daytime; but they are still there, and we continue to live under their influence. We have merely acquired on waking a critical attitude towards our own sensations; our thoughts are better co-ordinated, our actions more controlled, our impressions, sensations and desires more lively; but we are still in a state of non-consciousness. We are not now discussing the real 'awakened state' but what could be called a 'waking sleep'; and it is in that state that we spend practically the whole of our lives. We were taught that it is possible to become completely awake, and to be conscious of oneself. In this state, as I discovered during the experiment with the watch, I was able to have an objective knowledge of my thoughts and of a succession of images, ideas, sensations, sentiments and desires. While in that state, I could try to make a real effort to examine and even halt from time to time, or change this flow of sensations. And the very fact of making this effort, so I was told, created in me a certain subsistence. It did not actually result in anything definite. The mere fact of its having been made was enough to call into being and accumulate in me the very substance of my being. I was assured that I could then, having a fixed 'being', acquire an 'objective consciousness', and that I would then be in a state to have a completely objective and total knowledge not only of myself, but of other men and things and of the whole world.*

3. RAYMOND ABELLIO'S STORY

WHEN, in the 'natural' attitude which is that of all normal existing beings, I 'see' a house, my perception is spontaneous, and it is that house that I see, and not my own perception of it. On the other hand, if my attitude is 'transcendental', then it is my perception itself which is perceived. *But this perception of a perception radically changes my primitive approach.* The state of actually experiencing something, uncomplicated to begin with, loses its spontaneity from the very fact that the new contemplation has for its object something that was originally a *state*, and not an object, and that the elements which make up my new perception include not only those pertaining to the house 'as such', but those pertaining to the

* Extract from *Monsieur Gurdjieff*. Ed. du Seuil, Paris, 1954.

perception itself, considered as an actually experienced flux. And an essentially important feature of this 'alteration' is that the concomitant vision I had, in this bi-reflexible, or rather 'reflective-reflexible' state (*'état bi-réflexif, ou plutôt réfléchi-réflexif'*) of the house that was my original 'motif', so far from being lost, displaced or blurred by this interposition of 'my' second perception in front of 'its' original perception, *is, paradoxically, intensified*, becoming clearer, more 'actual' and *charged with more objective reality than before*. We are here confronted with a fact that cannot be accounted for by pure speculative analysis: namely, the transfiguration of the thing as consciously experienced, its transformation, as we shall call it later, into a 'super-thing', its passage from being something 'known about' to something 'known'. This fact is insufficiently appreciated, although it is the most remarkable in the whole field of phenomenological experimentation. All the difficulties met with in ordinary phenomenology and, indeed, in all the classic theories of knowledge, stem from the fact that they consider the duality consciousness – knowledge (or more precisely, consciousness – science) as being self-sufficient and able to absorb the whole of experience; whereas the triad knowledge – consciousness – science alone can provide a genuinely ontological foundation for phenomenology. Certainly, nothing can make this transfiguration apparent except the direct and personal experience of the phenomenologist himself. But no one can claim to have understood real transcendental phenomenology unless he has had this experience and been 'illuminated' as a result. No one, not even the most subtle of dialecticians or the most cunning logician, who has not actually experienced this and has therefore not seen things-beneath-things, can do more than talk about phenomenology; he cannot actively participate in any phenomenological experience. Let us take a more precise example:

As long as I can remember, I have always been able to recognize the colours blue, red, yellow. My eye saw them, and I had a latent knowledge of them. Certainly 'my eye' did not ask itself any questions about them; how could it have? Its function is to see, not to see itself in the act of seeing; but my brain itself was as if asleep; it was not in any sense the 'eye of the eye', but merely a prolongation of that organ. And so I simply said, almost without thinking: that's a beautiful red – or a faded green – or a brilliant white. One day some years ago while walking among the vines in the Canton of Vaud overlooking the Lake of Geneva – one of the most beautiful sites in the world – so beautiful, in fact, and so vast that the 'Ego' first expands at the sight of it, then dissolves and finally recovers and attains a state of exaltation – I had a most extraordinary experience. The ochre of the steeply descending slope, the blue of the lake, the violet of the mountains in Savoy, and in the distance the glistening glaciers of the Grand-Combin – all this I had *seen* a hundred times. I now knew for the first time that I had never *looked at* them. And yet, I had been living there for three months. It is true that, from the very first, this landscape

274

had profoundly affected me; but it had only produced in me a vague feeling of exaltation. No doubt the 'I' of the philosopher is stronger than any landscape. The poignant sensation of beauty we experience is only the 'I' measuring and deriving strength therefrom, the infinite distance that separates us from that beauty. But on that day, suddenly, I knew that it was I who was creating that landscape, and that without me it would not exist: 'It is I who sees you, and who sees myself seeing you and in so doing creates you.' This cry from the heart is the cry of the demiurge when creating 'his' world. It is not only the suspension of an 'old' world but the projection of a 'new' one. And in that instant, indeed, the world was re-created. Never had I seen such colours. They were a hundred times more vivid, more delicately shaded, more 'alive'. I knew that I had just acquired a colour-sense – that I was seeing colour for the first time, and that until then I had never really seen a picture or penetrated the world of painting. But I knew also that by this awakening of consciousness, this perception of my perception, I held the key to that world of transfiguration which is not a mysterious sub-world, but the true world from which we are banished by 'Nature'. This has nothing to do with attention. Transfiguration is complete; attention never is. Transfiguration knows itself in its positive sufficiency; attention aims at attaining some day such sufficiency. It cannot be said, of course, that attentiveness is empty. On the contrary, it craves fullness. But this craving is not fulfilment. When I returned to the village that day, the people I met were mostly 'attentive' to their work; yet to me they all seemed to be walking in their sleep.*

4. GUSTAV MEYRINCK

The Green Face (Extract)

THE key that will make us masters of our inner nature has been rusty ever since the Flood. The secret is to be awake. To be awake is everything.

Man is firmly convinced that he is awake; in reality, he is caught in a net of sleep and of dreams which he has woven himself. The tighter the net, the heavier he sleeps. Those who are trapped in its meshes are the sleepers who walk through life like cattle being led to the slaughterhouse, indifferent and without a thought in their heads. Seen through the meshes, the world appears to the dreamers like a piece of lattice-work; they only see misleading apertures, act accordingly, and are unaware that what they see are simply the crazy débris of an enormous whole. These dreamers are not, as you might perhaps think, dwellers in a world of fantasy and poets; they are the workers, the restless ones, consumed by a mad desire for action. They are like those beetles which laboriously climb all the way up a long pipe, only to plunge down into it again as soon as they have reached the top. They say they are awake,

* Raymond Abellio: *Cahiers du Cercle d'Etudes Metaphysiques.* Privately published, 1954.

275

but what they think is life is really only a dream, every detail of which is fixed in advance and independent of their free will.

There have been, and still are, a few men who have known that they were dreaming – pioneers who have advanced as far as the barrier behind which lies hidden the eternally awakened 'I' – seers like Descartes, Schopenhauer and Kant. But they did not possess the equipment necessary to capture the fortress, and their call to arms failed to awaken the sleepers.

To be awake is everything.

The first step towards this state is so simple that any child could take it. Only those who have been misled have forgotten how to walk, and stay paralysed on their two feet because they do not want to throw away the crutches they have inherited from their predecessors.

To be awake is everything.

Keep awake whatever you are doing! Do not imagine that you are already awake. No; you are asleep and dreaming.

Gather all your strength together, and fill your body for a moment with the feeling: Now I am awake!

If you can do this, then you will at once perceive that the state in which you were before was merely one of somnolence.

This is the first step on the long, long journey that leads from servitude to being all-powerful.

Go on, then, advancing from one awakening to another. There are no tormenting thoughts that you cannot in this way get rid of. They will be left behind and will not be able to trouble you any more. You will be as high above them as the crown of a tall tree is above the withered branches below.

Your pains will fall away from you like dead leaves from a tree when you feel your whole body is awake.

The Brahmans' icy baths, the sleepless nights of the disciples of Buddha and the Christian ascetics, the self-inflicted tortures of the Hindu fakirs are nothing other than the fixed rites which indicate that it was here that the temple of those who strove to stay awake originally stood.

Read the sacred writings of all the peoples of the Earth. Through all of them runs, like a red thread, the hidden science of maintaining wakefulness. It is the ladder of Jacob who fought all through the 'night' with the angel of the Lord until the 'day' broke and he was victorious.

You must climb from one rung to another if you want to conquer death.

The lowest rung is called: genius.

What are we to call the higher ones? They are hidden from the mass of mankind and looked upon as legends.

The story of Troy was thought to be a legend until one day a Man had the courage to start excavating by himself.

The first enemy you will meet with on this road to wakefulness will be your own body. It will fight you until the first cock-crow. But if you can glimpse the dawn of eternal wakefulness which will put a gulf between you and those somnambulists who think that they are men and who are unaware that they are gods asleep, then sleep will leave your body too, and the Universe will be at your feet.

Then you will be able to work miracles, if you wish, and you will no longer be compelled, like a humble slave, to wait until a cruel false god is kind enough to shower gifts upon you, or to cut off your head.

Naturally the happiness of a good and faithful dog – which is to serve a master – will no longer be yours; but be frank with yourself: would you, even now, want to change places with your dog?

Do not be afraid that you may not be able to attain your goal in this life. He who has found the way always returns to this world with an internal maturity that enables him to continue with his work. He is born a 'genius'.

The path I am pointing out to you is strewn with strange happenings: dead people you have known will rise up and talk with you! These are only images! Luminous silhouettes will appear to you and give you their blessing. They are only images, forms conjured up by your body which, under the influence of your newly transformed will, will die a magical death and become spirit, just as ice, when attacked by fire, dissolves in steam.

When you have got rid of the corpse within you, only then will you be able to say: Now sleep has left me for ever.

Then will come to pass the miracle which no Man can believe – because, deceived by their senses, they do not understand that matter and force are the same thing – the miracle that, even if you are buried, there will be no corpse in your coffin.

Then only will you be able to distinguish between reality and appearance. Whoever you may meet can only be one of those who have preceded you on this road.

All the others are shadows.

Up to now you do not know if you are the happiest or the unhappiest of creatures. But fear not. Not one of those who have followed the path that leads to the waking state, even if he has lost his way, has ever been abandoned by his guides.

I would like to give you a sign which will enable you to recognize whether an apparition is reality, or only an image: if it approaches you, if your conscience is troubled, if the things of the external world are vague or disappear – then beware! The apparition is only a part of yourself. If you do not understand it, it is only a spectre without substance, a thief who is robbing you of part of your life.

Thieves who steal your soul's strength are worse than worldly thieves. They attract you like will-of-the-wisps into the marshes of a false hope, only to abandon you in the darkness before disappearing for ever.

Do not allow yourself to be blinded by any miracle they may appear to perform for you, by any sacred name by which they may call themselves, or by any prophesy they may utter – not even if it comes true; they are your mortal enemies, driven out from the inferno of your own body, against whom you are fighting for victory.

Know that the marvellous strength they possess is your own – which they have stolen so that they may keep you as their slave. They cannot live outside your life; but if you defeat them they will collapse and be your dumb and docile tools for you to use according to your needs.

They have made innumerable victims among men. Read the history of the visionaries and sectarians and you will see that the path you are following is strewn with skulls.

Unwittingly, humanity has erected against them a wall of materialism. This wall is an infallible protection; it is an image of the body, but at the same time a prison wall that blocks the view.

Today they are all dispersed, and the phoenix of the inner life is resuscitated from the ashes where it has for long been lying as if dead; but the vultures of another world are also beginning to flap their wings. This is why you must be careful. The scales in which you place your consciousness will show you when you can trust these apparitions: the more 'awakened' it is, the further the scales will go down in your favour.

If a guide, a brother from another spiritual world, wishes to make himself known to you, he should be able to do so without making inroads on your consciousness. You can place your hand on his side, like doubting Thomas.

It would be easy to avoid the apparitions and their dangers. You have only to behave like an ordinary man. But what will you have gained by that? You will remain a prisoner in the jail of your body until Death, the executioner, comes to lead you to the scaffold.

The desire of mortal men to see supernatural beings is a cry that wakes even the ghosts of the underworld, because such a desire is not pure; because it is greed, rather than desire; because it wants to 'take' in some way or other, instead of learning to 'give'.

All those who look upon the Earth as a prison – all the pious folk who pray for deliverance,.evoke, without knowing it, the world of ghosts. Do the same yourself, but knowingly.

For those who do it unwittingly, is there an invisible hand to guide them out of the morass in which they are engulfed? I do not think so.

When, on your way to the 'awakened' state, you cross the kingdom of the shades, you will gradually come to see that they are simply thoughts that you are suddenly able to see with your eyes. That is why they are strangers to you, and seem to be creatures; for the language of forms is different from the language of the brain.

Now the moment has arrived when the transformation takes place: the men around you will become ghosts. All those whom you have loved will suddenly turn into worms. Even your own body.

It is impossible to imagine a more terrible solitude than that of the pilgrim in the desert who cannot find a well of pure water and dies of thirst.

Everything I have said here can be found in the writings of holy men of all nations: the advent of a new kingdom; wakefulness; the conquest of the body and of solitude. And yet an unbridgeable gulf separates us from these holy men: they believe that the day is coming when the good will enter into Heaven and the wicked will be cast down into Hell. We know that the time is coming when many will wake up, and will be set apart from the sleepers who cannot understand what it means to be 'awake'. We know that there is no good or bad; only right or wrong. They believe that to be 'awake' means keeping their senses alert and their eyes open during the night so that a man can say his prayers. We know that to be 'awake' is the 'awakening' of the immortal 'I', and that physical insomnia is a natural consequence of this. They believe that the body ought to be neglected and despised because it is sinful. We know that there is no such thing as sin; the body is the beginning of our work, and we have come down to Earth to transform it into spirit.

They believe that we ought to live in solitude with our bodies in order to purify our spirits. We know that our spirits must first retire into solitude in order that the body may be transfigured.

It is for you, and you alone, to choose what path to take: theirs or ours. You must act according to your own desires.

It is not for me to advise you. It is more salutary to pluck of your own free will a bitter fruit from a tree than to look at a sweet fruit hanging there that someone else has recommended.

But do not do as so many do who know the saying: examine everything, and only retain the best. You must go ahead; examine nothing, and cling on to whatever comes first.

IX

THE POINT BEYOND INFINITY

From Surrealism to Fantastic Realism – The Supreme Point – Beware of images – The madness of Georg Cantor – The Yogi and the mathematician – A fundamental aspiration of the human spirit – An extract from a story by Jorge Luis Borges

IN the preceding chapters I have tried to give some idea of possible ways of studying the reality of *another* state of consciousness. In that other state, if it exists, every man who is tormented by the demon of a desire for knowledge would perhaps find an answer to the following question, which never fails to arise:

'Is there not a place to be found in myself where everything that *happens to me* would be immediately comprehensible; a place where everything that I see, know or feel could be instantly deciphered, whether it be the movement of the stars, the way in which the petals of a flower are arranged, developments in the civilization to which I belong, or the most secret movements of my heart?

'Is it not possible that this immense and mad desire to understand which pursues me, as if in spite of myself, through all the vicissitudes of my life might not one day be completely and once for all assuaged? Is there not in Man, in myself, a path which leads to a knowledge of all the laws by which the world is governed? Do I not possess, deep down within myself, the key to total knowledge?'

André Breton, in the second Surrealist Manifesto, believed that he could return a definite answer to this question: 'There is every reason to believe that there is a certain point within the mind from which life and death, the real and the imaginary, the past and the future, the communicable and the incommunicable, the high and the low are no longer perceived contradictorily.'

It goes without saying that I do not, in my turn, claim to return a positive answer. In place of the methods and apparatus of surrealism, Bergier and I have aimed at substituting the more modest methods and heavier apparatus of what we call 'fantastic realism'. I therefore propose, in my study of these questions to have recourse to several different levels of knowledge: esoteric tradition; *avant-garde* mathematics; unusual trends in modern literature. Our method, in fact, consists in carrying out a survey on different levels (those of the spirit of magic, of pure intelligence and poetic intuition), establishing a connection between these three, verifying by comparison the truths belonging to each, and finally putting forward a hypothesis in which these truths will be integrated. This fat book of ours is nothing but a first attempt to justify and illustrate this method.

The quotation from André Breton above dates from 1930. It achieved an extraordinary notoriety; and is still often quoted and commented on. For the fact is that one of the chief characteristics of the contemporary spirit is the growing interest now being taken in what might be termed: the point beyond infinity.

This concept is to be found in the most ancient traditions as well as in the most advanced mathematics. It haunted the poetic inspiration of Paul Valéry, and one of our greatest living writers, the Argentinian Jorge Luis Borges, has made it the theme of his finest and most astonishing short story, entitled, significantly, *Aleph*.*

This is the name of the first letter of the alphabet in sacred language. In the Cabbala it indicates the *En-Soph*, the centre of total knowledge, the point from where the spirit, or mind, perceives in a flash the totality of all phenomena, their causes and their significance. This letter is said, in a great many texts, to be in the form of a Man who is pointing to Heaven and Earth so as to show that the world below is the mirror and map of the world above. The point beyond Infinity is the supreme point mentioned in the second Surrealist Manifesto, the 'Point Omega' of Father Teilhard de Chardin and the fulfilment of the alchemists' 'Great Work'.

* Published in *Les Temps Modernes*, June 1957, translated from the Spanish by Paul Benichou. An extract from it will be given at the end of this chapter.

280

How can this concept be clearly defined? Let us make an attempt. There exists in the Universe a point, a privileged spot from where the Universe as a whole is revealed. We observe creation with instruments, telescopes, microscopes, etc. But if an observer could be in this privileged spot everything that is or has ever been would appear to him in a flash, and space and time would be revealed in the totality and ultimate significance of all their aspects.

In order to give his sixth-form pupils some idea of the concept of eternity, a Jesuit teacher in a celebrated college employed the following image: 'Imagine that the Earth is made of bronze and that a swallow brushes it with its wing once every thousand years. When the Earth has been demolished in this way, only then will eternity begin. . . .' But eternity is not only an infinite length of time. It is something other than mere duration.

Images are not to be trusted. They help to transpose down to a lower level of consciousness an idea which could only survive at another altitude. They deliver a corpse to the cellar. The only images capable of conveying a lofty idea are those which create in one's consciousness a state of surprise and insecurity calculated to raise this consciousness to the level of the idea in question, where it can be grasped in all its freshness and strength. Magic rites and genuine poetry serve no other purpose.

For this reason we shall not try to provide an 'image' of this concept of the point beyond Infinity. We prefer to refer the reader to Borges' magic and poetical text.

Borges, in his story, has drawn on Cabbalistic and Alchemist sources and on Muslim legends. Other legends, as old as humanity, evoke this Supreme Point, this Privileged Spot. But it is a characteristic of the times in which we live that the efforts of pure intelligence, engaged in research of a completely non-mystical and non-metaphysical nature, have led to mathematical conceptions which enable us to rationalize and understand the idea of the 'transfinite'.

The most important and remarkable achievements in this field were made by a mathematician of genius, Georg Cantor, who died mad. His work is still discussed by mathematicians, some of whom maintain that Cantor's ideas are logically indefensible. To which the partisans of the 'Transfinite' theory reply: 'No one shall drive us out of the Paradise opened up by Cantor!'

Cantor's thought could be roughly expressed as follows: Let us imagine on this piece of paper two points A and B one cm. apart.

Now draw a segment joining A to B. How many points are there on this segment? Cantor demonstrates that there is more than an infinite number of points. To fill the segment completely would require a number of points greater than Infinity: the number *Aleph*.

This number Aleph is equal to all its parts. If we divide the segment into ten equal parts, there will be as many points in one of these parts as on the whole segment. If we make a square on the base of this segment, there will be as many points on the segment as on the surface of the square. If we make a cube, there will be as many points on the segment as in the whole volume of the cube.

If we build from the cube a four-dimensional solid, a tessaract, there will be as many points on the segment as in the four-dimensional volume of the tessaract. And so on and so on, to Infinity.

In this mathematical conception of the 'Transfinite', involving a study of the 'Alephs', the part is equal to the whole. From the point of view of classical reasoning this is completely mad; and yet it is demonstrable. Equally demonstrable is the fact that an Aleph multiplied by any number will always be an Aleph. Thus there is something in common between contemporary higher mathematics and the Emerald Table of Hermes Trismegistus ('that which is above is like that which is below'), or the intuition of poets like William Blake ('the Universe in a grain of sand').

There is only one way of going beyond Aleph, and that is to raise it to a power of Aleph (we know that A to the power of B means A multiplied by A B times; similarly, Aleph to the power of Aleph equals another Aleph).

If we call the first Aleph zero, the second is Aleph one, the third Aleph two, etc. Aleph zero, we said, is the number of points contained on a *segment de droite* or in a volume. It has been demonstrated that Aleph one is the number of all the possible rational curves in space.

As for Aleph two, already it corresponds to a number which would be greater than anything one could conceive in the Universe. There are not enough objects in the whole Universe which, if counted, would amount to an Aleph two. And the Alephs extend to Infinity. The human mind, then, is capable of reaching beyond the confines of the Universe and of forming concepts which the Universe could never fulfil. This is a traditional attribute of God; but no one had ever imagined that the human mind could encroach upon this attribute. It was probably the contemplation of the Alephs in excess of two that drove Cantor mad.

Modern mathematicians, of stronger fibre or, perhaps, less inclined to succumb to metaphysical delirium, handle concepts of this nature, and even deduce certain applications arising therefrom.

Some of these applications are a challenge to reason and common sense – for example, the famous paradox of Banach and Tarski.*

According to this paradoxical theory, it is possible to take a sphere of normal dimensions, such as an apple, for example, or a tennis ball, and to cut it up into slices and then to reassemble the slices so as to produce a sphere smaller than an atom or bigger than the Sun.

It is not possible to perform physically this experiment, because the cutting has to be done with special surfaces which have no tangent plane and is thus technically impracticable. Most specialists,

* Two contemporary Polish mathematicians. Banach was murdered by the Nazis at Auschwitz; Tarski is still alive and is now translating into French his monumental treatise on mathematical logic.

however, believe that this inconceivable operation is theoretically sound, in the sense that, although these surfaces do not belong to the tangible Universe, the calculations relating to them are valid and effective in the Universe of nuclear physics. The neutrons in an atomic pile move in curves which have no tangent.

The work of Banach and Tarski has led to conclusions which resemble to an hallucinating degree the powers claimed by Hindu experts in the *Samadhi* technique: they declare that they are able to grow as big as the Milky Way, or to shrink to the dimensions of the smallest conceivable particle. Nearer to us, Shakespeare causes Hamlet to exclaim: 'O God! I could be bounded in a nutshell, and count myself a king of infinite space. . . .'

It is impossible, in our opinion, not to be struck by the resemblance between these distant echoes of magical thouhgt and modern mathematical logic. An anthropologist taking part in a seminar on parapsychology at Royaumont in 1956 declared: 'The *siddhis* of the Hindu Yogis are extraordinary, since they include the faculty of being able to make oneself as small as an atom, or as big as the Sun or the whole Universe! Among these fantastic claims, we encounter positive facts which we have every reason to believe are true, and facts like these which seem to us incredible and beyond the bounds of any sort of logic.' But we can only suppose that this anthropologist was ignorant not only of Hamlet's cry, but of the unexpected forms assumed recently by the purest and most modern branch of logic: mathematical logic.

In what precisely lies the profound significance of these resemblances? As always in this book, we shall confine ourselves to formulating hypotheses. The most romantic and exciting, but the least 'integrating' hypothesis would be to admit that the *Samadhi* techniques are real, that the initiate can in fact make himself as small as an atom and as big as a sun, and that these techniques are derived from knowledge handed down from ancient civilizations which had mastered the mathematics of the 'Transfinite'. In our opinion, we are dealing here with one of the fundamental aspirations of the human mind which finds expression in the Yogis' *Samadhi* as well as in the advanced mathematics of Banach and Tarski.

If the revolutionary mathematicians are right, if the paradoxes of the 'Transfinite' are valid, then the most extraordinary perspectives are opened up for the human mind. It is conceivable that there exist in space Aleph points, like the one described in Borges' story. In these points the whole space-time continuum is represented, and the spectacle ranges from the interior of an atomic nucleus to the remotest Galaxy.

One may go still further: one can imagine that as a result of manipulations involving at the same time matter, energy and mind, any point in space whatsoever can become a 'Transfinite' point. If such a hypothesis corresponds to a mathematical-psycho-physical reality we have the explanation of the Alchemists' 'Great Work', and of the supreme ecstasy met with in certain religions. The idea of a 'Transfinite' point from which the whole Universe would

283

become perceptible, is prodigiously abstract. But the basic equations of the theory of relativity are equally abstract – and yet they have produced the sound movie, television and the atomic bomb.

Moreover, the human mind is incessantly progressing towards higher and higher levels of abstraction. Paul Langevin has already pointed out that the electrician's apprentice is perfectly at home with the highly abstract and delicate notion of the 'potential', and even has a word for it in his slang: he speaks of 'the juice'.

It is again possible to imagine that, in the more or less distant future, the human mind, having mastered the mathematics of the 'Transfinite', will succeed, with the aid of certain instruments in constructing, in 'Aleph' space, 'Transfinite' points from which it will be able to perceive the infinitely small and the infinitely great in their totality and ultimate significance.

Thus, the traditional quest for the 'Absolute' will have at last been crowned with success. It is tempting to dream that the experiment has already partially succeeded. We mentioned in an earlier chapter in this book the alchemistic experiment in which the operator oxidizes the surface of a molten bath of metal. When the film of oxide dispersed, it was said that an image of our Galaxy with its two satellites, Magellan's clouds, appeared against an opaque background. Legend or fact? In any case, this is an example of the earliest 'Transfinite Instrument' making contact with the Universe by means other than those provided by normal instruments.

It was perhaps through an operation of this sort that the Mayas, who did not know the telescope, discovered Uranus and Neptune. But we must not let our imagination run away with us. Let us be content to take note of this fundamental aspiration of the mind, so neglected in classical psychology, and at the same time to observe the connection between ancient traditions and one of the most important trends in modern mathematics.

Now follows the extract from the story by Borges: *The Aleph*.

'When I reached the house in the Rue Garay the maid asked me if I would mind waiting. Monsieur, as usual, was in the cellar developing his photographs. Near a vase empty of flowers on the unused piano stood smiling (more untemporal than anachronistic) the large portrait of Beatriz with its clumsy colouring. No one could see us, and impelled by an impulse of tender despair I went up to it and murmured: "Beatriz, Beatriz Elena, Beatriz Elena Viterbo, Beatriz darling, Beatriz lost forever, it is I, I, Borges."

'Carlos entered a moment later. He spoke abruptly: I understood that he was incapable of thinking of anything except the loss of the Aleph.

' "A small glass of pseudo-cognac," he ordered; "then down you go to the cellar. You know that the dorsal decubitus is indispensable. So are darkness, immobility and a certain visual accommodation. You are to lie on the ground, on the tiles, and gaze fixedly at the nineteenth step of the stairway I shall show you. Then I shall go away, shut the trap-door, and you'll be alone. Perhaps you'll be scared by some rodent – easily done! In a few minutes you will see the Aleph. The microcosmos of the alchemists and Cabbalists, our concrete and proverbial friend, the *multum in parvo!*"

'When we were in the dining-room he added: "It's understood that if you don't see it, your incapacity will not invalidate my experience. . . . Now go down; very soon you'll be able to start a conversation with *all* the images of Beatriz."

'I went downstairs quickly. The cellar, scarcely wider than the stairway, was very like a well. I looked in vain for the trunk which Carlos Argentino had mentioned. A few cases with bottles and some coarse sacking were piled up in one corner. Carlos took a sack, folded it and placed it in a particular position.

' "It's not much of a pillow," he explained; "but if I raise it an inch higher you won't see anything at all, and you'll be ashamed and embarrassed. Spread your great carcass on the ground and count nineteen steps."

'I complied with his ridiculous demands, and at last he went away. He carefully closed the trap-door; the darkness, in spite of a chink which I noticed later, seemed complete. Suddenly I realized the danger I was in; I had allowed myself to be buried by a madman, after having absorbed some poison. All Carlos's blustering failed to conceal his terror lest the miracle should not be revealed to me; Carlos, to justify his delusions and so as not to know that he was mad, was *bound* to kill me. I felt a vague *malaise* which I tried to put down to my stiffness, and not to the effect of a narcotic. I closed my eyes, then opened them. It was then that I saw the Aleph.

'I come now to the ineffable climax of my story; and this is where my despair as a writer begins. All language is an alphabet of symbols, whose use presupposes an experience which is shared by both parties; but how can I convey to others the infinite Aleph of which my timid memory has hardly any recollection? The mystics, in cases like this, abound in symbols; to indicate a divinity, a Persian speaks of a bird which, in some way, is all birds; Alanus de Insulis, of a sphere whose centre is everywhere and the circumference nowhere; Ezekiel, of an angel with four faces facing simultaneously North, South, East and West. (I have a reason for recalling these inconceivable analogies, as they have something in common with the Aleph.) Perhaps the gods would allow me to use an image of this kind; but then this story would be tainted with literature and falseness. In any case, the central problem is insoluble; it is impossible to enumerate, even partially, an infinite number of things. In that gigantic instant, I saw millions of actions, both delectable and atrocious; but none of them astonished so much as the fact that they all occupied the same point, without being either superimposed or transparent. What my eyes saw was simultaneous: my transcription of it will be successive, because language has to be. I want, however, to give some account of it.

'At the bottom of the step, to the right, I saw a little mottled sphere almost intolerably bright. At first I thought it was revolving round itself; afterwards I realized that this movement was an illusion due to the vertiginous spectacle it enclosed. The diameter of the Aleph must have been about two or three inches, but the whole of cosmic space was inside it, unreduced. Everything (the glass in the mirror, for example) was a multiplicity of things, because I could see it clearly from every point in the Universe. I saw the populous sea; I saw the dawn and the evening; I saw the multitudes swarming in America; I saw a silver spider-web in the centre of a black pyramid; I saw a broken labyrinth (it was London); I saw interminable eyes gazing one upon the other inside me as palpable as if seen in a mirror; I saw all the mirrors on the planet, and not one reflected my image; I saw in a backyard in the Rue Soler the same paving-stones that I had seen thirty years ago in a house at Fray Bentos; I saw clusters of grapes, snow, tobacco, veins of metal, steam; I saw convex deserts under the Equator and each of their grains of sand; I saw at Inverness a woman whom I shall not forget; I saw her dishevelled hair and haughty carriage; I saw a cancer of the breast; I saw a ring of dried earth on a pavement where there had been a tree; I saw in a country house at Adrogue a copy of the first English translation of Pliny by Philemon Holland; I saw every letter on every page at the same time (as a child I had always wondered why when a book was closed, the letters did not get mixed up and lost during the night); I saw the night and day together; I saw a sunset at Queretaro which seemed to reflect the colour of a Bengal light; I saw my bedroom with no one in it; I saw in a room at Alkmaar a terrestrial globe between two mirrors which multiplied it to Infinity; I saw horses with shaggy manes on a beach by the Caspian Sea; I saw the delicate bone-structure of a hand; I saw the survivors of a battle sending off post-cards; I saw in a shop-window at Mirzapur a pack of Spanish playing-cards; I saw the sloping shadows of ferns on the floor of a greenhouse; I saw tigers, pistons, bisons, heaving seas and armies; I saw all the ants on the Earth; I saw a Persian astrolabe; I saw in a drawer (and the handwriting made me tremble) obscene letters – precise, unbelievable – that Beatriz had addressed to Carlos Argentino; I saw an adored monument in the cemetery at Chacarita; I saw the ghastly remains of what had deliciously been Beatriz Viterbo; I saw the circulation of my dark blood; I saw the connection between love and the transformations of death; I saw the Aleph from every point; I saw the Earth in the Aleph and in the Earth again the Aleph, and in the Aleph the Earth; I saw my face and my entrails; I saw your face, and I was giddy and I wept, because my eyes had seen that secret and conjectural object whose name men utter improperly, but which no man has ever seen: the inconceivable Universe.

'I felt an infinite reverence, and an infinite sorrow. ... "You must be feeling a bit dazed after poking your nose into what is no concern of yours," said a jovial and detested voice. "Even if you empty your whole brain you'll never in a hundred years be able to repay me for that revelation. What a terrific observatory, eh? Borges!"

'Carlos Argentino was standing at the top of the staircase. 'In the sudden half-light I managed to raise myself and stammer: "Terrific – Yes, indeed. . . ."' 'The note of indifference in my voice surprised me. Carlos went on anxiously: "You saw absolutely everything – in colour?" 'In that moment I planned my revenge. Nervously and evasively, with a show of friendliness, I thanked Carlos Argentino Daneri for the hospitality of his cellar, and urged him to take advantage of the demolition of his house to leave the pernicious capital which never forgives anyone! I quietly but firmly refused to discuss the Aleph; I embraced ˙him on leaving, and reminded him again that the country and tranquility were the best doctors.

'In the street, in the stairways of Constitucion and in the metro all the faces seemed familiar. I was afraid that there was nothing left in the world that could surprise me, and that all my life I should be haunted by the feeling that I had seen everything before. Fortunately, after a few sleepless nights, I had forgotten everything.'

X

SOME REFLECTIONS ON THE MUTANTS

The child astronomer – A sudden access of intelligence – The theory of mutation – The myth of the Great Superior Ones – The Mutants among us – From Horla to Leonard Euler – An invisible society of Mutants? – The birth of the collective being – Love of the living

DURING the winter of 1956, Dr. J. Ford Thomson, a psychiatrist at the Education Office at Wolverhampton, received in his consulting room a small boy of seven who was causing great anxiety to his parents and to his teacher.

'He obviously could not have access to any specialist literature on the subject,' wrote Dr. Thomson. 'And even if he had, would he have been able even to read them? And yet, he knew the right answers to the most complicated problems of astronomy.'

Greatly impressed by his study of this case, the doctor decided to investigate the level of intelligence among school-children, and undertook to test 5,000 children all over England, with the assistance of the British Medical Research Council, the physicists at Harwell and a number of University professors. After eighteen months work, he came to the conclusion that there had been 'a sudden rise in the level of intelligence'. He went on to say:

'Among the last 90 children from seven to nine years of age whom we questioned, 26 had an I.Q. of 140, which is practically that of a genius. I believe that strontium 90, a radio-active substance that penetrates the body, could be responsible for this. This substance did not exist before the first atomic explosion.'

Two American scientists, C. Brooke Worth and Robert K.

Enders, in an important work entitled *The Nature of Living Things*, believe that there is proof that the gene groups have been disturbed and that, under the influence of forces that are still mysterious, a new race of men is appearing, endowed with superior intellectual powers. This is, of course, a subject to be approached with caution. The genetician Lewis Terman, however, after thirty years study of infant prodigies, has reached the following conclusions: Most infant prodigies used in the past to lose their faculties on becoming adult. It would seem today that they tend to become a superior kind of adult, gifted with an intelligence that has nothing in common with that of ordinary human beings. They are thirty times as active as a normal man of talent. Their 'success index' is multiplied by twenty-five. Their health is perfect, as well as their sentimental and sexual balance. Finally, they escape the psycho-somatic diseases, notably cancer. Is this certain? One thing is certain, and that is that we are now witnessing a progressive acceleration throughout the world of the mental faculties, and this is true also of the physical. The phenomenon is so evident that another American scientist, Dr. Sydney Pressey, of the University of Ohio, has just drawn up a plan for the instruction of precocious children capable, in his opinion, of producing 300,000 superior intelligences a year.

Does this point to a mutation of the human species? Shall we see a new race of beings who resemble us outwardly, but yet are different? This is the formidable problem we must now examine. What is certain is that we are witnessing the birth of a myth: that of the Mutant. That this myth should arise in our technical and scientific civilization must have some significance and dynamic value.

Before tackling this subject, it should be noted that this access of intelligence that has been observed among children carries with it the simple, practical and reasonable notion of a progressive improvement in the human race brought about by techniques.

Modern sporting techniques have shown that Man possesses physical resources that are far from being exhausted. The experiments now being carried out on the behaviour of the human body in interplanetary rockets have proved the existence of formidable powers of resistance. The survivors from the concentration camps have learned to what extremes it is possible to go to preserve life, and have discovered sources of strength in the interaction of psychic and physical forces. Finally, as regards the intelligence, the imminent discovery of mental techniques and chemical products capable of stimulating the memory and reducing to zero the strain of memorizing, opens up some extraordinary perspectives. The principles of science are not inaccessible to a normal intelligence. If school-children and students could be relieved of the enormous effort of memory they have to make, it will become quite possible to teach the structure of the nucleus and the periodical table of the elements to elementary pupils, and to explain the relativity and quantum theories to undergraduates. Moreover, when the principles of science are widely diffused in all countries and there are fifty or a hundred times as many research workers, the multiplication of new ideas, their mutual fecundation, and multiple points of contact will produce the same effect as an increase in the number of geniuses. Even greater, because genius is often unstable and anti-social. It is probable, too, that a new science, the general theory of information, will soon make it possible to express quantitatively the ideas we are now expounding qualitatively. By distributing equitably among men the knowledge mankind already possesses, and by encouraging them to exchange their knowledge so as to produce new combinations, we shall increase the intellectual potential of human society no less rapidly and surely than by multiplying the number of geniuses. This vision must be borne in mind along with the other more fantastic one of the Mutant.

Our friend Charles-Noël Martin, in a sensational communication, has revealed the accumulated effects of atomic explosions. The effects of the radiation generated in the course of the tests increase in geometrical proportion. Thus the human race is in danger of being exposed to unfavourable mutations. Moreover, for the last fifty years radium has been used all over the world without any serious precautions being taken. X-rays and certain radio-active chemical products are exploited in a great many industries. How, and to what extent does this radiation affect modern man? We know nothing about the system of mutations. Could there not also be favourable mutations? Speaking at an atomic conference at Geneva, Sir Ernest Rock Carling, a Home Office pathologist, declared: 'It is also to be hoped that, in a limited proportion of cases, these mutations will have a favourable effect and produce a child of genius. At the risk of shocking this distinguished company, I affirm that the mutation that will give us an Aristotle, a Leonardo da Vinci, a Newton, a Pasteur or an Einstein will largely compensate for the ninety-nine others which will have much less fortunate effects.'

First, a word as to the theory of mutations.

At the end of the last century, A. Weisman and Hugo de Vries instilled new life into the old ideas about evolution. The atom was then fashionable, and its effects were beginning to make themselves felt in physics. They discovered the 'atom of heredity', and localized it in the chromosomes. The new science of genetics thus created brought to light again the work done in the second half of the nineteenth century by the Czech monk, Gregor Mendel.

Today it appears to be an established fact that heredity is transformed by the genes. These are strongly protected against their outside environment. It seems, however, that atomic radiations, cosmic rays and certain violent poisons such as colchicine are able to attack them or cause the number of chromosomes to be doubled. It has been observed that the frequence of the mutations is proportional to the intensity of the radio-activity.

Now, today, the radio-activity in the world is thirty-five times higher than it was at the beginning of the century. Exact examples of selection in bacteria operating through genetic mutation under the action of antibiotics have been furnished in 1943 by Luria and Debruck, and in 1945 by Demerec. These studies show that mutation-selection is operating just as Darwin had imagined. The adversaries of the Lamarck–Mitchurine–Lyssenko theory as to the inheritance of acquired characteristics would therefore seem to be right. But can one generalize from bacteria to plants, animals or man? This is no longer doubted.

Are there any genetic mutations in man that can be controlled?

Yes. A case in point, as to which there appears to be no doubt, is the following: quoted from the archives of the Hospital for Sick Children in London: Dr. Louis Wolf, the Director of this hospital, estimates that thirty phenyl-cetonic mutants are born in England every year. These mutants possess genes which do not produce in the blood certain ferments that are normally found there. A phenyl-cetonic mutant is incapable of dissociating phenile-alamine. This inability renders the child vulnerable to epilepsy and eczema, turns his hair ash-grey, and renders an adult liable to mental disorders. A certain phenyl-cetonic race of men, distinct from normal human beings, is therefore living amongst us. . . . This is an example of an unfavourable mutation; but must one refuse to believe in the possibility of a favourable mutation? Some mutants could have in their blood substances capable of improving their physical equilibrium and raising their intelligence-coefficient to a level higher than our own. Their blood might contain natural tranquillizing agents which protect them from the psychic shocks of social life and anxiety complexes. In this way they would form a race different from ordinary humans and superior to them. Psychiatrists and doctors try to find out what makes things go wrong. How are they to act when things go exceptionally well?

Mutations are of various kinds. Cellular mutation, which does not attack the genes and has no effect on heredity, is known to us in its unfavourable forms: cancer and leukaemia are cellular mutations. To what extent could there be cellular mutations, generalized throughout the organism which would be beneficial? The mystics speak of the apparition of a 'new flesh', a 'transfiguration'.

We are also beginning to know something about unfavourable genetic mutations (e.g. the phenyl-cetonic cases). Could there not, here too, be beneficial mutations? Here again we must distinguish between two aspects of the phenomenon, or rather two interpretations.

(1) This mutation, this apparition of another race could be due to chance. Radio-activity, among other causes, could induce a modification of the genes in certain individuals. The protein in the gene, if slightly affected, would no longer, for example, produce certain acids which cause us to feel anxiety. We should see another species of Man – a race of tranquil men who would not know fear or have any negative sensations. Men who would go tranquilly to

war, and kill without anxiety and have no complexes in their pleasures – a sort of robot devoid of any internal emotions. It may well be that we are witnessing now the coming of this race.

(2) Genetic mutation is not, it would seem, due to chance, but directed in some way, perhaps towards a spiritual regeneration of humanity – a bridge, as it were, between a lower and a higher level of consciousness. The effects of radio-activity may be ordained as a means of improving the race. The modifications we mentioned just now are merely a slight indication of the profound changes that humanity may be destined to undergo in the future. The protein of he gene may be structurally affected so that we should see the birth of a race whose intelligence would be completely transformed – a race of beings capable of mastering time and space and of extending the domain of the intellect beyond Infinity. Between these two conceptions there is as much difference as there is between hardened steel and steel subtly transformed into a magnetic band.

The second conception (above) which is responsible for a modern myth which science-fiction has adopted, is curiously reflected in various manifestations of contemporary spirituality. In the Satanic camp we have seen how Hitler believed in the existence of Superior Beings, and heard him reveal his secret: 'The mutation of the human race has begun; there are already super-men.'

Representing the new Hindu school of thought, the master of the Pondicherry Ashram, Sri Aurobindo Ghose, founded his philosophy and his commentaries on the sacred texts on the certitude that the upward evolution of humanity would be accomplished by means of mutations. And Teilhard de Chardin, representing a Catholicism open to scientific speculation affirmed that he believed in 'a force capable of impelling us towards some form of super-humanity' ('Ultra-Humain').

André Breton, the Father of Surrealism, a pilgrim on the road of strangeness, sensitive to every transient current of disquieting ideas, spectator rather than creator, but a hyper-lucid observer of the most extreme adventures of the modern mind, wrote as follows in 1942: 'Man is not, perhaps, the centre, the principal protagonist of the Universe. It is permissible to believe that there are beings above him in the animal scale whose behaviour is as different from his as his own is from that of whales or butterflies. There is no reason why there should not be beings altogether outside his field of sensory perception, thanks to some form of camouflage possibly of the kind adopted by mimetic animals. There is no doubt that this idea opens up a vast field for speculation, despite the fact that it tends to reduce man's interpretation of his own universe to a modest scale, not unlike that of an ant in an anthill which a child has trampled on. When we think of catastrophes such as a cyclone, where Man can only be either a victim or a spectator, or war, about which notoriously inadequate opinions have been expressed, it should be possible in the course of an extensive study of a rigorously inductive nature, to succeed in giving a plausible picture of the structure and complexion of such hypothetical beings which haunt our imagination and fill us with obscure apprehensions.

'In this, I must point out, my thought is not far removed from that of Novalis who wrote: "We are really living inside an animal whose parasites we are. What we are, our constitution, depends on this animal, and vice-versa." I also find myself in agreement with William James, who asked: "Who knows but that we may occupy in Nature as small a place by the side of beings of whom we know nothing as the cats and dogs who live beside us in our houses?" Scientists themselves would not contradict this point of view: "All round us there may be beings, built on the same model as ourselves, but different – men, for example, whose albumins may be straight".*

'A new myth? Should we try to persuade these beings that they are nothing but a mirage, or give them an opportunity to reveal themselves?'

Are there really beings among us who resemble us externally, but whose behaviour is as far removed from ours as 'that of whales or butterflies'? Common sense answers that, if so, we should be aware of it, and that if such beings were living among us, we should certainly see them.

We know of a writer, John W. Campbell, who more or less demolished this common-sense argument in an editorial in the review *Astounding Science Fiction* in 1941. This is the gist of what he wrote:

No one goes to see his doctor to tell him that his health is magnificent. No one would go to a psychiatrist to inform him that life is an easy and delicious game, or visit a psycho-analyst to declare that he is not suffering from any complex. Unfavourable mutations can be detected. But what about the favourable ones?

Ah, but – objects common sense – the superior mutants would be revealed by their prodigious intellectual activities.

Not at all, replies Campbell. A man of genius, of the same species as ourselves – an Einstein, for example – publishes the fruits of his researches. He attracts attention. This often causes him a lot of trouble in the form of open hostility, incomprehension, threats and perhaps exile. Einstein at the end of his life declared: 'If I had known, I should have been a plumber.' Above Einstein's level, the mutant is clever enough to conceal himself. He keeps his discoveries for himself. He lives as discreetly as possible, and only tries to remain in contact with other intelligences like his own. A few hours of work each week are enough to ensure the necessities of life; the rest of his life he spends in activities of which we can have no conception.

An attractive hypothesis, but one that it is impossible to check in the light of science as it is today. No anatomic examination can tell us anything about intelligence. Anatole France had an abnormally light brain. Moreover, there is no reason why a mutant should

* Emile Duclaux, former Director of the Pasteur Institute.

be the subject of an autopsy, except in the case of an accident; in which case, how would it be possible to detect a mutation affecting the cells of the brain? It is not, therefore, completely mad to admit the possible existence of Superior Beings in our midst. If mutations are governed by chance alone, some of them are probably favourable. If they are governed by an organized natural force, or correspond to a living man's will to better himself, as Sri Aurobindo, for example, believed, then there must be many more. Our successors may be here already.

There is every reason to believe that they are exactly like us, or rather that we have no means of distinguishing them. Some science-fiction writers naturally imagine that mutants have some anatomical peculiarities. Van Vogt, in his celebrated *In Pursuit of the Slans* imagines they have a special kind of hair: a sort of antennae used in telepathic communications; and he makes this the basis of a fine but terrible story about hunting down Superior Beings, modelled on the persecution of the Jews. Storytellers, however, sometimes add to Nature to simplify the problems.

If telepathy exists, it is probably not transmitted by waves, and has no need of antennae. If we believe in a controlled evolution it is reasonable to suppose that the mutant, to ensure his own protection, is able to camouflage himself to perfection. In the animal kingdom it is a commonplace that the predatory species are deceived by their prey disguising themselves as dead leaves, twigs, even excrement, with an astonishing perfection. Some succulents are even cunning enough to imitate the colour of other uneatable species.

As André Breton said, when imagining the presence among us of 'Great Transparent Beings', it is possible that they escape our observation 'thanks to some form of camouflage of the kind adopted by mimetic animals'.

'The New Man is living amongst us! He is there! What more do you want? I will tell you a secret: I have seen the New Man. He is intrepid and cruel! I was afraid in his presence!' Thus spake a trembling Hitler.

Another example: Maupassant, in an access of terror, and madness, in blood and sweat wrote in precipitate haste one of the most disturbing texts in the whole of French literature: *Le Horla*:

'Now I know, I can guess the truth. Man's dominion is a thing of the past! *He* has come, the being who was an object of fear to primitive races, whom anxious priests tried to exorcize, whom sorcerers called up at midnight without ever yet seeing him in visible form, to whom the temporary lords of creation attributed in imagination the shape monstrous or attractive, of gnomes, spirits, fairies or goblins. After the vulgar ideas inspired by prehistoric fears, scientific research has clarified the outlines of Man's presentiment. Mesmer guessed it, and in the last ten years doctors have discovered the exact nature of this being's power before its manifestation. They have experimented with this weapon of the

293

new lord of the world, the imposition of a dominant will on the human soul, which thus becomes its slave. To this power they have given the name of magnetism, hypnotism, suggestion, and what not. I have seen them playing with it like silly children playing with fire. Woe to us! Woe to mankind! He has come . . . what is his name ? . . . yes, he is shouting it and I can't hear . . . say it again! . . . Le Horla, I've got it at last . . . Le Horla . . . that's his name. . . . Le Horla has come!'*

In his interpretation of this vision of horror and wonder, Maupassant, true to the age he lived in, endowed the mutant with hypnotic powers. Modern science-fiction literature, nearer to the work of Rhine, Soal, MacConnel than to that of Charcot, tends to endow the mutants with para-psychological powers: telepathy, or telekinesis. Other writers go further and show us the Superior Being floating in the air or going through walls; but this is pure fantasy, an agreeable echo of the archetype of all fairy-stories. Just as the island of the mutants, or the galaxy of the mutants correspond to the old dream of the Islands of the Blest, so do paranormal powers correspond to the archetype of the Greek gods. But from the standpoint of reality, it is obvious that all these powers would be completely useless to beings living in a modern civilization. Why have telepathy when the radio exists ? Why telekinesis, when you have the aeroplane. If the mutant exists as we are tempted to believe, he has powers greater than any that we can imagine. Powers that an ordinary man seldom uses: he is gifted with intelligence.

Our actions are irrational, and intelligence plays only a very small part in our decisions. One can imagine the Ultra-Human, representing a new stage of life on this planet, as a rational being, no longer merely a reasoning one, and as being endowed with a permanent objective intelligence, only taking decisions after having examined lucidly and thoroughly all the information at its disposal. A being whose nervous system is immune to any negative impulses. A being with a cold and swiftly calculating brain, equipped with a completely infallible memory. If the mutant exists it is likely to have a physical resemblance to a human being, but to be different in all other respects owing to the fact that it controls its intelligence and uses it unceasingly.

This seems a simple enough vision. Nevertheless, it is more fantastic than anything in science-fiction literature. The biologists are beginning to understand the chemical modifications which would have to precede the creation of this new species. Experiments with tranquillizing drugs, lysergic acid and its by-products have shown that very feeble traces of certain organic compounds still unknown to us would be enough to protect us against the excessive permeability of our nervous system, and enable us in this way to exercise on all occasions an objective intelligence. Since there are phenyl-cetonic mutants in existence whose chemical

* Extract from *Le Horla*, a short story by Guy de Maupassant. Penguin Edition; translated by H. N. P. Sloman.

composition is less well adapted to life than our own, it is legitimate to suppose that there are mutants whose chemical composition is better adapted than ours to life in this world in process of transformation. It is these mutants, whose glands would spontaneously secrete tranquillizers and substances capable of stimulating the activity of the brain, who would be the forerunners of the new species destined to replace Man. Their place of residence would not be some mysterious island or forbidden planet. Life has been able in the past to produce creatures adapted to dwell in the depths of the ocean or in the rarefied atmosphere of the highest mountains. It is also capable of creating the 'Ultra-Human' whose ideal habitation would be the Metropolis, 'the Earth of smoking factories, and teeming multitudes, the Earth that vibrates with a hundred new kinds of radiation. . . .'

Life is never perfectly adapted, but it tends towards perfect adaptation. Why should it relax this tension since the creation of Man? Why should it not prepare the way for something better than Man, through Man? And it may be that this Man-after-Man is already born. 'Life,' says Dr. Loren Eiseley, 'is a great dreamy river which flows through every opening, changing and adapting itself as it advances.' Its apparent stability is an illusion engendered by the brevity of our own life. Just as we do not see the hands of a clock going round, so do we fail to see one form of life flowing into another.

The object of this book is to reveal facts and suggest hypotheses, but not in any way to promote any particular belief. We do not claim to know any mutants. Nevertheless, if we accept the idea that the perfect mutant is perfectly camouflaged, we can accept the idea that Nature sometimes fails in her efforts to improve creation and puts into circulation some imperfect mutants who, unlike the others, are visible.

In such mutants you may find a combination of exceptional mental qualities and physical defects, as, for example, in the case of a great many lightning calculators. The greatest specialist in this field, Professor Robert Tocquet, has stated his views as follows: 'Many calculators were at first thought to be backward children. The Belgian prodigy Oscar Verhaeghe at the age of seventeen expressed himself like a two-year-old baby. Zerah Colburn, moreover, showed symptoms of degeneration: he had an extra finger on each hand. Another lightning calculator, Prolongeau, was born without arms or legs. Mondeux was subject to hysteria. . . . Oscar Verhaeghe, born on 16th April, 1862, at Bousval in Belgium to parents of humble origin, belongs to the group of calculators whose intelligence is far below average. The raising to different powers of numbers consisting of the same figures was one of his specialities. Thus, he could find the square of 888,888,888,888,888 in 40 seconds, and raise 9,999,999 to the fifth power in 60 seconds, the resulting numbers running to 35 figures. . . .'*

* *New York Herald Tribune*, 23rd November, 1959.

295

Degenerates, or imperfect mutants?

Here, now, is perhaps an example of a perfect mutant: Leonard Euler, who was in contact with Roger Boscovitch (whose story we related in the preceding chapter).*

Leonard Euler (1707–83) is generally considered one of the greatest mathematicians of all time. But this qualification is too narrow to convey the supra-human qualities of his mind. He could skim through the most complex treatise in a few minutes, and could recite from memory *all* the books he had ever handled since he had learned to read. He had a thorough and complete knowledge of physics, chemistry, zoology, botany, geology, medicine, history and Greek and Latin literature. In all these fields he was without a rival among his contemporaries. He had the power of isolating himself completely at will from the outside world, and of following a train of thought in any circumstances whatever. He lost his sight in 1766, but this did not affect him. One of his pupils has recorded that during a discussion relating to calculations involving 17 decimal places, there was some disagreement with regard to the fifteenth place. Euler then, with his eyes closed, performed the whole calculation again in a fraction of a second. He saw relationships and connections which had escaped the notice of other cultivated and intelligent beings throughout the ages. Thus, he discovered in the poetry of Vergil new and revolutionary mathematical ideas. He was a simple and modest man, and all his contemporaries agree that his one desire was to remain unnoticed. Euler and Boscovitch lived at a time when men of learning were honoured, and ran no risk of being imprisoned for their political opinions, or of being forced by governments to manufacture arms. If they had lived in our century, perhaps they would have taken steps to camouflage themselves completely. Maybe there are Eulers and Boscovitchs among us today.

Intelligent and rational mutants, endowed with an infallible memory, a constantly lucid intelligence are perhaps working beside us disguised as country schoolmasters or insurance agents.

Do these mutants form an invisible society? No human being lives alone. He can only develop himself within a society. The human society we know has shown only too well its hostility towards an objective intelligence or a free imagination: Giordano Bruno burnt, Einstein exiled, Oppenheimer kept under observation. If there are indeed mutants answering to our description, there is every reason to believe that they are working and communicating with one another in a society superimposed on our own, which no doubt extends all over the world. That they communicate by means of superior psychic powers, such as telepathy, seems to us a childish hypothesis. Nearer to reality, and consequently more fantastic, is the hypothesis that they are using normal human methods of communication to convey messages and information for their exclusive use.

* The diary of the father of the science of astronautics, Ziolkovsky, was published in U.S.S.R. in 1959. In it he states that he borrowed most of his ideas from the work of Boscovitch.

The general theory of information and semantics proves fairly conclusively that it is possible to draw up texts which have a double, triple or quadruple meaning. There are Chinese texts in which seven meanings are enclosed one within the other. One of the heroes in Van Vogt's *In Pursuit of the Slans* discovers the existence of other mutants by reading the newspapers and deciphering apparently inoffensive articles. A similar network of communication in our own Press and literature, etc., is quite conceivable. The *New York Herald Tribune* published on 15th March, 1958, an analysis from its London correspondent of a series of advertisements appearing in the Personal column of *The Times*. These messages had attracted the attention of professional cryptographers and the police in various countries, because they obviously had a hidden meaning. But this meaning was never deciphered. There are, no doubt, other still less decipherable means of communication. Who knows but that some fourth-rate novel, or some technical textbook, or some apparently obscure philosophical work is not a secret vehicle for complex studies and messages addressed to higher intelligences, as different from our own as we are from the great apes.

Louis de Broglie, in an article in *Nouvelles Litteraires* on 2nd March, 1950, entitled 'What is Life?', wrote as follows:
'We must never forget how limited our knowledge must always be, and in what unexpected ways it is likely to develop. If our human civilization endures, the physics of the future a few centuries hence could well be as different from the physics of today as the latter is from the physics of Aristotle. The greatly extended range of knowledge to which we shall have access by then will perhaps enable us to incorporate in a general synthesis, in which each will have its place, the whole body of physical and biological phenomena. *If human thought, which by that time may have had its powers extended by some biological mutation,* can one day rise to those heights, it will then perceive in its true perspective, something of which, no doubt, we have no idea at present, namely, the unity of the phenomena which we distinguish with the help of adjectives such as "physico-chemical", "biological" or even "psychic".'
And what if this mutation has already taken place? One of the greatest French biologists, Morand, the inventor of the tranquillizers, admits that mutants have made their appearance all through the history of humanity.*
'These mutants, among others, were called Mahomet, Confucius, Jesus Christ. . . .' Many more exist, perhaps. It is by no means inconceivable that, in the present evolutionary period, the mutants think it would be useless to offer themselves as an example, or to preach some new form of religion. There are better things to do at present than to appeal to the individual. Again, they may think that it is both desirable and necessary that our humanity should

* P. Morand and H. Laborit: *Les Destins de la Vie et de l'Homme.* Ed. Masson, Paris, 1959.

297

move towards collectivization. Finally, it may well be that they think it a good thing that we should be suffering now the pains of childbirth, and would even welcome some great catastrophe which might hasten a better understanding of the spiritual tragedy represented in its totality by the phenomenon of Man. So that they may act more efficiently and so as to obtain a clearer view of the current that is perhaps sweeping us all upwards to some form of the Ultra-Human to which they have access, it is perhaps necessary for them to remain hidden, and to keep their coexistence with us secret while, despite appearances and thanks, perhaps, to their presence, a new soul is being forged for the new world which we long for with all our heart.

We have arrived now at the frontiers of the imaginary. It is time to stop. We only want to suggest as many not unreasonable hypotheses as possible. Many of them, no doubt, will have to be rejected. But if some of them have opened doors to research that have hitherto been hidden, we shall not have laboured in vain; we shall not have exposed ourselves uselessly to ridicule. 'The secret of life can be discovered. If I had an opportunity to do this, I should not allow myself to be deterred by ridicule.' These words were spoken by Loren Eiseley.

Any reflections on the question of the mutants must lead to speculation with regard to evolution, and the destiny and nature of Life and Man. What is Time, in regard to the cosmic scale by which the history of the Earth must be measured? Has not the future, so to speak, been with us from all eternity? The appearance of the mutants would seem to suggest that our human society is from time to time given a foretaste of the future, and visited by beings already possessing a knowledge of things to come. Are not the mutants the memory of the future with which the great brain of humanity is perhaps endowed?

Another thing: the idea of a favourable mutation is clearly linked with the notion of progress. This hypothesis of a mutation can be dealt with on a strictly scientific level. It is known for certain that the areas most recently affected by evolution, and the least specialized – namely, the silent zones of cerebral matter – are the last to mature. Some neurologists think with reason that this points to possibilities which the future of the species will reveal. There may be individuals with 'other' possibilities; a superior kind of individualization. And yet the general trend of societies would seem to be towards a greater degree of collectivization. Is this contradictory? We do not think so. Existence, in our view, does not mean contradiction, but complementing and going beyond.

In a letter to his friend Laborit, the biologist, Morand wrote these words: 'The perfectly logical man who has abandoned all passions and all illusions will become a cell in the vital continuum constituted by a society arrived at the peak of its evolution; we have obviously not reached that stage yet; but I do not think there can be evolution without it. Then, and then only, will there emerge that "universal consciousness" of the collective being which we are all tending to become.'

Confronted with this vision, which seems highly probable, we are well aware that those who remain faithful to the old humanism that has moulded our civilization, will be filled with despair. They picture Man, henceforth deprived of any aim in life, entering into his decline. '. . . Perfectly logical, and having abandoned all passions and all illusions. . . .' How could a Man transformed into a being radiating intelligence be on the point of a decline? It is true that the psychological 'I', which we call 'personality' is likely to disappear. But we do not think that this 'personality' is Man's richest possession. It is only one of the instruments he has been given to enable him to pass into the 'awakened' state.

When the goal has been attained, the instrument disappears. If we had mirrors capable of revealing to us that 'personality' which we value so highly, we could not bear to look at our reflection so disfigured would it be by all sorts of monstrous excrescences. Only a truly 'awakened' man could look into such a mirror without being in danger of dying from fright, because then the mirror would reflect nothing and be absolutely pure. The true face is one which in the mirror of truth is not reflected We have not yet acquired, in this sense, a face. And the gods will not speak to us face-to-face until we have one ourselves.

Rejecting the fluid and limited psychological 'I', Rimbaud long ago said: 'I is another.' This is the pure, transparent, immobile 'I' endowed with infinite understanding: in all traditions, Man is taught to give up everything to attain this state. Maybe we are living at a time when the near future speaks the same language as the distant past.

Apart from these considerations on the 'other' possibilities of the mind, our thinking, even at its most tolerant, perceives only contradictions between the individual and the collective conscience, and between a personal and a collective life. But thinking which perceives contradictions in living things is wrong thinking. The individual conscience, when truly 'awakened', enters into the universal. Personal life, if regarded and used wholly and solely as an instrument of 'awakening', can be merged with impunity in a collective life.

This does not mean, however, that the formation of this collective being is the ultimate aim of evolution. The spirit of the Earth and the individual soul have not yet fully emerged. The pessimist, seeing the great upheavals which are caused by this secret emergence, say that we ought at least to try to 'save Man'. But this Man does not want saving, but changing. Man, as projected in orthodox psychology and current philosophy, has already been left behind, condemned as inadaptable. With or without mutation, we must envisage a different kind of human if we want to bring the phenomenon of Man into line with the present trend of our destiny.

From now on, it is no longer a question of pessimism or optimism: it is a question of love.

At the time when I thought I could possess truth in my soul and in my body, when I imagined I should find the solution of everything at the school of the philosopher Gurdjieff, there was one word which I never heard pronounced, and that was: love.

Today there is nothing about which I feel absolutely certain. I could not guarantee the validity of even the most timid hypothesis put forward in the course of this book. Five years of study and work in collaboration with Jacques Bergier have only taught me one thing: a determination to keep my mind prepared for surprises, and to have confidence in life in all its forms, and in intelligence wherever and however it may be manifested in living things around me. These two states: surprise and confidence are inseparable. The determination to attain them and to remain in them undergoes, in the end, a transformation. It ceased to be an act of will, in other words compulsion, and becomes love, in other words, joy and liberty. To sum up, all that I have gained is that I now bear within myself a love, which can henceforth never be uprooted, for all things living, in this world and in every world ad infinitum.

In order to express and pay homage to this powerful and complex love Jacques Bergier and I have, no doubt, not confined ourselves, as prudence would have dictated, to strictly scientific methods. But is there such a thing as prudent love? Our methods have been those familiar to scientists, but also to theologians, poets, sorcerers, magicians and children. In a word, we have behaved like barbarians, preferring invasion to evasion. This is because something told us that we were indeed a part of the strange armies, transparent cohorts and phantom hordes, heralded by ultra-sonic trumpets, which are beginning to descend upon our civilization. We are on the side of the invaders, on the side of the life that is coming, on the side of a changing age and changing ways of thought. Error? Madness? A man's life is only justified by his efforts, however feeble, towards better understanding. And to understand better is to become more attached. The more I understand, the more I love; for everything that is understood is good.